# Global Issues in Mediation

**Jacqueline Nolan-Haley**
*Professor of Law*
*Fordham University School of Law*
*Director of ADR & Conflict Resolution Program*

**Ellen E. Deason**
*Joanne Wharton Murphy/Classes of 1965 and 1973*
*Professor of Law*
*The Ohio State University Moritz College of Law*

**Mariana Hernandez-Crespo Gonstead**
*Professor of Law*
*University of St. Thomas School of Law*
*Executive Director*
*The International Dispute Resolution Research Network*

**GLOBAL ISSUES SERIES®**

WEST ACADEMIC PUBLISHING

444 Cedar Street, Suite 700
St. Paul, MN 55101
1-877-888-1330

Printed in the United States of America

**ISBN: 978-1-68328-619-6**

*To Annie, with much love and*
*hope for the future.*
J.N.H.

*To all the colleagues, friends, and*
*family who have made my life's*
*experiences more global.*
E.E.D.

*To those who have shown us the power of*
*unconditional love, and to those who will leverage*
*this power, that we may all contribute our unique*
*gifts and together reach new levels of*
*innovation and growth.*
M.H.C.G.

# Acknowledgments

We gratefully acknowledge permission to reprint excerpts from the following:

Harold Abramson, Crossing Borders into New Ethical Territory: Ethical Challenges When Mediating Cross-Culturally, 49 S. Tex. L. Rev. 921 (2008).

Harold I. Abramson, Protocols for International Arbitrators Who Dare to Settle Cases, 10 Am. Rev. Int'l Arb. 1 (1999).

Gerry Adams, To Cherish a Just and Lasting Peace, 22 Fordham Int'l L. J. 1179 (1998).

John Barkai, What's a Cross-Cultural Mediator to Do? A Low-Context Solution for a High-Context Problem, 10 Cardozo J. Conflict Resol., 43 (2008).

Jacob Bercovitch, Mediation Success or Failure: A Search for the Elusive Criteria, 7 Cardozo J. Conflict Resol. 289 (2006).

Klaus Peter Berger & J. Ole Jensen, The Arbitrator's Mandate to Facilitate Settlement, 40 Fordham Int'l L.J. 887 (2017).

Wayne D. Brazil, Court ADR 25 Years After Pound: Have We Found a Better Way?, 18 Ohio St. J. on Disp. Resol. 93 (2002).

Christine Kang, Oriental Experience of Combining Arbitration with Conciliation: New Development of CIETAC and Chinese Judicial Practice, 40 Fordham Int'l L. J. 919 (2017).

Kevin C. Clark, The Philosophical Underpinning and General Workings of Chinese Mediation Systems: What Lessons Can American Mediators Learn? 2 Pepp. Disp. Resol. L. J. 117 (2001).

James R. Coben, My Change of Mind on the Uniform Mediation Act, Disp. Resol. Mag., Winter 2017, at 6.

Jack J. Coe Jr., Toward a Complementary Use of Conciliation in Investor-State Disputes—A Preliminary Sketch, 12 U.C. Davis J. Int'l L. & Pol'y 7 (2005), copyright 2005 by the Regents of the University of California, All Rights Reserved.

Amy J. Cohen, Debating the Globalization of U.S. Mediation: Politics, Power, and Practice in Nepal, 11 Harv. Negot. L. Rev. 295 (2006). Please note that the copyright in the Negotiation Law

Review is held by the President and Fellows of Harvard College, and that the copyright in the Article is held by the Author.

Ellen E. Deason, Predictable Mediation Confidentiality in the U.S. Federal System, 17 Ohio State J. on Dispute Resol. 239 (2002).

Ellen E. Deason, Procedural Rules for Complementary Systems of Litigation and Mediation—Worldwide, 80 Notre Dame L. Rev. 553 (2005).

Ellen E. Deason, Combinations of Mediation and Arbitration with the Same Neutral: A Framework for Judicial Review, 5 Y.B. Arb. & Mediation 219 (2013).

Ellen E. Deason, Enforcement of Settlement Agreements in International Commercial Mediation: A New Legal Framework?, Disp. Resol. Mag., Fall 2015, at 33.

Ellen E. Deason, Beyond "Managerial Judges": Appropriate Roles in Settlement, 78 Ohio St. L. J. 73 (2017).

Giuseppe De Palo and Romina Canessa, Sleeping? Comatose? Only Mandatory Consideration of Mediation Can Awake Sleeping Beauty in the European Union, 16 Cardozo J. Conflict Resol. 713 (2014).

Roberto Echandi & Priyanka Kher, Can International Investor-State Disputes be Prevented? Empirical Evidence from Settlements in ICSID Arbitration, 29 ICSID Rev. 41 (2014).

Susan Nauss Exon, Ethics and Online Dispute Resolution: From Evolution to Revolution, 32 Ohio St. J. on Disp. Resol. 609 (2017).

John D. Feerick, The Peace-Making Role of a Mediator, 19 Ohio St. J. on Disp. Resol. 229 (2003).

Jacqueline N. Font-Guzmán, Moving 'Beyond Neutrality' and Cross-cultural Training: Using World Café Dialogue to Address End-of-life Care Inequalities, 21 Peace & Conflict Stud. 49 (2014). This Journal is sponsored by the Department of Conflict Resolution at Nova University in Fort Lauderdale, Florida. The copyright holder is NSUWORKS ©2014.

Susan D. Franck, Integrating Investment Treaty Conflict and Dispute Systems Design, 92 Minn. L. Rev. 161 (2007).

Susan D. Franck, Arbitration Costs: Myths and Realities in Investment Treaty Arbitration (forthcoming 2019).

Rebecca Golbert, An Anthropologist's Approach to Mediation, 11 Cardozo J. Conflict Resol. 81 (2009).

Julia Ann Gold, ADR through a Cultural Lens: How Cultural Values Shape Our Disputing Processes, 2005 J. Disp. Resol. 289 (2005).

Melanie Greenberg, Mediating Massacres: When "Neutral, Low-Power" Models of Mediation Cannot and Should not Work, 19 Ohio St. J. on Disp. Resol. 185 (2003).

Isabelle R. Gunning, Diversity Issues in Mediation: Controlling Negative Cultural Myths, 1995 J. Disp. Resol. 55 (1995).

Mariana Hernandez Crespo, A Systemic Perspective of ADR in Latin America: Enhancing the Shadow of the Law through Citizen Participation, 10 Cardozo J. Conflict Resol. 91 (2008).

Mariana Hernandez Crespo, Building the Latin America We Want: Supplementing Representative Democracies with Consensus-Building, 10 Cardozo J. Conflict Resol. 425 (2009).

Mariana Hernandez Crespo, From Paper to People: Building Conflict Resolution Capacity and Frameworks for Sustainable Implementation of IIAs to Increase Investor-State Satisfaction, in United Nations Conference on Trade and Development, Investor-State Disputes: Prevention and Alternatives to Arbitration II 55 (Susan D. Franck & Anna Joubin-Bret eds., 2011). Reprinted with the permission of the United Nations.

Mariana Hernandez-Crespo, From Noise to Music: The Potential of the Multi-Door Courthouse (Casas de Justicia) Model to Advance Systemic Inclusion and Participation as a Foundation for Sustainable Rule of Law in Latin America, 2012 J. Disp. Resol. 335 (2012).

Mariana Hernandez-Crespo, 30 Years of Dispute Resolution in Latin America, Disp. Resol. Mag. Spring 2015, at 48.

Mariana Hernandez Crespo G., A New Chapter in Natural Resource-Seeking Investment: Using Shared Decisions System Design ("SDSD") to Strengthen Investor-State and Community Relationships, 18 Cardozo J. Conflict Resol. 551 (2017).

Mariana Hernandez Crespo Gonstead, A New Dance on the Global Stage: Introducing a Cultural Value-Based Toolbox to Optimize Problem-Solving, Innovation, and Growth, 34 Ohio St. J. on Disp. Resol. (forthcoming 2019).

Kathryn Hendley, Resistance, Indifference or Ignorance? Explaining Russians' Nonuse of Mediation, 32 Ohio St. J. on Disp. Resol. 469 (2017).

Anna Joubin-Bret, International Dispatch: Investor-State Disputes, Disp. Resol. Mag., Fall 2013, at 37.

Paul F. Kirgis, Status and Contract in an Emerging Democracy: The Evolution of Dispute Resolution in Ghana, 16 Cardozo J. Conflict Resol. 101 (2014).

Fan Kun, An Empirical Study of Arbitrators Acting as Mediators in China, 15 Cardozo J. Conflict Resol. 777 (2014).

John Lande, Using Dispute System Design Methods to Promote Good-Faith Participation in Court-Connected Mediation Programs, 50 UCLA L. Rev. 69 (2002).

Michelle LeBaron, Transforming Cultural Conflict in an Age of Complexity, in Berghof Handbook for Conflict Transformation 1 (2000), online version, Berlin: Berghof Foundation, www. berghof-foundation.org/handbook.

Joel Lee, Culture and its Importance in Mediation, 16 Pepp. Disp. Resol. L.J. 317 (2016).

Elisabeth Lindenmayer & Josie Lianna Kaye, A Choice for Peace? The Story of Forty-One Days of Mediation in Kenya (International Peace Institute 2009).

David J. Ludlow, Preventive Peacemaking in Macedonia: An Assessment of U. N Good Offices Diplomacy, 2003 BYU L. Rev. 761 (2003).

Fernando Vieira Luiz, Designing a Court-Annexed Mediation Program for Civil Cases in Brazil: Challenges and Opportunities, 15 Pepp. Disp. Resol. L. J. 1 (2015).

Tracy Walters McCormack, Susan Schultz & James McCormack, Probing the Legitimacy of Mandatory Mediation: New Roles for Judges, Mediators, and Lawyers, 1 St. Mary's J. on Legal Malpractice & Ethics 150 (2011).

Carrie Menkel-Meadow, Correspondences and Contradictions in International and Domestic Conflict Resolution: Lessons from General Theory and Varied Contexts, 2003 J. Disp. Resol. 319 (2003).

Carrie Menkel-Meadow, Exporting and Importing ADR "I've Looked at Life from Both Sides Now," Disp. Resol. Mag., Spring 2006, at 5.

Jacqueline Nolan-Haley, Court Mediation and the Search for Justice through Law, 74 Wash. U. L. Q. 47 (1996).

Jacqueline Nolan-Haley, Informed Consent in Mediation: A Guiding Principle for Truly Educated Decisionmaking, 74 Notre Dame L. Rev. 775 (1999).

Jacqueline Nolan-Haley, Harold Abramson & Pat K. Chew, International Conflict Resolution: Consensual ADR Processes (2005).

Jacqueline Nolan-Haley, Self-Determination in International Mediation: Some Preliminary Reflections, 7 Cardozo J. Conflict Resol. 277 (2006).

Jacqueline Nolan-Haley, Mediation Exceptionality, 78 Fordham L. Rev. 1247 (2009).

Jacqueline Nolan-Haley, Mediation: the Best and Worst of Times, 16 Cardozo J. Conflict Resol. 731 (2014).

Jacqueline Nolan-Haley, Is Europe Headed down the Primrose Path with Mandatory Mediation? 37 N.C. J. Int'l L. & Com. Reg. 981 (2012).

Jacqueline Nolan-Haley, Mediation: The "New Arbitration," 17 Harv. Negot. L. Rev. 61 (2012), Reproduced with permission of Harvard University Law School.

Jacqueline M. Nolan-Haley, Designing Systems for Achieving Justice after a Peace Agreement: Northern Ireland's Struggle with the Past, 13 U. St. Thomas L.J. 315 (2017).

Louise Otis & Eric H. Reiter, Mediation by Judges: A New Phenomenon in the Transformation of Justice, 6 Pepp. Disp. Resol. L. J. 351 (2006).

Ian R. K. Paisley, Peace Agreement-Or Last Piece in a Sellout Agreement? 22 Fordham Int'l L. J. 1273 (1998).

Don Peters, Can We Talk? Overcoming Barriers to Mediating Private Transborder Commercial Disputes in the Americas, 41 Vand. J. Transnat'l L. 1251 (2008).

Orna Rabinovich-Einy & Ethan Katsh, Digital Justice: Reshaping Boundaries in an Online Dispute Resolution Environment, 1 Int'l J. Online Disp. Resol. 5 (2014).

Jeswald W. Salacuse, Is There a Better Way? Alternative Methods of Treaty-Based, Investor-State Dispute Resolution, 31 Fordham Int'l L.J. 138 (2007).

Timothy Schnabel, The Singapore Convention on Mediation: A Framework for the Cross-Border Recognition and Enforcement of Mediated Settlements, 19 Pepperdine Disp. Resol. L.J. 1 (2019).

Jernej Sekolec & Michael B. Getty, The UMA and the UNCITRAL Model Law: An Emerging Consensus on Mediation and Conciliation, 2003 J. Disp. Resol. 175 (2003).

Omer Shapira, Conceptions and Perceptions of Fairness in Mediation, 54 S. Tex. L. Rev. 281 (2012).

Thomas Stipanowich, The International Evolution of Mediation: A Call for Dialogue and Deliberation, 46 Victoria Univ. Wellington L. Rev. 1191 (2015).

Thomas J. Stipanowich & Zachary P. Ulrich, Commercial Arbitration and Settlement: Empirical Insights into the Roles Arbitrators Play, 6 Y.B. on Arb. & Med. 1 (2014).

S.I. Strong, Beyond International Commercial Arbitration? The Promise of International Commercial Mediation, 45 Wash. U. J. L. & Pol'y 11 (2014).

U.N. Secretary General, Strengthening the Role of Mediation in the Peaceful Settlement of Disputes, Conflict Prevention and Resolution: Report of the Secretary-General, U. N. Doc. A/66/811 (June 25, 2012) Annex I: United Nations Guidance for Effective Mediation (2012).

Ellen Waldman & Lola Akin Ojelabi, Mediators and Substantive Justice: A View from Rawls' Original Position, 30 Ohio St. J. on Disp. Resol. 391 (2016).

Nancy Welsh, the Place of Court-Connected Mediation in a Democratic Justice System, 5 Cardozo J. Conflict Resol. 117 (2004).

Nancy A. Welsh & Andrea K. Schneider, Becoming "Investor-State Mediation", 1 Penn. St. J.L. & Int'l Aff. 86 (2012).

Leah Wing, Ethical Principles for Online Dispute Resolution: A GPS device for the Field, 3 Int'l J. Online Dispute Resol. 12 (2016).

Bobette Wolski, Arb-Med-Arb (and MSAs): A Whole Which is Less Than, Not Greater Than, The Sum of its Parts?, 6 Contemp. Asia Arb. J. 250 (2013).

Robert Yazzie, Life Comes from It: Navajo Justice Concepts, 24 N.M L. Rev. 175 (1994).

William Zartman, Cowardly Lions: Missed Opportunities for Dispute Settlement, 18 Ohio St. J. on Disp. Resol. 1 (2002).

# Summary of Contents

# Table of Contents

# Table of Cases

**The principal cases are in bold type.**

# Global Issues in Mediation

# Chapter 1

# MEDIATION OVERVIEW

## I. INTRODUCTION

Why should you be concerned with global issues in mediation? With international and comparative perspectives on mediation? One obvious reason is that the world is changing and many lawyers today practice in legal environments that have both cross-cultural and cross-border dimensions. It is a world of increasing economic globalization where conflict is inevitable and attempting to manage or resolve it can be costly. Thus, there is a growing demand for efficient, consensual, interest-based methods of dispute resolution. Among the most notable of these processes is mediation which is relevant to both private and public international conflict settings.

Mediation is used to manage or resolve disputes and conflicts. It is a consensual process in which a neutral third party, the mediator, helps to facilitate an agreement between disputing parties but does not decide the outcome of the dispute. Mediation, arbitration, and negotiation together compose modern alternative dispute resolution (ADR) and offer a flexible combination of processes in a creative mix and match among the component features of ADR. With the advent of modern dispute resolution and, since the 1980s, the development of dispute systems design (DSD), mediation has achieved increased prominence as an interest-based method of dispute resolution, offering stakeholders an alternative to rights-based processes such as arbitration and court adjudication. The practice of mediation has roots in ancient times but mediation occurs today because of pre-dispute agreements, agreements to mediate existing disputes and, in some cases, when ordered by a court. Mediation also occurs because arbitrators are trending toward settlement and bringing mediators into the room. Most recently, mediation principles are being applied in new forms that are shaped by technology, in which is called ODR or online dispute resolution.

Mediation has evolved into a constituent part of the architecture of international dispute resolution as a confidential, efficient process that saves costs, preserves on-going relationships, gives parties control over their disputes, provides transparency and creative solutions, and often results in greater levels of satisfaction than litigation. These features make mediation attractive to global companies searching for consensual, interest-based methods of dispute resolution that help them to avoid conflict and manage their disputes. Mediation emphasizes cooperative communications between parties and offers abundant flexibility as it is not bound by rules of civil procedure and evidence. The mediation mindset changes the paradigm in dispute resolution from a positional bargaining stance characteristic of the adversary system to a more problem-solving approach focused on underlying needs and interests.

In the private commercial context, global companies are searching for methods of avoiding conflict and managing disputes efficiently. Private provider organizations, formerly devoted to arbitration, now promote mediation in their rules and practices. In the political arena, the United Nations and most sovereign States support projects to promote mediation as a means of conflict prevention and resolution because mediators can re-focus political disputes away from adversarial posturing in the direction of interest-based communications. There are also on-going efforts to integrate mediation into investment treaty dispute resolution. Beyond the political arena, creative uses of mediation appear in several settings from managing international parental kidnapping cases to online mediation of cross-border commercial disputes.

One might wonder, why the popularity of mediation at this time in history? What drives the growing interest in mediation and motivates parties to attempt to resolve their differences through this non-adversarial process? There are several responses to these questions. One major concern is with what has happened to arbitration, which traditionally has been the most common dispute resolution process for commercial matters. Today, however, in many respects arbitration is beginning to resemble litigation with its adversarial focus, attendant delays and costs. This can have a negative impact on maintaining long-term commercial relationships and developing cross-border initiatives. A second concern with arbitration is the difficulty of judicial enforcement of arbitration awards in some cases. Whether this is due to lack of judicial independence, corruption, or inability to locate the assets of the award debtor, it is a factor leading some parties away from arbitration and towards the mediation process.

The purpose of this book is to give you an overview of the mediation landscape from a global perspective. While mediation has assumed increased relevance in the field of international dispute resolution, it is still developing as a profession; it is newly institutionalized in legal cultures; and, it is relatively new to the canon of legal education. National legal traditions have responded in differing ways to the implementation of mediation. Therefore, it is important for lawyers to have an appreciation of the differences and nuances in mediation law and practice in multiple traditions if they are to be effective in the transnational dispute resolution arena. They must consider several questions related to geography and choice of law. For just as in the practice of international arbitration, there are strategic decisions that have to be made about where to have mediation take place and what laws will govern the mediation.

As we will see in the following chapters, mediation rules and both "soft" and "hard" laws are emerging rapidly throughout the world and it is critical for lawyers to understand which jurisdictions provide the optimal regulatory environment. Some of the considerations on which lawyers must reflect include questions related to confidentiality, enforceability of both agreements to mediate and agreements which result from mediation, and the effect of a refusal to mediate when requested by the court or by another party.

The following sections introduce some basic definitional concepts related to both law and mediation. Part II explores the connections between mediation and access to justice while Part III offers basic definitions for the terms "international," "transnational," and "comparative." The mediation process is discussed in Part IV, and Part V describes several models of mediation practice, including non-western models. The role of mediation and technology is described in Part VI, while Part VII offers considerations as to when mediation is the appropriate process to use. The role of perceptions in mediation is discussed in Part VIII and finally, in Part IX, mediation is distinguished from other consensual problem-solving processes.

## II. ACCESS TO JUSTICE AND MEDIATION

Mediation is frequently referred to as a vehicle for providing access to justice. This is true in developed as well as developing countries. The following excerpt discusses the historical background of mediation's evolution from an informal method of dispute resolution to a claimed vehicle for access to justice.

## JACQUELINE NOLAN-HALEY, *IS EUROPE HEADED DOWN THE PRIMROSE PATH WITH MANDATORY MEDIATION?*

37 N.C. J. Int'l L. & Com. Reg. 981, 986–87 (2012).

The idea of access to justice encompasses multiple meanings, all focused on empowering individuals to exercise their rights in the civil justice system. Under customary international law, access to justice refers generally to an individual's right to seek a remedy before an impartial court of law or tribunal. Access to justice has been a longstanding priority for European states. Along with the right to life, the duty to respect human rights, the prohibition against torture, slavery, and forced labor, and the right to liberty and security, the right to a fair trial through access to justice is a major part of the architecture of the European Court of Human Rights.

The idea of access to justice is also part of a worldwide law reform movement described more than thirty-two years ago by Cappelletti and Garth in their international study of access to justice. These authors identified what they labeled as three "waves" of reform: (1) making legal aid accessible to the poor; (2) developing procedural devices that would allow a single lawsuit to resolve multiple claims; and (3) promoting systemic reform of the legal system through ADR. Today, ADR is a strong wave of reform in the United States and throughout the world.

Much of Europe's embrace of mediation has been under the banner of the third ADR wave, as the European Parliament has included within the concept of access to justice "access to adequate dispute resolution processes for individuals and businesses." In this sense, mediation and other ADR processes are part of a network of access to justice systems. It is assumed that mediation will provide what EU Commissioner of Justice, Viviane Reding, calls "alternative and additional access to justice in everyday life."

---

In some countries where the legal system functions inefficiently, ADR processes such as mediation may not be an *alternative* to the courts because these processes operate without a practical judicial option. Thus, mediation may be the sole source of access to justice for the more vulnerable members of a population. The following excerpt provides an example of this situation in the context of many Latin American countries.

## MARIANA HERNANDEZ CRESPO, *A SYSTEMIC PERSPECTIVE OF ADR IN LATIN AMERICA: ENHANCING THE SHADOW OF THE LAW THROUGH CITIZEN PARTICIPATION*

10 Cardozo J. Conflict Resol. 91, 92, 99, 114, 115 (2008).

In the United States, ADR generally works as an alternative to the judiciary within the framework of the legal system, operating under what has been described as "the shadow of the law." This concept has become a general assumption in the U.S. ADR field. However, this assumption does not hold in most Latin American countries. In Latin America, there is a marked gap between the laws on the books and laws in action. Although most Latin American constitutions and laws guarantee the protection of citizens' rights, more specifically the right of access to justice, by and large these rights are simply aspirational for most Latin Americans because enforcement mechanisms are weak. Thus, dispute resolution in Latin American operates under a pale shadow of the law.

* * *

.... Even though "extra-judicial agreements" are reached between parties (represented or unrepresented) outside the court system, the current backlogs of ten years or more mean that courts are unable to offer practical or effective recourse. In order to circumvent judicial backlogs, there has been a general trend towards the use of arbitration for international and domestic business disputes, and mediation for low-income communities, with little practical recourse to a functioning judiciary for review or enforcement. Nonetheless, backlogs still remain because the judiciary is the only institution with the power of enforcement.

This state of affairs falls hardest on the disenfranchised majorities. These citizens live in the *favelas*, or slums, that encircle the large cities of Latin America. Most of the residents are immigrants from rural areas or small cities, many earning less than one dollar a day. They lack licit channels or connections—in other words, power—that would allow them to advance economically or socially. They have inadequate access to government social services, including dispute resolution.

* * *

[B]ecause [these] reform efforts have not been sufficiently participatory, nor have they taken into account the relationship and attitudes of the various stakeholder groups to the government, they have instead led to greater social and political fragmentation. A clear illustration of the fragmentation is that affluent sectors of society are accustomed to providing for themselves many basic services provided by governments, such as health, safety and education, but the low-income citizens have no choice but to rely on governmental or pro-bono services. In matters of justice, the affluent stakeholders now have a private justice arbitration or mediation option to circumvent the judicial system. Government and donor-funded mediation services have become the primary method used to resolve conflict in low-income communities, particularly neighborhood and small-claims disputes. However, justice is an intrinsic function of the government, and donor-funded mediation centers cannot be the sole means for resolving disputes, particularly if there is little recourse in the event of an unfair agreement.

In sum, the introduction of ADR into dispute resolution systems that lack functional and effective courts, which is the case for most Latin American countries, has had the unintended effect of exacerbating problems of access to justice by creating three tiers of justice: private arbitration, for those who can afford an arbiter; the justice system, for those who can afford a lawyer; and mediation centers, mainly for those in low-income communities who can afford neither.

---

## III. DEFINITIONAL CONCEPTS

### A. "International"

Throughout this book, there are references to "international," "transnational" and "comparative," mediation. There are multiple definitions of these terms but for purposes of this book, the term "international" refers to systems, treaties, agreements, and model laws which transcend national boundaries. Two good examples of this definition are found in the UNCITRAL Model Laws:" Article 3(2) UNCITRAL Model Law on International Commercial Mediation and International Settlement Agreements Resulting from Mediation, 2018 (amending the UNCITRAL Model Law on International Commercial Conciliation, 2002) and Article 1(3) of the UNCITRAL Model Law on International Commercial Arbitration.

Article 3(2) of the UNCITRAL Model Law on International Commercial Mediation provides that: "A mediation is international if:

(a) The parties to an agreement to mediate have, at the time of the conclusion of that agreement, their places of business in different States; or

(b) The State in which the parties have their places of business is different from either:

(i) The State in which a substantial part of the obligations of the commercial relationship is to be performed; or
(ii) The State with which the subject matter of the dispute is most closely connected."

Similarly, Article 1(3) of the UNCITRAL Model Law on International Commercial Arbitration states that: "An arbitration is international if:

(a) the parties to an arbitration agreement have, at the time of the conclusion of that agreement, their places of business in different States; or (b) one of the following places is situated outside the State in which the parties have their places of business:

(i) the place of arbitration if determined in, or pursuant to, the arbitration agreement;

(ii) any place where a substantial part of the obligations of the commercial relationship is to be performed or the place with which the subject-matter of the dispute is most closely connected; or

(c) the parties have expressly agreed that the subject matter of the arbitration agreement relates to more than one country."

### B. "Transnational"

With the expansion of international business and the development of cross-border relationships in recent years, there has been a growing interest in studying laws and policies that regulate actions which extend across national boundaries. This is true in the area of both private and public international and domestic law. In attempting to conceptualize transnational law, Harold Koh defines it as representing "a kind of hybrid between domestic and international law that can be downloaded, uploaded, or transplanted from onc national system to another."[1] International commercial mediation may be considered an example of transnational law.[2]

### C. "Comparative"

The term "comparative mediation" refers to the domestic mediation cultures and systems of other countries. We study these cultures and systems to understand how they achieve the goals and express the values of mediation. Comparative mediation focuses then on the study of similarities and differences between mediation approaches in different countries. The contrast can shed light on existing laws. The points raised in the following excerpt about the study of comparative civil procedure are equally true for the study of comparative mediation perspectives.

> Comparative law is often described as providing both a window into other cultures as well as a mirror for one's own. Increased tolerance, respect, and understanding are among the "soft" values that comparativism promotes; that others can do things differently yet still succeed is an important reminder. But there are also benefits that might be characterized as "hard" values. To be an effective advocate, students must be prepared to deal effectively with foreign systems and foreign lawyers. Moreover, foreign legal systems can be sources for data and ideas about the causes of and solutions to universal problems. . . . . Understand that any procedural system is a complex and dynamic amalgam with interconnected parts influenced by culture, language, and other forces.[3]

## IV. UNDERSTANDING THE MEDIATION PROCESS

Mediation is an extension of the negotiation process in which a neutral third party helps disputing parties resolve or manage their disputes and conflicts. The term "impartial" is often used interchangeably with the term "neutral" when describing the third party facilitator in the mediation process. However, these terms may be understood as having distinct meanings. In this Chapter we follow those scholars who define mediator impartiality as not being biased

---

1 Harold H. Koh, *Why Transnational Law Matters,* 24 Penn State Int'l L. Rev. 745, 753 (2006).

2 *See generally* Nadja Alexander, International and Comparative Mediation: Legal Perspectives (2009).

3 Thomas O. Main, Global Issues in Civil Procedure 5 (2006).

towards any particular party, while neutrality suggests that the mediator is indifferent towards any outcome reached by the parties.[4]

Mediation is a highly contextual process. How it is conducted depends upon a host of variables ranging from subject matter and mediator style to whether legal or judicial review is required. While there are a range of possible models of practice, there are specific activities associated with the mediation process that are constant. These core activities consist of identifying interests, exchanging information and bargaining between the parties. This may occur in joint sessions with all the parties, in private meetings known as caucuses or in a combination of both.

## A. Defining Mediation

In the domestic (western) setting, the concept of mediation contemplates a private, informal, consensual process in which a neutral third-party, without power to impose a settlement, helps disputing parties to reach a mutually satisfactory resolution. Lon Fuller's classic formulation reminds us of mediation's "capacity to reorient the parties toward each other, not by imposing rules on them, but by helping them to achieve a new and shared perception of their relationship, a perception that will redirect their attitudes and dispositions toward one another."[5] In the international context, Jacob Bercovitch defines mediation as a "process of conflict management related to but distinct from the parties' own negotiations, where those in conflict seek the assistance, or accept an offer of help from an outsider (who may be an individual, an organization a group or a state) to change their perceptions of behavior and to do so without resorting to physical force or invoking the authority of the law."[6]

An important norm governing (facilitative) mediation practice is party self-determination. As will be seen in Chapter 2, understanding of this norm may vary in different cultures. The following excerpt describes the core values and major characteristics of mediation. Some of these concepts will also be discussed in later chapters dealing with legal and ethical issues in mediation.

---

[4] *E.g.*, Douglas N. Frenkel & James H. Stark, The Practice of Mediation 88 (3rd ed. 2018). See Chapter 5 for a further discussion of neutrality and impartiality.

[5] Lon L. Fuller, *Mediation—Its Forms and Functions*, 44 S. Cal. L. Rev. 305, 325 (1971).

[6] Jacob Bercovitch, *Mediation in International Conflict: An Overview of Theory, a Review of Practice*, in Peacemaking in International Conflict: Methods & Techniques 130 (I. William Zartman & J. Lewis Rasmussen eds., 1997).

## JACQUELINE NOLAN-HALEY, *MEDIATION: THE "NEW ARBITRATION"*

17 Harv. Negot. L. Rev. 61, 68–70 (2012).

Mediation's core values of self-determination and party participation have been its traditional and essential selling points. Most ethical codes and practice standards define mediation as a voluntary process grounded in self-determination. In fact, it is the notion of self-determination and party control of the outcome that distinguishes mediation from arbitration. This aspect of mediation is part of the decision making process where the participants themselves decide the outcome, in contrast to the arbitration process where the neutral third party decides the outcome. Self-determination enhances the development of parties' problem-solving capacities, their ability to craft individualized justice on their own terms based on their own interests and values. It is what helps parties move beyond mere justice to achieving a sense of peace in resolving their disputes. Peace in mediation includes interior peace, offering opportunities for apologies, forgiveness and reconciliation. For these reasons, mediation is a way out of a rule-bound, formal justice system.

The central ideology and distinguishing feature of mediation is its voluntariness, as reflected in mediation rhetoric that focuses on empowerment and recognition. In contrast to arbitration, voluntariness in mediation is pervasive. It operates from the very beginning of the process, when the parties agree to mediate, and continues until the end of the process, when the parties decide whether or not to resolve their dispute, and the terms upon which it will be resolved. . . . .

Mediation also offers protection from exposure in public forums. Confidentiality, an almost sacred canon in the mediation process, is protected by statutes, ethical codes and agreements between the parties. Finally, the mediation preference can be attributed to its compliance effects, cost efficiency, and therapeutic benefits. In this regard, mediation's "voice" and participation features provide a welcome antidote to the American civil justice system where litigants are provided little opportunity for personal expression. Unlike the adjudication process, mediation is not bound by evidentiary and procedural rules. Parties' narratives are honored and their interests are valued. Finally, with open communication, mediation offers possibilities for cooperation and creative problem solving. Parties are oriented towards a collaborative search for mutually agreeable solutions.

## B. Role of the Mediator

We earlier defined mediation as an extension of the negotiation process in which a neutral third party assists disputing parties in resolving or managing their disputes. The role of the mediator is essentially to facilitate and help design the process for the parties' negotiations. The following excerpt expands upon this understanding of the mediator's role. (See Chapter 3 for a discussion of the role of co-mediators)

### JACQUELINE M. NOLAN-HALEY, *COURT MEDIATION AND THE SEARCH FOR JUSTICE THROUGH LAW*

74 Wash. U. L. Q. 47, 53–55 (1996).

There are, today, a number of differing views about the mediation process, and this, in turn, has generated a variety of opinions about the appropriate role of the mediator. The label "mediation" is attached to a wide variety of practices ranging from court conferences strongly suggesting settlement to exercises in moral development. At one end of the spectrum is the instrumentalist vision of mediation as an efficient means of managing court calendars—a perfunctory process which settles cases and clears dockets. At the other extreme is a more noble vision of mediation as a process of moral development which helps individuals realize their ends and develop a stronger sense of efficaciousness. Somewhere in between is the ethical pragmatists' view that mediation is a good method of resolving some disputes when it is responsive to human needs.

Depending upon one's philosophy of mediation, the cardinal virtues of this process can be self-determination, autonomy, empowerment, transformation, and efficiency. Mediation is thought to enhance parties' self-determinative capabilities because it permits them to structure and consent to the outcome of the bargaining process. Unlike decision making by a neutral third party in the adjudication process, decision making in mediation rests solely with the disputing parties. Some commentators consider mediation to be a fairer process than adjudication because the affected parties have complete authority in selecting what values will govern the resolution of their dispute. Finally, mediation is thought to result in greater litigant satisfaction than does judicial adjudication of disputes. There has been a significant amount of scholarly activity directed toward testing and validating these assumptions.

## C. Process Design

Mediators face multiple challenges in designing a mediation process when parties do not share the same cultural background. In the following excerpt, Mariana Hernandez Crespo Gonstead, introduces the concept of a Cultural Value Discernment that can assist mediators in aligning processes to the values of the parties.

### MARIANA HERNANDEZ CRESPO GONSTEAD, *A NEW DANCE ON THE GLOBAL STAGE: INTRODUCING A CULTURAL VALUE-BASED TOOLBOX TO OPTIMIZE PROBLEM-SOLVING, INNOVATION, AND GROWTH*

34 Ohio St. J. on Disp. Resol. (forthcoming 2019).

[T]he global landscape enables parties to connect more easily than ever before with those from different backgrounds and cultures. While this presents tremendous opportunities for collective innovation and growth, it also poses unprecedented challenges for effective interactions. Despite the current levels of interconnectivity, the capacity to combine our differences has not yet reached its full potential. This is due in part to the lack of understanding of our different cultural values. In other words, what is truly important in one culture might not have the same significance, if any, in another. The fact that we might be able to speak the same language does not mean that we have gained a deep understanding of what is being said. This lack of understanding has the potential to not only affect the issue at hand, but also the relationship between the parties.

Without a deeper understanding of our personal and cultural values, we might be able to conduct transactions and, to a certain extent, problem solve, but we will not have a complete picture of the underlying motivations or values. Also, the full potential of the business relationship might not be fully realized, because to capitalize on synergies, it is necessary to have an understanding of where we are coming from—our values as a critical driving force. If we continue to connect mainly on common ground, we might miss opportunities that can only be created by integrating our differences.

* * *

However, the current mediation models used in different parts of the world might not be ideal to accomplish this complex task because dispute resolution processes reflect the values of the cultures from where they emerge. Tailored processes that are congruent with the values of all parties are essential in order to more fully engage the parties and gain a broader picture of the conflict and what matters the most to them. Therefore, in order to have processes that reflect the values of the parties, it might be necessary to first conduct the Cultural Value Discernment (CVD), to identify what each party deeply cares about, and then through process or system design, select, tweak, combine, or craft a culturally tailored method for resolution.

* * *

In order to fully take advantage of this increasing level of interconnectivity in our global economy, we will need to develop the necessary cultural capacities that allow us to interact more effectively with each other. The quality of the process, the parties' level of engagement, and the sustainability of the final agreement are at stake. What worked before might not work now, as we are continually interacting with those from different cultures and background. This is just a glimpse of what could become the new normal—a fully globalized and integrated world.

---

# V. MODELS OF MEDIATION PRACTICE

Related to the discussion of the mediator's role is the manner in which the mediator carries out that role or which practice model is used. There are several models of mediation practice through which this may be accomplished.

## A. Western Models of Mediation Practice

1. **Facilitative:** A facilitative mediator assists parties with their communications and negotiations. The mediator's strategies are designed to help parties identify the issue in dispute, understand their real needs and interests, and formulate options for settlement. Several models have emerged along the continuum of the facilitative mediation framework.

2. **Evaluative:** This model goes beyond facilitative behaviors and usually involves some type of professional assessment. This may consist of an opinion or prediction by the mediator regarding a court outcome or legal advice on an issue or recommendation of a specific settlement. The practice of mediator evaluation is a topic of considerable debate. In general, the argument in favor of evaluation argues for flexibility in the mediator's role while the opposing view holds that evaluation compromises the mediator's neutrality.

3. **Narrative:** The narrative model has been described as both an approach and a methodology. It focuses on culture and shared stories as the forces which shape parties' interests and positions. Parties are encouraged to resolve problems through a deep understanding of their shared narratives and culture. Absolute neutrality is not required of the mediator where issues of oppression exist. In general, substantive issues are less important than the relational needs of the parties.[7]

4. **Transformative Mediation:** The role of the transformative mediator is to establish a context for party empowerment and recognition. Rather than taking responsibility for helping parties to reach an agreement or taking a directive approach that focuses on settlement, the transformative mediator supports the parties' own decision-making. In this regard, the mediator is nonjudgmental and assumes that the parties are acting in good faith.

5. **Understanding-Based Mediation:** This is a non-caucus model that aims to resolve conflict through deeper understanding by the parties of their own and each other's perspectives. It emphasizes the parties' responsibility for their own decisions and the concept that parties are best served by working together in reaching a solution. It relies primarily on the power of understanding rather than on any coercive behaviors to organize and manage the process.[8]

6. **Guided Choice:** Recognizing that most cases result in a settlement, the Guided Choice process uses mediation to shorten the period prior to settlement. With the benefit of confidentiality protections in the background, the mediator begins the process by focusing on procedural issues and identifying potential impediments to settlement. The mediator then helps the parties understand the causes of their dispute and assess what information they need for settlement purposes.[9]

---

[7] John Winslade & Gerald D. Monk, Narrative Mediation 149 (2000).

[8] Gary Friedman and Jack Himmelstein, Challenging Conflict, Mediation Through Understanding (2008).

[9] Paul M. Lurie & Jeremy Lack, *Guided Choice Dispute Resolution Process: Reducing the Time and Expense to Settlement*, 8 Disp. Resol. Int'l 167 (2014).

## B. Non-Western Models of Mediation Practice

Earlier in this Chapter, we referred to mediation as a process in which a neutral third party helps disputing parties to reach a mutually satisfactory resolution. Neutrality, however, is not a universally shared value in mediation. In some countries and cultures a mediator is expected to share her wisdom with the parties and offer them a solution. For example, some Middle Eastern countries might turn to the ancient tradition of "*wassata*" in which a tribal elder attempts to influence parties in resolving their disputes. Similarly, in some Native American and in some African tribal communities, a respected elder may conduct the mediation and strongly influence the outcome.

The following excerpt describes what Professor Harold Abramson has labeled the "wisely directive mediator."[10]

## JACQUELINE NOLAN-HALEY, HAROLD ABRAMSON & PAT K. CHEW, INTERNATIONAL CONFLICT RESOLUTION: CONSENSUAL ADR PROCESSES

132, 136–37 (2005).

*Wisely Directive Mediators*

In some countries, disputing parties have experience with a "wise" third party who is a source of the "right" answers and is assertively directive. The wisely directive mediator investigates the dispute, evaluates it, and formulates and promotes solutions based on the wisdom for which he or she was selected. That wisdom could be informed by local cultural norms, religious values, and the mediator's leadership position, age, and legal knowledge. Parties expect to receive the evaluations and answers; parties also are expected to accept them. Therefore, while the role of the wise third party may be to "mediate," the third party effectively functions as a quasi-adjudicator imposing a resolution on the parties. Wisely directive mediators can be found in some Islamic countries, and China, among other places.

* * *

*Distinguish Wisely Directive Mediation from Other Settlement Processes*

The distinctive function of the wisely directive mediator should appear familiar to people in the United States knowledgeable about

---

10 See Harold Abramson, *Selecting Mediators and Representing Clients in Cross-Cultural Disputes*, 7 Cardozo J. Conflict Resol. 253, 265–270 (2006).

*evaluative mediation* in which the mediator assesses the merits of the dispute or solutions, *judicial settlement conferences* in which a judge hints at what she might do in court or urges a particular settlement, and *nonbinding arbitration* where an arbitrator issues a decision on the merits. The function of the third party in these three familiar settlement processes and the wisely directive process are similar. The third party offers evaluations.

But parties' responses to third party evaluations in the U.S. are not similar to parties' responses to wisely directive evaluation in other countries. An evaluation from a U.S. mediator can provide valuable input but parties are relatively free to reject the recommendation as well as resist any pressure if the mediator is also directive. Parties can reject and resist with little consequence. An evaluation from a settlement judge can be riskier to repel especially if the parties want to avoid alienating the judge that might decide the case. Nevertheless, parties are not shy about resisting pressure when they must to protect their interests—a proud trait for those brought up in an individualistic society. And, a nonbinding decision by an arbitrator who will not be further involved in resolving the dispute can be freely rejected by the parties.

In contrast, an evaluation and pressure from a wise third party is received quite differently. Various case studies suggest that, based on history and experience in a collectivist society, disputing parties expect the wisely directive mediator to steer them toward the right solution, a solution that they are expected to accept. The third party may dress like a mediator but act more like an arbitrator.

Although wisely directive mediation may no longer be embraced intact by either mediators or parties in modern societies, its cultural influence can still be felt in the mediation practice of some regions around the globe.

---

## VI. MEDIATION AND TECHNOLOGY

One result of the Internet's rapid growth over the last thirty years has been the expansion of digital technology and the development of online dispute resolution (ODR). ODR refers to procedures for resolving disputes through the use of information technology. It requires the use of an electronic platform that is dedicated to facilitating the dispute resolution process. Early use of ODR involved the use of human mediators who used the platform network instead of face-to-face meetings but the mediation skills they used were traditional offline skills. However, the future of mediation use in ODR is now pointing in a different direction.

The following excerpts discuss how ODR has the potential to alleviate some of the problems with the traditional justice system. They illustrate some examples of cutting edge online mediation practices and offer predictions as to how ODR may be expanded in the future with the introduction of technological "fourth" parties in mediation.

## THOMAS J. STIPANOWICH, *THE INTERNATIONAL EVOLUTION OF MEDIATION: A CALL FOR DIALOGUE AND DELIBERATION*

46 Victoria Univ. Wellington L. Rev. 1191, 1226–28 (2015).

### *Technology, Mediation and Conflict Management*

In every aspect of our lives, communication is increasingly digital and virtual, and the implications for managing and resolving conflict are immense. In an age when clients demand greater value for money and rapid results, technology offers many opportunities for achieving efficiency and economy and, hopefully, providing fair and satisfactory experiences and outcomes. It also presents many new challenges.

As a primary means of communication across distances, and even within homes and offices, email has become an indispensable element in conflict and its resolution. Electronic interchange is the backbone of modern business transactions . . . . Email is also a prime ancillary tool for dispute resolution professionals in mediation and arbitration.

Since the beginning of the 21st century, a variety of existing and would-be dispute resolution service providers have promoted online dispute resolution (ODR) in the form of "cybermediation". Although growth was initially slow, ODR has found an initial and expanding niche with the growth of e-commerce, as it proved to be a means of addressing concerns regarding the reliability of online sellers or products, and the availability of accessible recourse, in the event of a dispute.

The cutting edge of online mediation is presently in the arena of high-volume, low-value online transactions. The most visible and notably successful of online systems is the one designed by SquareTrade as the ODR provider for eBay, a system that has facilitated the settlement of millions of disputes between online buyers and sellers.

The advent of ODR prompted UNCITRAL to establish a Working Group to draft procedural rules on Online Dispute Resolution for Cross-Border Electronic Commerce Transactions (ODR For E-Commerce). While there are serious questions about the eventual outcome of this effort, change is proceeding apace. This is certainly the case in China, the home of more than 600 million Internet users (comprising almost half the population of the PRC as of the end of 2013).

The Chinese Internet company, Sina, established a team of 5,000 mediators for its Weibo social media platform. Taobao, the Chinese counterpart of eBay, now sponsors its own equivalent of the ODR system designed by SquareTrade for eBay. In 2014, Baidu, the Chinese web-services corporation, established the Baidu People's Mediation Committee in order to properly respond to disputes from consumers and enterprises they link to through Baidu. . . . . [S]everal Chinese courts authorised the Mediation Center of the Internet Society of China to mediate domain name disputes. The Mediation Center of the Internet Society of China (ISC) has partnered with various institutions to promote new online dispute coordination and resolution mechanism for Internet-based claims. These developments suggest that mediation through online platforms represents a looming cutting edge of change for mediation of online transactions as well as court-connected mediation in the PRC. It will be interesting to see how these changes affect perceptions and practices in Chinese mediation.

## ORNA RABINOVICH-EINY & ETHAN KATSH, *DIGITAL JUSTICE: RESHAPING BOUNDARIES IN AN ONLINE DISPUTE RESOLUTION ENVIRONMENT*

1 IJODR. 5, 25, 26, 32 (2014).

We can expect the use of ODR to expand even further in light of three developments: (1) changing views towards the online medium and digital communication, (2) development of ever more powerful software and (3) ongoing dissatisfaction with the functioning of courts and ADR. The first development has to do with the growing reliance on digital communication in people's lives in modern day society. Initially, these tools were used to communicate with and shop from distant strangers. We currently use digital communication to interact with those closest to us, touching on mundane but also more sensitive and complicated matters. As the online-offline distinction continues shifting and the line separating the online 'space' from the physical surroundings is being blurred, our understanding on what can be performed online is also changing, making ODR more appealing for offline, potentially more complex and intimate disputes.

The second development concerns evolving, indeed accelerating, innovation in the use of data. The rapidly growing field of Big Data focuses on finding meaning in data that in the past was never collected or examined. In the ADR field, data was routinely discarded when a dispute was resolved, and in the dispute prevention arena data was often not available.

* * *

The third development has to do with the potential of technology to remedy some of the persistent problems we have been experiencing with our justice system. Despite hopes that informal justice and the concept of a 'multi-door courthouse' could improve court efficiency and result in more satisfactory processes and imaginative outcomes, the institutionalization of ADR was accompanied by fierce critiques ranging from the dangers posed to parties belonging to disadvantaged groups to the curtailment of law development and precedent-setting. Criticism extended to proponents of ADR who were disappointed as hopes of increased speed and efficiency remained unrealized and the quality of ADR processes was questioned. In recent decades it has become evident that technology could dramatically enhance the efficiency of both court proceedings and alternatives through automation and 24/7 access to files from afar. Over time, other features of ODR that were initially viewed as shortcomings, such as documentation, have been seen as potentially advantageous in remedying some of the other problems associated with traditional ADR processes by allowing better monitoring, quality control, consistency and a higher degree of transparency.

* * *

The introduction of technology into the design of the process in the form of the technological 'fourth party' has both generated completely new types of processes unimaginable in the face-to-face era and separated some familiar dispute resolution processes from qualities and traits previously considered significant, if not essential, to their design and operation. A clear example of a new process is the emergence of automated and technology-assisted negotiation/mediation approaches, which include problem identification processes (eBay), mechanisms for matching problems and solutions (SquareTrade), automated negotiation support systems (SmartSettle) and blind bidding tools (CyberSettle). These processes escape previously accepted clear-cut distinctions between direct negotiation and third-party dispute resolution, giving rise to another *sui generis* category in which the 'fourth party' displaces the third party. These applications have been employed mainly in relatively simple disputes but can be expected to evolve and play a useful role and be a force for change in the managing of highly complex disputes.

## VII. WHEN IS MEDIATION THE APPROPRIATE PROCESS?

Not every case is appropriate or even ripe for mediation and there is some debate about the benefits of mediation generally. Advocates favor mediation as a process which reduces the transaction costs and acrimony associated with litigation. Critics argue that when mediation is unsuccessful in resolving a dispute, it increases the transaction costs of a dispute. Earlier critics claimed that mediation disadvantaged the poor and minority populations. The following excerpt discusses the suitability of mediation, particularly in cases that are international in character.

### JACQUELINE NOLAN-HALEY, HAROLD ABRAMSON & PAT K. CHEW, INTERNATIONAL CONFLICT RESOLUTION: CONSENSUAL ADR PROCESSES

97–98 (2005).

1. *Disputes Suitable for Mediation*

The suitability of a dispute for mediation does not depend on the dispute's substantive content; it depends on whether your client's process interests can be met in mediation. A client may prefer mediation because it might meet her interests in:

a. Controlling the outcome. She may want a process that gives her the power to retain control over the outcome of the dispute.

b. Selecting a forum that addresses all issues. She may want a process that can produce a global solution that goes beyond resolving the narrow legal issues that brought the parties to arbitration or court.

c. Preserving or improving a continuing relationship with the other party.

d. Avoiding establishing a binding precedent.

e. Developing creative remedies. She may want to search for remedies that are not restricted to what an arbitrator or judge is likely to order.

f. Forming an enduring settlement. She may desire a process that fosters implementation by involving parties in the nuanced shaping of the settlement terms.

g. Maintaining confidentiality. She may need an assurance of confidentiality before she will share critical information and settlement ideas with the other side.

h. Saving time and money.

i. "Cleaning-Up" the case. Even when she does not expect the case to settle fully in the mediation she may want to gain a better understanding of her interests, clarify what issues need to be resolved, dispose of some issues, solidify a discovery schedule, and develop a plan for resolving any remaining issues.

j. Examining and discussing conflicting views of the facts or the law. This preview of the facts and the law in mediation can provide a valuable reference point for parties who are trying to assess whether to accept a proposal on the table or continue litigating.

k. Venting. A party may need a forum where she can feel that the other side has heard her or she can constructively discharge any built up anger.

l. Overcoming communication problems between participants.

m. Dealing with an unskilled negotiator.

n. Overcoming conflicts between her and her attorney or conflicts between the opposing attorney and his client.

*2. Disputes Less Suitable for Mediation*

Some party's process interests are less suitable for mediation. Even though these interests can occasionally be met in mediation, they are usually more meaningfully satisfied in other forums such as a court or possibly in arbitration. Interests that are less suitable for mediation include:

a. Establishing precedent to guide future conduct.

b. Deterring future litigation.

c. Securing vindication.

d. Going for the jackpot before a jury, judge, or arbitrator.

e. Overcoming particular impediments that are especially difficult to overcome in mediation such as:

   i. Preserving a Principle. Your client may be unwilling to agree to any settlement in which he must compromise a personal principle or value.

   ii. Other party is inadequately represented.

   iii. Critical party is not participating.

   iv. Other party is engaging in bad faith negotiations

---

## VIII. ROLE OF PERCEPTIONS IN MEDIATION

As discussed earlier in this Chapter, mediation generally involves managing or resolving either disputes or conflicts. Frequently, conflict does not lie in objective reality but in how people think about or perceive a situation. Thus, how conflicts are framed and how narratives are constructed can have a substantial impact both on parties' perceptions of conflict and how the conflict is managed or resolved.

When parties have different views of a conflict situation, the mediator is required to manage the tensions between the two conflicting perceptions. This was the challenging task that confronted former Senator George Mitchell who mediated the peace talks in Northern Ireland that led to the signing of the Good Friday/ Belfast Agreement in 1998. This Agreement began the process of ending a 30 year era of violent conflict known as "The Troubles." The following excerpts describe the reactions of the leaders of two dominant political groups in Northern Ireland to the signing of this Agreement. One party views the peace process with confidence and optimism while the other labels it a "counterfeit peace."

### GERRY ADAMS, *TO CHERISH A JUST AND LASTING PEACE*

22 Fordham Int'l L. J. 1179, 1195–99 (1998).

In the opening line of the diary that he kept during the first three weeks of his hunger strike, republican prisoner Bobby Sands, who died after fifty-five days on strike, wrote: "I am standing on the threshold of another trembling world." We in Ireland also stand on the threshold of a new beginning—of a new world that holds enormous potential for all Irish people.

History occasionally grants each of us a unique opportunity to contribute to the future well-being of our family, friends, and neighbors, and of children yet to be born. The people of Ireland are at a defining point in our history and everything depends on how we respond to the opportunities and difficulties that lie before us.

Sinn Fein's peace strategy and the many political and personal risks that we have taken, along with the efforts of nationalists, the Irish government, Irish America, U.S. government, and most recently the Blair government in London, have brought about a situation that only a few short years ago would have been unthinkable. This process has been a difficult one, but Irish republicans have demonstrated repeatedly our capacity to overcome adversity and advance our struggle for freedom and justice against enormous odds.

* * *

There will be many difficulties ahead for all of us, but we must look forward with confidence and optimism. This is a watershed moment in our history, one that we cannot allow to slip away. It must be seized with both hands. The decisions and actions of the next few months will determine whether we move forward. History has placed a challenge at all our doors. We must succeed, for all our people and for generations yet to be born.

## IAN R.K. PAISLEY, *PEACE AGREEMENT—OR LAST PIECE IN A SELLOUT AGREEMENT?*

22 Fordham Int'l L. J. 1273, 1318–19 (1998).

In Northern Ireland today there prevails an unbelievable situation. British democracy has been trampled into the ground. The civil rights and cultural heritage of the Protestant and Unionist majority are being systemically eroded because of Government that has totally failed to deal with Irish Republican terrorism is instead continuing its headlong capitulation to the violence and threats of the IRA and its political wing, Sinn Fein.

Northern Ireland is paying for England's peace. In order to avoid repetition of the atrocities of the Warrington and Canary Wharf bombs, the British Government is selfishly appeasing the crocodile of a violent terrorist minority. Britain has shamelessly abandoned its support for the democratic and constitutional rights of a peaceful majority, which it is attempting to sedate with the contrived propaganda of a counterfeit peace.

The depth of political depravity to which the British government has sunk in its self-destructive urge to appease the forces of the pan-

Nationalist conspiracy is perfectly symbolized in the current mass release of terrorist prisoners onto the streets of Northern Ireland, many of them guilty of vile maiming, butchering, and murdering of their innocent victims, and all of them now enabled to return to and to use their intact stockpile of weaponry and explosives when their fascist aims are not achieved—an arsenal that, despite the provisions of the so-called Good Friday Agreement, the IRA now says that it will not decommission.

This situation is the fruit of three decades of appeasement of the Irish Republican agenda.

* * *

This agreement is a reprehensible deal. It is an insult to the victims of terrorism and is a two-fingered salute to the democratic community of Northern Ireland. Little wonder the IRA rejoiced in the deal and the UFF called on their one-time enemies to embrace it. It allows for the throwing open of our jails, for the replenishing of the ranks of the terrorist organizations, and for the strengthening of the IRA. The *Daily Telegraph* rightly commented: "Over the whole scene hangs the dark cloud of Sinn Fein/IRA—as strong, as armed, as unreconciled to peace as in the past and, perhaps, freer than ever. No, these are not good days for the union."

---

## IX. DISTINGUISHING MEDIATION FROM OTHER PROBLEM-SOLVING PROCESSES USING THIRD PARTIES

### A. Processes Aligned to Mediation

As discussed in the previous section, the mediation process involves the use of a third party who intervenes in a situation for the purpose of assisting parties in managing or resolving their disputes or conflicts. Other processes such as consensus building, dialogue, public peace processes and fact-finding also use third parties to help manage conflicts and disputes. However, the processes discussed in the following excerpts, third-party consultation, good offices, and conciliation, are more closely aligned to mediation.

## JACQUELINE NOLAN-HALEY, HAROLD ABRAMSON & PAT K. CHEW, INTERNATIONAL CONFLICT RESOLUTION: CONSENSUAL PROCESSES

34–36 (2005).

*Third-Party Consultation*

Consultation is a preliminary form of negotiation in which parties discuss issues and exchange views. Professional writings increasingly recognize consultation as a process for resolving disputes relating to the interpretation of treaties or as a pre-negotiation phase in the settlement of disputes. Most recently, the use of consultation has increased with the growth of international trade. For example, the four part Dispute Settlement system of the World Trade Organization (WTO) begins with a flexible consultation process conducted by the parties. The purpose of consultation is to help the parties resolve their dispute by giving them a better understanding of the conflict and the legal claims on both sides. WTO statistics show that more than half of the cases are either resolved, settled, or abandoned at the consultation phase.

Effective consultation requires the parties' voluntary good faith cooperation. When disputing parties use consultation as a mere formality or in bad faith, the process lacks integrity and it will not achieve effective results.

*Good Offices*

The traditional understanding of "good offices" refers to the use of third-parties—such as States, international organizations, or individuals—to assist two conflicting countries in negotiating a resolution of their dispute. The use of "good offices" is a traditional method of diplomatic assistance with longstanding historical roots. Its legitimacy was affirmed in the Hague Convention or the Pacific Settlement of International Disputes (1907) which provides that "strangers to the dispute have the right to offer good office or mediation even during the course of hostilities" (Art. 3, para. 2). Acting under the auspices of "good offices," individuals use a variety of means to facilitate the resolution of disputes and conflicts, including informal contacts, friendly suggestions, or mediation. More recently, the use of good offices has been expanded to include the intervention of international organizations, particularly the Secretary General of the United Nations, to end human rights violations.

---

## B. Conciliation

In some legal cultures, mediation is distinguishable from the more directive conciliation process where the neutral third party may be more actively involved in moving disputing parties towards agreement by offering legal information and proposals for settlement. For this reason, some commentators suggest that the conciliation process should be positioned between mediation and arbitration. Linda Reif offers further elaboration upon the differences between mediation and conciliation:

> . . . . [T]he concept of conciliation stemmed from and resembles mediation, with both methods using a third party to facilitate a nonbinding result through the medium of communication with the disputants. Indeed, the two terms are occasionally used interchangeably. In the transnational system, a distinction between the two can be made in the degree of formality and level of initiative imposed on the third party. A mediation is more informal and the mediator, when making proposals, is expected to construct them based purely on the information provided by the parties. Comparatively, a conciliation is more formal in structure and procedure, yet retains a nonadversarial environment. The central objective of the conciliator is to facilitate an amicable settlement of the conflict by communicating with the parties, typically through structured conciliation proceedings, and by submitting written proposals for a resolution of the dispute.[11]

In some other legal cultures, however, conciliation is a less directive process than mediation.

## C. Combinations of Mediation and Arbitration

Mediation is sometimes combined with arbitration in what can be called a "mixed mode" or "hybrid" process. Ellen Deason introduces the concept and its advantages:

---

[11] Linda C. Reif, *Conciliation as a Mechanism for the Resolution of International Economic and Business Disputes*, 14 Fordham Int'l L. J. 578, 584 (1990).

## ELLEN E. DEASON, *COMBINATIONS OF MEDIATION AND ARBITRATION WITH THE SAME NEUTRAL: A FRAMEWORK FOR JUDICIAL REVIEW*

5 Y.B. Arb. & Mediation 219 (2013).

The combined process typically takes the form of mediation followed by arbitration ("med-arb"), arbitration followed by mediation ("arb-med"), or arbitration with the possibility of a break in the proceedings for mediation ("mediation window"). A major advantage of these combinations is that they offer parties not only the opportunity to structure and control their own resolution, but also the certainty that if the parties do not agree to a settlement in mediation their dispute will be resolved in a final and binding award. The processes can be fully separated and conducted by different neutrals, but using the same neutral is an attractive way for parties to reduce costs. It eliminates the need for the parties to identify and appoint an additional neutral, and they can start the second process without having to educate a new neutral about the case.

---

Attitudes about combining mediation with arbitration differ around the world and the practice raises numerous issues. These topics are covered in Chapter 6.

# X. NOTES AND QUESTIONS

1. In the "wisely directive mediator" model, the mediator promotes a specific form of settlement for the parties. How does this approach take into account the principle of party-self-determination?
2. What are some benefits of using ODR? Are there any circumstances when you believe the use of ODR is not appropriate?
3. What are the underlying values of the mediation process? Do you think that autocratic societies would be able to truly accept mediation with its assumptions about party self-determination?
4. Do you have a preference for any one of the western models of mediation described in this chapter? Discuss the reasons for your choice.
5. What is the difference between the two UNCITRAL definitions of the term "international"? Of what significance are the differences?
6. Compare the radically different perceptions of the leaders of the two dominant political groups in Northern Ireland regarding the peace agreement that was signed in 1998 after 30 years of violent conflict

in that country. What are some of the challenges for the mediator in a conflict situation such as this one?

7. In your opinion, would the "wisely directive mediator" model described in this Chapter have been effective in mediating the conflict in Northern Ireland?

# Chapter 2

# COURT-CONNECTED AND MANDATORY FORMS OF MEDIATION

## I. INTRODUCTION

A variety of mediation regimes have been adopted by several countries as part of modern civil procedure reforms. In an effort to control case dockets, reduce costs and provide more streamlined, efficient justice, court administrators and some private provider organizations are turning to mediation. Proponents argue that institutionalized mediation programs reflect a public policy of encouraging parties to engage in solving their own disputes. They help to remove the perception that using mediation is a sign of weakness, and they support a lawyer's decision to recommend mediation to her clients. Others argue that these mediation programs provide access to justice.

Persuaded by the time and cost savings of mediation (and unhappy at its low usage) many countries have adopted a variety of mandatory regimes which require parties to attend mediation as a precondition to having a trial in court. In the United States, for example, courts have the power to require parties to participate in mediation. This power arises from a number of sources including individual court rules, laws, the parties' contractual obligations to mediate, and the Federal Rules of Civil Procedure. Other countries, such as Italy, have instituted mandatory mediation of certain categories of cases through legislation. The Court of Justice of the European Union (EU) has upheld Italy's approach, holding that EU law does not preclude national legislation which provides that, in disputes involving consumers, mandatory mediation should take place before any court proceedings.[1]

---

[1] Court of Justice of the EU, Judgment in Case C-75/16, Livio Menini and Maria Antonia Rampanelli v. Banco Popolare Societa Cooperativa (June 14, 2017).

There is a great deal of diversity within court-connected and mandatory mediation programs. Within these broad frameworks, there are programs with opt-in and opt-out provisions, and with various incentives for participation. An opt-in structure allows parties to have a preliminary meeting with the mediator and then decide whether or not to engage in the mediation process. In contrast, with opt-out provisions, parties attend an initial mediation session and then they may decide to withdraw at the beginning of the process. In a very real sense, these programs of integrating mediation into the litigation system are redefining the relationship between mediation and litigation. It is important to keep in mind, however, that while mandatory mediation programs exert various pressures on parties to participate in mediation, it is never permissible for programs or mediators to coerce or otherwise pressure parties with respect to their decisionmaking. This is because the essence of mediation is party self-determination.

## II. BRINGING MEDIATION INTO THE COURT SYSTEM

### A. Historical Development in the United States

The origins of court-connected mediation programs can be traced back to the 1976 National Conference on the Causes of Popular Dissatisfaction with the Administration of Justice, also known as the Pound Conference. At that conference, scholars, judges and practitioners explored ways to improve the traditional justice system. The late Frank Sander in his seminal article, *Varieties of Dispute Processing*[2] proposed the idea of a "multi-door courthouse" where disputes would be referred to appropriate dispute resolution (ADR) processes such as arbitration, mediation, or negotiation, rather than the traditional, automatic referral to the trial process. Over the years since the Pound Conference, the use of court-connected ADR processes has grown dramatically with mediation becoming the most common form of ADR used in state and federal courts in the United States. In the following excerpt, Magistrate Wayne Brazil reflects on the benefits of court ADR programs.

---

[2] Frank E. A. Sander, *Varieties of Dispute Processing*, Address delivered at the National Conference on the Causes of Popular Dissatisfaction with the Administration of Justice (Apr. 7–9, 1976), in 70 F.R.D. 79, 111–34 (1976).

## WAYNE D. BRAZIL, *COURT ADR 25 YEARS AFTER POUND: HAVE WE FOUND A BETTER WAY?*

18 Ohio St. J. on Disp. Resol. 93, 94–96 (2002).

The questions are as follows: "Court ADR 25 years after Pound: have we found a better way?" "ADR outcomes: saves what—has court ADR kept its promise?" "Has the integration of ADR into the litigation process improved the administration of justice?" "What has been gained?" "What has not been gained?" "Where do the perils lurk?" "What are the primary challenges that court ADR faces and what are the most threatening dangers on the road ahead?"

* * *

*Have We Found a Better Way?*

My answer is a resounding "No." We have not found "a" better way. We have found nothing in the singular. What we have found is in the plural. And if what we have does not remain in the plural we will have seriously compromised our capacity for gains.

Moreover, we contravene the spirit of ADR if we insist on "winning"—if we insist on establishing that ADR is necessarily better than traditional litigation. ADR is *not* about being better than; it is about being in addition to. ADR is *not* about subtracting; it is about adding. And the perils we face will be much more threatening if we fail to make this point clear to those who see ADR as subtraction—especially those who see it as subtraction from the Seventh Amendment.

* * *

Has court ADR kept its promise? In addressing this question, we must begin by weaning ourselves from the suggestion that the answer necessarily has anything to do with "savings," unless what we are talking about saving is public trust in and respect for the system of justice.

Has there ever been just one promise of court ADR? Haven't there been many different promises? And haven't those promises changed, appropriately, over time?

Who are the primary promisees? The courts? Legislators and administrators trying to protect the public fisc? Lawyers? Professional neutrals? Or the people—especially people who need dispute resolution services?

Let me be clear from the outset about my core views on this matter. One of the defining beauties of court ADR is that it is not built on any one promise, but on many different kinds of promises promises that can and should evolve over time. Another notion that is fundamental to court ADR is that the parties should decide for themselves which promises are most important to them.

As a matter of public policy, however, I believe that not all of the promises of court ADR are equal. Instead, there are among those promises two that are most significant. These are the promises of opportunity and of process integrity.

At the core of every court ADR program worthy of its name is one dominating set of messages. Through its ADR program, the court reaches out to the parties and says: "we acknowledge you, we acknowledge your needs, we acknowledge your entitlement to define for yourself what is most important to you, and we acknowledge that in some circumstances the established system of litigation serves some legitimate needs poorly. Just like when we provide you with a trial, we cannot and do not guarantee any particular outcome or achievement; we cannot and do not guarantee that if you use an alternative process you will be successful, by whatever criteria you define success. We cannot guarantee that you will save time or money. We cannot guarantee that you will achieve a better result than you would through litigation. Instead, the promise we make through our ADR program is to provide you with an opportunity, an opportunity to see if some other way might serve you better."

---

## B. The Relationship Between Court-Mediation and Democracy

The growth of mediation programs within the judicial system has given rise to a greater prominence for the core values of autonomy and party self-determination. These values suggest the possibility of greater democratic participation in decision making. In theory, this means that parties who are affected by a dispute decide the outcome of that dispute. But what has this meant in practice? Has mediation actually begun to transform the court system with a new vision of democracy? In the follow excerpt, Nancy Welsh reflects on these questions with both a critical and hopeful perspective.

## NANCY A. WELSH, *THE PLACE OF COURT-CONNECTED MEDIATION IN A DEMOCRATIC JUSTICE SYSTEM*

5 Cardozo J. Conflict Resol. 117, 135–38, 143–44 (2004).

### *The Current Place of Mediation in the Evolution of the Judicial System*

Within the last decade, another dispute resolution process—mediation—has become the "darling" of the courts. Court-connected mediation programs began to appear in the 1980's and, at this point, can be found in nearly all state and federal courts. Magistrate Judge Wayne Brazil has urged that the process "democratized our institution [the courts] in potentially profound ways because mediation permitted, in fact actively encouraged, the parties to decide for themselves which values were most important to them, then to use ADR to pursue those values."

* * *

There can be little doubt that the "contemporary mediation movement" of the late 1970's and early 1980's was inspired by the principles of democracy. Mediation proponents emphasized the central role to be played by citizens in disputes. *Citizens*—not judges or attorneys or other professionals-would communicate and negotiate directly with each other, identify the issues to be discussed, determine the substantive norms that were legitimate and relevant (including the pursuit of harmony and reconciliation if they wished), create the options for settlement, and control the final decision regarding whether or not to settle and on what terms. The mediator's role was to facilitate and to help these disputing parties find their own voices and solutions. Ultimately, mediation "seemed to embody both a faith in the dignity and autonomy of individual citizens and a skepticism regarding the legitimacy of government authorities and professionals."

Certainly, there are ways in which court-connected mediation has stayed true to this democratic spirit. Consistent with the values of self-determination and accountability, there is no binding outcome in mediation unless the parties agree to it. Attorneys, who generally attend these mediation sessions, report that their understanding of their clients' goals and potential solutions are influenced by the clients' presence. No doubt, some mediation sessions result in creative resolutions that reflect the particular needs, abilities, and preferences of parties. Court-connected mediation also offers citizens at least some degree of participation. At most mediation sessions, the parties attend and contribute to the discussion either directly or through their attorneys. The parties thus are not forced to rely blindly on their attorneys to conduct separate, bilateral settlement negotiations.

But substantial data also suggests that mediation is *not* infusing the courts with a new manifestation of democracy. Instead, as the courts have come to rely on mediators as the next set of judging adjuncts, the mediation process and the roles of both mediators and parties have changed. When parties failed to make significant voluntary use of mediation, courts made the process mandatory. Thus, citizens lost the ability to decide for themselves whether or not to try mediation. As attorneys have become more frequent participants in mediation sessions and have assumed responsibility for selecting mediators, the process has become less focused on empowering citizens and more focused on forcing these citizens to confront and become reconciled to the legal, bargaining and transactional norms of the courthouse. Attorneys select fellow attorneys as mediators and especially value those who possess substantive expertise and the ability to value cases and conduct "reality testing" with the parties. Many of these mediators maximize their own influence by minimizing the time spent by the parties in joint session. These mediators quickly separate the parties and become their sole channel of communication and negotiation, shuttling back and forth with the information and descriptions of offers and counter-offers that will facilitate settlement. Attorneys also now dominate the discussion and negotiation in mediation sessions. Indeed, in many personal injury and medical malpractice cases, the defendants are not expected to attend mediation sessions, and in some courts, parties generally are discouraged from attending. These changes in the implementation of mediation, though often understandable, generally have the effect of constricting, not celebrating, citizens' ability to engage in self-governance *and* demand accountability from the mediators, the mediation process and mediated outcomes. In sum, court-connected mediation has evolved from a process that focused on enhancing individual citizens' voice, control and assurance of accountability into a mechanism that resolves cases by reconciling these citizens to the institutional reality (or at least mediators' and attorneys' perception of the reality) of the courts and litigation.

* * *

The judicial system of the United States seems to be changing, and mediation is playing one small part in that change. Yet, change should be tempered by context, and even as the judicial system changes, it should reflect the values of our democracy. Our courts draw their legitimacy from their accountability to, and the responding support of, a democratic people. Within the context of democracy, judicial adjuncts exercising public functions must also be held accountable for the justice of their decision-making procedures and outcomes.

Perhaps mediation, which has so far played a relatively small role in the judicial system's larger evolution, can play a much more significant part in helping the courts reconcile the need for delegation (or more pejoratively, "outsourcing") *and* accountability. Mediation may then become an important complement that helps the courts play *their* appropriate role in the lives of the citizens in a democratic nation.

---

### C. Good Faith Requirements

The growth of mandatory court-connected mediation programs has met with some resistance by parties and their attorneys. As a result, many countries have enacted rules that require good faith participation in mediation. But, how should good faith be defined? How should violations of the rules be monitored? There is much debate about the merits of good faith requirement and in the following excerpt, John Lande offers a summary of the debate.

## JOHN LANDE, *USING DISPUTE SYSTEM DESIGN METHODS TO PROMOTE GOOD-FAITH PARTICIPATION IN COURT-CONNECTED MEDIATION PROGRAMS*

50 UCLA L. Rev. 69, 70–75 (2002).

What can be done to prevent people from behaving badly in mediation? One litigator described his approach to mediation this way:

> "[I]f. . . . I act for the Big Bad Wolf against Little Red Riding Hood and I don't want this dispute resolved, I want to tie it up as long as I possibly can, and mandatory mediation is custom made. I can waste more time, I can string it along, I can make sure this thing never gets resolved because . . . . I know the language. I know how to make it look like I'm heading in that direction. I make it look like I can make all the right noises in the world, like this is the most wonderful thing to be involved in when I have no intention of ever

resolving this. I have the intention of making this the most expensive, longest process but is it going to feel good. It's going to feel so nice, we're going to be here and we're going to talk the talk but we're not going to walk the walk."

In her study of Ontario litigators, Professor Julie Macfarlane found that rather than using mediation to try to reach a settlement in good faith, some lawyers use mediation to make misleading statements, " 'smoke the other side out,' " gain leverage for later negotiations, drag out litigation, increase opponents' costs, and generally wear down the opposition. Bad-faith tactics include purposely wasting time and money to demoralize parties less able to afford litigation. Attorneys can do this while using mediation jargon and creating phony issues to appear sincerely interested in settling the case.

* * *

The debate over good-faith requirements is related to the growth of court-ordered mediation. In recent decades, courts increasingly have ordered cases to mediation to help parties settle cases without trial and relieve pressure on court dockets. In general, participants have been satisfied with court-connected mediation programs. Predictably, however, some people do not want to participate in mediation, at least not at the time and under the circumstances ordered by the court. In the past decade, numerous reported cases have adjudicated claims of bad faith in mediation. This may reflect a growing reaction against mandated mediation, especially in areas where the legal culture promotes heavy settlement pressure.

The controversy over good-faith requirements is part of a larger debate over the purpose and nature of court-connected mediation programs. This debate focuses on competing program goals and ideas about what is needed to ensure the programs' integrity. On one side of the debate, people view mediation programs as mechanisms to dispose of a portion of court dockets. Courts order parties to spend time and money for mediation and want to be sure that the time and money are well-spent. Courts also want to ensure that parties and attorneys comply with their orders and cooperate with the courts' case management systems. From this perspective, a good-faith requirement seems to be the logical way to ensure the integrity of court-connected mediation programs.

On the other side of the debate, people focus on the integrity of the mediation process, defined as an adherence to mediation practice norms. Many mediators are especially concerned that people participate in mediation without coercion, take advantage of opportunities for open discussion and problem-solving, and receive assurance that courts will honor confidentiality protections. From this perspective, good-faith requirements seem to violate mediation norms and thus *undermine* the integrity of court-connected mediation programs. Although this brief summary oversimplifies the debate, it captures a real tension in the debates about the future of court-connected mediation programs.

---

# III. MODELS OF COURT-CONNECTED AND MANDATORY MEDIATION

Court-related mediation programs may be voluntary or compulsory. Mediators may be appointed by the court or chosen by the parties and in some jurisdictions, judges may act as mediators. In China, for example, mediation is embedded in judicial and arbitral proceedings. There are several varieties of compulsory or "mandatory mediation." Programs may require that parties participate in mediation as a pre-requisite to trial. In Italy, for example, parties are required to meet with a mediator for a preliminary hearing. Other programs give judges the power to refer parties to mediation while some programs categorically refer cases to mediation by subject matter. Some programs allow for mediation at an early stage of the litigation process before formal discovery has occurred. Consider the following forms of mandatory mediation.

## A. Opt-out Provisions

Opt-out provisions are a feature of mandatory mediation which initially require parties to participate in mediation but then allow them to leave the process or opt out. An example of such a model used by a private provider of mediation services is found in the American Arbitration Association's Commercial Arbitration Rules and Mediation Procedures where there is a claim or counterclaim that exceeds $75,000.00. Rule R-9 provides:

> In all cases where a claim or counterclaim exceeds $75,000.00, upon the AAA's administration of the arbitration or at any time while the arbitration is pending, the parties shall mediate their dispute pursuant to the applicable provisions of the AAA's Commercial Mediation Procedures, or as otherwise agreed by the parties. Absent an agreement of the parties to the contrary, the mediation shall take place concurrently with the arbitration and shall not serve to delay the arbitration proceedings. However,

any party to an arbitration may unilaterally opt out of this rule upon notification to the AAA and the other parties to the arbitration. The parties shall confirm the completion of any mediation or any decision to opt out of this rule to the AAA. Unless agreed to by all parties and the mediator, the mediator shall not be appointed as an arbitrator to the case.

## B. Mandatory Mediation of Specified Category of Cases

Italy leads the European community in establishing compulsory pre-trial mediation programs in certain categories of disputes. After an unsuccessful attempt at instituting pre-trial mediation in a wide variety of cases, the Italian government passed a regulation, Law Decree 69 of June 1, 2013, that effectively requires pre-trial mediation in cross-border and domestic disputes of certain categories of cases including some insurance matters, and medical and hospital liability. There is an opt-out provision that allows parties to withdraw from mediation if they do not believe that the mediation is likely to be successful. Thus, mediation has become, in specified cases, a condition precedent to judicial proceedings.

## C. Quasi-Compulsory Mediation

In some jurisdictions such as England and Wales, Hong Kong and Singapore, there is the potential for significant adverse cost consequences for parties who unreasonably refuse to mediate. The leading cases in this regard are *Halsey v. Milton Keynes General NHS Trust* and *Steel v. Joy* wherein the English Court of Appeal held that it should not require truly unwilling parties to mediate their cases, because in the court's view, compulsory referral would violate a litigant's fundamental rights to have access to the courts and run afoul of Article 6 of the European Convention on Human Rights. The court's reasoning is discussed in the following excerpt.

### JACQUELINE NOLAN-HALEY, *MEDIATION EXCEPTIONALITY*

78 Fordham L. Rev. 1247, 1259–60 (2009).

*Halsey's* rationale for not imposing a mandatory scheme was practical and pragmatic. Compulsory referral "would achieve nothing except to add to the costs to be borne by the parties, possibly postpone the time when the court determines the dispute and damage the perceived effectiveness of the ADR process." In short, the court held that its role was to encourage but not compel parties to engage in ADR.

While compulsory referral to mediation was considered unacceptable, encouragement to use ADR could be "robust." Accordingly, *Halsey* upheld a court's right to impose costs on a party who has unreasonably refused consent to mediate. In so doing, it readily acknowledged that this was a departure from the general rule on costs:

> In deciding whether to deprive a successful party of some or all of his costs on the grounds that he has refused to agree to ADR, it must be borne in mind that such an order is an exception to the general rule that costs should follow the event. In our view, the burden is on the unsuccessful party to show why there should be a departure from the general rule. The fundamental principle is that such departure is not justified unless it is shown . . . . that the successful party acted unreasonably in refusing to agree to ADR.

The court offered a nonexhaustive list of six factors in determining the reasonableness of a party's refusal to participate in mediation:

> (a) the nature of the dispute; (b) the merits of the case; (c) the extent to which other settlement methods have been attempted; (d) whether the costs of the ADR would be disproportionately high; (e) whether any delay in setting up and attending the ADR would have been prejudicial; and (f) whether the ADR had a reasonable prospect of success.

Reasonableness was considered a relevant factor.

> In our judgment, it would not be right to stigmatise as unreasonable a refusal by the successful party to agree to a mediation unless he showed that a mediation had no reasonable prospect of success. That would be to tip the scales too heavily against the right of a successful party to refuse a mediation and insist on an adjudication of the dispute by the court. It seems to us that a fairer balance is struck if the burden is placed on the unsuccessful party to show that there was a reasonable prospect that mediation would have been successful.

---

## D. Party-Initiated Mediation

In some court-connected mediation programs, court rules provide that one of the parties may move to refer a case to mediation.

Courts, exercising their inherent right to order mediation, may approve such a motion even over the objection of the opposing party. Consider the competing arguments made in the following case from the Court of International Trade in favor of and against referring a case to mediation.

## UNITED STATES V. TENACIOUS HOLDINGS, INC.

6 F. Supp. 3d 1374 (Ct. Int'l Trade 2014).

CARMAN JUDGE:

Before the Court is the Motion for Referral to Court-Annexed Mediation ("Mot.") filed by Defendant Tenacious Holdings, Inc. ("Tenacious"). . . . . Plaintiff United States ("United States" or "Government") opposes the motion. . . . . For the reasons that follow, the Court will grant the motion and an Order of Referral to Court-Annexed Mediation will issued separately.

*Background*

The United States brought this penalty case against Tenacious seeking penalties for negligent misclassification of work gloves.

* * *

Because the Court finds the potential benefits of mediation outweigh the risks, the motion will be granted.

*Discussion*

Tenacious claims referral to mediation is appropriate here for six reasons. First, Tenacious claims that penalty actions are inherently suited to mediation because they often settle, given that the Court has wide latitude over the central issue of whether the defendant importer exercised reasonable care in classifying the goods at entry. Second, Tenacious notes that the approximately $50,000 amount sought by the government in penalties and unpaid duties could be exceeded by litigation expenses, giving the parties an incentive for early resolution. Third, Tenacious claims that the relevant provision of the tariff schedule is so ambiguous as to make it unlikely that the negligence penalty would be found appropriate. Fourth, Defendant notes that the classification provision at issue expired in 2009, so the parties have no interest in a court judgment to guide its future application. Fifth, Tenacious contends that the confidential forum of mediation may permit resolution without the waiver of attorney-client privilege that would be necessary if Tenacious were to invoke an advice-of-counsel defense to the negligent misclassification charge. While Tenacious states that it has not yet asserted an advice-of-counsel defense, it recognizes that it may eventually have to do so. Tenacious states that it "would prefer to seek a mediated resolution to this claim, if possible, so that a waiver will not become necessary," . . . . . Tenacious notes that "referral to mediation may likely enhance communication between the parties because there will be no risk that evidentiary privileges will be waived in the process" given the strict confidentiality of mediation discussions. Finally, Tenacious contends that referral to mediation will promote the goal of "just, speedy, and inexpensive" resolution embodied in the Court's rules.

The United States opposes mediation. Noting that Tenacious' motion was filed the same day that Tenacious was due to produce certain discovery materials, the government claims that "Tenacious filed the present motion in hopes of avoiding its obligation to answer the Government's outstanding discovery requests." The government argues that it would be "a waste of time" to enter mediation before Tenacious produces discovery. From the government's perspective, the merits of the case cannot be properly weighed in mediation without full discovery. The government states that it is "not interested in a mediation in which Tenacious would provide a hand-picked sample of its attorney-client communications" related to a potential advice-of-counsel defense, since that would allow Tenacious to "reveal favorable advice while withholding unfavorable advice" as well as "the information that its attorneys considered before providing advice." The government also views the case "very seriously," disagreeing with Tenacious' view that the case's relatively small dollar value and lack of precedential value for future imports make it unimportant.

* * *

Here, the Court's power to order mediation is grounded in Rule 16.1 and the Guidelines, which do not establish any express limitations on that authority. The matter is left to the Court's discretion, limited by the bounds of its inherent powers. In deciding how to exercise that discretion, it seems wise to accept guidance from the Court of Appeals for the First Circuit, which identified four limits to a district court's exercise of its inherent power to order mediation in *Atlantic Pipe:* (1) "inherent powers must be used in a way reasonably suited to the enhancement of the court's processes, including the orderly and expeditious disposition of pending cases"; (2) "inherent powers cannot be exercised in a manner that contradicts an applicable statute or rule"; (3) "the use of inherent powers must comport with procedural fairness"; and (4) "inherent powers must be exercised with restraint and discretion." *Atlantic Pipe,* 304 F.3d at 143 (internal quotations and citations omitted).

In evaluating whether mediation may assist in the orderly and expeditious disposition of this case, the Court has given careful consideration to the objections of the government. Although the government is opposed to the idea that mediation may be successful, the Court is mindful that "the results of mandatory mediation resemble those achieved in voluntary mediation in terms of settlement rates and party satisfaction." . . . . Tenacious is correct that mediation is more likely to be successful given that the amount in dispute here is relatively low and the tariff provision at issue is no longer in effect and therefore resolution of this case is unlikely to impact future cases. Noting these practical factors does not suggest that the case is unimportant, merely that it may be amenable to early resolution. Ordering mediation is consistent with Rule 16.1 and the Guidelines. Since there are no fees for court-annexed mediation in the CIT, the financial concerns that sometimes arise with mediation referrals are inapplicable. Referral to mediation will not cause any procedural unfairness, since the discovery issues at the core of the government's concerns will be fully addressable by order of the Court should mediation be unsuccessful. Although the Court acknowledges the government's concerns about mediating without the robust information that it would have after the completion of discovery, the Court does not agree that mediation is bound to fail at this stage. Many cases are resolved in mediation prior to the production of all discovery, and Rule 16.1 and the Guidelines clearly contemplate referrals to mediation prior to the completion of discovery. The government cannot accurately prejudge what information Tenacious may produce in the confidential setting of mediation; if the government approaches the process with good faith, as the Court expects it to do, it may be surprised to find that the case is more amenable to disposition than the government fears.

*Conclusion*

For the foregoing reasons, Defendant's motion will be granted. An Order of Referral to Court-Annexed mediation will issue separately.

### E. Case Settlement

A variation of mediation used in some court systems is *case settlement*. Israeli mediator Mordehai Mironi describes that process as follows:

> Case settlement and mediation engage different participants and assign them different roles. Other than the third-party facilitator, the main actors in case settlement are the lawyers. The third party who facilitates the process attempts to convince the lawyers and the parties to accept her offer for a compromise solution. . . . The discourse of case settlement tends to be narrowly focused, rights-based and backward looking.[3]

### F. Judicial Mediation

Judicial mediation is a form of highly institutionalized dispute resolution in which sitting judges act as mediators in court mediation programs that are closely connected to the traditional adjudicative court system. The following excerpt discusses the benefits of judicial mediation and offers reasons for using a judge to mediate. It is based on the experience of Quebec's voluntary judicial mediation program which was instituted in 1997.

## LOUISE OTIS & ERIC H. REITER, *MEDIATION BY JUDGES: A NEW PHENOMENON IN THE TRANSFORMATION OF JUSTICE*

6 Pepp. Disp. Resol. L. J. 351, 362–71 (2006).

In our view, for disputes that are already within the adjudicative system or that have proved resistant to extrajudicial resolution, judicial mediation presents a powerful alternative to the often blunt instrument of an adversarial trial. It offers a *via media*, combining some of the legal and moral *gravitas* of adjudication with the flexibility and adaptability of ADR. It thus represents not just an efficiency reform but also a reconceptualization of the role of the courts and judges in dispensing justice.

* * *

Why use judges to mediate? This is a frequent question and an understandable one, given the relatively high cost of scarce judicial

---

[3] Mordehai Mironi, *Mediation v. Case Settlement: The Unsettling Relations between Courts and Mediation—A Case Study*, 19 Harv. Negot. L. Rev. 173, 179–180 (2014).

resources and the already heavy demands on judges' time. Mediation need not be conducted by a judge, of course, even within a courthouse setting. In many jurisdictions trained mediators are kept as courthouse staff, acting as officers of the court to perform mediations in much the same way as court clerks hear motions. Even in Quebec's judicial mediation system, the parties are free to choose private mediation if they so desire; the choice to mediate with a judge—like the choice to mediate at all—is entirely up to the parties

* * *

Judges are well-suited for the role of mediator for several reasons, relating both to the perceptions of the parties and to the specific skills possessed by judges. Of particular importance is the perception of the judicial office as one of impartiality and independence, which confers on judges a degree of moral authority. This can function to keep the process on track and to prevent abuses of the process by the parties or their representatives. Exercising this moral authority is extremely delicate, however: the consent of the parties is a central pillar of any mediation system, and judge-mediators must never use their position to manipulate this consent. The judge-mediator is not there to extract a settlement or to steer the process towards a particular result but instead to help the parties come to their own resolution of their conflict. The judicial office and the parties' opinion of it can lend credibility to the process and keep it moving when it might otherwise stop, but to use the office to control the process is to subvert it.

A more subtle advantage of judicial mediation—particularly at the appellate level—arises from its institutional relationship to the adjudicative system. A judge well-trained as a mediator is ideally placed to uphold the integrity of the adversarial system during the course of a mediation session by showing appropriate curial deference to the decision of the trial judge. Indeed, to allow a private mediator—even one attached to the courts—to consider a first-instance decision pending on appeal brings up delicate issues of confidence in the courts and could potentially affect public perceptions of the authority of judicial decisions.

The judicial mediation model effectively keeps the review process in-house. Following the trial judge's decision, a fellow judge mediates the dispute; if a settlement agreement is reached, it is ratified by an independent panel of judges from the court of appeal. Public perception of the judicial process can be fragile; an integrated system of judicial mediation for cases already being litigated ensures that neither process—adjudication nor mediation—undermines the other.

Besides the perceptions of the parties, judges bring to the table many particular qualities and skills that make them effective mediators. First, judges have long experience in intervening between disputing parties. This practical experience is buttressed by a second factor, namely the judge's commitment both to achieving resolution and to dispensing justice. Third, the judge is already part of the subsidized public court system. This provides an enormous benefit to parties for whom both adjudication and private mediators are too expensive; in the Quebec system, for example, there is no cost to the parties associated with judicial mediation beyond preparation expenses. Such programs thus have the potential to offer the best of both worlds; they provide the flexibility of alternative dispute resolution but do so by employing existing adjudicators at no extra cost.

A fourth, and obviously important, factor is the judge's knowledge of the law. While this, too, flows from the judge's experience, this knowledge goes beyond simply discerning how to handle parties to a dispute. Judges have an understanding of legal issues that permits them cogently to focus on the issues underlying the dispute and to bring these to the fore during discussions between the parties, even if this necessarily must stop short of expressing an opinion on the case. In this way, the presence of a judge provides the ideal foil to agency costs and efficiency losses between the parties and their attorneys by providing an experienced supervisory presence during the negotiations.

* * *

Adjudication is of course a natural reflex of experienced judges, as is forming opinions on the matters before them; both, however, present grave threats to the integrity and viability of a voluntary system of judicial mediation. For this reason, a judicial mediation system must provide judge-mediators with strategies to help them shift gears between adjudication and mediation and must provide supervision as a continuing complement to the initial training provided. Letting the parties control the process and the outcome is a challenge for a mediator in any mediation. For judge-mediators this challenge is intensified, since they will always remain judges in the eyes of the parties, even when they are in the informal setting of the mediation room.

* * *

[There is a] uniquely complementary relationship between adjudication and *judicial* mediation. Mediation involves preparation time for the judge-mediator, of course, as well as the time devoted to the session itself. Because the judge-mediator plays a facilitative rather than adjudicative role, however, and because the parties are free to come to their own terms (subject only to public order and other legal imperatives), the amount of preparation required of the judge-mediator is usually less than in adjudication. In contrast to adjudicative hearings, where in many cases the oral arguments are little more than summaries of the written submissions, in mediation it is the negotiations and the dynamics of the session itself that play the largest role. As a result, preparation time is less, particularly when we recall that appellate adjudication requires preparation by three justices.

Furthermore, a successful mediation results in an immediate settlement rather than deliberations, another enormous savings of time. Finally, a mediation can address the parties' conflict globally, thus resolving the principal dispute at the same time as side issues, each of which might otherwise land before the courts. In short, experience at the appellate level has shown that the investment of the time of one judge results in freeing up two other judges to hear other matters and, in many cases, clears the docket prospectively of a number of procedural or even substantive matters related to the parties' dispute that would otherwise require separate litigation.

An integrated system of mediation by judges also creates a synergy between courts, as different courts collaborate in the global resolution of conflicts. A case before an appellate court often includes other related matters pending before courts of first instance; a case before a trial court might likewise include interlocutory or other matters pending in appeal. Parties can grant a judge seized of one aspect of their litigation the mandate to settle all connected aspects, even those pending before other courts or tribunals. The prospect of a complete resolution of their conflict can convince otherwise reluctant parties to mediate rather than to continue multiple court proceedings; the advantages of efficiency, cost, and finality are strong inducements.

* * *

In summary, the presence of a judge brings certain benefits to the mediation process and makes judicial mediation a highly efficient complement to classical adjudication. Since judicial mediation is a voluntary process, the role of a judge-mediator is not to compel the parties to settle by holding the law over their heads like a sword but rather to guide the parties to a better understanding of their differences in order to resolve the conflict between them. The presence of a judge reminds the parties of what is at stake, ensures that the process is capably run in all instances, and allows continued vigilance of issues like the balance of bargaining power. Judicial mediation amounts to a new way of rendering justice, one that empowers the parties and provides justice better suited to their needs.

---

## IV. MEDIATION AND JUDICIAL SETTLEMENT CONFERENCES

In some jurisdictions judges may mediate cases before them or conduct judicial settlement conferences with the same goal of resolving the dispute and avoid the time and costs of going to trial. Despite the blending of boundaries by some judges, mediation and judicial settlement are different processes as explained in the following excerpt by a judge from Brazil. Note that this is a more critical view of judicial involvement in mediation than the Quebec perspective offered in the previous section with the Otis and Reiter article.

### FERNANDO VIEIRA LUIZ, *DESIGNING A COURT-ANNEXED MEDIATION PROGRAM FOR CIVIL CASES IN BRAZIL: CHALLENGES AND OPPORTUNITIES*

15 Pepp. Disp. Resol. L.J. 1, 14–19 (2015).

Regardless of the model, even though it is possible, it is not desirable for a judge to sit as a mediator and, worse still, when he is the one assigned to adjudicate the case if it is not settled.

* * *

Judicial settlement conferences differ from mediation in the same way that the mediation differs from litigation. For different purposes and processes, it is natural that different persons with different backgrounds, training, and abilities are needed. Therefore, the first pitfall of having judges settle cases—which makes judicial settlement conferences distinct from mediation—is the lack of competency and training. Mediation and litigation call for different skills. Judges are trained to master the law and apply it to a certain situation. The Constitution, statutes, and case law are the raw materials that will be filled out by the particular facts of each dispute. The goals of litigation are establishing facts and narrowing down legal issues, so consequently the judge is the personification of such attributes. The judge guarantees these goals and avoid proceedings that stray from those objectives. In the end, there will be a clear ruling for the plaintiff or the defendant with no room for compromise in between. Even though legal texts are not disregarded in mediation, they are not the main point of the process. While a judge is a well-versed interpreter of the law, the mediator is an expert interpreter of people. The mediator's focus is on the parties' interests, not their legal positions; the mediator should master the psychological aspects of the conflict to enhance dialogue that will lead to an amicable environment propitious for producing creative solutions. In this sense, "there are times when a sophisticated, knowledgeable neutral can be much better than a judge."

Some lawyers still prefer judicial settlement conference over mediation, arguing that the judges' authority and lack of time make the process faster because judges force parties to get straight to the point. The absence of a specific fee for the conferences makes it cheaper than mediators' fees, and a judge's experience from the bench and knowledge of recovery in similar cases make the process better. I do not agree with that perspective. Actually, those factors make a judge an unsuitable third party neutral for a number of reasons.

First, if a judge has a limited amount of time and parties are expected to spend not more than one or two hours with the judge, it is clear that the judge is not the best person to resolve the problem because there will not be enough time to explore all the legal and extralegal issues around the relationship between the parties. Short of time and using a going-straight-to-the-point approach, no one can build up trust, which is essential for disclosure of all the information needed and for a sound evaluative approach.

Second, a judge's "status and authority do not trump skill and experience as a neutral." In a mutually accepted agreement the last thing parties wants is a judge displaying authority by superseding the free will of the parties and imposing a solution. Research suggests that "former judges who serve as mediators tend to adopt a 'bashing' style," which exemplifies a tendency to display such authority. In this regard, judges or former judges need even more training to act as neutrals because they need "to unlearn or modify some tendencies."

As to fees, the estimate of which process is more expensive will vary from court to court and from jurisdiction from jurisdiction. In India, for instance, mediation is cheaper than judicial settlement because courts do not charge for their mediation program and return all the court's fees if the case is settled.

On the issue of experience, it is true that experience from the bench may be somehow useful. Knowing how juries behave in a specific area or how much damages one may usually get are assets when evaluating the options for a settlement. However, it is preferable to have someone who is experienced in the process, rather than someone experienced in the field of law discussed. Settlement methods involve more than how much one can get, and usually anyone without specific training is unable to see farther than that. They are structured processes that have certain distinct phases so as to guarantee the empowerment of every participant and to make sure the parties are well informed about their decisions. Therefore, having someone who has mastered negotiating techniques and is able to conduct the process in the right way is more important than having experience on the bench.

A confusion in the role they play may arise for judge, lawyers, and parties when the judge in charge of the negotiation process decides the case if it is not settled. How will a judge decide a case based on its legal aspects alone after urging the parties to observe their interests and not their position? How can the judge reduce the pie just trying to extend it? The judge—and everybody else—is expected to forget and simply dismiss everything said during the negotiating rounds to be able to perform ordinary function.

In my capacity as a trial judge, I experienced this problem recently. The case was the following: After the marriage of his son, the plaintiff let the new couple live on one of his properties, a medium-size apartment. Some twenty years later, the couple decided to get divorced and the former wife kept on living in the apartment even though no disposition was made on this in the divorce settlement. Some months after the husband left the place, his father, the owner, filed suit against his daughter-in-law, demanding his apartment back. He included in his injunctive relief pleading that he wanted to have the apartment back since the beginning of the lawsuit. In her answer, she argued that the plaintiff had verbally donated the apartment to the couple, and, therefore, she owned the place or half of it at least.

The parties, their lawyers, and I were at the preliminary hearing, where the main objective is trying to settle the dispute. After some hours of conversation in both joint and private sessions, the interests were clear. The woman needed a place to live, at least for six months in order to find a smaller place where she could afford the rental and some amount of money to start a new life. The plaintiff did not need the place for himself, although his son, the ex-husband, was living in a small rented bedroom in a poor neighborhood far from his job and amenities, such as supermarkets, drugstores, and gas stations. Therefore, the plaintiff wanted the place in order to let his son live there, and if he could not get the apartment back, the relationship with his son would be harmed.

As the one in charge of the process, I tried to show the parties the advantages and disadvantages of both settlement and a future trial, and satisfy them with a speedy resolution. Also, I stimulated the parties to find creative solutions. For instance, the proposition of letting the defendant live in the apartment for four months with no recovery of money was seriously considered by both parties. However, I knew from the outset that the defendant's defense was very weak, and if not settled, the injunction would be granted almost immediately. Brazilian law does not accept the verbal donation of real estate. There are certain formalities that must be observed, and one of them is a written instrument. Therefore, even if the verbal donation were proven, injunctive relief would be granted because the alleged donation was not legally enforceable.

At the end of the hearing, the parties did not settle the case, and I found myself in a most difficult situation. According to Brazilian law, I could not recuse myself for the case. I spent hours trying to find creative solutions that would have some mutual gains for the parties' interests and convincing them of the advantages of a negotiated agreement, even proposing some of the possible outcomes. Afterwards, as a trial judge, I was quite simply unable to use any of the remedies I suggested to the parties earlier. I could decide on the injunction, but I could never arrive at any solution that would be at least minimally acceptable to one of the parties. I could not enforce even the solution I proposed to them in the hearing.

This case is one example of millions that might happen where the roles of judges are in conflict, generating problems for the judge but also for lawyers, and especially the parties. Particularly regarding the parties' confusions, I cannot imagine the reaction of both plaintiff and defendant when they were reading my decision after listening to my suggestions in the hearing.

---

In the following excerpt, Ellen Deason, writing from a U.S. perspective, describes the growing influence of mediation on judicial settlement activity and the risks for parties when their mediator is also the decisionmaker in their case.

## ELLEN E. DEASON, *BEYOND "MANAGERIAL JUDGES": APPROPRIATE ROLES IN SETTLEMENT*

78 Ohio St. L. J. 73, 97, 115–18 (2017).

[T]here is some evidence that in recent decades mediation has exerted an increasing influence on judicial settlement activity. Mediation practices and norms appear to have had a discernable effect on how many judges conceive their role—and on what they actually do—when they act as settlement neutrals. These developments in the way judges exercise this role make separating it from their adjudicatory and management functions all the more important.

* * *

For judges functioning as mediators, information gathering from the parties is central to the process of reaching an agreement. Mediators do not just hear inadmissible information; they hear personal information, and they hear it from parties as well as from their attorneys. To help the parties settle their dispute, it is important for a mediator to learn "about the parties' feelings, motivations, relationships, values, standards and priorities—topics generally irrelevant to a judge." It is commonplace, for example, for parties in meditation to describe their personal interests. For example, a mediator may learn why a party needs to settle quickly, or why a party needs a particular sum of money. And this is not dry information; parties often express their personal situation in emotional terms, which makes it especially salient and more accessible in the judge's memory. A mediator is also likely to become privy to parties' strategies, priorities, and trade-offs as she discusses their bargaining concessions. Moreover, in the course of these discussions she is bound to gain an impression of each party's degree of cooperation and willingness to settle. Perhaps most significantly, the discussion is likely to cover extensively the attorneys' assessments of their cases: their view of the most likely outcome, the litigation cost, and the bottom line for reaching an agreement. Indeed, it "would be difficult . . . . to conduct a settlement conference without at some point dealing with the issue of value." The key point is that exposure during settlement to the parties, to their strategies, and to the settlement value of a case go far beyond what judges usually learn in their adjudicatory and managerial roles.

The potential effect of this knowledge on a judge's subsequent decisionmaking needs to be taken seriously. As recognized in an American Bar Association (ABA) ethics opinion on settlement, such disclosure to the judge of a client's settlement position significantly increases the potential for an unsatisfactory disposition of the case. The Judicial Conference's Committee on Codes of Conduct concurs, concluding that information from settlement that is not likely to be presented at trial "may undermine the judge's objectivity as a fact finder and give rise to questions about impartiality." Standards for recusal and disqualification are not, however, tailored for settlement and do not provide an effective vehicle for considering the effect of information from settlement on subsequent decisionmaking. While there are court decisions that condemn mediator reports to assigned judges or testimony that reveals information learned in mediation, such knowledge does not usually lead to disqualification of the judge. Even when a judge gains knowledge about what transpired in mediation directly from his role as the settlement neutral, the effect of that knowledge tends to be treated as benign. Courts have interpreted the federal statute on disqualification and recusal for bias or prejudice in light of the "extrajudicial source" doctrine. The judge's favorable or unfavorable opinion must be wrongful either because it is "excessive in degree" or based on extrajudicial knowledge. This means the bias cannot be "derived from the evidence or conduct of the parties that the judge observes in the course of the proceedings." A judge's knowledge acquired from participating in a settlement proceeding is not "extrajudicial," and thus does not necessitate recusal.

A party may choose to avoid the risk of sharing information that might affect future decisions of the neutral, but the cost of reticence can be high. The reason this information is shared is that it is helpful to the settlement process. Withholding it handicaps a mediator and very likely reduces the chances of settlement, or at least the responsiveness of the settlement to the party's needs. Thus a party whose mediator is also the decisionmaker in a case faces a difficult choice: accept the risks to impartiality of sharing sensitive information with a looming trial, or risk a less effective settlement process.

---

# V. MANDATORY MEDIATION

## A. EU Directive on Mediation

Mediation's gradual evolution from a voluntary to a compulsory process can be illustrated through the lens of developments with the

EU Directive on Mediation (2008).[4] By way of background, in 2002 the European Commission issued a Green Paper that identified ADR as a "political priority." The purpose of the paper was to encourage use of ADR as a means of increasing access to justice in cross-border disputes. The paper initiated a wide-spread consultation with Member States and interested parties on possible measures to promote the use of mediation. In October 2004, following enthusiastic responses to the Green Paper, the Commission of the European Communities issued a draft proposal for a Directive on mediation in civil and commercial matters in cross-border disputes. It was intended to promote the use of mediation in the EU without making it compulsory. A Mediator Code of Conduct was developed by the European Commission and finalized in July 2004 and in 2008 the Commission issued a final Mediation Directive to be applied in cross-border commercial disputes. The Directive provided that Member States should authorize courts to suggest mediation to parties but not compel them to mediate. A significant feature of the Directive is its voluntary nature. The decision to mediate must be based on a voluntary agreement between parties to a cross-border dispute, and the actual mediation process must be voluntary and based on party self-determination. Despite the voluntary nature of the Directive, Member states are free to enact national legislation making mediation compulsory. Member states had three years in which to comply with the Directive, and there was very slow progress with implementation. Italy was alone in its adoption of extensive mandatory mediation.

Following low usage of mediation after the Mediation Directive, (mediation was used in less than 1% of cases in court),[5] the EU commissioned a study to examine the situation. The report, "Rebooting the Mediation Directive: Assessing the Limited Impact of Its Implementation and Proposing Legislative and Non-Legislative Measures to Increase the Number of Mediations in the EU (2015)[Rebooting Study], called for mandatory mediation with opt-out provisions. In September 2017, the EU Parliament issued a resolution on the implementation of the Mediation Directive,

---

[4] Directive 2008/52/EC, of the European Parliament and of the Council of 21 May 2008 on certain aspects of mediation in civil and commercial matters.

[5] Prof. Giuseppe De Palo and Dr. Leonardo D'Urso, *Achieving a Balanced Relationship between Mediation and Judicial Proceedings*, *in* EUROPEAN PARLIAMENT, THE IMPLEMENTATION OF THE MEDIATION DIRECTIVE 4 (2016).

encouraging Member States to increase their efforts to encourage the use of mediation in commercial disputes.[6]

The following excerpt, critical of mandatory-type mediation programs, describes what Europe might expect from engaging with mandatory mediation structures.

## JACQUELINE M. NOLAN-HALEY, *IS EUROPE HEADED DOWN THE PRIMROSE PATH WITH MANDATORY MEDIATION*

37 N. C. J. Int'l L. & Com. Reg. 981, 1006–09 (2012).

*What Europe Can Expect with Mandatory Mediation Regimes*

Before EU Member States consider adopting more aggressive approaches to mediation as a possible remedy for its low usage, they should take note of other countries' experiences with compulsory regimes, particularly the United States. One of the major mediation debates in the United States for over twenty-five years has been whether mediation, which is essentially a voluntary process, should be made compulsory. Proponents of mandatory regimes have argued that diversion to mediation is a sensible move, particularly when considering the desirability of reducing the dockets of overcrowded courts. To honor the understanding of mediation as a voluntary process, proponents have adopted Professor Frank Sander's theory that there is a difference between requiring parties to enter into a mediation process, a permissible practice, and requiring them to reach an agreement in mediation, an impermissible form of coercion. Another justification proponents have invoked in developing compulsory regimes is the need to remedy the low usage problem caused by unfavorable views of mediation, which are shared by potential users. Some clients and lawyers have perceived of mediation as a sign of weakness, while other critics have viewed it as a form of "second class justice."

In an effort to promote and legitimize mandatory mediation, the Law and Public Policy Committee of the Society of Professionals in Dispute Resolution (SPIDR) issued a report in 1990 stating that "[m]andatory participation in non-binding dispute resolution processes often is appropriate." Federal legislation soon followed. The Civil Justice Reform Act of 1990 and its progeny in the states made mandatory mediation part of the ADR landscape, and courts upheld

---

[6] Directive 2008/52/EC of the European Parliament and of the Council of 21 May 2008 on Certain Aspects of Mediation in Civil and Commercial Matters, 2008 O.J. (L 136) 3.

its legitimacy. After mediation was implemented as a cure for the inefficiencies of the justice system, mandatory mediation programs were adopted in numerous contexts, particularly for custody and divorce disputes. Some studies reported that parties remained satisfied with mediation, even when their participation was required.

Today in the United States, there is a substantial amount of literature that criticizes mandatory mediation programs with their frequent requirements of good faith participation. While mandatory mediation programs were adopted in large measure for efficiency reasons, experience has demonstrated that in some respects these programs have been false economies. Given the number of parties returning to court to challenge the validity of agreements made in mediation, the efficiency rationale has lost some of its luster. Paradoxically, while mediation has been offered as a means of access to justice, some scholars have argued that it has become a barrier to accessing justice and that it should be phased out. Other critiques include claims that mediation has outlived its usefulness, is antidemocratic, has reduced the number of trials, has lacked the substantive and procedural protections of court, and can be "destructive to many women and some men" in the divorce context.

Apart from these policy and process critiques, mandatory mediation programs also implicate ethical issues. When forced to engage in mediation, some lawyers push back by using the mediation process as a free discovery tool or by simply going through meaningless motions. Confidentiality may also be compromised, particularly when rules requiring good faith bargaining allow the mediator to report on what happens during mediation. Good faith bargaining requirements can also pressure parties to settle. Some parties who are referred to mediation may fear that if they do not settle, there will not be a favorable outcome from the judge.

---

## B. The On-Going Debate over Mandatory Mediation

There are considerable differences of opinion about the merits of mandatory mediation regimes. The following readings, one of which is authored by one of the authors of the EU Rebooting Study, offer a flavor of that debate. Notwithstanding the debate, the significant consideration is not the label "mandatory" or "voluntary" but making sure that parties' retain their right of access to the court system.

## GIUSEPPE DE PALO & ROMINA CANESSA, *SLEEPING? COMATOSE? ONLY MANDATORY CONSIDERATION OF MEDIATION CAN AWAKE SLEEPING BEAUTY IN THE EUROPEAN UNION*

16 Cardozo J. Conflict Resol. 713, 727–730 (2014).

Over the past few decades many people in the field of ADR, particularly mediation, have become jaded by their version of mediation—a version that is increasingly being referred to as a Sleeping Beauty. Actually, in light of many decades of stagnation, and despite the generous injection of enthusiasm and repeated efforts to revive her, the consensus seems to be that mediation in its current state is, unfortunately, more than just asleep. The Rebooting Study concluded that a certain degree of *mandatoriness* is the necessary ingredient in the magic remedy for Sleeping Beauty.

* * *

Just like any other good policy, good dispute resolution policy is about encouraging and rewarding good behaviors. Sometimes it is necessary for this to happen by law, at least in the initial phases; history shows us that human beings often resist change, even when they know it is good for them. People did not simply stop smoking in public places when they knew smoking would not only damage their health, but also that of others. And what about using seat belts in the car, or helmets on a motorcycle? What would happen to the majority of human beings if those rules were cancelled? Since they reflect behaviors that are individually and societally beneficial, will these behaviors be followed spontaneously? The answer is probably not.

When faced with a lawsuit, people demonstrate similar resistance to beneficial change: in particular, the notorious two "F's"—fight or flight—come into play. When suing, or being sued, the immediate, natural instinct is not to mediate, despite repeated demonstrations that overall mediation remains the most effective way of dealing with lawsuits. People know that wearing a seat belt or helmet is good for them and for society, still there are laws compelling that behavior. In this case mediation culture alone will not be sufficient either.

* * *

Most importantly, if people really did not want to resort to mediation, why is mediation then so successful? Why would one out of two cases settle, as is the situation in Italy? Or why, in the US, would otherwise similar foreclosure mediations programs register a 25% mediation rate, when the system is "opt-in", and over 70% when it is opt-out? Part of the success of mandatory mediation elements can be attributed to the fact that people often take the path of least resistance.

It is also interesting to note several recent trends in mediation all advocating similar models to the one advocated in the Rebooting Study. These trends all involve different mandatory elements, thus further emphasizing that voluntariness and a mediation culture alone is not enough.

* * *

It is now commonly agreed by mediators that something is necessary to "wake" mediation up from its dormant state. The Rebooting Study ultimately concluded that unless the law introduces "elements of mandatory mediation", mediation would not ever be revitalized, at least in the EU. Voluntariness, therefore, is the false Prince Charming as far as dispute resolution policy is concerned, as litigants are not enchanted by the vision of mediation, and mediation must be woken up by other, real-world means.

First, nothing short of mandatory elements has worked, at least in the EU, in terms of increasing mediations. Second, where mandatory elements are there, people hardly think of going back. Third, the trend, as discussed above, seems clearly to be headed in that direction, legislation-wise, in Europe and elsewhere.

In short, mediation is a beauty (at least, as compared to its alternative), and she is in a coma. There is presumably more than one wicked witch. People, who are often, blinded by the philosophically and scientifically mistaken view of voluntariness, are waiting for the wrong Prince to come and wake her up. Smart forms of mandatory mediation—a more flexible approach than most recognize—increase the number of mediations. Rejecting that reality, and wishing that a more idealistic approach would work, is the fairy-tale, idealistic vision that has kept us in the situation we confront today for too long. It has been shown time and again that the only real Prince Charming capable of waking Sleeping Beauty is mandatory consideration of mediation.

## JACQUELINE NOLAN-HALEY, *MEDIATION: THE BEST AND WORST OF TIMES*

16 Cardozo J. Conflict Resol. 731, 737–38 (2014).

We should not separate consent from mediation. I propose a return to a consensual understanding of mediation, so that we may recover at least plausible account mediation's joy, and its powerful connections to human dignity. Hopefully, this will attract potential users to engage with her once again. Mediation is a voluntary process based on party self-determination. Acknowledgement of this first principle honors the consensual nature of mediation both at entry into the process, during the process and at the outcome.

Pushback from potential users is often the result of unwanted pressure. Some parties' discomfort with mediation comes from being pressured into participation. Coercion appears in many disguises—from telling parties that mediation is an automatic part of the litigation process to imposing costs and fees if they refuse to mediate. Non-consensual mediation may help to clear dockets, but it is a poor substitute for the real thing. It compromises a party's ability to influence how her dispute is resolved, and may minimize the potential for meaningful settlement. There is some research which shows that cases are more likely to settle at mediation if the parties enter into the process voluntarily rather than being pressured into the process.

* * *

Court-connected programs have been a breeding ground for non-consensual mediation practices with variations of mandatory regimes operating in many countries. In the United States, for example, courts have upheld programs where parties may be required to participate in mediation while England has adopted a more indirect approach through the imposition of costs. In the seminal case of *Halsey v. Milton Keynes General NHS Trust,* Lord John Dyson considered the question of whether courts could compel unwilling parties to mediate and he concluded that while courts could not force unwilling parties to mediate, they could use robust means to encourage mediation. Thus, parties who unreasonably refused to mediate could be liable for costs. *Halsey* generated much debate over the merits of compulsory mediation with courts extending its principle to refusals to negotiate, delays in agreeing to mediate, and taking unreasonable positions in mediation. Ten years after the *Halsey* decision, Lord Dyson reflected on the normative question of whether courts could order parties to mediate. His response is instructive on the issue of consent:

> [T]he real question is not whether or not a power exists to order mediation. Rather it is whether the court should exercise that power. Ten years on, I remain in the "carrot" camp; it is one thing to compel parties to consider mediation; it is another to frog march them to the mediation

table and deny them access to the courtroom if they refuse to participate in the mediation.

---

## TRACY WALTERS MCCORMACK, SUSAN SCHULTZ, AND JAMES MCCORMACK, *PROBING THE LEGITIMACY OF MANDATORY MEDIATION: NEW ROLES FOR JUDGES, MEDIATORS, AND LAWYERS*

1 St. Mary's J. on Legal Malpractice & Ethics 150, 159–60 (2011).

*Peeling Away the Curtain of Mandatory Mediation*

"No one gets in to see The Wizard, not no one. Not no how."

In The Wizard of Oz, Dorothy and her companions are sent away for further tests and hardships, even after they have completed their initial perilous journey to Oz. Litigants may feel much like Dorothy as they struggle to have a jury trial heard by a judge. Why has access to a judge and the court system become so difficult, and why do courts use mandatory mediation as one more obstacle before an audience with "the great and powerful Oz?" Is it really a constitutional function of the judiciary to create an extra hoop through which litigants must first jump in order to get what they originally sought when they filed suit or an answer? Is judicial time really so scarce that courts need to deflect people from using it? Do we believe that litigants are not capable of choosing between a judge or jury and mediation so we choose for them? Is mediation a better solution than a jury trial or judicial decision? Are darker unconscious forces at play? Could it be that a lack of confidence in juries lingers among many participants, including lawyers and judges, and we continue to limit the jury's role accordingly? Do we no longer want to engage in the business of judging and declaring winners and losers? Are there so few actual trial lawyers left that clients must be funneled to a "kinder, gentler" solution that is more palatable for our "no losers, all winners" society, which is marketed as better for the would-be litigants as well?

Judicial efficiency is a legitimate concern, but we cannot keep reflexively invoking the concept to automatically relegate cases to a private resolution system without questioning why or even tracking what happens to these cases in and out of the courthouse. If judicial resources are scarce and must be rationed, why do we not prioritize their use? . . . .

---

## MARIANA HERNANDEZ CRESPO, *30 YEARS OF DISPUTE RESOLUTION IN LATIN AMERICA*

Dispute Resolution Magazine, 48, 50 (Spring 2015).

*Mandatory Court-Connected Mediation*

The tendency to promote court-connected mediation has also been a topic of debate in Latin America. Colombia and Argentina have significant experience in this area. Most recently, Chile experimented with a voluntary mediation process in the context of family law but ended up making mediation mandatory.

Even though some data suggests that mandatory court-connected mediation reduces the number of cases that end up in court, there is not enough information to establish a causal effect between mediation and the number of cases in courts. The drop in trials could be due to the cost of the process, the cost of legal representation, or general distrust in the judicial system.

---

# VI. NOTES AND QUESTIONS

1. Does the English Court of Appeal's rationale for not imposing mandatory mediation make sense to you? Does it support the claim that mandatory mediation deprives a litigant of access to the courts?
2. With respect to the English legal system, the Civil Action Working Group on ADR in its report, "ADR and Civil Justice," declined to recommend compulsory mediation as a pre-condition for participating in civil litigation, and it retained the cost sanctions approach endorsed in the *Halsey* case (discussed on pages 38–39 of this chapter). However, the report noted that a major criticism of the existing regime for costs sanctions where parties fail to engage in ADR is that the *Halsey* guidelines are too restrictive. The Working Group stated that it would welcome a review of these guidelines—"We think it should not be sufficient to say 'This is a complex case and I have just won' as a justification for not having at least attempted to explore ADR. . . ." Do you agree with this opinion? [Civil Justice Counsel, "ADR and Civil Justice," CJC ADR Working Group Interim Report October 2017 at p. 60.]
3. What arguments do you find most and least persuasive in the debate over mandatory mediation? Consider the points raised in *United States v. Tenacious Holdings*.

4. In the English case of Bradley v. Heslin [2014] EWHC 3267 (Ch) that involved a boundary dispute between two neighbors the court wrote:

> I think it is no longer enough to leave the parties the opportunity to mediate and to warn of consequences if the opportunity is not taken. In boundary and neighbor disputes the opportunities are not being taken and the warnings are not being heeded, and those embroiled in them need saving from themselves. The Court cannot oblige truly unwilling parties to submit their disputes to mediation: but I do not see why, in the notorious case of boundary and neighbor disputes, directing the parties to take (over a short defined period) all reasonable steps to resolve the dispute by mediation before preparing for a trial should be regarded as an unacceptable obstruction on the right of access to justice.

   Do you agree with the principle that there are certain categories of disputes that are appropriate for mandatory mediation? Boundary disputes between neighbors? What other categories of disputes would you assign to the same category?

5. Are there any benefits to having a judge serve as a mediator in a case to which she has been assigned to adjudicate?

6. Many countries today are institutionalizing mediation within their judicial systems, and in some cases, making a mediation mandatory pre-requisite to accessing the courts. Do you see any danger that if this trend continues, mediation will simply become a settlement device to achieve cheap justice?

7. What are your views on whether mandatory mediation is an obstacle to achieving access to justice?

8. Do you find the arguments in favor of judicial mediation persuasive?

# Chapter 3

# THE ROLE OF CULTURE IN INTERNATIONAL MEDIATION

## I. INTRODUCTION

In the dispute resolution field one of the contexts in which the impact of culture is most prevalent is international mediation. There are many different ways to define culture. This chapter will use the following definition: "Culture consists of the derivatives of experience, more or less organized, learned or created by the individuals or a population, including those images or encodements and their interpretations (meanings) transmitted from past generations, from contemporaries, or formed by individuals themselves."[1] Despite the fact that culture affects both domestic and international conflicts, its impact is more salient at the international level. In part, this is due to the potential lack of shared backgrounds between the parties, which may result in a substantial cultural gap. Therefore, when structuring transactions or addressing disputes, culture can become either an extraordinary asset or an insurmountable liability.

In adjudicative processes such as litigation or arbitration, while culture plays an important role in cognitive processes such as perception, interpretation, and decision-making, its impact can be more easily ignored, since these rights-based processes will often continue until a judgement or award is rendered. Yet it does not mean that the impact of cultural differences is not felt by the parties, especially because the legal system tends to reflect the culture of the majority. In contrast, in problem-solving processes, such as negotiation or mediation, cultural differences are more difficult to ignore because the parties—as decision-makers—are able to leave the table at any given point, without facing the same consequences as leaving an adjudicative process. However, ignoring culture may

---

[1] Kevin Avruch, Culture & Conflict Resolution 17 (1998) (citing Theodore Schwartz, *Anthropology and Psychology: An Unrequited Relationship*, *in* New Directions in Psychological Anthropology 324 (Theodore Schwartz, Geoffrey M. White & Anne C. Lutz, eds. 1992)).

not only cost the parties a valuable opportunity to enhance mutual understanding, but can also preclude the possibility of reaching a mutually satisfying agreement.

Parties usually find themselves in mediation when they are unable to overcome an impasse by themselves. A failed negotiation, a contractual agreement, or legal authority can channel conflicts to the mediation process. It is in this context that effectively addressing culture—especially in international settings—becomes critical. Increasing the parties' and mediator's awareness of the impact of culture can not only deepen the understanding between the parties to help them reach an effective resolution, but it can also potentially strengthen their relationship.

Often, an important first step in addressing cultural differences is to acknowledge and seek to understand them. This awareness can then help identify the effect of culture on the individual, others, and their interactions.[2] It also assists in the process of examining how culture affects the different social, political, legal, and economic constructions of a given society at a specific time. Finally, this deeper understanding of culture's impact on both daily interactions and the broader social-political structures can lead to varying levels of integration and, in some cases, increase the opportunity for innovation and growth.

Although culture is an integral part of every interaction—in any setting, both domestically and internationally—given its underlying, yet ubiquitous nature, it can be overlooked or inadequately addressed. This chapter explores the reasons why culture should not only be simply acknowledged or studied, but should also be recognized and then actively experienced and modified through our relationships with others and in our daily interactions. To this end, it first explores, in Part II, the importance of culture in mediation. Next, in Part III, it examines the impact of culture in our interactions and conflicts. Then, in Part IV it offers some suggestions for addressing cultural differences in mediation, and Part V explores how cultural differences impact process design and system design. Process design allows for the crafting of a culturally appropriate dispute resolution process, including mediation. System design focuses on designing processes to address streams of conflict.

---

[2] *See generally* Mariana Hernandez-Crespo, *Workshop 1: Global Opportunities and Conflicts: The Need for Cross-Cultural Mediation*, *in* Mediation: A one trick pony? Using Mediation in the Wider Context 48–59 (Chartered Institute of Arbitrators ed., 2013).

Mediation is an important potential element of systems design. Finally, in Part VI, this chapter discusses the impact that culture has on the mediator and the potential role of co-mediators as cultural interpreters in our multicultural world.

## II. THE IMPORTANCE OF CULTURE IN MEDIATION

Mediation is not a new phenomenon. In fact, in some regions of the world, mediation processes date back for centuries. These processes reflect the cultural values of a given society, which may evolve over time. For these reasons, the context in which mediation emerges will likely not be value-neutral. While one process may seem natural for the parties who belong to that particular culture, parties who do not share that culture may find the process to be foreign, as it might not be aligned with their cultural norms.

In order to understand how culture has affected the mediation processes in different regions of the world, it is necessary to grasp its dynamic, complex, and multidimensional nature. Kevin Avruch elaborates on this point, stating that culture is "the socially transmitted values, beliefs and symbols that are more or less shared by members of a social group. These constitute the framework through which members interpret and attribute meaning to both their own and others' experiences and behavior."[3]

In recent decades, it could be argued that North American mediation theories and practices have been one of the dominant influence worldwide.[4] This trend may lead to the false assumption that American mediation theories are the norm. Kenneth H. Fox has alerted us that failing to recognize other cultures poses a significant risk. He notes that this "can lead to distortions in our understanding of the very cultures we seek to know. It can also lead us to think of other cultures as if ours is the norm." Quoting George Bernard Shaw, he writes, "[p]ardon him, Theodotus: he is a barbarian, and thinks that the customs of his tribe and island are the laws of nature."[5]

---

[3] Kevin Avruch, *Culture as Context, Culture as Communication: Considerations for Humanitarian Negotiators*, 9 Harv. Negot. L. Rev. 391, 393 (2004).

[4] *See* Amy J. Cohen, *Debating the Globalization of U.S. Mediation: Politics, Power, and Practice in Nepal*, 11 Harv. Negot. L. Rev. 295, 309 (2006).

[5] Kenneth H. Fox, *Unanswered Questions, Future Opportunities: Reflections on an International Conversation About the Globalization of ADR*, 27 Hamline J. Pub. L. & Pol'y 297, 298–300, 302 (2006).

Because North American culture has been one of the significant influences in the development of modern mediation, what aspects should be considered to understand the values driving this mediation processes? What are some of the cultural clashes with members of other cultures? How do subcultures, such as the legal and business fields, present additional challenges to the mediation process? The following excerpts discuss how these value differences impact the development of the mediation process. First, Jacqueline Nolan-Haley, stresses the influence culture can have on the mediation process and suggests some questions that we can ask in order to bring awareness to this influence. Next, Thomas Stipanowich discusses some of the differences in mediation between Western and Asian cultures. Finally, Don Peters discusses how the subcultures within the American culture, such as those developed within the legal and business fields, add additional sets of values to the mediation process and pose additional challenges.

## JACQUELINE NOLAN-HALEY, *TEACHING COMPARATIVE PERSPECTIVES IN MEDIATION: SOME PRELIMINARY REFLECTIONS*

81 St. John's L. Rev. 259, 264–65 (2007).

Mediation practice does not exist in a vacuum. It is important to appreciate the cultural context in which mediation programs begin to develop and the extent to which dominant cultural values influence its growth in any given country. In this regard, there are a number of significant questions that can be developed for class discussion:

a) What are the major differences between civil and common law jurisdictions and how do they influence mediation's development?

b) To what extent do political and religious interests shape mediation's development?

c) How do cultural differences among groups impact the development of mediation?

d) Which needs of the justice system drive efforts to develop ADR and mediation programs in any given country?

e) Within the context of teaching comparative mediation in American law schools, how does the international community perceive Americans? What are common stereotypes and images of Americans and how do these perceptions impact on international mediation practice?

---

## THOMAS STIPANOWICH, *THE INTERNATIONAL EVOLUTION OF MEDIATION: A CALL FOR DIALOGUE AND DELIBERATION*

46 Victoria Univ. Wellington L. Rev. 1191, 1214 (2015).

There is no question that the United States "modern mediation" model and variants developed in places like the United Kingdom and Australia have been very influential throughout the world. As with religion and other conceptual exports, however, there is always the matter of translation into cultures that sometimes have much older traditions of mediation, as in Asia. In "relearning mediation from the West," as Singapore Professor Joel Lee explains, Asian mediators have a challenge in translating a Western mediation approach founded on the primacy and autonomy of individuals and the furtherance of individual interests, with a traditional orientation toward, among other things, social hierarchy, societal harmony and obedience to authority. The challenge might include not only figuring out what techniques and approaches mediators should employ, but also embracing the very notion that a mediator might be an independent paid professional, as opposed to an adjudicator or other authority figure.

---

## DON PETERS, *CAN WE TALK? OVERCOMING BARRIERS TO MEDIATING PRIVATE TRANSBORDER COMMERCIAL DISPUTES IN THE AMERICAS*

41 Vand. J. Transnat'l L. 1251, 1275–78, 1289–90 (2008).

A decision to mediate a commercial dispute typically involves businesspersons and their legal counsel, both outside and inside. Culture supplies a frequently used analytical metaphor for examining belief patterns, shared expectations, and behavioral norms of individuals and groups acting within organizations. This perspective suggests that barriers to the use of mediation arise from both business and legal cultures in America.

Contentious, competitive business cultures exist, and they generate disputes initially while erecting barriers to efficient resolution. Company lawyers note that their "business people think that they are right all the time." Key individuals in companies often get personally and emotionally invested in disputes in ways that influence selection of resolution methods. Corporate lawyers explain that angry businesspersons with strong emotions often dictate the choice of adjudication, even though this is not the most effective method of dispute resolution. . . . .

The professional culture of U.S. lawyers also erects barriers to recommending and using mediation to resolve transborder disputes in ways that transcend the cognitive biases of partisan perception, fixed-pie assumptions, and win-lose thinking. Professional expectations regarding the extent of information needed before counseling clients about resolution options, for example, often inhibit recommending mediation. . . . .

* * *

Decisions to mediate transborder disputes usually involve businesspersons and lawyers from different cultures, and often from different legal systems. Cultural differences—reflecting dynamic, growing, interrelated, and shared mental perceptions about what is appropriate in human interaction—present additional barriers to mediating transborder commercial disputes. These shared perceptions contain categories and implicit rules that persons use to interpret events, behaviors, and communications. They influence attitudes, action habits, and behavioral norms regarding how disputes are perceived, expressed, managed, and resolved.

Commonly encountered cultural differences stem primarily from fundamental distinctions between emphasizing individual or collective values, and preferring to communicate directly or indirectly. Most wealthy Western countries, for example, have individualistic traditions of direct communication, while most Latin American countries possess collectivistic traditions and tendencies toward indirect communication. These fundamentally different orientations create common misunderstandings regarding win-lose or win-win orientations, emphasizing contracts or relationships, formality or informality, time sensitivity, risk taking, and top-down or consensus-based team organization. These and other cultural differences create gaps between what persons using one set of cultural assumptions intend by actions, and the meanings others using different shared mental precepts attribute to these behaviors.

These differences create enormous challenges to consensual resolution of disputes through negotiation and mediation.

* * *

Culturally fluent mediators can identify and correct miscommunications that prolong resolvable conflicts. Skilled transnational dispute mediators are attuned to subtle cultural patterns and nuances, which allows them to spot signals that suggest the existence of barriers and misunderstandings.

---

## III. CULTURE IN INTERACTIONS AND CONFLICTS

In order to fully understand the role of culture in the mediation process, it is important to first explore how culture affects our own daily interactions and conflicts, as they will influence the process. John Paul Lederach reminds us that conflicts are deeply imbedded in culture, and he asserts that, "Conflicts are, in every sense of the word, cultural events. They are perhaps one of the most intriguing and complex social accomplishments we humans construct. . . . [Conflicts include our] lifetime of knowledge about what is right and wrong to do, how to proceed, whom to turn to, when, where, and with what expectations."[6] Yet Sanda Kaufman, Christopher Honeyman, and Andrea Kupfer Schneider, remind us that "[w]e still think we understand others' cultures and circumstances and even offer advice on how to handle cross-cultural negotiations. However, there is a hefty dose of hubris in this belief."[7]

Given the complexity of conflict as cultural events, it is important to keep in mind that culture itself, as a prevailing yet invisible factor, has many dimensions to consider. While culture affects our behaviors, traditions, and institutions, it also encompasses the mindsets that produce them. These mindsets are not only passively transmitted, but actively modified by the members of the various social groups in each society. Therefore, to fully understand the impact of culture, it is necessary to recognize how it evolves within the context of relationships.

---

6 John Paul Lederach, *Of Nets, Nails, and Problems: The Folk Language of Conflict Resolution in a Central American Setting*, *in* Conflict Resolution: Cross-Cultural Perspectives, 165–66 (Kevin Avruch, Peter W. Black & Joseph A. Scimecca, eds., 1998).

7 Sanda Kaufman, Christopher Honeyman & Andrea Kupfer Schneider, *Should They Listen to Us? Seeking a Negotiation/Conflict Resolution Contribution to Practice in Intractable Conflicts*, 2017 J. Disp. Resol. 73, 95 (2017).

## A. Behaviors and Cultural Values

One of the most evident forms of how cultural differences can be appreciated is through their manifestation in social constructions. Jeanne Brett has used the analogy of an iceberg in order to make this distinction more tangible. In her analogy, the iceberg's waterline separates the visible from the invisible, with the behaviors and institutions above the waterline and the knowledge structures: values, beliefs, norms, and fundamental assumptions hidden below.[8]

A culturally shared psychology and knowledge structure, illustrated by the submerged portion of the iceberg, differentiates one culture from another. In the following excerpt, Julia Ann Gold draws on the work of Edward Hall and Geert Hofstede to summarize the different dimensions of cultural value patterns and styles of communication that play a significant role in dispute resolution processes, such as mediation.

### JULIA ANN GOLD, *ADR THROUGH A CULTURAL LENS: HOW CULTURAL VALUES SHAPE OUR DISPUTING PROCESSES*

2005 J. Disp. Resol. 289, 295–301 (2005).

Cultural values become visible through behaviors, operating as a set of unwritten rules that guide the ways we communicate and interact. In discussing and comparing national groups, researchers have identified characteristic behaviors within those groups. Similarities and differences across societies are explained and predicted theoretically using dimensions of cultural variability, called cultural value patterns.

Value patterns are constructs for discussion of cultural differences among national groups and individuals. While everyone within a particular national group will not share the same values, a majority of individuals within that group will conform to similar values, creating what we call the "dominant culture." Those who do not conform to the dominant culture will exhibit different cultural values, creating subcultures and co-cultures. Within the dominant culture and subcultures, individuals inhabit multiple levels of culture, from national identity to family, professional or workplace identity, or regional, gender and generational affiliations. These layers of cultural affiliation affect everything we do, including how

---

[8] Jeanne Brett, Negotiating Globally: How to Negotiate Deals, Resolve Disputes and Make Decisions Across Cultural Boundaries (2001).

we resolve conflict for ourselves and our beliefs about how others should resolve conflict.

* * *

[Value Patterns and Communication Patterns]

*1. Individualism-collectivism.* This dimension describes the relationship between the individual and larger society. Individualists believe that it is important to satisfy the needs of the individual before those of the group. Individual identity is more important than group identity; and individual rights are more important than group rights. One is expected to look after oneself, be self-sufficient, autonomous and independent. Personal freedom is highly valued in an individualistic society. Privacy is respected, and personal information is not shared except with close friends or family. . . .

In a collectivist culture, identity is tied to a primary group, usually the family. Members of a collectivist society believe that the survival of the group will ensure each member's survival because the success of the group benefits the individual. . . . . In a collectivist society, one is rarely alone. The level of interdependence means that harmony is highly valued. . . . .

* * *

2. *Universalism-particularism.* . . . . A universalist believes that what is right is right, regardless of the circumstances or who is involved. Certain absolutes exist and the same rules should apply to similar situations. To a universalist, fairness means treating everyone the same, and one should not make exceptions for family, friends, or members of one's ingroup. Universalists believe it is important to put feelings aside and look at situations objectively. Making exceptions to rules should be avoided. . . . .

In contrast, particularists believe that circumstances should be taken into account, and that what is right in one situation may not be right in another. . . . . Rather than being laid aside, personal feelings should be relied upon. . . . . To a particularist, being fair means treating each person as unique. . . . .

3. *Communication patterns.* Communication styles, and the meaning attached to nonverbal messages and time also vary across cultures, and are rooted in cultural values. Two style dichotomies are relevant to this discussion: low-/high-context and monochronic/polychronic time orientation, which vary along continua similar to value patterns.

a. *Low-/high-context communication.* Anthropologist Edward T. Hall identified the communication style continuum called "low-context" to "high-context." Low and high-context refer to how much of the meaning of a communication comes from the surrounding context, as opposed to the actual words exchanged. In a low-context culture, people tend to say exactly what they mean rather than to suggest or imply. The spoken word carries most of the meaning. People are not expected to read into what is not said or done to embellish the meaning. The goal of most communication is getting or giving information, as opposed to preserving the relationship, which is the goal in high-context communication.

* * *

In a high-context culture, much of the meaning of a communication is already "programmed" into the receiver of the message as a result of the shared experience, connection and history of the sender and the receiver. People are more likely to infer, suggest and imply than say things directly. Often no words are necessary to carry the message—a gesture or even silence is sufficient to communicate meaning. A critical component of most communication is to preserve the relationship and face-saving is important. This leads to a tendency to be indirect and avoid confrontation.

* * *

b. *Monochronic—polychronic.* Hall also identified two time orientations that vary and affect communication across cultures. A monochronic culture perceives time as linear, quantifiable, and in limited supply. In these cultures people believe that it is important to use time wisely and not waste it. Efficiency is important, which leads to a sense of urgency. The needs of people are adjusted to suit the demands of time, resulting in schedules and deadlines. It is considered most efficient to do one thing at a time. Unforeseen events should not interfere with plans, and interruptions are seen as a nuisance. . . .

In a polychronic culture, time is perceived as limitless, and not quantifiable. There is a sense that there is always more time. Time is adjusted to suit the needs of people. Schedules and deadlines get changed. People may need to do several things simultaneously. It is considered okay to split attention between several people or tasks, and it is not necessary to finish one thing before starting another. Strictly speaking, there is no such thing as an interruption. . . .

4. *Power distance.* Measured from low to high, power distance refers to the extent to which the less powerful members of a society

"expect and accept that power (e.g. wealth, prestige, access to education and other benefits that enhance power) is distributed unequally." In a low power distance culture, individuals see inequities as man-made and largely artificial. Those with power tend to deemphasize it, minimize differences between themselves and subordinates, and delegate and share power to the furthest extent possible. Subordinates are encouraged to take initiative and are rewarded for it. Informality is encouraged. In a low power distance culture, criticism of authorities is considered appropriate, and discussion and consultation are desirable.

* * *

In a high power distance society, people tend to accept inequalities in power and status as natural. The prevailing attitude is that some individuals will have more power and influence than others, just as some people are taller than others. Those with power emphasize their status and avoid delegating or sharing it. They distinguish themselves from those without power or with less power. Criticism or disagreement with those in authority by subordinates is viewed as undesirable. The powerful are also expected to accept the responsibilities that go with power, including looking after those beneath them. Subordinates are not encouraged to take initiative and are closely supervised.

* * *

5. *Uncertainty avoidance.* A fifth dimension is uncertainty avoidance—the degree of comfort with the unknown or unpredictable. This dimension was one of the four dimensions identified by Hofstede. . . .He defined it as "the extent to which the members of a culture feel threatened by uncertain or unknown situations." "This feeling is, among other things, expressed through nervous stress and a need for predictability: a need for written and unwritten rules." As Hofstede wrote, "[e]xtreme uncertainty creates intolerable anxiety." One of the ways that society alleviates this anxiety is developing laws, which govern the behavior of others, and decrease uncertainty.

Uncertainty avoidance is measured from low to high. In a society low on this dimension anxiety levels are relatively low. Showing emotion or aggression is frowned upon, and those who behave emotionally are viewed negatively. Hofstede describes the effect of these cultures as "quiet, easy-going, indolent, controlled, lazy." Ambiguity is not cause for concern. Experimenting is viewed as necessary to learn and improve. People view what is different as interesting, and tradition is not valued for its own sake. The "way we have always done things" is not seen as the best way and new ideas are encouraged. Rules or norms are informal and allow for a wide range of personal interpretation in application. Formal rules are established only when necessary, but once established they are respected. People are tolerant and not threatened by deviant ideas. Conflict is viewed as potentially positive. Initiative and flexibility are valued and structure is avoided. . . .

People in high uncertainty avoidance cultures are more expressive. Hofstede describes the effect of people in these cultures as "busy, fidgety, emotional, aggressive, active." Talking loudly accompanied by gesturing is common. Showing aggression or emotions at the proper time and place is viewed as acceptable. Conflict and change are viewed as threatening. People believe there is a good reason for "the way we do things around here," and structure is valued. Tradition, rules and laws are respected and followed, and provide predictability and guidance for how to handle every possible situation. . . .

These cultures tend to be less accepting of differences because people believe that what is different may be dangerous. High uncertainty avoidance cultures tend to have more formal "rules, planning, regulations, rituals and ceremonies, which add structure to life." . . .

6. *Locus of control.* Locus of control, measured from internal to external, refers to the extent to which people believe that they control their fate. Individuals with an internal locus of control believe that they control their own destinies. These people believe that most things can be changed, and that there are no limits to what one can do or what one can become. Anything one sets one's mind to can be achieved. One is responsible for what happens to oneself . . . .

At the other end of the continuum, people with an external locus of control believe that some things in life are predetermined. Fate, destiny and acceptance are part of life. They believe that success is a combination of good fortune and one's effort. Life is what happens to you.

---

## B. People Who Make Culture

Given the notable differences between cultures, the focus of attention has been on studying these differences in an effort to gain cultural competency. A number of publications have compiled the distinctions in behaviors and customs between countries, with the goal of informing the reader on what to expect when interacting with members of those cultures, and how these differences can affect communication and business opportunities.[9] While these books provide a foundation to raise awareness of some of the perceivable and significant characteristics of each country, it is critical to also realize that cultures are not monolithic.

Furthermore, in order to fully grasp the impact of culture, knowledge of the other is not enough, knowledge of one's own culture is also important. In this regard, experts in the dispute resolution field have noted that "[t]he more one engages in cross-cultural experiences, the more one gets to understand oneself. There is an apparent inherent irony, a paradox, which easily eludes one who is untrained in cross-cultural ways."[10] For these reasons, it is not only necessary to move from cultural competency, where knowledge of other cultures is essential, to cultural sensitivity, where the focus is on gaining intellectual awareness of the impact of one's own culture, but to go beyond to cultural sensibility. Cultural sensibility focuses on the reflection and change that may occur because of our interactions with people from different cultures.[11]

In the following excerpt, Carrie Menkel-Meadow alerts us to some of the risks of limiting our focus to cultural competency. She suggests that culture is not something that should only be passively studied, but rather is actively shaped because people make culture.

## CARRIE MENKEL-MEADOW, *EXPORTING AND IMPORTING ADR "I'VE LOOKED AT LIFE FROM BOTH SIDES NOW"*

12 Disp. Resol. Mag. 5, 6–7 (Spring 2006).

On the one hand, we are all human; on the other hand, we live in a world of amazingly different cultural beliefs, understandings and practices. I have long abhorred those popular books on "how to negotiate with the . . . . (Japanese, Chinese, Russians, New Yorkers," fill in the blanks with your favorites).

---

9 *See, e.g.*, Olegario Llamazares, How to Negotiate Successfully in 50 Countries (2008); Terri Morrison & Wayne A. Conaway, Kiss, Bow, or Shake Hands: The Bestselling Guide to doing Business in More than 60 Countries (2d ed. 2006).

10 Bee Chen Goh, Habib Chamoun-Nicolas, Ellen E. Deason, H. Jay Folberg & Sukhsimranjit Singh, *As We See It*, *in* Educating Negotiators for a Connected World 104 (2012).

11 Andrea Anne Curcio, Teresa E. Ward & Nisha Dogra, *A Survey Instrument to Develop, Tailor, and Help Measure Law Student Cultural Diversity Education Learning Outcomes*, 38 Nova L. Rev. 177 (2014).

More recently, radical differences have been the vogue, such as in Samuel Huntington's famous "Clash of Civilizations" argument. My own views are closer to those of Kevin Avruch and Frank Sander and Jeff Rubin. Culture is not some stereotypic, monolithic, reified "thing" out there which can be learned by reading a few books, watching a few movies, or having a few meals and then "technically" managed as a communication or translation problem.

Rather, people make cultures, and people form institutions, and there may be as much variability within "national" or "group" cultures as between them. . . .

* * *

Every individual belongs to many cultures, so it is dangerous to make assumptions about individuals and the groups they form (especially where age and educational training may trump more "traditional" aspects of culture).

* * *

Culture is not out there—it is in all of us. So crude cultural assumptions should be avoided, and that includes thinking about one's own "culture."

---

## C. The Relational Aspect of Culture

If we are to view ourselves as people who make culture, then it is essential to understand not only that we are active participants in developing culture, but also that it is important to examine how culture evolves through the interactions that occur within our relational systems. Given its "dynamic and complex nature," it can be beneficial to gain insight on how culture is both engrained in—and transforms—who we are, our environment, and our interactions with others.

To illustrate how culture operates at both the individual and collective level, and how it develops within the context of relationships, Michelle LeBaron presents three metaphors: culture as lenses, as a medium, and as a relationship. At the individual level, comparing culture to lenses, she notes that culture "colors" our worldview. Given the variety of experiences each person has, these *lenses* are different for each of us. At the collective level, she describes culture as a *medium*, where behaviors and values emerge, grow, and are transferred. Finally, she compares culture to a relational system which "shapes and reflects" who we are, who we associate with, and how we interpret the world around us. These metaphors highlight the impact culture can have on what we consider "natural and right" and what is "unnatural and incorrect." In the following excerpt, through the use of these metaphors, Michelle LeBaron explores how culture operates in our daily interactions.

## MICHELLE LEBARON, *TRANSFORMING CULTURAL CONFLICT IN AN AGE OF COMPLEXITY, IN* BERGHOF HANDBOOK FOR CONFLICT TRANSFORMATION

1, 2–4, 6–7, 9–10 (2000).

All conflicts entail interpersonal interactions that occur in the context of cultures. The exact influence of culture will differ from person to person as no two individuals from the same country, region, religion, socio-economic class, gender or generation will exhibit the same constellation of cultural behaviours and attitudes. Power further complicates conflicts, operating at the symbolic level to shape what seems natural or reasonable in any given situation. A history of inequitable interactions between dominant and subdominant groups leads to emotionally charged communication and increases the likelihood of conflict escalation.

An adequate response to conflict requires a sophisticated understanding of culture, borrowing from many disciplines and extensive experience. Culture shapes not only the possibilities for resolution or transformation, but also the naming, interpretation, enactment and course of conflicts. Culture is many things: it is a set of lenses through which all parties to a conflict necessarily see. Resulting from the lenses' omnipresent, we are usually unaware of their existence. Culture is also the medium in which behavioural patterns and values grow and are passed on one generation to the next. Deep-rooted conflicts become embedded in cultural stories and myths and thus more resistant to transformation. Finally, culture shapes and reflects identity formation and the way we make and assign meaning. Humans are essentially creatures who assign meaning, or 'meaning-making', we seek to explain, to understand, to make sense of our worlds and ourselves in our worlds. Because we do this frequently in the context of relationships, I have chosen the metaphor of intimate relationship to convey the dynamics of culture at this symbolic level.

Each of these metaphors expresses the complexity and unconscious dynamics rooted in culture. [Harry] Triandis (1990) reminds us that all groups tend to define what happens in their own culture as "natural" and "right", and what happens in other cultures as "unnatural" and "incorrect". In-group norms are usually perceived as applicable to others, even to those outside the national or cultural group. Members of one culture group are inclined to believe that it is expected and natural to help and favour one another, and to feel pride towards their own. Unfortunately, this pride is often coupled with hostility towards outsiders. Resulting from these perceptual and attitudinal biases, clarity about culture and conflict is elusive, yet important to any transformative process.

* * *

[Culture as a Lens]

Culture colours everything we see. It is impossible to leave our cultural lenses at the door to a process; without perspective and experiences through which we interpret and intuit the way forward, we would be impotent to transform conflicts. Our cultural legacy gives us a range of behaviours from which to choose; it gives us a "common sense" of conflict and how to approach it. . . . .

* * *

[Culture as the Medium for Behaviour and Values]

Sometimes, trying on the lenses of another is not enough. In long-term or deep-rooted conflicts, it is important to get beyond the lenses to values and cultural logic. . . . .

* * *

Even when one medium is similar to another, it will respond differently when environmental factors vary. Even when a similar value is shared by two groups, it may be manifested very differently determined by culture. . . . .

* * *

Three implications follow from conceptualising culture as a medium that sustains the mental, moral and economic equipment for life. First, culture is always relevant, just as the medium in a biological experiment is significant to whether and how a specimen will grow. Secondly, the medium changes as the environment around it changes. No cultural group is immune to pressure, influence and ideas from other groups. Power dynamics, in particular, play a key role in affecting how change comes about and in which directions. Finally, the medium is life-sustaining. It is essential for the ongoing development of the group and therefore must be respected and protected. . . . .

* * *

[Culture as Intimate Relationship]

Culture, like intimate relationships or deep friendships, is dynamic, multidirectional, and interactive. It is constantly changing, adapting, reshaping and engage in a continuous exchange with other cultural systems. . . . . Culture in this view is more than a medium; it is a complex relational system with multiple dimensions.

I chose the metaphor of intimate relationship because it conveys the constant change and multileveled interaction that characterizes cultures. . . . . Furthermore, behaviour adopts textures and meanings over time because a relationship has symbolic dimensions in addition to its physical and relational ones. Similarly, cultural influences both shape and reflect those things that are precious to us: our identity, our bonding with others and the ways we make meaning.

---

# IV. ADDRESSING CULTURAL DIFFERENCES IN MEDIATION

It is important to identify and address both cultural similarities and differences during the mediation process because culture affects the way each person interacts at the table, which can hinder or enhance the process. In this regard, it is particularly beneficial to pay attention to how participants' cultures affect their narratives, positions, interests, and values.

In order to take into account the different cultures of the parties in the mediation process, this section first introduces the significance of competing narratives. Next, it suggests the need to identify the underlying values that are the core of what matters to each party. This can be accomplished through a tool called the Cultural Value Discernment (CVD). Finally, it presents another tool, the Cultural Value Glasses (CVG), as a vehicle to gain awareness of the impact of culture at each stage of the mediation process.

## A. The Influence of Culture upon Parties' Narratives

In the mediation process, the parties' narratives play a critical role, as each party tells their story in a way that is consistent with their own lenses, medium, and relationships.[12] In this way, the mediation process becomes an "interaction of narratives" competing

---

[12] This is the essence of the narrative model of mediation, discussed earlier in Chapter 1.

for "legitimacy" or "primacy." These narratives, in part, derive from the particular cultures of each party. They articulate the interpretive frameworks that assign value to behaviors, and portray them in a positive or negative light.

In the context of adjudication, competing narratives are ultimately decided by a third-party neutral. However, in the mediation process, where the parties are the decision makers, to try to convince each other to agree with their own interpretive framework, is a challenging exercise. Because only one narrative can prevail, the interpretative framework that the narrative follows will be reflected in the resulting agreement. In order to overcome this clash of narratives, it is necessary to examine them to open the door to transformation and understanding. How does this competition of narratives play out at the mediation table? Why are these narratives so powerful? What is the role of culture in informing these narratives? These are some of the questions that Isabelle Gunning examines in the following excerpt.

### ISABELLE R. GUNNING, *DIVERSITY ISSUES IN MEDIATION: CONTROLLING NEGATIVE CULTURAL MYTHS*

1995 J. Disp. Resol. 55, 68–71 (1995).

What is often noted as unique and even magical about mediation is the opportunity for parties to tell their own stories and have them be heard. But the process of story-telling or narratives, while it has its positive aspects, may also be at the heart of the problem of bias in mediation. Narratives must interact or compete for legitimacy or primacy in a mediation. In doing this, parties will understand and craft their stories in relation to other pre-existing stories and cultural myths with which all the participants, parties and mediators are familiar. Disadvantaged group members will have more negative cultural myths uniquely related to them, i.e. stereotypes, that undermine the ability of their narratives to compete effectively.

Two mediation scholars, Sara Cobb and Janet Rifkin, have described narratives as "re-representations of the past in the present, through which identities, moral orders and relational patterns are constructed and negotiated," and the mediation process itself as the interaction of narratives. The first story told, the "primary narrative," describes the conflict by relating, generally, a sequential series of events, the plot, with characters and their roles and an overall theme or moral code. Subsequent speakers generally employ the same series of events and moral code or interpretive framework. In part they do this because it is a conversational practice that requires speakers to connect or relate their stories to the primary narrative. In part, they do this because the primary narrative in identifying a moral code will determine what behavior constitutes "goodness" and "badness" and will generally assign subsequent speakers a "bad" character role or a "negative position." People assigned a negative position will act to reposition themselves in a more positive light and, in doing so, they will connect to the primary narrative and employ stories of "justification, denial or excuse." By repositioning themselves through the use of the primary narrative events and moral codes, subsequent speakers, unwittingly, strengthen the legitimacy of the primary narrative. The narrative and accompanying interpretive framework which is repeated the most, generally the primary narrative, becomes the strongest and will most likely provide the framework for any resultant agreement. To actually transform a narrative, one must change its context, i.e. the moral code and characters must be altered.

* * *

These interpretive frameworks or competing definitions are drawn from the history and norms of the larger society. This interpretive framework is itself constructed by bits and pieces of larger cultural myths . . . .; myths that are themselves cultural and historical artifacts. "There are, in any given culture, stocks of stories that actors may draw on to 'nest' their narratives inside of pre-existing narratives that are already legitimized in the wider culture."

All of the participants must juggle these "bits and pieces of larger cultural myths" during the process of the mediation. The parties bring whatever bits and pieces most legitimate their view of the conflict. The mediator, too, has lived in the wider culture and does not have a "teflon" mind. So she, too, will bring in her own bits and pieces of larger cultural myths which provide her with the ability to even recognize that there is a conflict and understand what the parties are arguing about.

* * *

The larger cultural myths evoked by the relevant identity or group categories provide the participants with a series of preexisting possible stories within which the parties' narratives may fit. The myths can be positive or negative. And whether they are positive or negative will affect the ability of the party who draws upon that myth to legitimate her own narrative.

---

## B. The Need to Identify Underlying Values and to Engage Culturally Diverse Parties

Besides competing narratives, the parties may also have conflicting goals or visions of what the outcome should be, which might be driven not only by individual interests, but also the parties' underlying personal and cultural/collective values. In the following excerpt, Mariana Hernandez Crespo Gonstead introduces the CVD as a tool to incorporate values in problem-solving. She first argues that in problem-solving processes, such as interest-based negotiation or facilitative mediation, it might be necessary to go beyond identifying positions and interests, to also explore the underlying values in order to realize what is really at stake for each party. This is of particular importance when the parties do not share a similar cultural background. Next, she suggests a second tool, called the CVG, to assist the process of gaining awareness of the impact that our personal and cultural/collective values have on each stage of the mediation process.

### MARIANA HERNANDEZ CRESPO GONSTEAD, *A NEW DANCE ON THE GLOBAL STAGE: INTRODUCING A CULTURAL VALUE-BASED TOOLBOX TO OPTIMIZE PROBLEM-SOLVING, INNOVATION, AND GROWTH*

34 Ohio St. J. on Disp. Resol. (forthcoming 2019).

In order to integrate the logic of problem-solving and understanding, it is necessary to connect parties' interests to their underlying values. Expanding the focus from a position-based approach to an interest-based approach has been essential for resolving disputes in a more satisfactory way, as it has promoted value creation rather than mere compromise. While this is of critical importance, it may not be sufficient when the situation requires some understanding of the parties' distinct personal and cultural/collective values, and how those values affect their relationship.

To this end, when the dispute occurs in the context of an ongoing relationship, it might be useful to incorporate the Cultural Value Discernment (CVD) tool into the problem-solving process. The Cultural Value Discernment (CVD) is the process through which each identified interest is connected to its underlying value by asking why it is important to that particular party. Learning why parties care about a particular interest opens the door to understanding what truly matters to them. Values are the driving force behind the parties' articulated positions and interests that guide the decisionmaking process. These values are the core of who we are and the cultures to which we belong. Therefore, this additional inquiry is often worth the effort, as it can enhance understanding of the parties' motivations.

* * *

Culture has generally been treated as one factor to consider during the problem-solving process, rather than an intrinsic and fundamental component. However, it is necessary to develop a framework that treats culture as a transversal aspect that affects every single stage of the process, rather than treating it as an isolated element. Culture not only has implications at the external level (non-verbal signals, words, behaviors), but it also deeply impacts our cognitive processes (perceptions, expectations, interpretations).

To illustrate this, the metaphor of cultural lenses [examined above], has been used to facilitate the notion of how culture shapes our understanding of the objective world. Gaining awareness about our cultural lenses allows us to gain a deeper knowledge about ourselves, others, and our interactions. These lenses are formed and shaped over time, and are fluid and ever-present. Cultural lenses are engrained in who we are, and given their intrinsic nature, cannot be disregarded during the mediation process without leaving potential value on the table, or in some cases, failing to reach an agreement at all. Each of us is wearing a set of unique cultural glasses that is composed of a multiplicity of lenses that reflect the values of the cultures to which we belong.

When there are multiple glasses at the table, parties will face especially unique challenges and opportunities. On the one hand, if the parties are wearing completely different sets of glasses, it can make communications and interactions more difficult due to the array of possible perceptions, expectations, and interpretations of what is happening. On the other hand, if the parties have the necessary awareness and guidance, this variety of glasses can instead broaden the parties' mutual understanding and lead to collective innovation and growth.

In this regard, Steven Weller, John A. Martin, and John Paul Lederach have asserted that "one method of dispute resolution that should be able to provide a culturally sensitive forum is mediation." Therefore, in order to maximize the opportunities for cultural understanding that mediation could provide, I suggest supplementing the Cultural Value Discernment with an additional practical tool, the Cultural Value Glasses (CVG). This tool can be used to assess the impact of culture throughout the mediation process. In this context, cultural differences can either be harnessed to produce a mutually satisfying agreement or ignored, which risks an escalation of the conflict.

The Cultural Value Glasses (CVG) provides guidelines for assessing how personal and cultural values affect the information gathering, generation of options, selection of options, and the drafting of agreements. Without a tool such as the Cultural Value Glasses (CVG), that allows us to recognize the impact of our cultural lenses at each stage of the process, we might ignore or misinterpret important information that may be critical for both the present agreement and the ongoing relationship.

---

## V. THE INFLUENCE OF CULTURE IN PROCESS AND SYSTEM DESIGN

Culture is not only influential in the different stages of the mediation process, but it is also relevant in process and system design. Process design provides an opportunity to tailor a culturally appropriate dispute resolution process, such as mediation, in order to meet the needs of the parties and the organization. In contrast, dispute system design (DSD) allows for the selection and creation of processes, including mediation, to address streams of disputes, so that each process reflects the values of the parties. While process design refers to a single process, system design has been described as "the applied art and science of designing the means to prevent, manage, learn from, and resolve streams of dispute or conflict."[13]

Even though culture is an intrinsic part of DSD, its prevalence has not always been emphasized by the field. The initial groundbreaking literature in dispute system design had only occasional references to culture.[14] However, later developments incorporated organizational culture in the context of design within institutions.[15] Also an early symposium on DSD held at

---

[13] Lisa Blomgren Amsler, Alexander B. Avtgis, & Michael Scott Jackman, *Dispute System Design and Bias in Dispute Resolution*, 70 SMU L. Rev. 913, 915, 916 (2017); *see also* Cathy A. Costantino & Christina Sickles Merchant, Designing Conflict Management Systems (1996); William L. Ury, Jeanne M. Brett & Stephen B. Goldberg, Getting Disputes Resolved: Designing Systems to Cut the Costs of Conflict (1988); Stephanie Smith & Janet Martinez, *An Analytic Framework for Dispute Systems Design*, 14 Harv. Negot. L. Rev. 123, 126 (2009).

[14] William L. Ury, Jeanne M. Brett & Stephen B. Goldberg, Getting Disputes Resolved: Designing Systems to Cut the Costs of Conflict (1988).

[15] Cathy A. Costantino & Christina Sickles Merchant, *Preface* to Designing Conflict Management Systems (1996).

Northwestern University in 1989 focused the relevance of culture in dispute system design. Furthermore, more recent works discuss the relevance of culture as one of the fundamental elements of system design.[16]

## A. The Need to Address Cultural Differences in Mediation Process Design

Whenever there is an opportunity to not only participate in a pre-established mediation process but also to design a dispute resolution process, it will be equally important to incorporate, to the extent possible, the culture of the parties. In this way, the mediation process design may allow for an opportunity to align the process choice with the values of the parties.

The multiplicity of cultural perspectives profoundly affects the expectations the parties bring to the mediation process. In the following excerpt, Rebecca Golbert reflects on the need to address the different assumptions and social constructions regarding the understanding of conflict itself, and how to design a process that takes into account these differences.

### REBECCA GOLBERT, *AN ANTHROPOLOGIST'S APPROACH TO MEDIATION*

11 Cardozo J. Conflict Resol. 81, 83–84 (2009).

. . . . An examination of mediation as it is perceived and practiced in other national and cultural settings, and in cross-cultural and international settings, may place these and other issues within a broader comparative framework and allow us to rethink some of our assumptions about what makes mediation work in differing cultural contexts. . . .

* * *

. . . . This essay . . . . looks at conflict and conflict resolution as culturally constructed categories. While all cultures experience conflict, they may understand and manage conflict very differently and may have differing legal and social mechanisms for resolving it. Mediation appears to be one of the most common forms of conflict resolution applied across a diverse range of cultures; however, this

---

16 *See* Nancy H. Rogers, Robert C. Bordone, Frank E.A. Sander & Craig A. McEwen, Designing Systems and Processes for Managing Disputes (2013); Lisa Blomgren Amsler, Janet K. Martinez & Stephanie E. Smith, Dispute Systems Design (forthcoming) (draft on file with the author).

wide application of mediation raises the question of what is locally understood by the concept and practice of mediation. . . .

* * *

. . . . In such mediated contexts, more than one cultural perspective may shape the understanding and expectations of the mediation process. How can mediation accommodate the differing social and cultural needs and aspirations of the parties to the mediation? . . . [B]eyond raised awareness, the field of mediation as developed in the United States and exported abroad, may need to adjust its own assumptions, philosophies, and practices to create an approach to international and cross-cultural mediation that is more responsive to both context and culture.

---

## B. Considerations for Mediation Process Design

Process and system design are embedded in a broader social and political context. As Lisa Blomgren Amsler, Janet K. Martinez, and Stephanie E. Smith have noted, relying on the work of Eleanor Ostrom, processes and systems are "nested" within broader systems, and therefore are affected by and affect each other as parts of the whole.[17] In this regard, Amy Cohen reminds us of the need to examine the "complexity on the ground" in which the system operates, and the narratives and struggles of the stakeholders.

### AMY J. COHEN, *DEBATING THE GLOBALIZATION OF U.S. MEDIATION: POLITICS, POWER, AND PRACTICE IN NEPAL*

11 Harv. Negot. L. Rev. 295, 352–53 (2006).

We are a field dedicated to fixing problems, not least of all our own. Yet in our desire to articulate certain methods, and in our subsequent critiques of these methods, we have produced an academic debate that has become so tightly locked that we are, I fear, missing a breathtaking amount of complexity on the ground—complexity that often amounts to nothing less than struggles over justice. To borrow from David Kennedy, "[i]f we set aside our preoccupation with the suitability of formal or informal legal

---

17 Lisa Blomgren Amsler, Janet K. Martinez & Stephanie E. Smith, *Christina Merchant and the State of Dispute System Design*, 33 (S7, S9) Conflict Resol. Q. (2015) (applying Eleanor Ostrom's concept that structures are nested to dispute system design).

structures, substantive or procedural legal rules . . . . we might find our way to asking how we wish to transform the distribution of power, status, and authority in society to humanitarian ends."

For those of us who wish to link the mediated resolution of disputes to outcomes that are more fair and egalitarian for social groups who share less in society's resources and power, we still know little about what possibilities, variations, costs, and benefits mediation is producing in developing countries. We might therefore begin with a research agenda and with a method of analysis that proceeds through case studies similar to those presented here. Questions we ask might examine both the forms and effects of ADR in the lives and practices of those who utilize it; what larger social narratives these are strengthening and subverting; and how culture is used and to what distributional ends. Culture as it features in the CVICT [Centre for Victims of Torture] mediation project is a site at which villagers deploy and contest visions of dispute resolution as it links to social change.

Finally, if we are willing to re-orient our understanding of ADR interventions as sources of norm-generation and of social and cultural change, we might also become willing to articulate the normative goals that motivate our interventions and to examine the effects, both procedural and substantive, that result in light of those goals. I offer here a description of an actual practice of a mediation—its hybrid methods and complex effects—as one example of an expressly interventionist model of mediation driven by shared commitments to evolving visions of social justice.

---

Expanding on the importance of taking into account the context in which the design takes place, Amy Cohen and Ellen Deason compare the interaction of culture and process design to the interdependence that occurs in any ecosystem. In the following excerpt, they argue the need to explore the "functions, context and consequences"[18] of various dispute resolution processes in order to understand their social and political foundation and impact. They suggest that a comparative analysis of the goals, structures, and methods of a process can assist in the examination of design options.

---

[18] Amy J. Cohen & Ellen E. Deason, *Comparative Considerations: Toward the Global Transfer of Ideas about Dispute System Design*, 12 Disp. Resol. Mag. 23, 23 (2006).

## AMY J. COHEN & ELLEN E. DEASON, *COMPARATIVE CONSIDERATIONS: TOWARD THE GLOBAL TRANSFER OF IDEAS ABOUT DISPUTE SYSTEM DESIGN*

12 Disp. Resol. Mag. 23, 23 (2006).

[F]ew methods exist to transmit ideas about dispute system design across systems and cultures in ways that pay careful attention to context-specific variables. Although there has been a significant amount of scholarship examining how individuals communicate and negotiate differently across contexts, far less attention has been paid to the differences in the legal, political and social norms and processes that shape and are shaped by dispute resolution institutions.

Consider an analogy from the plant kingdom. Surely, for a rainforest plant to survive in the desert it would need to incorporate water-conserving adaptations. Yet if the plant were able to take root, its method of attracting insects for pollination might prove successful among desert fauna.

But plants not only adapt to their ecosystem, they also influence the nature of that ecosystem, altering temperature, humidity and the level of nutrients—possibly even transferring genetic material to existing plants. Thus the new plant must be seen as an integral part of the environment, not as an independent product of environmental factors.

Similarly, although dispute resolutions institutions are socially and culturally embedded, some of their characteristics may spark innovation in other settings. However, to encourage the cross-pollination of ideas about dispute resolution institutions, we need to examine dispute resolution institutions themselves as social and cultural processes. Such analysis would compare how dispute resolution institutions work, why they work the way they do, how they get deployed in the service of ideology or social struggles, how they interact with other institutions to create the political and social conditions to realize their goals and to what distributional ends.

With the aim of comparing functions, context and consequences, we examined several dozen dispute resolution institutions around the globe. To permit comparisons of dissimilar institutions across contexts, we extracted "design elements," which we describe in generalized terms and organize in series of continua grouped into three schematic categories: (1) goals; (2) structure; and (3) methods.

Points along these continua represent idealized possible design choices.

---

## C. Integrating Culture in System Design

In addition to the above considerations, when integrating culture into system design, it is essential to be aware that neither processes nor systems are value-neutral. In the following excerpt, Carrie Menkel-Meadow brings attention to the "fundamentally different belief systems"[19] that are found not only across the globe, but also within our own communities. She suggests that the search for resolution should include inquiry as an essential method to compare and contrast differences rather than "assuming uniformity."[20]

### CARRIE MENKEL-MEADOW, *CORRESPONDENCES AND CONTRADICTIONS IN INTERNATIONAL AND DOMESTIC CONFLICT RESOLUTION: LESSONS FROM GENERAL THEORY AND VARIED CONTEXTS*

2003 J. Disp. Resol. 319, 350–52 (2003).

While I continue to admire those who attempt to create "acontextual" theory in our field (now focused on elaborating the differences between bi-lateral and multi-lateral negotiation), applying economic, mathematical, or even psychological models to human decision making, I can't help but think, especially in light of current events (and many actors, including terrorists committed to fundamentally different belief systems, as well as our own leaders, who seem equally insensitive to global well-being), that human conflict makers and conflict resolvers will not easily be "contained" in universal boxes or categories. Because I think these things, I offer the following suggestions for future "contextualized" studies for moving our field productively along, in theory and in practice, with the hope that even without universal theories we can learn more about how to prevent deadly and dangerous conflict and violence:

1. Under what social, political, cultural, and economic conditions do particular forms of conflict resolution

---

[19] Carrie Menkel-Meadow, *Correspondences and Contradictions in International and Domestic Conflict Resolution: Lessons from General Theory and Varied Contexts*, 2003 J. Disp. Resol. 319, 350 (2003).

[20] *Id.*

(adversarial, competitive, violent or collaborative, cooperative, and problem solving) emerge?

2. What kinds of interventions/actors/circumstances change the course, scope, or method of conflict resolution?

3. What kinds of circumstances require different forms of conflict resolution activities? (e.g., how does "short-term" violence prevention or amelioration differ from longer term reconciliation and relationship-developing action)?

4. What roles can "insiders" (stakeholder participants) to a conflict play?

5. What roles can "outsiders" ("interested parties," "affected parties," or "neutral parties") to a conflict play?

6. How does the locus (familial, local, national, cultural, intercultural, international) of the conflict affect the possible processes and outcomes that are available (a form of "level" or unit of analysis "reality testing")?

7. How much commitment to similar goals, "world views," values, or processes, is required to create a "conflict resolution" process?

8. How can we develop structures, concepts, and languages that are protean enough to have explanatory purchase across domains, but "open" enough to be studied and examined across levels of disputing and conflicts?

9. What varieties of interventions and dispute processing are possible and how are they related to each other (sequencing, series, continuing, multiple or parallel tracks)?

10. How can dispute processes be "elicited" from those in dispute (rather than "laid down" by those outside or "on top" of a dispute)?

11. What kinds of dispute or conflict resolution processes can be "institutionalized"? Which work better when maintained in "ad hoc," flexible forms?

12. What is the relation of formal "international relations" or "civil or criminal litigation" (state-based processes)

theory and practices to more informal, flexible, and ad hoc processes or institutions (NGOs, "problem solving workshops," etc.)? How much multiple level action is beneficial/tolerable and how much leads to difficulties of coordination?

* * *

Learning to live with differences within national boundaries or regional trade zones may provide a variety of "exemplars" for different modes of co-existence. If we are truly looking for "solutions" to domestic and international conflicts, disputes, and problems, than we should be open to as many different and contextually specific ideas as it will take. Though I doubt that there is a single theory to fit all human problems for decision, I think we can get better at it by "comparing and contrasting" specifics, rather than assuming uniformity or generality.

---

Besides the need for contextualization and inquiry, Jacqueline Nolan-Haley suggests the need to engage all stakeholders in order to build trust and attempt to reconcile their goals for the system. In order for sustainable implementation, especially in the context of identity-based disputes, she argues that there is a need to wrestle with not only the present conflict, but also with the issues of the past. In the following excerpt, she examines the conflict in Northern Ireland, and stresses the importance of building trust through active participation.

## JACQUELINE M. NOLAN-HALEY, *DESIGNING SYSTEMS FOR ACHIEVING JUSTICE AFTER A PEACE AGREEMENT: NORTHERN IRELAND'S STRUGGLE WITH THE PAST*

13 U. St. Thomas L.J. 315, 331–33 (2017).

Three major deficiencies prevent the successful implementation of DSD principles in dealing with the legacy of the past in Northern Ireland.

*1. Lack of Consensus Regarding Goals.* One of the challenges in implementing DSD principles in Northern Ireland's transitional justice regime is reaching a consensus on a strategic approach to achieving goals. While there is general agreement about the need to deal with the legacy of the past, there is no consensus on what approach to take or whose narrative of events controls the thinking and policy that goes into design of that project. Moreover, there is no consensus on whether reconciliation needs to be a part of truth recovery efforts. Achieving consensus will require active engagement by representatives of all stakeholders.

*2. Lack of Resources.* A second DSD challenge relates to the availability of resources. Establishing a mechanism for truth recovery has costs, and these costs need to be measured against competing fiscal concerns. . . .

*3. Lack of Trust.* Finally, trust is a key missing element which needs to be either discovered or recovered. . . . Lack of trust is consistent with identity-based conflicts which are rooted in the past. It is a problem encountered in many post-conflict regimes. And this is where our field of dispute resolution has been deficient. We have not developed adequate responses for dealing with conflicts rooted in the past. Frequently, mediation is considered the default process. But much of traditional mediation and other conflict-resolution thinking, at least in the United States, is not inclined to focus very much on the past. Mediation is considered a forward-looking process that does not try to place any blame for past harmful events. This is problematic when the goal is to recover the truth about the past. It is possible, however, that more consideration of transformative and narrative models of mediation might be useful in helping parties engage with the past and restore relationships.

* * *

As new approaches are considered in designing a truth recovery system with traction, all signs point toward independence as a critical value in the design. Independence does not necessarily mean neutrality. It is not even clear the extent to which DSD is a neutral activity or whether neutrality is possible in a country such as Northern Ireland. But with independence, a sustainable truth recovery process is possible. The divided communities in Northern Ireland can begin to build trust—the missing link in earlier efforts to recover truth. Within an atmosphere of trust, DSD principles have breathing space and are able to offer a participatory framework for guiding the development of a sustainable truth recovery model. Without trust, no amount of creative process design will achieve that goal.

In imagining how DSD principles can help to build trust, there are more questions than answers. Given so many past attempts at truth recovery, it takes a certain degree of courage and hope to believe that a process can be designed with transparency, legitimacy, and a framework for reconciliation. Identifying and then including representatives of *all* stakeholders in the design of an independent truth recovery process is a good place to begin.

---

One process that can promote the active participation of stakeholders and begin the building of the trust needed for a culturally appropriate dispute system design is the World Café. This process could be a powerful tool to explore the cultures of the different stakeholders and enhance understanding. In the following except, Jacqueline Font-Guzman summarizes the process, and brings attention to its potential use in the dispute resolution field. She argues that through this process it is possible to create a space for powerful conversations, new experiences, and synergies.

## JACQUELINE N. FONT-GUZMÁN, *MOVING 'BEYOND NEUTRALITY' AND CROSS-CULTURAL TRAINING: USING WORLD CAFÉ DIALOGUE TO ADDRESS END-OF-LIFE CARE INEQUALITIES*

21 Peace and Conflict Stud. 49, 50–51 (2014).

The .... World Café participants were welcomed into a room with background music, snacks, round tables, and tablecloths. At the tables there were colored markers, different color post-it notes, and flip chart paper for participants to write notes summarizing the main points in the discussion and/or doodle. There were three rounds of conversations driven by questions, previously drafted, and every twenty minutes or so, music alerted the participants that it was time to relocate to another table with a newly formed group and share their ideas. The three questions that served as discussion starters in each successive round were: What is important to our group? What does the group need in order to be energized and feel engaged in these efforts? What conversations could create ripples and create new possibilities for engagement? After finalizing all three rounds, the facilitators led a group discussion to share as a group the patterns and themes that had emerged. Contrary to brainstorming, where the main goal is usually to generate solutions or strategies to solve a problem, through these questions our aim was to foster deep listening, enable a diverse group of people to connect with each other, and tap into their inner wisdom. A graphic artist captured the narratives that emerged in the conversations.

Within minutes, strangers were actively engaged in powerful conversations. They were sharing their intimate experiences, frustrations, fears, hopes, values, expectations, and feelings ..... These conversations not only served as a communication tool, they were creating experiences. You could feel the intensity of the synergy in the room. . . . .

I argue that through dialogue processes, conflict practitioners can pose a challenge to oppressive power structures by educating those with power about the mutual benefit of altering relationships so that they can lead using "power with" and not "power over."

---

Processes such as the World Café are an effective method for identifying and understanding the key underlying cultural differences of the stakeholders. However, in order to use this knowledge gained from the World Café, a tool which has been termed the Cultural Value Integration Spectrum (CVIS) be helpful. The Cultural Value Integration Spectrum (CVIS) allows for an assessment of the level of stakeholder cultural compatibility, and aims to realize expectations, determine the goals for the system, and assist the development of culturally tailored processes. It builds upon the information gained through the Cultural Value Discernment (CVD) and the Cultural Value Glasses (CVG), (discussed earlier in this chapter) and applies it in the context of process and system design. In the following excerpt, Mariana Hernandez Crespo Gonstead introduces the Cultural Value Integration Spectrum (CVIS), and argues that it can be a powerful tool to better address cultural differences in system design.

## MARIANA HERNANDEZ CRESPO GONSTEAD, *A NEW DANCE ON THE GLOBAL STAGE: INTRODUCING A CULTURAL VALUE-BASED TOOLBOX TO OPTIMIZE PROBLEM-SOLVING, INNOVATION, AND GROWTH*

34 Ohio St. J. on Disp. Resol. (forthcoming 2019).

The greater the cultural gap is between parties, the more the Cultural Value Discernment (CVD) needs to become an intrinsic part of process and system design. Without a thorough understanding of what matters the most to the parties, it would be nearly impossible to design a process or system that is culturally compatible with their values. If the values of the parties are ignored, the quality of the processes or systems will be diminished, especially for those who do not share the culture that the process reflects. This may in turn affect the parties' level of engagement and satisfaction.

Once the values of the parties have been identified by the Cultural Value Discernment (CVD), then the value compatibility between the stakeholders can be explored using another tool, the

Cultural Value Integration Spectrum (CVIS). Through this compatibility assessment, the Cultural Value Integration Spectrum (CVIS) aims to realize expectations, determine the goals for the system, and assist the development of culturally tailored processes. In this way, stakeholders can make informed decisions after determining, through the Cultural Value Integration Spectrum (CVIS), the desired level of cultural integration sought before designing a process or system.

On one end of the Cultural Value Integration Spectrum (CVIS), when cultures are less compatible due to their core values, processes and systems can be designed with the goal of creating harmonious co-existence. In the middle, when cultures are more compatible because they share a common goal, then systems can be designed to promote collaboration. On the other end, when cultures are most compatible because they share core values, systems can be designed to promote complementarity. The parties themselves will have to engage in a process of mutual discernment with regard to the level of cultural value integration they desire. In other words, which, if any, values from each culture will be fused to give rise to a new shared culture.

* * *

If parties do not assess their values to determine the level of cultural integration before systems are designed, processes can become a path for assimilation, where the dominant culture becomes the norm. This could force the parties or stakeholders who are not of the dominant culture into uniformity. From the perspective of the dominant culture, achieving harmony through uniformity is easier, faster, and cheaper, because it is simply preserving the status quo. But, for the subordinate culture, achieving harmony through uniformity is harder, slower, and more expensive because it requires a decrease in autonomy, by having to operate under imposed cultural norms that might feel foreign. Therefore, ignoring the impact of cultural norms may only be beneficial as long as you share the dominant culture and do not have to assimilate. However, if you share the subordinate culture the cultural norms cannot be as easily ignored because you are forced to operate in a way that may not feel "normal." If assimilation is the primary way to achieve harmony, it could become a "power-over" struggle with temporary wins that are not sustainable, because they are based on exclusion. Instead if parties are able to integrate, to some degree, their values, a fusion of cultures emerges, potentially producing a higher level of unity. While this might not always be possible, and even when it is possible, it may not be as easy, fast, or cheap, if the parties can operate within a "power-with" mindset, the outcomes can be more sustainable.

If parties or stakeholders continue to primarily assimilate rather than integrate, their level of engagement is likely to decrease significantly because it requires adopting the dominant culture. This passive manner of interaction not only wastes a unique opportunity for innovation, but also hinders the potential for individual and collective growth. Therefore, using the Cultural Value Integration Spectrum (CVIS) as a tool to identify the level of compatibility becomes critical because if the values have some degree of compatibility, and a certain level of integration is desirable, then the process or system design can be used as an opportunity to allow the parties or stakeholders to make unique contributions to the whole. Ultimately, this increases unity though participatory processes (i.e. facilitative processes). Alternatively, the Cultural Value Integration Spectrum (CVIS) might help the parties gain awareness of their unwillingness or inability to integrate. In this case, processes that lead to assimilation through persuasion might be the preferred option (i.e. adjudicative processes).

Cultural compatibility has different implications in the private and public spheres. Generally, in the private sphere, process and system design affects parties that, to some degree, can select who they want to associate with. In other words, in private design there is an assumption of some common bond or shared identity. In contrast, in the public sphere, process and system design is generally more complex because communities are composed of a diverse variety of stakeholders and there might be fewer shared values present. Therefore, when designing interest-based systems in the public square, the assessment of stakeholder value compatibility is even more critical in order for parties to be able to make informed decisions on the preferred level of integration. When values are diametrically opposed, parties might have to resort to a rules-based system.

## VI. THE IMPACT OF CULTURE ON THE MEDIATOR

Cultural differences not only impact the meditation process and its design, but also the mediator's or mediators' role. Moreover, the mediator's identity, which is informed by her or his own cultural lenses, can be a significant factor in the mediation process and in process and system design. The culture of the parties, the attorneys, and the mediator(s) are important variables that should be considered.

## A. Cultural Values and the Identity of the Mediator

Our cultural identity is formed by the impact of the cultures to which we belong. As such, the influence of our primary culture predetermines what cultural tendencies are familiar and which are unfamiliar. In the following excerpt, John Barkai shares the struggles of a mediator wrestling with her or his own cultural identity. He explores the origin of these limitations, and suggests that our abilities to operate within one culture, presupposes the inability to operate within a different culture. In a series of tables, he highlights these cultural differences, by comparing the tendencies of low-context and high-context cultures, and also contrasting the cultural differences between Western and Asian cultures in negotiation and mediation. This visual representation emphasizes how profound cultural differences are, and why the identity of the mediator is important and needs to be a part of the decision-making process.

### JOHN BARKAI, *WHAT'S A CROSS-CULTURAL MEDIATOR TO DO? A LOW-CONTEXT SOLUTION FOR A HIGH-CONTEXT PROBLEM*

10 Cardozo J. Conflict Resol., 43, 49–50, 52–53, 59, 85 (2008).

Although I write this article with the hope of offering a cross-cultural mediation guide for all mediators, I am sure that I am a bit like 'Popeye the Sailor Man' in this situation. Popeye said, 'I am what I am and that's all that I am.' Popeye's words remind me that I am an American, who is an American-trained mediator, who speaks only one language (English), and who, despite rather extensive travel, has lived outside the United States for less than one year. To use terms further developed later in this article, this means that, in many ways, my behavior is that of the typical American stereotype in that I am an individualist, egalitarian, informal, low-context communicator who makes extensive use of jokes and humor, and uses a rationally-based, problem-solving approach to resolve conflicts.

Because of our culture, myself and most other American mediators have a difficult time (and perhaps a true inability) radically shifting our cultural perspective and behavior ninety degrees or more to see and do mediation differently. This is what I call 'Popeye's Problem': lacking the ability to be what you are not and consequently not being able to relate to people from other cultures as they might prefer to be related. As Popeye says, 'I am what I am and that's all that I am.' For cross-cultural mediation, as I will explain in greater depth later, I am a low-context communicator, and I cannot relate or communicate well in a high-context manner. However, as I shall also explain, I believe that reaching wise, desirable, and long-lasting solutions to cross-cultural problems can be accomplished by using a low-context communication approach even with high-context communicating disputants. . . . .

* * *

Perhaps the three most effective tools for mediating cross-cultural disputes are pre-mediation meetings (joint or private), caucuses during mediation, and the Socratic method of questioning. All three of these tools can be used in any mediation, but they may take on a different form or focus in a cross-cultural mediation.

* * *

**Cultural Variations Between Low-Context and High-Context Cultures (according to Edward T. Hall, 1976)**

| LOW-CONTEXT CULTURE | HIGH-CONTEXT CULTURE |
|---|---|
| Overtly displays meanings through direct communication forms | Implicitly embeds meanings at different levels of the sociological context |
| Values individualism | Values group sense |
| Tends to develop transitory personal relationships | Tends to take time to cultivate and establish permanent personal relationships |
| Emphasizes linear logic | Emphasizes spiral logic |
| Values direct verbal interaction and is less able to read nonverbal expressions | Values indirect verbal interaction and is more able to read nonverbal expressions |
| Tends to use "logic" to present ideas | Tends to use more "feeling" in expression |
| Tends to emphasize highly structured messages, give details, and place great stress on words and technical signs | Tends to give simple ambiguous non-contexting messages |
| Perceive highly verbal persons favorably | Perceives highly verbal persons less favorably |

* * *

## Contrasting Cultural Differences in Negotiation and Mediation

| WESTERN | ASIAN |
|---|---|
| Low Context (direct) Communication | High Context (indirect) Communication |
| Low Power Distance | High Power Distance |
| Individualism | Collectivism |
| Low Uncertainty Avoidance | High Uncertainty Avoidance |
| Masculinity (Assertive) | Femininity (Cooperative) |
| Short-Term Orientation | Long-Term Orientation |
| Monochronic Time | Polychronic Time |
| Space—far apart | Space—close |
| Risk Takers | Risk Avoiders |
| Universalism | Particularism |
| Achievement | Ascription |
| Specific | Difuse |
| Brief Rapport building time (short) | Extensive Rapport building time (long) |
| Aggressive | Passive |
| Contract focused | Relationship focused |
| Win-lose approach | Win-win approach |
| Informal approach | Formal approach |
| Show emotions | Hide emotions |
| Preference for specific agreement | Preference for general agreement |
| Contract is fixed | Re-negotiation is possible |
| Individual Decision-making | Group Decision-making |
| Logical decision-making | Emotional decision-making |
| All equals | One leader |
| Face Saving | Face Giving |
| Inductive logic | Deductive logic |
| Low Government involvement | High Government involvement |
| Linear-Active | Multi-Active Reactive |

While mediators can confront many functional and logistical challenges when mediating across cultures, there may be ethical challenges as well. In this regard, Carrie Menkel-Meadow and Harold Abramson, stress the need to consider when cultural clashes between the mediator and the parties could become "ethical conundrums." They note that "[a]lthough all ethical problems are challenging because they present compelling values in ineluctable tension, cross-cultural ethical dilemmas are particularly agonizing because they seem to require a choice between deeply felt cultural traditions."[21] Therefore, they stress the importance of mediators being aware of their own cultural identity and values and how this might impact their suitability to participate in the process. In the following excerpt Harold Abramson suggests guidelines for mediators to address cultural diversity in terms of understanding the different cultural practices.

## HAROLD ABRAMSON, *CROSSING BORDERS INTO NEW ETHICAL TERRITORY: ETHICAL CHALLENGES WHEN MEDIATING CROSS-CULTURALLY*

49 S. Tex. L. Rev. 921, 925 (2008).

Cross-cultural mediators live under the constant threat of cultural imperialism charges. Mediators do not want to be guilty of parochial ignorance and arrogance when objecting to what might be a cultural practice. Mediators want to avoid claiming that they are right and the parties wrong. In order to reduce this risk, cross-cultural mediators should approach mediations with a healthy respect for cultural pluralism and a clear understanding of the other cultural practice. This sequence of four initiatives is designed to guide mediators along this pathway.

First, a cross-cultural mediator should understand his or her own cultural practices.

Second, the mediator should research the other cultural practice to be sure that the mediator understands its terms and its rationale.

Third, the mediator should try to bridge any cultural gap between the mediator and parties by posing questions to the parties

---

[21] Carrie Menkel-Meadow & Harold I. Abramson, *Mediating Multiculturally: Culture and the Ethical Mediator*, *in* Mediation Ethics: Cases & Commentaries 305 (Ellen Waldman ed., 2011).

to be sure that the parties are making informed and voluntary decisions free of coercion.

Fourth, if the mediator cannot bridge the gap and finds the practice to be fundamentally abhorrent, then, as a last resort, the mediator should consider withdrawing if the mediator concludes that the practice violates an internationally recognized norm or compromises the mediator's impartiality or the mediation process.

---

## B. Addressing Cultural Differences Through Co-Mediation

Having more than one mediator at the table can pose both advantages and disadvantages. Lela P. Love and Joseph P. Stulberg have pointed out that while having two or more mediators can enhance "expertise, insights, and listening capacity,"[22] the use of co-mediation can also require more time and adds an additional layer of complexity as the mediators need to coordinate with each other. Also, Frank Sander has also questioned whether the proposed benefits outweigh the increased financial cost of co-mediation.[23] Yet in the international context, co-mediators as interpreters can assist the parties in bridging a cultural gap. In the following excerpt, Mariana Hernandez Crespo Gonstead notes that co-mediators could play an essential role in not only enhancing understanding at the table, but also assisting in aligning the cultural preferences with the process design.

### MARIANA HERNANDEZ CRESPO GONSTEAD, *A NEW DANCE ON THE GLOBAL STAGE: INTRODUCING A CULTURAL VALUE-BASED TOOLBOX TO OPTIMIZE PROBLEM-SOLVING, INNOVATION, AND GROWTH*

34 Ohio St. J. on Disp. Resol. (forthcoming 2019).

Another area in which our cultural glasses play a significant role—and in which the Cultural Value Glasses (CVG) could be of critical importance—is in the selection of experts. When the parties at the table do not share the same culture, the identity of the mediator becomes an especially important factor, as she or he has the potential to assist in bridging the cultural gap between the parties.

---

22 Lela P. Love & Joseph P. Stulberg, *Practice Guidelines for Co-Mediation: Making Certain that "Two Heads are Better than One,"* 13 Mediation Q. 179, 179–81 (Spring 1996).

23 Frank Sander, *Some Concluding Thoughts,* 17 Ohio St. J. on Disp. Resol. 705, 707 (2002).

In this regard, in co-mediation, the presence of multiple mediators can increase the potential for bridging the cultural gap by sharing parties' cultural ties. Our cultural glasses are composed of a multiplicity of lenses that reflect the variety of cultures each of us belongs to. Therefore, while we all have a unique set of glasses, we may share at least one set of lenses with those with whom we share a cultural tie. For this reason, the parties might need to assess what is or are the most relevant cultural ties for the selection of the mediator.

An analogous scenario is found in the arbitration field, where the identity of the arbitrator seems to play a significant role. There, despite the additional cost, parties sometimes prefer to have an arbitration tribunal in which two of the three arbitrators are party-appointed. One benefit is that these arbiters can serve as translators of the parties' legal and cultural differences. Despite the fact that mediators are facilitators rather than decision-makers, as is the case with arbiters, the identity of the mediator can also impact the mediation process.

As facilitators, co-mediators can address parties' cultural differences as an intrinsic part of the process. [Jeswald] Salacuse compares culture to a "silent language" that those who are in a community share. This shared "silent language" allows them to understand each other and operate in auto-pilot when making decisions, which enables more fluid interactions. He describes culture as a shared pool of information which guides the group member's understanding and behaviors.

The power of this silent language cannot be overlooked, or underestimated. Problems can emerge when we interact with those who do not share our "silent language." The lack of a shared pool of cultural knowledge creates a gap that may just make interactions more cumbersome when there is no common reference point. In other cases, these gaps may hinder understanding completely. It is in these contexts, where there is little to no understanding, that co-mediation may be an important option to consider. Having two mediators, who could each have cultural ties with at least one of the parties, can facilitate interactions at the mediation table. In this way, mediators can act as interpreters of the silent language to help align the process to the cultural values of the parties, and also assist with the impact culture has on each part of the process.

# VII. NOTES AND QUESTIONS

1. What arguments do you find most and least persuasive for why culture matters? Why? What do you think would happen if we decided to ignore culture in our daily interactions? In the mediation process? In process and system design?

2. The culture as an iceberg analogy notes that the behaviors, processes, and traditions are what manifest above the surface, but they are driven by the underlying cultural values. Can you think of some examples of the underlying culture values that are reflected in the institutions, behaviors, and traditions in your own communities and countries?

3. Given the dynamic and complex nature of culture, can you identify a couple of examples of how culture has changed in your family, community, or country within your lifetime?

4. As people who make culture, think of a time when you have been involved in a relationship or group where you were interacting with people of different cultures. Was there a dominant culture and did its values prevail? Were you a member of the dominant culture or the subordinate culture? Did the members of the subordinate culture make a conscious decision to adopt the dominant culture or was it challenged?

5. Daniel Shapiro alerts us to the danger of polarization, what he describes as the "tribes effect." He defines a tribe as "any group to which we see ourselves as similar in kind, whether based on religion or ethnicity or even our place of work. We feel a kinlike connection to the tribe; we emotionally invest in it. This means a religious community or nation can feel like a tribe."[24] After reading this chapter on the importance of culture, what impact do you think the "tribes effect" can have on mediation?

6. This chapter introduced the Cultural Value Discernment (CVD) as a tool to enhance understanding in problem solving processes, such as mediation, and system design. The CVD allows us to connect the positions and interests of the parties to the underlying values that drive their decision-making process. Learning the other's values and motivations, allows us to know each other better, which can increase predictability for future interactions. Can you think of a situation when it would be useful to not only ask "what do you want and why?" (positions and interests) but also "why is that important

---

[24] Daniel Shapiro, Negotiating the Nonnegotiable: How to Resolve your Most Emotionally Charged Conflicts 6 (2017).

to you?" (values)? What difference could that make for the agreement and the relationship?

7. The Cultural Value Glasses (CVG) was presented in this chapter as a tool that can be used to gain awareness of the cultural impact on each stage of the mediation process. Imagine that you go to a foreign country and you find yourself in a mediation process where your expectations are not met at each stage of the process. For example, in the information gathering stage you may have expected meditator to ask certain questions and react in a certain way. How would that make you feel? What impact do the cultural glasses of the parties and mediators have on the process?

8. When designing a system for dispute resolution, mediation processes are one of the available options. In this context, the Cultural Value Integration Spectrum (CVIS) could be a useful tool to assist in assessing the level of stakeholder cultural compatibility in an effort to explore stakeholder's expectations, goals, and values. What would be some of the benefits and constraints in trying to design a system that aligns different cultural values of the parties? For example, if some of the stakeholders come from a culture that values efficiency and others value relationships, how would you design a system that takes into account both values?

9. If there is a default mediation process in a contract, who determines what the process looks like? What would be the criteria? How would the subject matter of the dispute, the geographical region, the type of conflict, and the goals of the parties be taken into account?

10. What are your views on how to select a mediator or mediators? What factors would you take into account? What would you look for in a co-mediator? Would you like to select the mediator or have one appointed?

11. Imagine a situation where you are called to be a mediator between two parties that share a different faith or culture that clashes with your own. If you were in this position, would this affect how you proceed? Do you think you could be an effective mediator? Why or why not?

# Chapter 4

# LEGAL ISSUES AND REGULATION OF MEDIATION

---

## I. INTRODUCTION

Mediation is celebrated for its flexibility and the opportunity for participants in many different contexts to tailor the procedures they use, as well as the resolutions they reach, to their own particular circumstances. Detailed regulation of the mediation process could not only impair this aspect of party autonomy, but could also limit approaches to mediation and diminish its versatility and usefulness. Perhaps for this reason, mediation—both domestic and international—is far less constrained by formally enacted legal rules and regulations than the litigation process, with its detailed procedural rules and codes. Instead, private contracts are important determinants of mediation processes. They are supplemented by "soft law" developed by organizations in the form of ethical codes and standards. Together, parties' contracts and soft law play an important role in mediation regulation.

There is, however, growing legal regulation of mediation, which has been motivated by a desire to benefit participants and encourage mediation use by improving consistency, predictability, and quality. Surveys indicate that mediation users value the enforceability of mediated agreements, strong protection for confidentiality, and the availability of competent mediators. Commentators suggest that legal measures that promote these goals will encourage disputants to use mediation, and regulatory frameworks are being developed in many countries. While few laws extensively regulate the procedures employed by mediators, in numerous jurisdictions legislation or court rules now determine important aspects of the relationship between mediation and the legal system.

In Part II, this chapter introduces the sources of law that govern mediation. It then examines three key legal issues that arise in mediation: (1) enforcing agreements to mediate disputes (Part III); (2) protecting the confidentiality of communications in mediation (Part IV); and (3) enforcing settlement agreements reached in mediation (Part V). It concludes in Part VI by identifying several other aspects of mediation that are sometimes subject to regulation: mediator qualifications, the effect on limitation periods, and the roles of judges with regard to mediation. Taken as a whole, these developments in legal regulation of mediation can be seen as an important element in the evolving balance between a diversity of approaches and harmonization in global approaches to mediation.

## II. SOURCES OF LAW FOR THE REGULATION OF MEDIATION

Mediation has been governed predominantly by two categories of rules. The first type, discussed in Part A, consists of those that the parties themselves select by agreement. Those agreements can also incorporate by reference rules and soft law that have been developed by mediation institutions. The second category of rules governing mediation, introduced in Part B, consists of external rules provided by the applicable national law and court rules. National laws may, in turn, need to be consistent with a regional regulatory framework. In Europe, the European Union (EU) Mediation Directive,[1] which has been implemented in the national laws of the EU Member States, sets minimum requirements for mediation regulation. National laws can also be influenced by model laws, which are designed to promote consistent legal regulation of mediation. Part C explains that both institutional rules and national law are typically a mix of mandatory and default provisions, which maximizes the opportunity for parties to exercise their autonomy in designing their mediation process.

Party-created rules and national law governing mediation have now been joined by a third category—international law—with recent developments in this arena. In December 2018, the United Nations General Assembly adopted the United Nations Convention on International Settlement Agreements Resulting from Mediation.[2] This treaty, which is discussed in Part V, will be opened for signature in 2019 and will be called the Singapore Convention. Once the Convention is widely ratified, it will govern the enforcement of settlement agreements reached in international commercial mediation.

---

1 Directive 2008/52/EC of the European Parliament and of the Council of 21 May 2008 on Certain Aspects of Mediation in Civil and Commercial Matters [hereinafter *EU Mediation Directive*].

2 Available at https://uncitral.un.org/en/texts/arbitration.

### A. Party Agreements and Institutional Rules

Many aspects of mediation are controlled through private contracting between the parties, which is an expression of party autonomy as well as an important form of self-regulation. Examples of types of contracts that relate to the conduct of mediation include:

- dispute resolution clauses in commercial contracts that trigger the use of mediation in the future if a dispute arises;
- agreements to mediate a specific dispute after it arises, which typically contain provisions on how the mediation will be conducted; and
- confidentiality agreements.

Parties may decide to make arrangements for how they plan to mediate a dispute and set forth these procedures in an agreement. At the start of a contractual relationship, however, parties tend to be focused on the promise of the new enterprise and frequently do not consider carefully the possibility of future disputes. This natural tendency is ironic given the importance of contracts in determining the specifics of how a mediation will be conducted.

As an alternative to negotiating the specifics of a design for their dispute resolution process themselves, parties may instead select a set of institutional rules and procedures to govern their mediation. These rules become binding on the parties when they incorporate them by reference in their contract. They may also decide to have an organization administer their mediation, in which case they would typically designate the rules of that organization. (Many of these organizations also administer arbitrations as well.) Or, the United Nations Commission on International Trade Law (UNCITRAL) Conciliation Rules were developed in 1980 for parties to use in what are called *ad hoc* or non-administered mediations, i.e. conducted without institutional supervision. Other sets of rules are tailored for specific subject matter, such as disputes about intellectual property or investor-state disputes. (See Box 1 for examples of rules designed for international mediations.)

In addition, parties' mediation agreements may also include references to soft law, such as ethical codes for mediators, which are discussed in Chapter 5. They include the European Code of Conduct for Mediators and, in the United States, the Model Standards of Conduct for Mediators. Even when they are not incorporated into a party agreement, these instruments set standards for the professional behavior of mediators and thus serve to promote the quality of mediation.

### 1. Examples of International Mediation Rules

- UNCITRAL Conciliation Rules
- International Chamber of Commerce (ICC) Mediation Rules
- International Centre for Dispute Resolution (ICDR/AAA) Mediation Rules
- London Court of International Arbitration (LCIA) Mediation Procedure
- World Intellectual Property Organization (WIPO) Mediation Rules
- International Bar Association (IBA) Rules on Investor-State Mediation

## B. Mediation Frameworks, Model Laws, National Laws, and Court Rules

In addition to party self-regulation through agreement and by adopting institutional rules, mediation is increasingly regulated by national legislatures and regional authorities, with influence from international bodies. This regulation takes the form of mediation frameworks, national laws, and court rules. There are also model laws, which have been enacted or have influenced legislation in a number of jurisdictions. Globally, there is a great deal of diversity in national laws governing mediation, and this chapter can include only selected examples to provide a feel for the variability. Along with this diversity, however, there is a countervailing effort to harmonize mediation law using mediation frameworks and model laws.

An important example of a mediation framework is the European Union Mediation Directive, which, as discussed in Chapter 2, came into force in 2008. The Directive aims to "promote the amicable settlements of disputes by encouraging the use of mediation and by ensuring a balanced relationship between mediation and judicial proceedings." [3] It established parameters that European countries can implement using a variety of forms of regulation.

---

[3] *EU Mediation Directive, supra* note 1, art. 1.1.

Under its guidance, all the European States were required to enact national legislation on the mediation of cross-border civil and commercial disputes. Furthermore, almost all of them went even further and extended their legislation to include domestic mediation.[4] Framework regulation such as the EU Directive is a step in the direction of harmonization and standardization, but one that allows individual countries flexibility in the measures they adopt so long as they meet the minimum standards of the framework. As described throughout this chapter, there is a great deal of variation in the national laws that implement the Directive.[5]

Variation in mediation regulation is also noteworthy *within* some countries, as in the United States. The federal ADR Act of 1998 (5 U.S.C. §§ 651–658), requires all federal district courts to provide alternative dispute resolution. But the ADR Act leaves the choice of dispute resolution and its implementation to individual courts, resulting in different approaches among the federal courts. Moreover, outside the court system, almost all regulation of mediation takes place at the state level. The most important effort at harmonizing state provisions is the Uniform Mediation Act (UMA), adopted jointly by the American Bar Association and the Uniform Law Commission.[6] It provides a model for legislation that, as of 2018, had been enacted in 12 jurisdictions. The UMA primarily concerns the confidentiality of the mediation process.

There has also been a major effort to provide a vehicle intended to harmonize national mediation laws in the international context. In 2002, the United Nations endorsed the UNCITRAL Model Law on International Commercial Conciliation, which provides a model for national legislation governing transboundary commercial mediations. In 2018, the Model Law was amended to be consistent with the Singapore Convention and renamed the UNCITRAL Model Law on International Commercial Mediation and International Settlement Agreements Resulting from Mediation (Mediation Model

---

[4] Report from the Commission to the European Parliament, The Council and the European Economic and Social Committee on the Application of Directive 2008/52/EC of the European Parliament and of the Council on Certain Aspects of Mediation in Civil and Commercial Matters, COM(2016) 542final, 26 August 2016.

[5] For thorough coverage of national law on mediation in the European Union, see EU Mediation Law Handbook: Regulatory Robustness Ratings for Mediation Regimes (Nadia Alexander, Sabine Walsh, & Martin Svatos, eds. 1917).

[6] Uniform Mediation Act (2001, amended 2003), available at https://www.uniformlaws.org/home.

Law).[7] (Note that the Model Law treats mediation as equivalent to conciliation.) The Model Law is also suitable for regulating domestic mediation. UNCITRAL reports that, as of 2018, the original Model Law on Conciliation or close variants had been enacted by 33 countries. In the United States, the UMA was amended to add coverage for international commercial mediations that coordinated with the original Model Law.

Regulation governing mediation can be both comprehensive, governing broad categories of mediation, or piecemeal, with a more restricted application to specific types of mediation. The EU Mediation Directive is an example of an instrument with a comprehensive scope. It includes measures on ensuring the quality of mediators, encouraging courts to promote mediation, providing for the enforceability of agreements reached in mediation, protecting confidentiality, and suspending statutes of limitations during mediation. Laws with a more limited scope may be designed for the mediation of disputes within a particular industry or sector, or tailored for a specific type of mediation program. For example, in many jurisdictions there are separate rules for court-connected mediation programs, which are discussed more fully in Chapter 2.

### C. Default and Mandatory Regulatory Provisions

Mediation laws and institutional rules are both typically a mix of two categories of provisions: default and mandatory. Default provisions operate only if the parties have not expressly agreed on their own provision. That means they open the door for private contracts to play a major role in regulating mediation by allowing the parties to implement their preferences. One can think of these default rules as "back-up" provisions that fill in the gaps where parties have neglected, or been unable, to agree on procedures. In contrast, mandatory rules govern mediations regardless of anything the parties have agreed; parties cannot contract out of these provisions. Because party autonomy is a central principle for mediation, mandatory provisions tend to cover only fundamental tenets. Default provisions tend to dominate, giving parties the flexibility to adjust the details of mediation to their particular context. By allowing individual tailoring, default provisions promote

---

[7] Model Law on International Commercial Mediation and International Settlement Agreements Resulting from Mediation, 2018 (amending the UNCITRAL Model Law on International Commercial Conciliation, 2002), UNCITRAL, Report on the Work of its 51st Sess., U.N. Doc. A/73/17 annex II (2018), available at https://uncitral.un.org/en/texts/arbitration/.

a goal of self-determination. But they do not foster consistency or uniformity.

The UNCITRAL Mediation Model Law provides an excellent example of the interplay between default and mandatory provisions. First, the entire law is a default provision except for the provisions on enforcing mediated agreements; it applies to transboundary mediations *unless* the parties agree to exclude its application. (See Article 3(5).) Second, if the parties do not exercise their opportunity to opt-out of the law entirely, many of its provisions take the form of default rules. Compare the wording of one of the Model Law's mandatory provisions, which sets forth the principle of fair treatment in mediation, to a typical default provision on appointing a mediator, which allows the parties to shape the mediation process by agreement. (See Box 2.)

**2. Illustration of Mandatory and Default Statutory Provisions**

**UNCITRAL Model Law on International Commercial Mediation and International Settlement Agreements Resulting from Mediation**

**Article 7. Conduct of mediation**

3. In any case, in conducting the proceedings, the mediator shall seek to maintain fair treatment of the parties and, in so doing, shall take into account the circumstances of the case.

**Article 6. Number and appointment of mediators**

1. There shall be one mediator, unless the parties agree that there shall be two or more mediators.

The UNCITRAL Model Law is not alone in its emphasis on party autonomy and use of default provisions. For example, both the U.S. Uniform Mediation Act and the EU Mediation Directive similarly grant parties the ability to agree that the legislative limitations on using mediation communications in subsequent litigation or arbitration will not apply at all to their mediation.

## III. AGREEMENTS TO MEDIATE

Agreements to mediate come in two forms. First, when parties initiate a relationship, they may plan for dispute resolution and insert a provision into their contract. This provides them with an opportunity to design a resolution process before a dispute arises, while their relationship is positive. While arbitration has been the traditional choice in international commercial endeavors, parties are now turning more frequently to mediation or to combinations of mediation with other processes. Parties are choosing to combine mediation with arbitration in hybrid processes or agreeing to multi-tiered dispute resolution clauses that include negotiation or mediation as the initial consensual step in a multi-step process. Chapter 6 explores combining mediation with other processes in more detail.

As mentioned in Section II, when entering into a relationship, parties have an opportunity to plan for dispute resolution. They can design a process to fit their specific situation and the types of disputes they anticipate. Or they can designate a dispute resolution institution to administer the mediation process and use its standard rules and mediation clause. Whether the parties design an individual ad hoc process or use an institution, a mediation clause commits the parties to the process and thus serves a triggering function once a dispute arises. One of the barriers to using mediation is that some parties feel that suggesting mediation for an existing dispute signals weakness. In this situation, a pre-commitment in a contract clause is a useful strategy for getting disputing parties to the mediation table. (See Box 3 for some useful provisions to include in when drafting a mediation clause.)

**3. Elements of a Mediation Clause for Transboundary Disputes:**

- a triggering mechanism (how and when the mediation will be initialized, including notice provisions);
- the scope of mediation (what disputes are covered by the agreement);
- the choice of procedural and substantive law;
- a method for mediator selection;
- a method for allocating costs and fees;
- the language of the mediation;
- description of mediation procedures

Second, parties may enter into an agreement to mediate after their dispute arises. Post-dispute agreements typically define the conflict to be mediated and either incorporate institutional rules or set forth details for the procedure. They often serve as an appointment contract between the parties and the mediator and they typically contain confidentiality provisions. In practice, parties may use both pre-dispute mediation contract clauses and post-dispute mediation agreements, and the content of these two types of agreements often overlaps.

With arbitration, the Convention on the Recognition and Enforcement of Foreign Arbitral Awards (New York Convention) and national laws mandate that courts must send disputes to arbitration when parties have entered into an agreement to arbitrate. There is no comparable legal framework to enforce mediation clauses at the international level. In fact, the law in this area could be described as still at an embryonic stage. There are no enforcement provisions for agreements to mediate in either the EU Mediation Directive or the U.S. Uniform Mediation Act. Moreover, the new Singapore Convention (discussed in Section V) does not include any provisions on the enforcement of agreements to mediate.

There is a very limited provision on enforcing mediation agreements in the UNCITRAL Mediation Model Law. It applies only when parties have entered into an explicit agreement that they will not initiate arbitral or judicial proceedings while mediation is pending. In that situation, the arbitral tribunal or the court must bar arbitration or litigation from proceeding in violation of the parties' agreement. There is, however, an exception: a party may disregard the mediation agreement "to the extent necessary, in its opinion, to preserve its rights." This exception has been criticized as being so broad that it undermines enforcement of an agreement to mediate, even in the narrow circumstances contemplated by the Mediation Model Law.

Most mediation clauses are never tested in court because parties typically fulfill their agreement to participate in mediation. And even if it is not legally enforceable, an agreement can be effective due to the psychological value of an advance commitment to use mediation. The enforcement issues that do arise usually occur when one party files a court case without fulfilling its obligation to mediate and the other seeks performance of the mediation agreement. Because settling a dispute in mediation is a voluntary process, some commentators question the wisdom of enforcing contractual obligations to mediate when one party resists the process.

The Australian case of *Hooper Bailie Associated Ltd v Natcon Group Party Ltd* enunciates a strong rationale for ordering parties to follow through on their agreement even when one party opposes mediation. In that case, the parties had an arbitration agreement, but before initiating arbitration they exchanged correspondence specifying issues for conciliation and discussing conciliation procedures. They were able to resolve several matters in conciliation and then they adjourned so that they could gather additional information. Natcon subsequently tried to invoke the parties' arbitration agreement without returning to conciliation. Hooper Bailie sought a stay of the arbitral proceedings, which was granted by the Supreme Court of New South Wales. The judge explained his decision to enforce the agreement to conciliate (which he saw as contained in the correspondence) as follows:

> Conciliation or mediation is essentially consensual, and the opponents of enforceability contend it is futile to seek to enforce something which requires the co-operation and consent of a party when co-operation and consent can not be enforced; equally, they say that there can be no loss to the other party if for want of co-operation and consent the consensual process would have led to no result. The proponents of enforceability contend that this misconceives the objectives of alternative dispute resolution, saying that the most fundamental resistance to compromise can wane and turn to co-operation and consent if the dispute is removed from the adversarial procedures of the court and exposed to procedures designed to promote compromise, in particular where a skilled conciliator or mediator is interposed between the parties. What is enforced is not co-operation and consent, but participation in a process from which co-operation and consent might come.[8]

The trend in many countries is to enforce mediation clauses, provided that contract-law requirements are met. This trend is particularly strong in Anglo-American jurisdictions, but also includes civil law countries such as France and Germany. In contrast, in jurisdictions such as Austria and Hungary, a mediation clause does not prevent a party to the contract from filing legal proceedings even if the dispute is covered by the terms of the clause.[9]

Agreements to mediate are interpreted—in most countries—based on the general law of contract. Because the requirements for a

---

[8] (1992) 28 NSWLR 194 at 209.

[9] For a detailed account of how different countries approach issues relating to the enforcement of mediation clauses, see Nadja Alexander, International and Comparative Mediation: Legal Perspectives 174–213 (2009).

legally binding contract vary greatly among jurisdictions, the law chosen by the parties to govern their agreement assumes a great importance in this context. (For example, consideration is a contract issue that arises only in common-law countries; the doctrine is not recognized in other legal traditions.) Mediation clauses must also meet the specific form and content requirements for contracts in the jurisdiction where they are to be enforced.

In the United States, courts will, in general, enforce unambiguous mediation clauses by staying or dismissing litigation when one party has failed to comply with a mediation clause. The trend is toward applying ordinary contract law to enforce agreements by treating the mediation clause as a condition precedent to litigation.[10] This is similar to the approach of other common-law countries. (See Chapter 6 for a discussion of enforcing agreements to mediate when mediation is combined with other processes either in a multi-step dispute resolution agreement or as a hybrid process.)

## IV. CONFIDENTIALITY IN MEDIATION

Chapter 1 described confidentiality as "an almost sacred canon in the mediation process." But it is important to recognize that this view is held more strongly in the context of Western models of mediation where confidentiality is protected by statutes, court rules, ethical standards, and party agreements. There are, however, cultural contexts in which mediations take place in a public group setting and confidentiality is not the norm. In some societies, disputes, even those between individuals, are seen as community concerns. Thus community members may participate as stakeholders in resolutions. (See Chapter 3 for more on the role of culture in mediation.)

Nonetheless, protecting confidentiality in mediation, and balancing it with the values of transparency and access to evidence that are associated with adjudication, has been a major motivation for the development of mediation law, both domestically and internationally. These confidentiality laws address issues such as:

- To what extent should mediation confidentiality be protected? In general? In legal proceedings?

---

[10] See Chapter 6 in Sarah R. Cole, Craig A. McEwen, Nancy H. Rogers, James R. Coben, & Peter N. Thompson, Mediation: Law, Policy & Practice (Thompson Reuters 2018) for a more detailed account of enforcing mediation clauses in contracts under U.S. law.

- Who should control the extent of the protection? The parties? The mediator? A judge? The legislature?
- What legal mechanisms are most effective and appropriate to protect confidentiality?

First, in Part A this section explains the reasons for protecting confidentiality. Second, it outlines different methods for protecting mediation communications in three settings: 1) confidentiality between the parties during the mediation process; 2) general confidentiality outside mediation; and 3) special restrictions on disclosures in subsequent legal proceedings.

There are significant differences among jurisdictions in the legal methods of confidentiality protection they employ, the scope of protection they offer, and the exceptions to confidentiality they recognize. These variations reflect how different legal systems have grappled with competing values between maintaining confidentiality and supporting public policies that would be furthered by disclosure. In practical terms, the differences in how jurisdictions have resolved questions about the appropriate limits on confidentiality protection for mediation mean that the choice of location for a mediation and the selection of governing law can have important consequences for the parties.

### A. Rationales for Protecting Confidentiality in Mediation

Confidentiality is important from three perspectives: those of the parties, the mediator, and (when the dispute is in litigation) the court. From the parties' perspectives, confidentiality is often necessary to encourage parties to exchange information with their adversary and with the mediator. A dispute is a setting where, without confidentiality protection, such disclosures could be used to a party's detriment. The following excerpt underscores the importance of confidentiality in mediation and the reasons why two important models for mediation legislation—the Uniform Mediation Act in the United States and the UNCITRAL Model Law on International Commercial Mediation—provide protections for confidentiality. It emphasizes the importance to the success of mediation of exchanging information with an adversary. By preventing an adversary's harmful use of mediation communications, legal safeguards thus encourage the parties to participate in mediation without reservation. These protections allow them to share their interests and needs in ways that lay the groundwork for creative outcomes that go beyond the scope of the remedies available in court.

## JERNEJ SEKOLEC & MICHAEL B. GETTY, *THE UMA AND THE UNCITRAL MODEL LAW: AN EMERGING CONSENSUS ON MEDIATION AND CONCILIATION*

2003 J. Dispute Resol. 175, 188–89 (2003).

To optimize chances of success, the scope of discussion between the parties and conciliator must allow for an exploration and understanding, as much as possible, of the issues between the parties, the background and circumstances that gave rise to the issues (including the reasons for which the parties were unable to reach agreement), and the possibilities for the parties to overcome the existing issues and to settle the dispute. In many cases, this discussion could extend to matters beyond the immediate issues at the conciliation.

One of the main pillars of conciliation has been to allow parties to make statements that they would normally not make in court or arbitral proceedings, or delve into matters that would normally not be considered in arbitral or court proceedings, including those that the parties deem damaging to their position. If there was risk of the information reaching the public domain or [being] used against the party that provided the information as evidence in arbitral or court proceedings in the event the conciliation failed, then parties would not be as forthcoming with information during the conciliation process. This could potentially jeopardize the chances of success for the conciliation.

It is therefore critical that safeguards are afforded to parties, providing the desired degree of legal protection against unwanted disclosure of certain facts and information. These safeguards are "the centerpiece of the conciliation regime" and the single most important reason why legislation on conciliation is needed.

---

Limitations on mediator testimony are another important safeguard from the parties' perspective. In subsequent disputes that implicate a mediation, mediators are often regarded as the most credible source of information. In a mediation that used private sessions, they alone witnessed all the interactions. Even more importantly, they are not affiliated with either party. By keeping mediation communications confidential, a mediator prevents parties from being harmed by their communications and thus furthers the goal of encouraging parties to communicate.

In addition, mediators and courts have separate interests in confidentiality protection. From a mediator's perspective, the very neutrality that makes a mediator an attractive witness would be endangered if that mediator had to testify. This is a justification for providing mediators with their own legal tools to protect the confidentiality of mediation. And finally, when the mediated dispute is the subject of litigation, confidentiality can also be important to the court. The following excerpt explores the purposes of confidentiality from the perspectives of mediators and courts.

## ELLEN E. DEASON, *PROCEDURAL RULES FOR COMPLEMENTARY SYSTEMS OF LITIGATION AND MEDIATION—WORLDWIDE*

80 Notre Dame L. Rev. 553, 564–65 (2005).

Preventing disclosures is also crucial to another important aspect of mediation. Mediator neutrality, "a primary value of mediation," depends on the mediator's ability to avoid taking sides. Neutrality is impossible, however, if a mediator is called to testify about events in a mediation; in the win-lose posture of litigation, such testimony will always favor one party over the other. Such lapses in neutrality damage the mediation process itself, for its integrity depends on the institutional trustworthiness of mediators.

Procedural prohibitions on disclosures of mediation communications also safeguard the integrity of courts in a world of intertwined mediation and litigation. Judges need to stay separated from the content of mediations because they might adjudicate the underlying dispute or a dispute that arises out of a mediation. Procedures to limit disclosures protect judges from the perception of bias and impropriety that would be raised by the possibility of ex parte communications about a mediation. This is especially true when the court sponsors a mediation program and is thus linked institutionally to the mediation. Absent adherence to such rules, a suggestion that mediation communications served as unauthorized evidence in a case could undermine the promise of confidentiality made in court mediation programs and reduce public confidence in the courts that sponsor these programs. Because of courts' active role in sponsoring and recommending mediation, confidentiality provisions are necessary, not only to encourage mediation, but also to protect the stature of the adjudication system.

---

Mediation communications among the participants can be disclosed in three major contexts. The confidentiality protections in each context are described separately in the following three sections. First, Section B considers how confidentiality is maintained *within* the mediation process. This protection allows a party to communicate privately with the mediator in caucus with the assurance that the mediator will not disclose the information to the opposing party. Second, Section C describes the legal forms used to provide general protection against disclosures *outside* the mediation, such as to nonparticipants or to the public. Third, Section D covers legal mechanisms that also operate outside the mediation process, but in the special context of *subsequent legal proceedings*. The UNCITRAL Mediation Model Law provides safeguards in all three categories. Countries with other legislation often protect communications in only one or two of these three contexts. Section E looks at considerations for choosing mechanisms to protect confidentiality.

## B. Legal Protection for Confidentiality Within the Mediation Process

During a mediation, keeping information confidential between the parties becomes a concern when the mediator meets with parties separately in private sessions (often called caucuses). In that setting, a party may share information with the mediator that they have not revealed in a joint session with all the participants. The obligation for the mediator to keep this information confidential is frequently set forth in ethical codes for mediators. It is also included in some institutional rules and in the confidentiality provisions of some national laws.

There are two approaches to maintaining the confidentiality of information revealed in a caucus. The first approach assumes that the mediator can communicate anything she learns to the other party unless the disclosing party asks the mediator to keep something private. The original UNCITRAL Model Law on Conciliation selected this approach and it was retained in the revised Mediation Model Law. (See Box 4.) (Although notice that it is a default provision that can be changed by agreement of the parties.) This choice reflected a preference for "ensuring circulation of information between the various participants in the conciliation process" and a concern that requiring consent as a condition of sharing information would be "overly formalistic" and "likely to inhibit the entire conciliation process."[11]

[11] Report of the Working Group on Arbitration on the Work of its Thirty-Fifth Session, U.N. Doc. A/CN.9/506 (Dec. 21, 2001), at ¶¶ 78–79, *available at* www.uncitral.org.

**4. Examples of Confidentiality Protections Within a Mediation**

**UNCITRAL Model Law on International Commercial Mediation and International Settlement Agreements Resulting from Mediation (2018).**

**Article 9. Disclosure of Information.** When the mediator receives information concerning the dispute from a party, the mediator may disclose the substance of that information to any other party to the mediation. However, when a party gives any information to the mediator, subject to a specific condition that it be kept confidential, that information shall not be disclosed to any other party to the mediation.

**Model Standards of Conduct for Mediators (2005).**

**Standard V. Confidentiality**

B. A mediator who meets with any person in private session during a mediation shall not convey directly or indirectly to any other person, any information that was obtained during that private session without the consent of the disclosing person.

Under the second approach, the presumption is for confidentiality. There is an understanding that the entire discussion with the mediator is confidential *unless* the party identifies information that the mediator may share with the other party. An example of this approach is set forth in the Model Standards of Conduct for Mediators (described in Chapter 5), which is influential in the United States. (See Box 4.) This approach maximizes the parties' sense of security and allows a party to speak freely with the mediator during caucuses without keeping track of sensitive communications.

The different ways that the European countries treat this issue illustrate how the EU Mediation Directive permits variation when Member States implement its framework. In many countries, the national legislation is silent on this aspect of confidentiality, presumably leaving the choice to the mediator to determine in light of ethical guidance. In some countries, however, the law specifies that the mediator must maintain the confidentiality of information within the mediation unless the party who revealed the information gives permission to share it. The mediator may even be liable for damages if he breaches this obligation. In contrast, other European countries have selected the opposite approach. There, the mediator is free to share information within a mediation unless a party requests confidentiality for the communication.[12]

### C. General Protection from Disclosures Outside Mediation

Outside mediation, there is a risk that a party may disclose documents prepared for mediation or relate what was said during the mediation process. Often the concern arises during a subsequent legal proceeding. (Protections in this context are discussed below in Part D.) But a party can also be harmed more generally by disclosures. For example, reports that reach the public through the press or information passed on to competitors may harm a party's interests, even if the disclosures do not affect any legal proceedings. There are two different legal mechanisms that are commonly used to provide general protection for mediation communications. One is a duty of confidentiality that prohibits certain mediation participants from disclosing mediation communications to nonparticipants. A second way to provide this protection is by an agreement of the parties to maintain confidentiality.

As an example of the first approach, the UNCITRAL Mediation Model Law imposes a broad general duty of confidentiality. (See Box 5.) This duty applies to all participants in the mediation and it covers not only information disclosed during the mediation session, but more broadly "all information relating to the mediation proceedings." This means that the result of the mediation is protected, and also any discussions leading up to an agreement to mediate. There are two exceptions: 1) where disclosure is required by law, such as an obligation to disclose a criminal offense, and 2) where disclosure is needed to enforce a settlement agreement.

In contrast, in the United States, the Uniform Mediation Act takes the second approach. It does not impose a general duty of confidentiality, but rather leaves this decision to the parties. They can elect to impose confidentiality outside legal proceedings on themselves as a matter of contract. (See Box 5.) This agreement could require a general silence, or specify disclosures that parties may not make.

---

[12] Giuseppe De Palo, Leonardo D'Urso, Mary Trevor, Brian Banon, Romina Canessa, Beverly Cawyer, & L. Reagan Florence, 'Rebooting' the Mediation Directive: Assessing the Limited Impact of its Implementation and Proposing Measures to Increase the Number of Mediations in the EU 49, 62, 91, 98 (2014) (comparing the approach in Poland and Lithuania to that of Hungary and Slovenia) [hereinafter *Rebooting the Mediation Directive*].

**5. Examples of Provisions on a General Duty of Confidentiality**

**UNCITRAL Model Law on International Commercial Mediation and International Settlement Agreements Resulting from Mediation (2018).**

**Article 10. Confidentiality.** Unless otherwise agreed by the parties, all information relating to the mediation proceedings shall be kept confidential, except where disclosure is required under the law or for purposes of implementation or enforcement of a settlement agreement.

**Uniform Mediation Act**

**Section 8. Confidentiality.** Unless subject to the [open meetings act and open records act], mediation communications are confidential to the extent agreed by the parties or provided by other law or rule of this State.

The EU Mediation Directive provides for a baseline of confidentiality protection but permits states to enact stricter measures. Its basic protection does not include a general duty of confidentiality, but relates only to a mediator's evidence in judicial proceedings and arbitration (which will be discussed below). Many of the Member States, however, have imposed a general duty of confidentiality that applies beyond the Directive's coverage of legal proceedings. In France, for example, the decree implementing the Directive requires that mediation proceedings will be confidential unless the parties agree otherwise.[13]

Sometimes a statutory duty of confidentiality for mediators works in tandem with party agreements by relying on a combination of legislation and party autonomy to set the boundaries of general confidentiality. In some countries, for example, the national legislation on mediation imposes a general duty of confidentiality only on mediators. The parties do not have a corresponding general duty of confidentiality, but they can agree to such a duty by contract.[14]

---

13 *Rebooting the European Directive, supra* note 12, at 27.

14 *Rebooting the European Directive, supra* note 12, at 17, 32 (Austria and Germany).

## D. Confidentiality Protections in Subsequent Legal Proceedings

This category of confidentiality protection prevents communications made in mediation from being introduced in a legal proceeding such as a court case or arbitration. Evidence of information provided in mediation, either orally or in documentary form, can be relevant in legal proceedings in multiple ways. Some of the most important are:

- if the mediation does not produce a settlement during litigation, a party to the mediation may seek to introduce information disclosed in mediation in the court case or arbitration;
- the content of a mediation may be relevant in separate litigation brought by or involving third parties who did not participate in the mediation;
- a party may allege that the parties reached an agreement in mediation and seek to introduce evidence from the mediation in an attempt to enforce it;
- a party may challenge the enforceability of an agreement the parties reached in mediation;
- a party may seek to hold a mediator or an attorney responsible for alleged duress or other malpractice in the mediation.

The need for confidentiality in legal proceedings is generally accepted for mediation. However, this is an exception to the general rule that a judicial or arbitral tribunal should have access to relevant information in order to determine the facts accurately and render a just decision. Therefore, the importance of confidentiality must be balanced with other public policies that would be served by access to the information from the mediation.

One major issue is who should determine whether an exception to confidentiality protection is justified. Sometimes exceptions that allow disclosures are established in mediation legislation. In this situation, the legislators have weighed the policies served by disclosure against the benefits of maintaining confidentiality and decided in favor of disclosure as a blanket rule. Other situations are less clear cut in advance and the legislature may instead grant a judge the discretion to make a determination in favor of confidentiality or disclosure on a case-by-case basis.

The way a country regulates how information from mediation can be introduced as evidence in a legal proceeding is shaped in part by whether that country is a common-law or civil-law jurisdiction. Many common-law jurisdictions use the legal mechanism of privilege to protect mediation communications. In contrast, the civil-law tradition does not recognize this concept. Instead, civil-law countries tend to rely on evidentiary exclusions and various forms of restrictions on mediator testimony.

This section discusses several of the differing approaches that countries have adopted. It compares mechanisms to protect mediation confidentiality in legal proceedings, exceptions to those protections that allow disclosures, and the way that these exceptions are determined. The degree of protection for information shared in mediation differs among countries depending on the form and scope of the legal mechanisms they employ.

### *1. Restrictions on Mediator Testimony*

As described above, mediator testimony is one of the most persuasive sources of information about a mediation. Protecting it is important both to create incentives for parties to share information and to safeguard mediator neutrality. Thus it is not surprising that many enactments and doctrines protect confidentiality by restricting mediator testimony.

The legal framework for confidentiality provided in the EU Mediation Directive focuses on this protection; it requires that Member States prohibit compelling a mediator to testify in civil judicial proceedings or arbitration, subject to certain exceptions and unless the parties agree otherwise. (See Box 6.) The Directive's mandate protects a broad category of information: anything "arising out of or in connection with a mediation process." This protection, however, is under the control of the parties; if they agree to forgo it, the mediator has no means to resist giving testimony.

In terms of exceptions to the restrictions on mediator testimony, the Directive uses a combination of approaches. First, it invokes "overriding considerations for public policy" and specifies two areas of public policy of particular concern: protecting the best interests of children and preventing physical or psychological harm. But it leaves it to judges to decide if disclosure is necessary to protect those interests. Second, the Directive provides that enforcing an agreement reached in mediation is a justification for allowing mediator testimony about the content of the agreement, but again leaves it to the judge to determine if disclosure is necessary for enforcement.

### 6. Example of Confidentiality Protection in Legal Proceedings: Restriction on Mediator Testimony

**EU Mediation Directive**

**Article 7. Confidentiality of Mediation**

1. Given that mediation is intended to take place in manner which respects confidentiality, Member States shall ensure that, unless the parties agree otherwise, neither mediators nor those involved in the administration of the mediation process shall be compelled to give evidence in civil and commercial judicial proceedings or arbitration regarding information arising out of or in connection with a mediation process, except:

(a) where this is necessary for overriding considerations of public policy of the Member State concerned, in particular when required to ensure the protection of the best interest of children or to prevent harm to the physical or psychological integrity of a person; or

(b) where disclosure of the content of the agreement resulting from mediation is necessary in order to implement or enforce that agreement.

2. Nothing in paragraph 1 shall prelude Member States from enacting stricter measures to protect the confidentiality of mediation.

The Directive does not mandate any particular legal mechanism for protecting confidentiality, and the methods for restricting mediator testimony vary among the European States. One way is to classify mediators as incapable of testimony and preclude them from presenting evidence about mediation.[15] With this approach, the parties cannot release the mediator from this testimonial incapacity by agreement. An alternative used in some other countries merely exempts mediators from the obligation to give evidence in court proceedings or arbitration, but the parties can release them from this exemption and allow the mediator to testify.[16]

Many EU Member States, as permitted by the confidentiality article of the Directive, have enacted more stringent protections. Some have expanded the limitation on testimony beyond mediators

---

15 *Rebooting the European Directive*, *supra* note 12, at 17; Alexander, *supra* note 9, at 263–64 (Austria).

16 *Rebooting the European Directive*, *supra* note 12, at 32 (Germany).

to cover more participants. In some European countries, for example, mediators, parties, and anyone else involved in the mediation process, such as witnesses and experts, may not be compelled to produce evidence or be summoned as witnesses.[17]

### 2. *"Without Prejudice" Communications*

In some common-law countries, statements made in settlement negotiations are protected by the common-law doctrine of "without prejudice" that protects both written and oral settlement communications from disclosure. This rule, which is considered a type of privilege, governs the admissibility of evidence and rests on the public policy of encouraging settlement. An English court described the reasoning behind the doctrine as follows:

> [Parties] should not be discouraged by the knowledge that anything that is said in the course of such negotiations . . . . may be used to their prejudice in the course of the proceedings. They should . . . . be encouraged fully and frankly to put their cards on the table. . . . . [T]he public policy justification in truth, essentially rests on the desirability of preventing statements or offers made in the course of negotiations for settlement being brought before the court of trial and submissions on the question of liability.[18]

Without prejudice rules for negotiation have been applied to mediation in a number of common-law jurisdictions, including England, Australia, and Hong Kong. In essence, courts in these countries treat mediation as a "form of assisted without prejudice negotiation."[19] The doctrine protects confidentiality at the behest of the parties and is less protective of a mediator's interest in preventing disclosures. If the parties elect to waive an objection that they could bring under the without prejudice rule, the mediator may not resist an order to testify. As an alternative, if there is an agreement to mediate between the parties and the mediator containing a confidentiality provision, the mediator may be able to

---

17 *Rebooting the European Directive, supra* note 12, at 35, 73 (Greece and Belgium).

18 Cutts v Head [1984] Ch.290 (Law Judge Oliver).

19 Aird v. Meridian Ltd. [2006] EWCA Civ 1866 at 5. For detailed descriptions of how the without privilege doctrine has developed in these countries, see Nadja Alexander, International and Comparative Mediation: Legal Perspectives 266–71 (2009) and Penny Brooker, Mediation Law: Journey through Insitutionalism to Juridification 187–200, 222–24, 230–34 (2013).

enforce it as a matter of contract. But, even then, the English High Court has stated that a court can override confidentiality and order disclosure "in the interests of justice."[20]

The without prejudice rule is not absolute, and there are numerous exceptions. One of the traditional exceptions to the rule has significant implications for mediation: there is no protection from disclosure once an agreement has been reached. As a result, mediation evidence *will* be admitted when the issue is whether or not the parties reached an enforceable agreement.[21] In addition, the United Kingdom Supreme Court has recently been willing to expand the traditional list of exceptions to the without prejudice doctrine.[22] This potential for new exceptions makes the doctrine's boundaries somewhat uncertain. Moreover, difficulty in predicting the scope of mediation protection is magnified in the cross-border context because exceptions for mediations have developed differently in different jurisdictions. For example, Australian courts will admit evidence from a mediation when a party sues their solicitor in relation to professional misconduct, but this exception to the without prejudice rule has been rejected in England.[23]

### 3. *Evidentiary Exclusions*

Another way to regulate disclosures is through an evidentiary exclusion, which is a legal mechanism used in both civil- and common-law traditions. These are rules designed to exclude evidence for particular policy reasons and the general purpose is often to prevent litigation from discouraging socially desirable activity. For mediation, that socially desirable activity is settlement. Excluding testimony about what happened in mediation encourages settlement by giving parties the freedom to suggest compromises without fear that those proposals will be used against them if there is no settlement. The mechanism of evidentiary exclusion thus reflects a judgment that avoiding harm to confidentiality, and consequently encouraging parties to use the mediation process, is more valuable than certain types of evidence based on mediation communications.

---

20 Farm Assist Ltd (FAL) v Secretary of State for Environment, Food and Rural Affairs (DEFRA) (No. 2) [2009] EWHC 1102 (TCC) at 28–29 & 44(1).

21 Brown v Rice and Patel [2007] EWHC 625 (Ch), [2008] F.S.R. 3.

22 Oceanbulk Shipping & Trading SA v. TMT Asia Ltd [2010] UKSC 44.

23 *Compare* Tapoohi v Lewenberg and Ors (No 2) [2003] VSC 410 (21 Oct 2003) (Australia), *with* Cumbria Waste Management Ltd. v Baines Wilson [2008] EWCH 786 (QB) (England).

One form of evidentiary exclusion is a list of specific communications that may not be admitted into evidence. This is the approach adopted in the international context by the UNCITRAL Mediation Model Law, which contains an exclusion that applies broadly to all the participants in mediation: the parties, the mediator, and "any third person." (See Box 7.) The Model Law does not identify exceptions to the exclusion; presumably everything not included on the list of exclusions is admissible in evidence. One risk of using this format is that the list may not anticipate all appropriate circumstances for excluding evidence. Another is that it does not carefully define the scope of exceptions to the exclusions.

California's evidentiary exclusion is an example of a different approach. Rather than listing protected communications, it provides blanket protection for *all* communications in mediation. (See Box 7.) This makes the scope of the exclusion broader than the list found in the UNCITRAL Model Law. Moreover, the California statute does not recognize any exceptions, and courts have refused to read them into the absolute language of the provision.

**7. Examples of Confidentiality Protection in Legal Proceedings: Evidentiary Exclusion**

**UNCITRAL Model Law on International Commercial Mediation and International Settlement Agreements Resulting from Mediation (2018).**

**Article 11. Admissibility of evidence in other proceedings.**

1. A party to the mediation proceedings, the mediator and any third person, including those involved in the administration of the mediation proceeding, shall not in arbitral, judicial or similar proceedings rely on, introduce as evidence or give testimony or evidence regarding any of the following:

(*a*) An invitation by a party to engage in mediation proceedings or the fact that a party was willing to participate in mediation proceedings;

(*b*) Views expressed or suggestions made by a party in the mediation in respect of a possible settlement of the dispute;

(*c*) Statements or admissions made by a party in the course of the mediation proceedings;

(*d*) Proposals made by the mediator;

*(e)* The fact that a party had indicated its willingness to accept a proposal for settlement made by the mediator;

*(f)* A document prepared solely for purposes of the mediation proceedings.

* * *

**California Evidence Code**

**Section 1119. Written or oral communications during mediation process; admissibility**

* * *

(a) No evidence of anything said or any admission made for the purpose of, in the course of, or pursuant to, a mediation or a mediation consultation is admissible or subject to discovery, and disclosure of the evidence shall not be compelled, in any arbitration, administrative adjudication, civil action, or other noncriminal proceeding in which, pursuant to law, testimony can be compelled to be given.

* * *

### *4. Mediation Privileges*

Whereas an evidentiary exclusion is a blanket mechanism based on a policy judgment about categories of potential evidence, a privilege is a mechanism invoked at the discretion of the party who holds it. This common-law doctrine thus fits well with the principle of party autonomy in mediation: a party who holds a privilege can decide to exercise its privilege, or waive it and allow evidence from the mediation to be introduced. A privilege gives the holder two separate powers: 1) he can refuse to provide the evidence himself and 2) he can also block others from providing evidence.

In the United States, many states have enacted statutes with privileges for mediation. The most comprehensive mediation privileges are found in the Uniform Mediation Act. (See Box 8.) It provides three privileges of varying strengths for three different types of holders. All the mediation privileges apply to evidence at trial, but also protect against disclosures in discovery and arbitral proceedings. Parties have the strongest privilege: they can refuse to disclose, and block all others from disclosing, any mediation communication. "Mediation communications" are broadly defined to include both statements and actions during mediation or in preparation for mediation. The mediator holds a more limited privilege that allows her to refuse to testify about any mediation communications, but allows her to block other testimony only with regard to her own statements.

### 8. Example of Confidentiality Protection in Legal Proceedings: Privilege

**Uniform Mediation Act (UMA)**

**Section 4. Privilege Against Disclosure; Admissibility; Discovery.**

(a) Except as otherwise provided in Section 6 [on exceptions to the privileges], a mediation communication is privileged as provided in subsection (b) and is not subject to discovery or admissible in evidence in a proceeding unless waived or precluded as provided by Section 5.

(b) In a proceeding, the following privileges apply:

(1) A mediation party may refuse to disclose, and may prevent any other person from disclosing, a mediation communication.

(2) A mediator may refuse to disclose a mediation communication, and may prevent any other person from disclosing a mediation communication of the mediator.

(3) A nonparty participant may refuse to disclose, and may prevent any other person from disclosing, a mediation communication of the nonparty participant.

* * *

The third privilege, which is designed to encourage communications by other participants such as experts, allows them to protect their own communications, but gives them no power over party or mediator communications. The following excerpt describes how the different scope of the party and mediator privileges is based on the rationales (discussed earlier) for protecting mediation confidentiality.

## ELLEN E. DEASON, *PREDICTABLE MEDIATION CONFIDENTIALITY IN THE U.S. FEDERAL SYSTEM*

17 Ohio State J. on Dispute Resol. 239, 260–61 (2002).

The designation of a holder is important for connecting a mediation privilege to the rationales for protecting confidentiality. When the mediation parties hold the privilege, they can use it to protect their interests in confidentiality with a level of control over use of their communications that will encourage them to participate fully in the mediation. Because the parties' interests conflict in part, this assurance must include the ability to prevent later disclosure by the other participant(s). In contrast, a privilege that makes a mediator an independent holder as to her own communications protects the institution of mediation. It gives a mediator the tools to maintain neutrality and to protect against parties' fears that she will reveal their confidences if called to testify. A dual privilege protects both confidentiality goals.

---

The protections of the three types of UMA privileges interact. One party may decide that it would like to waive the privilege and testify, but the other party also holds a privilege for all mediation communications and can use it to block testimony. This means that the first party may introduce mediation evidence *only* if the second party also waives its privilege. Similarly, because the mediator holds an independent privilege, even if both parties waive their privilege they cannot compel the mediator to testify. And, while the parties may introduce evidence about their own communications, they cannot disclose the mediator' statements unless the mediator waives his privilege to block that testimony. These waiver provisions give the parties, the mediator, and other participants the power to protect their interests and the flexibility to tailor disclosures to the circumstances of the case.

The UMA mediation privileges are not, however, absolute. They give way to exceptions based on public policy.[24] The UMA includes two forms of exceptions. The first is a list of circumstances in which the legislature has predetermined, as a matter of policy, that the need for disclosure outweighs the reasons to maintain mediation confidentiality. Here is a paraphrase of these exceptions:

---

24 *See* Uniform Mediation Act, *supra* note 6, at § 6.

- a written agreement signed by all the parties (which is useful for enforcement);
- communications available under open meeting laws;
- a threat or statement of a plan to inflict bodily injury or commit a crime of violence;
- communications used to plan a crime or conceal ongoing criminal activity;
- communications offered to prove mediator misconduct that is alleged in a filed complaint;
- communications offered to prove professional misconduct by a mediation participant or party representative that is alleged in a filed complaint;
- communications offered to prove child or adult abuse or neglect under certain circumstances.

Second, the statute also includes two exceptions that are not predetermined by the legislature. They require a judge to hold a hearing in camera and make individualized determinations on a case-by-case basis. The mediation information will be kept privileged unless the party seeking to introduce it can show that the evidence is not available from any other source and there is a need for it "that substantially outweighs the interest in protecting confidentiality." These potential exceptions to the privilege are:

- evidence offered in a court proceedings involving a felony (or, in some states, either a felony or misdemeanor);
- evidence offered in a proceeding to enforce a contract agreed in mediation.

## E. Choosing Mechanisms for Protecting Confidentiality in Legal Proceedings

Given the great variety in protections for mediation confidentiality, as law develops in the transnational context there are question about which legal mechanisms are most effective, which are most appropriate, and what criteria should be used in the selection. Indeed, UNCITRAL was criticized when it selected an evidentiary exclusion to protect confidentiality in the original Model Law on conciliation. According to mediator Eric Van Ginkel, the Model Law "ended up with an evidentiary system of protection of certain types of communication that is unclear in its enumeration and subject to potentially broad exceptions that may vary from country to country. This was a missed opportunity to enhance the attractiveness of conciliation . . . . ."[25] Even though the exclusion in the UNCITRAL Model Law applies broadly to all participants in a mediation, Van Ginkel believes that it provides less effective confidentiality protection than a privilege.

But other factors, such as variations in legal culture, may be important. Privilege is a common-law doctrine that is unfamiliar in countries with other legal traditions. UNCITRAL chose the legal mechanism of evidentiary exclusion in an attempt to promote widespread adoption of the Model Law by making it acceptable to as many nations as possible. Legal culture and the traditions used in domestic regulation of mediation have an important influence on what nations may be willing to adopt in the international context.

Another factor that is relevant in comparing different forms of legal protections is their track record for generating court disputes about the application of confidentiality rules. A legal mechanism that generates litigation is certainly not efficient, and is moreover at odds with the basic purpose of using mediation to resolve disputes. The following excerpt compares a privilege and one form of an evidentiary exclusion on this score. The Uniform Mediation Act provides a set of multiple privileges with a long list of exceptions. (See Box 8.) It is detailed and complex. In contrast, California uses a broad blanket evidentiary exclusion that lists no exceptions. (See Box 7.) It is short and simple. One might assume that the implementation of the simpler statute would be more straightforward and would trigger fewer ancillary disputes. The data described in the following excerpt, however, offers evidence to the contrary in terms of the litigation that each approach has spawned.

## JAMES R. COBEN, *MY CHANGE OF MIND ON THE UNIFORM MEDIATION ACT*

Dispute Resol. Mag., Winter 2017 at 6, 6–8.

Generally, the more complex the rule universe, the more litigation is likely to occur. Surprisingly, that has not been the history of the UMA. Though it has been adopted in 12 jurisdictions . . . . there has been a dearth of litigation about its terms . . . .

* * *

---

[25] Eric Van Ginkel, *The UNCITRAL Model Law on International Commercial Conciliation: A Critical Appraisal*, 21 J. Int'l Arb. 1, 8 (2004).

[From] 2013 through 2015, [courts interpreted] the UMA to resolve a dispute about confidentiality in mediation only 16 times nationwide (just 8% of all state and federal cases addressing mediation confidentiality disputes in that three-year period). By comparison, in that same three-year time frame, California state and federal courts issued more than four dozen mediation confidentiality opinions (25% of all state and federal cases addressing mediation confidentiality disputes in that three-year period). As it turns out, California's more or less absolute confidentiality evidence regime has always been the source of a disproportionate share of mediation confidentiality disputes. . . . [I am] relatively confident that my treatise co-authors and I got it right when we praised the UMA drafters' decision to use a categorical approach—stating a broad privilege with exceptions (only two of which involve judicial balancing)—rather than an absolute or qualified approach without listed exceptions.

Equally important, to the extent that there is litigation about the UMA, nothing suggests it is due to the act's complexity or lack of clarity. Nor has the litigation track record suggested, as I feared, that the act would open the doors of the mediation room in potentially chilling ways. . . .

Despite my concern that a privilege approach with numerous exceptions might reduce people's confidence in the mediation process, to my knowledge not a single empirical study suggests that the UMA has triggered a decline in the use of mediation. If there are anecdotal reports, I have not heard them. And out of those hundreds of disputed confidentiality cases in state and federal court, I have yet to read a single judicial opinion critical of the act. That stands in stark contrast to the considerable judicial angst expressed in California courts . . . .

---

## V. MEDIATED SETTLEMENT AGREEMENTS

Many believe that the most important shortcoming of mediation in the cross-border context is the uncertainty of enforcement of a settlement agreement reached in mediation. The conventional wisdom is that mediation results in a high rate of compliance because parties are more willing to accept a consensual outcome they have crafted than an outcome imposed by an outside decisionmaker. Thus Lawrence Susskind and Jeffrey Cruikshank have called mediated agreements "nearly self-enforcing."[26] But enforcement litigation nonetheless arises in two postures: 1) a party refuses to comply with a mediated agreement and the other party attempts to enforce it, or 2) a party challenges a mediated agreement in court. The potential magnitude of the problem is indicated by an analysis of issues related to mediation in reported court cases in the United States: enforcement of mediated settlements was the most litigated issue, accounting for 46% of the U.S. cases concerning mediation between 1999 and 2003.[27] In fact, some believe that uncertainly about enforcement of agreements reached in mediation is a primary reason that mediation is not more prevalent in international dispute resolution.

The international legal framework for enforcing mediated agreements has historically relied on national approaches that vary greatly. However, as mentioned earlier in this Chapter, there are important new developments in this area. In 2018, the United Nations approved a convention on enforcing mediated settlement agreements—the United Nations Convention on International Settlement Agreements Resulting from Mediation—that opened for signature in August 2019. It is to be called the Singapore Convention. UNCITRAL also amended its Model Law on International Commercial Conciliation to be consistent with the Convention, and renamed it the UNCITRAL Model Law on International Commercial Mediation and International Settlement Agreements Resulting from Mediation. In the coming years, there will likely be an interim period of transition as nations consider adopting these instruments. In time, the Convention and provisions in the Model Law may change the landscape for enforcement of mediated settlement agreements. But in the meantime, the current legal mechanisms remain relevant because parties will need to rely on them in many countries.

The enforcement of mediated settlement agreements has been a challenging issue. Neither of the two most important instruments on cross-boundary mediation—the original UNCITRAL Model Law on International Commercial Conciliation (2002) and the European Mediation Directive—established uniform standards or procedures for enforcing mediated agreements.

---

[26] Lawrence E. Susskind & Jeffrey L. Cruikshank, Breaking Robert's Rules: The New Way to Run Your Meeting, Build Consensus, and Get Results 133, 134 (2006).

[27] James R. Coben & Peter N. Thompson, *Disputing Irony: A Systematic Look at Litigation about Mediation*, 11 Harv. Neg. L. Rev. 43, 73 (2006).

The original 2002 version of the UNCITRAL Model Law (which as of 2018 had been enacted in 33 countries) left this issue entirely to the individual States.[28] It merely invited them to provide their own method for enforcing settlement agreements. The Guide to Enactment that accompanied the Model Law on Conciliation indicated the difficulty of finding an acceptable international solution. It explained that the Model Law's approach of leaving the approach to enforcement to each country "reflects the smallest common denominator between the various legal systems" and noted that the variation among legal systems and domestic procedural law means that they "do not easily lend themselves to harmonization by way of uniform legislation."[29] By leaving enforcement to domestic law, UNCITRAL may have intended to maximize adoption of the Model Law, but it did so by silence on this issue.

The EU Mediation Directive went somewhat further than the original Model Law in that it requires Member States to provide a mechanism for enforcement of settlement agreements. But its requirement is limited. Member States must provide an enforcement mechanism only for the situation in which all the parties have first consented that a written agreement resulting from mediation should be made enforceable.[30] And, like the original UNCITRAL Model Law on Conciliation, the Directive leaves the legal mechanism for enforcement to each Member State. The result is a great deal of variability among national enactments.

There can also be uncertainty about enforcement in the domestic context that reflects the difficulty in finding common ground on the issue. In the United States, the Uniform Mediation Act is entirely silent on the subject. The Drafting Committees discussed multiple ways to provide for expedited enforcement of mediated agreements by the courts, but in the end recommended against adopting any of them. They concluded that if a summary enforcement provision was limited sufficiently to protect parties' rights, it would not aid appreciably in promoting enforcement when compared to existing contractual mechanisms.[31]

---

[28] UNCITRAL Model Law on International Commercial Conciliation Art. 14 (2002).

[29] Guide to Enactment and Use of the UNCITRAL Model Law ¶ 88 (2002).

[30] *EU Mediation Directive, supra* n. 1, Art. 6.

[31] Ellen E. Deason, *Procedural Rules for Complementary Systems of Litigation and Mediation—Worldwide,* 80 Notre Dame L. Rev. 553, 585 (2005).

With scant guidance from the major models for legislation and from the EU framework, until the Singapore Convention and revised UNCITRAL Mediation Model Law gain acceptance a party will need to rely on the enforcement procedures of the jurisdiction where it seeks to enforce the mediated agreement. There are only a few jurisdictions that provide special methods for enforcing agreements that stem from international mediations, so in many jurisdictions the enforcing party will need to use the same legal procedures that apply to settlements from domestic mediations.

In Part A this section first describes the law as it stands as of the beginning of 2019. It outlines the major forms of enforcement mechanisms, illustrating the variety of procedures and hurdles that may currently confront a party seeking to enforce a settlement from a cross-border mediation. Second, Part B introduces the Singapore Convention and the revised UNCITRAL Mediation Model Law with their new structures that provide for a more unified approach to enforcement of settlement agreements resulting from international commercial mediations.

## A. Legal Mechanisms for Enforcement of Mediated Settlement Agreements

The wide variety of legal frameworks that provide procedures and standards for enforcing mediated settlements poses a challenge for parties to international mediations and illustrate the need for harmonization. In many jurisdictions, settlements reached in mediation are enforced via ordinary actions for breach of contract, which can be time-consuming and expensive. Depending on the jurisdiction, there might be an alternative summary procedure. These include using a settlement deed, obtaining court approval, or converting the settlement into an arbitral award. Most of these mechanisms are domestic procedures and they highlight the great variation that can face a party who seeks to enforce a settlement agreement in a foreign jurisdiction.

### 1. *Mediated Settlements as Contracts*

In most jurisdictions, settlements may take the form of a contract and, absent any special procedure for enforcement of mediated agreements, they must be enforced by bringing a contract action in court. In both common-law and civil-law systems, this means that the settlement must satisfy ordinary principles of contract law and any special requirements that apply to settlement agreements or mediation. For example, a jurisdiction may require formalities that are not applicable to contracts in general, such as a writing, mediator or attorney signatures, or a statement that the parties intend the settlement to be enforceable.[32]

Enforcing a mediated settlement as a contract also means that traditional contract defenses can be used to object to the existence or the validity of an agreement.[33] Contract formation issues that can be raised to challenge the existence of a mediated agreement include the following grounds: lack of authority to settle, absence of legal capacity, no meeting of the minds, a mere agreement to agree, and lack of required formalities. And even when there is no dispute that a contract has been formed, its validity can be challenged on grounds for setting aside an agreement. These include fraud and misrepresentation, duress, undue influence, mistake, unconscionability, and attorney and mediator misconduct.

The ability to raise contract defenses is complicated in some jurisdictions by confidentiality protections for mediation communications. If a party's objection to enforcement implicates statements or actions that occurred during a mediation, testimony about those statements or actions may be inadmissible under the relevant confidentiality protections. This can make it impossible, as a practical matter, to prove a defense. The problems created by this aspect of mediated settlement enforcement vary greatly depending on the confidentiality protections under the applicable law. For example, in England, the without prejudice rules do not apply when the issue concerns an agreement reached in mediation. That means that confidentiality protections are not a barrier to enforcement. In contrast, in the United States, one can find three different applications of confidentiality protections to enforcement litigation. Some mediation statutes are written in absolute terms that make no exception to their confidentiality protections for the purpose of enforcing a mediation agreement. These statutes can block enforcement of an agreement or block a challenge to a flawed agreement. Some take a case-by-case approach with the judge weighing the need for the evidence against the value of protecting confidentiality. This process carries inherent uncertainty for enforcement. Yet other statutes include a broad exception to confidentiality that allows evidence from a mediation to support

---

[32] For a canvas of such requirements in the United States, see Ellen E. Deason, *Enforcing Mediated Settlement Agreements: Contract Law Collides with Confidentiality,* 35 U.C. Davis L. Rev. 33, 52–55 (2001).

[33] For an analysis of the contract defenses parties raise to the enforcement of mediated settlement agreements in the United States, see Coben &. Thompson, *supra* note 27, at 77–92, 95–97.

contract defenses to enforcement of a settlement agreement. This third approach yields a result that is similar to the English rules.

### 2. *Settlement Deeds and Related Settlement Formats*

Settlement deeds are a way to document a settlement in compliance with specific form requirements, and they confer a special status for enforcement. They are a common way to express mediated settlements in civil law jurisdictions. They go by a variety of names (e.g., "notorial deed") and the legal requirements vary. In most jurisdictions, the document must be in writing and signed by the parties. Often others must sign as well, such as witnesses, lawyers, notaries, judges, or some combination of these individuals. Involving others in these official roles serves to emphasize for the parties the significance of the commitment they are making in agreeing to a settlement. Moreover, in some jurisdictions, a notary or lawyer has a duty to review the agreement and to advise parties on the content of the deed, which should help produce an agreement whose quality supports enforceability.

When the relevant requirements have been met, settlement deeds can usually be enforced using an expedited procedure that does not require a contract action. For example, in some countries, if a settlement is executed as a notorial deed it can be enforced by a simple petition to a court.[34]

### 3. *Court Approval or Ratification*

In contrast to filing a contract action to enforce an agreement, some jurisdictions offer a summary procedure to seek court approval for settlements without an enforcement action. In France, for example, this involves submitting the settlement to a judge for validation through a process called homologation. After homologation, the settlement becomes enforceable as a judgment of the court. Many European countries offer a similar procedure, either as a stand-alone mechanism or as an option along with a notorial or settlement deed procedure. This process is often limited to settlements reached in court-ordered mediation, although in some countries it is now available for extra-judicial (contractual) mediations as well as court-ordered mediations.[35]

The European Directive's requirement for Member States to provide a mechanism for making mediated agreements enforceable

---

[34] *Rebooting the European Directive, supra* note 12, at 110 (Slovakia).

[35] *See, e.g.*, French Code of Civil Procedure arts. 1565–1568.

has also stimulated the creation of entirely new procedures. In England and Wales, parties who settle a cross-border dispute using mediation can now apply to a court for a "mediation settlement enforcement order" (MSEO). A MSEO enables a party to apply for a judgment on an expedited basis if the other party breaches the terms of the settlement.[36] A court will not issue a MSEO unless both parties consent to the application, but if this requirement is not met the aggrieved party can still nonetheless seek relief using a contract suit based on the settlement agreement.

### 4. *Mediated Settlements as Arbitral Awards*

Another method for providing for enforcement of a mediated settlement agreement is to convert it into an arbitral award, called a "consent award" or an "award on agreed terms." The purpose is to gain the advantages of the Convention on the Recognition and Enforcement of Arbitral Awards (New York Convention) and national laws that are favorable for the enforcement of awards rendered in international commercial arbitration. Parties may combine mediation with arbitration in various ways and the topic of these combinations is considered in more detail in Chapter 6. There are three main postures in which a settlement agreement can be treated as an arbitral award.

First, parties who are participating in an arbitral proceeding may decide to settle their dispute prior to receiving an arbitral award. In nations that have enacted the 1985 UNCITRAL Model Law on International Commercial Arbitration, an arbitral tribunal, if requested by the parties, can enter the settlement in the form of an award on agreed terms. Many other countries also have similar provisions for settlements reached during an ongoing arbitration.

Second, a dispute may be settled in mediation when there is no ongoing arbitration. The parties can then agree to institute arbitration and appoint an arbitrator to enter their settlement as an award. Or, they may agree that the mediator shall assume the duties of an arbitrator to enter the award. Some doubts have been raised, however, about whether awards created in this manner are eligible for enforcement under the New York Convention. The Convention covers "disputes" resolved in arbitration and one argument is that there is no "dispute" when the parties have agreed on a settlement prior to initiating arbitration.

---

36 *Rebooting the European Directive*, *supra* note 12, at 69.

Third, there are jurisdictions that treat certain settlement agreements as arbitral awards as a matter of law. The Arbitration and Conciliation Ordinance of India, for example, provides that a settlement agreement signed by the parties is final and binding and has the same effect as an arbitral award. In the United States, several state statutes treat a mediated settlement of an international commercial dispute as a final arbitral award as long as the settlement agreement is written and signed by both parties or their representatives, along with the mediator.

### B. UNCITRAL Negotiations on an International Instrument

This great diversity of enforcement methods for mediated agreements has made finding the commonality necessary for global harmonization difficult. For example, when UNCITRAL adopted its Model Law on Conciliation in 2002, it left enforcement provisions to national law rather than adopt a single approach that would be unacceptable in numerous legal systems. Since then, developments such as court-sponsored mediation programs, business contracts with multi-step dispute resolution clauses, and national mediation legislation have signaled mediation's growth and increased acceptance in many nations. This growth has been accompanied, moreover, by calls for a more efficient international framework for enforcing agreements reached in mediation. Businesses argue that the complexities and uncertainties of enforcement in transboundary settings discourage their use of mediation. And arbitration remains the favored method of resolution for transnational disputes, even though users complain that the cost can be high, the proceedings lengthy, and the process legalistic. Many see the enforcement regime for arbitral awards as the reason for the predominance of arbitration despite the many advantages of reaching a consensual agreement in mediation. As a result, they view the lack of an efficient enforcement mechanism for cross-border agreements reached in mediation as a major obstacle to the growth of global mediation, and favor the development of such a mechanism. In the following excerpt, S.I. Strong explores this comparison to arbitration and expresses the need for a comparable legal regime for mediation.

### S.I. STRONG, *BEYOND INTERNATIONAL COMMERCIAL ARBITRATION? THE PROMISE OF INTERNATIONAL COMMERCIAL MEDIATION*

45 Wash. U. J. L. & Pol'y 11, 27–28 (2014).

[M]any people believe that the key benefit of international commercial arbitration relates to the easy enforceability of arbitral awards. Over the last fifty years, the international legal community has established a highly effective system of treaties and other mechanisms that promote the recognition and enforcement of foreign arbitral awards. . . . .

International commercial arbitration is therefore distinguishable from both international litigation and international mediation with respect to enforceability issues. Furthermore, the experience of international commercial arbitration suggests that mediation may be more attractive to parties if international mediation and settlement agreements are as easily enforceable as international arbitration agreements and awards. Once the playing field is leveled with respect to enforceability, then the parties would be free to choose their dispute resolution mechanism based solely on process considerations (i.e., a preference for consensual over adjudicative processes or vice versa). The question, therefore, is how to create an international legal regime that supports the enforcement of commercial mediation as effectively as the web of international treaties that currently supports commercial arbitration.

---

There are dissenting voices who challenge this emphasis on enforceability as the key development needed to encourage the growth of global mediation. Based on a 2014 questionnaire on the use of mediation combined with arbitration, Dilyara Nigmatullina suggested that the importance of an enforcement mechanism may be overstated. She concluded that the lack of a "coherent enforcement mechanism" was not an obstacle to mediation based on the large number of mediated agreements that were not recorded as consent awards in combined processes.[37] (For more on combining mediation with other ADR processes, see Chapter 6.)

Noting that the use of mediation lags behind expectations, Nadja Alexander raises a more general question about the effectiveness of legal measures as a stimulus for mediation: "to what extent will legal and policy initiatives to address issues such as confidentiality, competency and enforceability change people's behavior?"[38] She proposes using the principles of choice architecture to encourage disputants to use mediation in cross-border settings. One option she

---

[37] Dilyara Nigmatullina, Combining Mediation and Arbitration in International Dispute Resolution 105 (2019).

[38] Nadja Alexander, *Nudging Users Towards Cross-Border Mediation: Is it Really about Harmonized Enforcement Regulation?*, 7 Contemp. Asia Arb. J. 405, 409 (2014).

suggests would be to incorporate opt-out provisions for using mediation in institutional rules rather than opt-in provisions. Default provisions are "sticky" in that parties tend to accept them rather than negotiating an alternative, so making mediation a default would likely increase its use.[39]

It may take more than legal frameworks to encourage fuller use of mediation, but the new Singapore Convention and the revised UNCITRAL Model Law on Mediation represent an emerging consensus that a global legal framework for enforcing mediated international commercial settlement agreements is an important step forward. When UNCITRAL began deliberations aimed at formulating such an international instrument there was no agreement on whether the product should be a convention or a model law. Eventually UNCITRAL took an unprecedented step and negotiated both instruments simultaneously. The following excerpt describes the motivations behind this effort and the initial debate about whether an international enforcement mechanism was needed. The excerpt also outlines issues that came up early in the deliberations regarding the desirable scope of an instrument and describes the conceptual challenges posed by the wide variety of enforcement procedures (discussed above in Part A). The Singapore Convention and revised Mediation Model Law represent compromise and consensus forged at UNCITRAL on these and many other issues.

## ELLEN E. DEASON, *ENFORCEMENT OF SETTLEMENT AGREEMENTS IN INTERNATIONAL COMMERCIAL MEDIATION: A NEW LEGAL FRAMEWORK?*

Dispute Resol. Mag., Fall 2015 at 33–35.

The motivation for proposing a convention to enforce mediated settlement agreements is straightforward: to encourage parties to use mediation for cross-border disputes because it can save time and money and help preserve ongoing commercial relationships. By signaling the importance of mediation internationally, and by creating a clear and uniform framework, a convention could generate greater certainty that settlements can be relied upon and readily enforced. This would promote the resolution of international commercial disputes through mediation.

At [an UNCITRAL Working Group] meeting, several business representatives and groups noted the burden and uncertainty of

[39] *Id.* at 413–15.

current cross-border enforcement mechanisms that rely on contract law and articulated a need for a more effective international legal framework. Many were from the United States, but they also represented multinational perspectives. In contrast, some countries' delegates, perhaps reflecting variations in the degree to which different legal cultures have embraced mediation for cross-border disputes, questioned the need for an enforcement framework for mediated settlements. . . .

Other countries' representatives maintained that current enforcement mechanisms are sufficient. Indeed, in many countries, settlements can be entered and enforced as court judgments. This procedure is, however, often limited to court-sponsored mediation or cases filed in court, and enforcing such court judgments across borders can be notoriously difficult. Alternatively, some national laws allow arbitral tribunals to convert mediated settlement agreements into awards on agreed terms, thus enabling the agreements to be enforced as arbitral awards. But again, this procedure is not always available for freestanding mediations, as some countries limit it to settlements reached during ongoing arbitrations.

* * *

Even more significantly, creating an arbitral award is not a practical solution for many parties in mediation. Unless they were already engaged in arbitration, they would need to initiate it—with the associated expense and delay—merely to rubber-stamp their settlement. This need to resort to arbitration would undermine the goal of promoting mediation as an independent, co-equal dispute resolution process.

* * *

*What Scope is Desirable?*

The United States proposes a convention that would govern enforcement of settlements resulting from conciliation of *international commercial* disputes. This restriction to commercial settings would exclude disputes arising out of consumer and employment contracts with non-business parties. . . . [A]bsent this exclusion, a convention would run afoul of mandatory laws protecting such parties, which frequently are stronger outside the United States.

There is, however, a more fundamental scope question: the United States proposes limiting the convention to settlements *resulting from mediation,* which raises thorny philosophical issues.

Many legal systems make no distinction between agreements reached with third-party assistance and those resulting from unassisted negotiation; both are subject to rules of contract law. So some States object to differentiating between them for purposes of enforcement. Even more broadly, some nations are concerned about the effect on contract law of treating enforcement of settlement agreements differently from that of ordinary contracts, such as sales agreements.

Limiting a convention to mediation is a pragmatic approach. If a country is hesitant to enact enforcement mechanisms for settlement agreements, ratifying a convention limited to mediation would be a narrower, less dramatic step than approving one that concerns all settlements. Furthermore, the distinction between mediated and negotiated settlements is familiar to many because confidentiality protections typically differ along that fault line. Hence instruments such as the Conciliation Model Law, which sets forth provisions on confidentiality, could serve as a precedent for singling out mediation as a settlement process.

The proposed convention is also limited to enforcement of *settlement* agreements. Although some scholars calling for a convention regard enforcement of parties' agreements to mediate as a high priority, the current focus . . . . is on enforcement of settlement agreements that result from mediation. [A]s a practical matter, garnering support for a less ambitious legal instrument would probably be easier. Moreover, it is not clear that enforcement is needed at the initiation of mediation. . . . .

* * *

*How to Deal with the Diversity of Practices?*

One of the challenges of crafting an effective convention is the wide variety of enforcement frameworks in use around the world. Current practices will influence nations' attitudes toward acceptable criteria for enforcement, and the procedures ultimately adopted in a convention will have to coexist with the full range of domestic mechanisms.

*Existing diversity.* The UNCITRAL Secretariat has compiled a valuable set of information on current national enforcement regimes for mediated settlements. Many nations treat such settlements as an ordinary contract, which often means that a party must file a suit claiming breach of contract to obtain enforcement. In other nations, a party can apply to a court to convert a settlement agreement into an enforceable legal instrument, but that often requires the court to approve the settlement or confirm its validity. Grounds for denying enforcement of the agreement include (depending on the country) lack of capacity, duress, undue influence, misrepresentation, mistake, fraud, unconscionability, illegality, or that the settlement is contrary to *ordre public*.

Some countries have special summary or expedited procedures for enforcement. In addition to the procedures for turning a settlement into an arbitral award . . . ., other mechanisms provide for expedited treatment in court. . . . In some civil-law countries, parties can use procedures that involve notaries: if they declare in their agreement that they consent to compulsory execution and record the agreement in a public document drawn up by a notary, they can obtain expedited enforcement. In other countries, mediated settlement agreements are directly enforceable if they meet certain criteria. In Ecuador, for instance, a mediated settlement agreement is an enforceable instrument if it is signed by the parties and the mediator and the mediation was conducted in compliance with Ecuadorian law.

These are, however, domestic procedures and, in the absence of treaties or the special framework of the European Union for recognition of court judgments, their application to international settlements is at best uncertain. Only a few countries have a specific legal framework for cross-border enforcement of settlement agreements.

*Relationship of a convention to domestic enforcement.* In determining which mediated settlements to enforce, one approach would be to rely on domestic frameworks to produce an instrument that could then be enforceable internationally. If a settlement has already passed muster by meeting the requirements for enforcement in the country where the mediation occurred (the seat), the enforcing jurisdiction could use an expedited procedure. But given the current range of enforcement procedures, this would seem to require either a herculean harmonization effort among jurisdictions or acceptance of a diverse set of enforceable instruments. More significantly, by requiring a domestic procedure as a prerequisite to international enforcement, this approach would impose a two-step approval process that would create undesirable burdens for parties seeking enforcement.

Alternatively, a convention could provide for direct enforcement of settlement agreements under specified criteria, with the enforcing jurisdiction evaluating compliance with those criteria. The New York Convention uses this general approach for enforcement of arbitral awards. In the context of mediation, such a system would eliminate the need to decide which of the many domestic mechanisms would be acceptable as a basis for enforcement in other countries. . . . .

---

The Singapore Convention and the revised UNCITRAL Mediation Model Law resolved the questions on scope discussed in the previous excerpt in a way that furthers the goal to promote the use of mediation in cross-border commercial disputes. In order to qualify for enforcement, an agreement must meet several criteria: it must be mediated, international, and commercial. Agreements that are enforceable as an arbitral award or as a court judgment are excluded. Settlements concerning consumer transactions, family, inheritance, and employment disputes are also excluded.

The instruments avoid the problems associated with the great diversity in domestic law by creating a new enforcement mechanism. It is intended to streamline practices and save parties from needing to turn an agreement into an arbitral award or rely on an enforcement process under domestic law. In the following excerpt, Timothy Schnabel, who headed the U.S. delegation to the UNCITRAL deliberations, explains the legal nature of this new enforcement mechanism.

## TIMOTHY SCHNABEL, *THE SINGAPORE CONVENTION ON MEDIATION: A FRAMEWORK FOR THE CROSS-BORDER RECOGNITION AND ENFORCEMENT OF MEDIATED SETTLEMENTS*

19 Pepperdine Disp. Resol. L.J. 1, 9–12 (2019).

[T]he Convention can be seen as creating a new category of legal instrument on the international plane, elevating what would otherwise be a mere contract to a sui generis status. In general, the Convention provides for international, mediated settlements to be treated in a manner comparable to arbitral awards. That this effect would occur was recognized early in the UNCITRAL discussions, and was controversial. Some delegations argued that settlements are only contracts and should not be given a different status solely because they are mediated. The ability of disputing parties to convert a mediated settlement into an arbitral award (a "consent award" or "award on agreed terms") was cited as an adequate workaround; some delegations suggested that such processes suffice to ensure enforceability . . . . .

By contrast, others argued that disputing parties should not have to go through the elaborate exercise of converting a settlement into an award, and that they should not have to depend on finding (and hiring) an arbitrator willing to enter it as an award. . . . . Moreover, in many jurisdictions, whether the New York Convention would apply to all such consent awards is an open question. . . . . Beyond these concerns about a legal gap, from a policy perspective, parties that prefer to use mediation should not be forced to engage in another form of alternative dispute resolution simply in order to receive equal legal protection of the outcome of the dispute resolution process.

Thus, rather than forcing disputing parties to shoehorn their mediated settlements into the existing legal framework governing arbitration, the Convention accords a new status to mediated settlements in their own right. It converts what would otherwise be seen as purely a private contractual act into an instrument that can circulate under a legally-binding international framework, and provides an entitlement to privileged treatment in other states, similar to a judgment. Thus, under the Convention, settlements are no longer merely subject to contract law, although some aspects of contract law may remain relevant in certain situations (and, of course, a party could still seek to rely on contract law, as mediated settlements do not lose their status as contracts). Such an approach makes sense, as a mediated settlement should receive more deference than a normal contract, given that parties have likely already given up contractual rights in settling their dispute, and have spent time and money on the mediation. More importantly, in arbitration, the disputing parties consent only to the process for resolving their dispute, but not to the ultimate outcome, yet the agreement to arbitrate and the arbitral award—which otherwise would only be private acts governed by contract law—are given privileged status under the New York Convention. In mediation, by contrast, the parties have agreed to not only the process for resolving their dispute but also to the ultimate outcome—thus suggesting a far stronger justification for according a privileged status to the mediated settlement agreement.

---

In nations that have ratified the Convention, courts *shall* enforce a mediated settlement agreement under the Convention unless it satisfies one of the grounds for refusing to grant relief. However, countries can make reservations to the Convention to limit its reach. First, they can declare that they will not apply the

Convention to settlement agreements to which the government is a party. This could affect the enforcement of settlements in investor-state disputes. (See generally Chapter 7.) Second, they can give parties the ability to determine whether they want to be able to enforce their agreement under the Convention. In States that make this reservation, the Convention will not apply by default. Courts will use the Convention procedures for enforcement only if the parties have "opted-in" by agreeing that they want the Convention to apply to their settlement.

The Convention and revised Model Law supply the only grounds a court or other competent authority may use to refuse to enforce a mediated settlement agreement. By requiring courts to enforce a mediated settlement agreements unless there is a ground to refuse enforcement, the Convention's structure is pro-enforcement. In addition, the Convention allows a party to rely on other applicable law in the jurisdiction where it seeks enforcement when that law permits the party to avail itself of the settlement agreement.[40] In other words, a party can take advantage of domestic law in the enforcing nation that is more favorable for enforcement than the Convention.

One question that needed to be resolved was the extent to which these grounds to refuse enforcement would displace contract law defenses. The Convention allows a court to deny enforcement if the settlement is "null and void, inoperative or incapable of being performed." [41] According to delegations' comments during the negotiations, this ground encompasses contract law concepts such as fraud and misrepresentation. It does not include arguments that a settlement agreement is invalid because it fails to comply with domestic requirements that are not recognized by the Convention. Examples include requirements for mediators to be licensed by certain bodies, that mediations must be conducted under certain rules, or formalities such as notarization.[42] For a complete list of the grounds a court can use to deny enforcement of a mediated settlement agreement, see Article 5 of the Convention.

Some of the terms of the Convention and the Model Law have generated controversy. One issue concerns the requirement to submit

---

[40] United Nations Convention on International Settlement Agreements Resulting from Mediation, G.A. Res. 73/198, annex, Art. 7 (Dec. 20, 2018).

[41] *Id.*, Art. 5(1)(b)(i).

[42] Timothy Schnabel, *The Singapore Convention on Mediation: A Framework for the Cross-Border Recognition and Enforcement of Mediated Settlements*, 19 Pepperdine Disp. Resol. L.J. 1, 44–45 (2019).

evidence that the settlement agreement was the result of mediation. (See Box 9.) This is necessary to distinguish mediations—which are covered by the Convention—from settlements that parties negotiate without the assistance of a third-party—which are not. When a mediation has not been administered by an institution, this evidence requirement will often involve documents signed by the mediator.

**9. United Nations Convention on International Settlement Agreements Resulting from Mediation**

**Art. 4. Requirements for reliance on settlement agreements**

1. A party relying on a settlement agreement under this Convention shall supply to the competent authority of the Party to the Convention where relief is sought:

(a) The settlement agreement signed by the parties;

(b) Evidence that the settlement agreement resulted from mediation, such as:

(i) The mediator's signature on the settlement agreement;
(ii) A document signed by the mediator indicating that the mediation was carried out;
(iii) An attestation by the institution that administered the mediation; or
(iv) In the absence of (i), (ii), or (iii), any other evidence acceptable to the competent authority.

* * *

Mediator F. Peter Phillips argues that these requirements are inconsistent with "fundamental attributes" of the practice of commercial mediation in many Western jurisdictions.

> Many mediators conscientiously refuse to sign a settlement agreement. Most American mediators follow the practice that, consistent with their mediation agreements providing that they not be subpoenaed as a witness, they neither draft nor execute any written memorial that may be interpreted as witness[ing] its execution or—even worse—including

them as a party to the rights and obligations set forth therein.[43]

# VI. OTHER SIGNIFICANT LEGAL ISSUES

This section identifies a selection of additional types of mediation regulation that have been enacted in some countries. Part A discusses regulation of mediator qualifications. Part B introduces the variation in national treatment of the interaction between a mediation proceeding and limitation periods for litigation. Part C considers the role of judges in settling cases using mediation. An additional legal issue, discussed in the context of ethics in Chapter 5, is whether lawyers have a duty to discuss mediation with their clients.

## A. Mediator Qualifications

Regulation of mediator qualifications can be a controversial topic. On one hand, some justify regulation as promoting quality mediation and advancing professionalism. On the other hand, some criticize it for restricting access to the profession and limiting party choice. Mediation law on this subject varies greatly in its scope and the landscape is still developing.

Countries in Europe employ a wide variety of approaches to ensuring the quality of mediation, and these include regulation of mediator qualifications. The EU Directive requires Member States to encourage training and quality control mechanisms to ensure "effective, impartial and competent mediation."[44] In some countries, a professional mediation association sets qualification standards for mediators.[45] Many countries, however, use national law to set training standards and regulate the profession, with an official government body such as the Ministry of Justice maintaining a list of registered or accredited mediators.[46] Other countries operate a two-tiered system with some mediators who qualify for Department

---

[43] F. Peter Phillips, Concerns on the New Singapore Convention (Oct. 9, 2018), http://www.businessconflictmanagement.com/blog/2018/10/concerns-on-the-new-singapore-convention/.

[44] *EU Mediation Directive, supra* note 1, Art. 4.

[45] *Rebooting the European Directive, supra* note 12, at 47 (Netherlands).

[46] *Rebooting the European Directive, supra* note 12, at 17, 24, 79, 92, 111 (Austria, Bulgaria, Cyprus, Hungary, & Slovakia).

of Justice certification and others who are certified under standards promulgated by private mediation organizations.[47]

The nature of the legal regime for mediator qualifications and the level of involvement of official governmental bodies can sometimes affect other aspects of mediation regulation. These include protections for confidentiality and enforcement of mediated agreements. In the Netherlands, for example, confidentiality protections in national law are limited. Due to concerns about extending a privilege to non-certified mediators, they are not provided by law. Instead, confidentiality is provided by party agreement, including protection for a mediator from the obligation to testify in subsequent legal proceedings.[48] In some other countries, the enforceability of a settlement agreement may depend on the choice of a mediator. One option for parties in Belgium, for example, is to have a mediated agreement from voluntary non-court mediation ratified by a court and treated as a court judgment. But this procedure is available only if the mediator is accredited under standards set by Belgian legislation.[49] In Estonia, if the mediator is an attorney or notary, a mediated agreement is enforceable following court authorization, and other expedited procedures are available depending on the type of claim. But, if the mediator is not a member of one of these two professions, an agreement can be enforced only if a court determines that the mediator's character ensures impartiality and independence.[50] In Finland, the Mediation Act requires the mediator to be trained in mediation as a condition of enforceability.[51] These provisions are presumably designed to improve the quality of mediation by setting standards for mediators.

In contrast, in the United States, there is far less regulation of the mediation profession. Some states have established state-wide requirements for court mediators, and in other states individual courts provide lists of approved mediators. There are professional organizations that certify mediators who meet education and experience standards but, aside from court-connected mediation, government certification is rare. While there are concerns about the training of mediators and the quality of the service they provide, appropriate standards for quality are hard to articulate and there is

---

47 *Rebooting the European Directive, supra* note 12, at 33 (Germany).

48 *Rebooting the European Directive, supra* note 12, at 45.

49 *Rebooting the European Directive, supra* note 12, at 73.

50 *Rebooting the European Directive, supra* note 12, at 85–86.

51 *Rebooting the European Directive, supra* note 12, at 88.

a concern that defining standards too narrowly will erect barriers that limit the diversity of mediators.[52]

## B. Effect of Mediation on Litigation Limitation Periods

There are important differences in the legal effect that mediation has on limitation periods for bringing legal proceedings. For example, in the United States, if parties attempt to resolve their dispute in mediation prior to filing a lawsuit, this has no effect on the statute of limitations. It continues to run until suit is filed and the normal requirements for tolling it are met. In contrast, European countries use a different legal rule as a way to encourage parties to use mediation. The EU Mediation Directive protects parties who choose to attempt to settle their dispute using mediation; they will not be prevented from initiating judicial or arbitral proceedings if the limitation period for the action expires during the mediation process.[53] As a result, the EU Member States suspend their limitation periods during mediation or provide an extension beyond the end of the mediation.

## C. The Role of Judges with Regard to Mediation

This is an unsettled area of the law with much variation among jurisdictions. Judges can be involved with mediation in several contexts: when they encourage mediation and refer parties to court mediation programs, when they act as mediators to settle a case themselves, and when they interact with mediators, especially those who work in court-connected programs. The traditional wisdom is that the role of judges in settling cases is very different in civil-law legal systems and in common-law countries. Civil law judges are more accustomed to an active role in settlement, whereas common-law judges have traditionally been more restrained. Some courts, for example in Germany, Austria, and China, have an especially strong practice of encouraging settlement. This has also influenced how arbitrators in those countries view their roles. (See Chapter 6 for a discussion of arbitrators' roles in settlement.)

In the latter half of the twentieth century, however, many judges in the United States became active in leading settlement conferences in their cases. Now, judges increasingly use mediation techniques in those conferences. There are concerns, however, (discussed in Chapter 2) when the judge who mediates the case is the same judge

---

[52] See Chapter 11 in Sarah R. Cole et al., *supra* note 10, for more information on regulation of mediator qualifications in the United States.

[53] *EU Mediation Directive, supra* note 1, Art. 8.

who will adjudicate it if the case does not settle. The worry is that the parties will feel coerced to settle and that the judge will learn information that should not be considered in making a decision.[54] In the United States, the Uniform Mediation Act does not include this situation within its ambit, in part because the drafters thought that parties would be so hesitant to share information with the judge assigned to their case that they would not need the benefits of confidentiality.

The UMA does, however, regulate the second context for judicial involvement. It imposes a firm separation between judges who will decide the case and mediators (whether the mediators are private individuals or other judges). This provision is particularly relevant for court-annexed mediation programs. Mediators are strictly limited in what they can communicate to the assigned judge. They are allowed to report only if a mediation was held, who attended, if a settlement was reached, and information that falls under an exception to the privileges.[55] This restriction serves the interest of the parties by avoiding a "back door" to informing the judge about mediation communications that may not be disclosed in the formal proceeding. In addition, it furthers the interests of a court in the integrity of its processes, as described above in Section IV(A).

## VII. NOTES AND QUESTIONS

1. As the use of mediation grows, but its popularity varies in different regions and countries, do you think it is important to promote uniformity and harmonization of legal regulation world-wide? Can you articulate the arguments for harmonization efforts and the competing values of local approaches? Perhaps it is more important to have consistency of regulatory approaches for some aspects of mediation than for others. Are there, for instance, some aspects of mediation that should not be governed by legal provisions at all?
2. Given the growth of legal rules that apply to mediation, what are the consequences for the role of lawyers in helping parties plan for dispute resolution and advising them about their options? How does the variation in regulatory approaches among the jurisdictions affect your answer? What about some subjects, such as a general duty of confidentiality, that are regulated in some jurisdictions but left to party agreement in others? Do you think that most lawyers

---

54 *See* Ellen E. Deason, *Beyond "Managerial Judges": Appropriate Roles in Settlement,* 78 Ohio State L.J. 73, 108–18 (2017).

55 Uniform Mediation Act, *supra* note 6, § 7.

are well-prepared for their role in cross-boundary dispute resolution as legal regulation of mediation grows?

3. What are the implications for the role of lawyers of the default frameworks used by many mediation statutes, which give parties the potential to select their mediation procedures by agreement? Are default provisions important given the tendency to avoid discussion of future disputes at the initiation of a commercial relationship? What is the effect of default provisions on the balance between uniformity and local approaches to mediation? Consider that while they allow parties to choose their own options, they are also known to be "sticky" and are often accepted by parties without modification.

4. The strong emphasis on party autonomy that led to heavy reliance on default provisions in the UNCITRAL Mediation Model Law has been criticized as inappropriate for provisions that regulate the intersection of mediation and adjudicatory systems. Mediator Eric Van Ginkel agrees that party autonomy is important for parties' control of the "inner workings" of conciliation procedure. He distinguishes this, however, from giving the parties the ability to set aside provisions on confidentiality or enforcement of a mediated agreement. "Both confidentiality and the enforcement of settlement agreements interact closely with the judicial, arbitral and/or administrative adjudicatory systems of the same or another country, and therefore ought to be mandatory law." *See* Eric Van Ginkel, *The UNCITRAL Model Law on International Commercial Conciliation: A Critical Appraisal,* 21 J. Int'l Arb. 1, 7 (2004). What do you think is the appropriate balance between mandatory and default provisions in legislation that regulates mediation? Is your answer affected by the important role in mediation for party self-determination? How far should this role reach?

5. The same criticism is relevant for the "opt-in" provision that States can choose to offer parties under the Singapore Convention. In addition, the default rule is the opposite of that recommended by Nadja Alexander. If parties are to be given a choice, what do you think should be the default—applying the Convention to enforcement or not using the Convention? Why does it matter? Which posture is more likely to result in an increased use of mediation for cross-border disputes?

6. When a mediator uses a caucus, compare the advantages and disadvantages of the two approaches to maintaining confidentiality among the parties—protecting all information unless the mediator has permission to share it or allowing the mediator to share everything except designated information. Which would you prefer as a party? As a mediator? Should statutes regulate this aspect of

mediation practice, or is the choice better left to the ethical rules, the mediator, and/or the parties?

7. What is the mediator's role in notifying the parties about mediation regulation? For example, how should a mediator in the United States deal with the complexity of the Uniform Mediation Act's confidentiality protections? Should she describe all the exceptions to the privilege in her opening statement? If the mediation is a transnational proceeding, how should the mediator approach this question given the variation in legal protections for confidentiality and for enforcement of mediated settlement agreements? Is a mediator obligated to know the applicable law in all the relevant jurisdictions? Can a mediator rely on counsel for the parties?

8. Assume you are a legislator considering legal mechanisms to protect confidentiality for mediation in cross-border disputes. What considerations do you think are important? How would you prioritize factors such as the local legal culture's familiarity with legal mechanisms, simplicity, comprehensive coverage, specific statements of public policy exceptions, tendency to trigger litigation, and other considerations?

9. One of the goals behind the UNCITRAL deliberations that led to the Singapore Convention and the revised Model Law providing for enforcement of mediated settlement agreements was a desire to increase acceptance and use of mediation in the international context. The goal of the EU Directive is similarly to encourage the cross-border use of mediation in Europe. Are legal regulations the best way to achieve these changes? Almost 10 years after issuing the EU Directive, the European Commission noted that "certain difficulties exist in relation to the functioning of the national mediation systems in practice, mainly related to the adversarial tradition and the lack of a mediation culture in the Member States, the low level of awareness of mediation in the majority of Member States, insufficient knowledge of how to deal with cross-border cases, and the functioning of the quality control mechanisms for mediators." Should nations implement additional legal regulations to promote mediation? What other approaches might be appropriate? For the recommendations of the European Commission, see European Parliament resolution of 12 September 2017 on the implementation of Directive 2008/52/EC of the European Parliament and of the Council of 21 May 2008 on certain aspects of mediation in civil and commercial matters (the 'Mediation Directive') (2016/2066(INI)).

# Chapter 5

# ETHICAL CHALLENGES

## I. INTRODUCTION

The materials in this chapter focus on the primary ethical concerns associated with mediation practice. With the growth of transnational and international mediation there has been greater attention focused on the ethical issues which arise in mediation. Questions related to party self-determination, informed consent, neutrality, impartiality, fairness, and good faith participation are as relevant in cross-border and transnational mediation as they are in domestic mediation practice. However, when these ethical issues are considered in the international and transnational context, the role of culture becomes increasingly relevant and the material in Chapter 3 should also be considered. Some issues, such as confidentiality, overlap the discussion of legal issues in Chapter 4, and the topic of good faith participation requirements is discussed in Chapter 2.

Perhaps the earliest and best known mediation ethical standards are the Model Standards of Conduct for Mediators, originally prepared in the United States in 1994 by the American Arbitration Association, the American Bar Association and the Association for Conflict Resolution and amended in 2005. Other ethics codes, such as the European Code of Conduct for Mediators followed suit. There is also a wide array of mediation rules established by international organizations such as the United Nations, the World Trade Organization, the International Centre for Settlement of Investment Disputes (ICSID), the International Chamber of Commerce (ICC) and the International Mediation Institute (IMI) which include ethical standards. Most mediation ethical codes address topics such as party self-determination, impartiality, conflicts of interest, confidentiality, competence, and quality of the process. More broadly, most ethical standards are concerned with the fundamental issues of justice and fairness in mediation.

The following sections in this chapter explore the broad issues of fairness and justice in mediation, and the core ethical values of self-determination, consent, impartiality, and neutrality, and distinguish impartiality from neutrality. They also discuss issues related to a lawyer's duty to inform clients about mediation. Finally, they address ethical issues associated with the growing practice of online mediation.

## II. FAIRNESS AND JUSTICE IN MEDIATION

Fairness and justice are essential concerns of mediation's ethical cannon, and there is a rich literature on the meaning of justice and fairness in mediation. [1] Frequently these two terms are used interchangeably and that is the approach taken in this chapter. It is difficult, however, to determine a universal meaning for the concepts of justice and fairness because they may vary depending upon cultural contexts.

Self-determination and party autonomy are given primary status in most mediation ethical codes wherein mediators are advised to pay attention to process concerns and procedural fairness and justice. In the following except, Omer Shapira reviews various meanings of procedural fairness from several mediation ethical standards and from the literature.

### OMER SHAPIRA, *CONCEPTIONS AND PERCEPTIONS OF FAIRNESS IN MEDIATION*

54 S. Tex. L. Rev. 281, 282–287 (2012).

Fairness is considered a fundamental principle of mediation. As one author noted, "Fairness is a predominant concern in the mediation community. Few commentators would disagree that it is the normative standard governing mediation. Determining what constitutes fairness, however, is a difficult question."

The reader of mediation literature and codes of conduct for mediators may be overwhelmed by the numerous aspects of fairness referred to and may wonder what these aspects of fairness have in common and what mediation academics and the code drafters have intended by the use of fairness terminology. Additionally, in the absence of a defined meaning of fairness, it is difficult to evaluate the strength of fairness-based arguments that commentators make. If, for example, a commentator argues that a particular action of the mediator is unfair, how can we evaluate his claim without first

---

1 *See e.g.*, Lela P. Love & Jonathan Hyman, *If Portia Were a Mediator: An Inquiry into Justice in Mediation*, 9 Clinical L. Rev. 157 (2002); Lisa Blomgren Amsler, *Designing Justice: Legal Institutions and Other Systems for Managing Conflict*, 24 Ohio St. J. on Disp. Resol. 1 (2008).

understanding the meaning of fairness? How can we determine whether the process of mediation is fair—or whether a mediation outcome is unfair—without a good understanding of the meaning of fairness?

* * *

*Codes of Conduct for Mediators*

Codes of conduct for mediators often use fairness terminology, though it is rare to find an independent standard of fairness in a code of conduct. A few codes do not mention fairness at all. The following review of selected codes of conduct aims to illustrate the numerous and bewildering meanings of fairness in the codes and the difficulty of finding a unifying rationale for these meanings.

Fairness according to the codes of conduct is connected to the mediator's competence to conduct the mediation and the duty to "exercise diligence in scheduling the mediation." Fairness requires the mediator to remain impartial, to avoid conflicts of interests, and to avoid unfair influence that results in a party entering a settlement agreement. Fairness is connected to the quality of the process and its integrity. Fairness requires that parties have an opportunity to participate, that their participation is meaningful, and that they have an opportunity to speak, be heard, and articulate their needs, interests, and concerns.

Fairness demands that parties make voluntary, uncoerced decisions without undue influence on the basis of knowledge or informed consent and have an opportunity to consider the implications of their decision. In a fair mediation, the parties may terminate the mediation at any time. The fairness of mediation is preserved when participation is not to gain an unfair advantage, when manipulative or intimidating negotiating tactics are not used, and when the parties avoid nondisclosure or fraud. Fairness is violated when the agreement is grossly or fundamentally unfair, illegal, or impossible to execute, and when the parties do not understand the agreement and its implications on themselves and on nonparticipants (third parties).

The numerous contexts in which fairness is used in codes of conduct indicate the importance which is attached to fairness concerns. Yet the question remains: What precisely is the meaning of fairness in mediation? What is common to all those aspects of fairness?

*Mediation Literature*

Issues of fairness and justice have received much attention in mediation literature. . . . . . Mediation literature often distinguishes between procedural fairness relating to the process of mediation, and substantive fairness relating to the outcome of mediation. According to the literature, a mediator acts fairly when the mediation is conducted impartially, without bias, evenhandedly, and indiscriminately, though the mediator is expected to take account of the parties' differences and power inequalities. A fair mediator treats the parties with dignity and respect, considers their views and concerns, and does not pressure or coerce them to settle. According to mediation literature, fairness requires the presence of parties in mediation sessions, party control of process, and that the parties have an opportunity for expression and voice. In a fair process, party decisions are voluntary, informed, based on adequate information, and the parties have access to independent legal advice. In a fair mediation, there are no significant power inequalities between the parties, the parties treat each other with dignity and respect and avoid intimidation and abusive behavior.

---

The concerns voiced by Omer Shapira raise the following questions. Are the values of self-determination and party autonomy the most important ethical bases for a mediator's conduct? Or, should the mediator also be responsible for the substantive fairness of an agreement? In the following excerpt, Ellen Waldman and Lola Akin Ojelabi point out the limitations of an exclusive focus on procedural justice and argue for the importance of substantive justice in mediation.

## ELLEN WALDMAN & LOLA AKIN OJELABI, *MEDIATORS AND SUBSTANTIVE JUSTICE: A VIEW FROM RAWLS' ORIGINAL POSITION*

30 Ohio St. J. Disp. Resol. 391, 413–419 (2016).

*Procedural and Substantive Justice*

Virtually every mediation code in existence, including the ones surveyed here, pay obeisance to the requisites of procedural justice. Affording parties equal time to speak and to be heard and treating parties with respect are standard fixtures in most mediation codes and align with the common mediation view that, if sufficient attention is paid to process, the resulting agreement will be substantively fair. Some mediation codes, however, adopt a somewhat paradoxical stance. They emphasize procedural justice and caution against excessive mediator influence. Yet, almost as a backdoor gesture, these same codes ask the mediator to be the last backstop against errant substantive injustice. While issuing no definite injunction, they allow the mediator to terminate the process if one party acts unconscionably or if an unconscionable agreement appears likely. Thus, while code authors are concerned that mediators not dominate or usurp party discussions, they remain uncomfortable with the threat that power imbalances, or other antecedent inequities, will turn the mediation setting into one of exploitation and abuse.

The U.S. Model Standards and the PMA [Professional Mediator's Association Singapore] Code illustrate the "pure procedural justice" approach where no mention is made of substantive justice. Standard VI of the U.S. Code, which is devoted to "Quality of the Process," directs the mediator to conduct the process "in a manner that promotes .... procedural fairness," but makes no mention of fairness of the outcome. A mediator has the option of withdrawing if the mediation is being used to further criminal conduct, if there is violence between the parties, or if the mediator feels she cannot remain impartial, but there is no option for withdrawal where the agreement appears to the mediator to be substantively unfair. An omnibus direction exists for the mediator to "take appropriate steps," including possible withdrawal if the mediator believes that participant conduct "jeopardizes conducting a mediation consistent with these Standards," but since the Standards set no ceiling or floor with regard to the terms of resulting agreements, it would appear that this provision relates to procedural matters only. The PMA tracks the U.S. Standards, except it includes an additional warning for the mediator who might be tempted to apply external criterion to the parties' discussions, cautioning that "the mediator must respect the culture, beliefs, rights and autonomy of the participants and should defer their own views to those of the participants . . . ."

The more ambivalent aspects of the Australian, IMI, EU, and Singapore codes are salient upon quick perusal. The Australian code, for example, contains an entire section on procedural fairness and cautions the mediator against evaluating outcomes reached by the probable "litigated outcomes." Although it does note that a mediator should support the parties in assessing the practicality and feasibility of any possible agreement, that assessment must be done according to the parties' subjective understandings of fairness. One might interpret this language to mean that any societal consensus as embodied in legal rights and entitlements are secondary to the parties' own ideas and thus, not relevant to the process. At the same time, the code does contain language that could be read to the contrary. The code states that when assessing a proposed agreement's feasibility, the interests of "vulnerable stakeholders" should be considered. An entire provision devoted to power imbalances requires mediators be trained to spot situations where the bargaining table is dangerously uneven and be alert to instances of subtle threat and intimidation. When discussing mediator competence, the code requires training in the ethics of assuring "fairness and equity" and when discussing the mediator's limited role as information-provider, the code suggests it is appropriate in some disputes for the mediator to turn attention to a proposed solution's impact on absent third party stakeholders. Most importantly, when discussing termination of the process, the code states that the mediator may terminate when, in the judgment of the mediator, the parties are reaching a substantively unconscionable agreement. Thus, despite the code's significant emphasis on mediator self-restraint, it ultimately places the mediator in the role of backstop, a final bulwark against the exploitation of the unwary by more knowledgeable and perhaps unscrupulous bargainers.

The IMI Code of Professional Conduct is similarly mysterious regarding the mediator's relationship to the substantive fairness of the mediation agreement. On the one hand, the focus of the code appears initially to lie with questions of procedural fairness. One section entitled "Fairness and Integrity of the [P]rocess" requires the mediator to "conduct the process with fairness to all parties." This requirement is further explained as ensuring the parties have an opportunity to be heard, be involved in the process, and consult with legal counsel. However, there is no corollary requirement that mediators attend to the terms of the agreement being discussed. However, the Code does vest the mediator with some duties of assessment in a provision discussing termination of the process. Like the Australian Code, the IMI Code provides that the mediator "may withdraw from a mediation if a negotiation among the parties assumes a character that to the mediator appears unconscionable or illegal." Obviously, this last provision vests the mediator with the authority and the burden to determine when suspension, termination, or withdrawal is necessary based on an evaluation of the possible outcome as substantively unfair or inequitable.

The EU Code of Conduct for Mediators appears designed to sensitize mediators to the threat of substantive unfairness, but provides little guidance regarding the mediator's role in preventing it. It notes helpfully that mediators should conduct the process "appropriately," keeping in mind the possible existence of power imbalances and the rule of law as well as the parties' possible desire to end the dispute quickly without affording themselves of all the protections that an adversary procedure might allow. "Process fairness" in this code means that each party will have an opportunity to speak and the mediator may terminate the discussions if the agreement reached appears illegal or unenforceable. It is notable that the last provision relating to termination places the mediator in the position of evaluating the outcome-fairness of the agreement reached, a position of critique or judgment that the remainder of the code provisions explicitly warns against. The Singapore Mediation Centre's Code of Conduct similarly does not explicitly hold the mediator responsible for the substantive fairness of any agreement reached. But, it does allow the mediator to terminate the mediation if "any of the parties acts unconscionably," thus suggesting that a mediator who brings her own assessments of what constitutes unconscionable behavior into the parties' dispute is nonetheless acting appropriately and within the bounds of ethical mediator behavior.

The codes we have surveyed reflect the vast majority of mediation ethics standards; they require mediators attend diligently to the requisites of procedural justice, but make few or no references to the substantive justice of the resulting agreement. Codes that do address the fairness of the mediation outcome do so in the context of terminating the mediation agreement. Some codes require the mediator to terminate the process if the resulting agreement is illegal, unfair, or unconscionable. Others simply raise termination as an option that remains at the mediator's discretion. These termination provisions suggest that the mediator can, and in some instances should, subject the proposed agreement to an assessment based on criteria that differ from the parties' own preferences.

* * *

[T]he provisions . . . . reveal a central tension within the codes. If a mediator's only ethical responsibility is to respect party autonomy and remain impartial, then, arguably, the mediator should not be assessing the fairness, legality, or unconscionability of the parties' proposed agreement. What these termination provisions acknowledge is that sometimes mediation negotiations can lead to harmful or exploitative outcomes and that the mediator should be on the lookout for these disturbing outcomes, work to modify them, or seek to disassociate from them. Not every code contains these termination agreements, but those that do suggest a more layered and complex set of responsibilities for the mediator than do codes that focus exclusively on procedural fairness to the exclusion of other concerns. Although self-determination or party autonomy is a fundamental value of facilitative mediation, the codes, to cater for circumstances that may lead to unjust outcomes, are shifting from complete reification of self-determination to an acknowledgement that the mediator may have a role to play in protecting against gross exploitation or unfairness. The critiques that have dogged mediation from its earliest days acknowledge the threat that power imbalances and systematic inequities pose to a quality process. That literature of critique confronts directly what some mediation ethics codes hint at covertly—that the mediator has a role to play in ensuring that mediation agreements meet some sort of minimal threshold of justice—both for each party and for affected parties outside the mediation room. In our view, existing codes should formally recognize that self-determination and party autonomy are crucial, but not the single ethical basis for mediator's conduct.

---

## III. CORE ETHICAL VALUES

### A. Self-Determination

The Model Standards of Practice for Mediators emphasize the importance of self-determination as a controlling principle of mediation. In theory, this principle means that the parties who are affected by a dispute decide the outcome of that dispute. However, theory and practice may not always be aligned. Research conducted in Australia regarding ethical challenges faced by mediators showed that despite common agreement on the importance of party self-determination, mediators do not act uniformly in honoring this principle. Rather they have individual moral compasses that reflect different views on the meaning of justice in mediation. This in turn leads them to varied responses to ethical dilemmas. The following excerpt illustrates some of the challenges of engaging with the principle of party self-determination.

### JACQUELINE M. NOLAN-HALEY, *SELF-DETERMINATION IN INTERNATIONAL MEDIATION: SOME PRELIMINARY REFLECTIONS*

7 Cardozo J. Conflict Resol. 277, 278–282 (2006).

Few concepts have generated as much discussion in the post-war international legal system as that of "self-determination." Scholars debate the proper identity of the "selves" endowed with this right, its boundaries and its normative relevance. When the focus turns to mediation, the discussion becomes murky because the concept of self-determination has both procedural and substantive components and is noticeably different in the private and public sectors.

* * *

*Self-Determination in Private Mediation*

The principle of self-determination in mediation offers procedural justice protections, providing parties with fairness and dignity. The inherent attraction of self-determination is its connection to self-governance and individual autonomy. In U.S. domestic practice, self-determination is widely accepted as the intrinsic value of mediation. The legal principle of informed consent provides the structure through which this value is measured. Informed consent promotes respect for human dignity through its emphasis on participatory, knowledgeable and consensual decision-making. Parties' perceptions of procedural justice are enhanced when they actively participate in the mediation process and voluntarily consent to an outcome that is free of any coercive influences. European mediation practice is similar in this regard. The proposed European Code of Conduct for Mediators advises mediators to give all parties adequate opportunity to be involved in the mediation process and to ensure that all agreements are reached through informed consent.

Notwithstanding the strong emphasis on self-determination in private mediation, scholars have observed a disconnect between its theory and practice. While self-determination appears to be an explicit value in private mediation, in fact, much depends upon the "frame" in which mediation is conducted and the place and the culture in which mediation takes place. Expressions of self-determination may look very different depending upon whether mediation is labeled facilitative or evaluative, transformative or narrative, and whether it occurs in a court-based facility or with private providers. More importantly, the lens of culture is a critical component in shaping and understanding party self-determination. Western, individualist cultures typically honor a form of self-determination that gives the disputing parties significant control over deciding the outcome. In contrast, more traditional, collectivist cultures value the interests of the community over those of the individual in deciding outcomes. Cultural considerations also influence mediator behavior. In Continental Europe, mediators' civil law orientation shapes their behaviors in influencing party decision-making. Likewise, in Islamic and some Arab cultures, the "wisely directive" mediator is expected to put pressure on the parties to reach an agreement. Thus, depending upon cultural contexts, moral persuasion and coercion can be justifiable practices in mediation.

Despite the various and sometimes conflicting modes of expressing self-determination in private mediation practice, there is a significant public discourse and a recognition of it as an explicit process value.

---

## B. Consent

Mediation has traditionally been considered a consensual process. Thus, it is understood that informed consent is a key aspect of mediation decisionmaking. For example, the Model Standards of Conduct for Mediators require that parties make "free and informed choices as to process and outcome" (Standard I). Likewise, the European Code of Conduct for Mediators (3.3) states that "the mediator must take all appropriate measures to ensure that any agreement is reached by all parties through knowing and informed consent, and that all parties understand the terms of the agreement. A variation of this explicit informed consent mandate is found in the International Mediation Institute (IMI) Code of Professional Conduct (3.2.1) which requires that the mediator "explain the mediation process to the parties and their advisers and be satisfied that they consent to the process being used and to the Mediator selected."

The following two excerpts discuss the values protected by informed consent in mediation and the important role of consent in mediating political conflicts.

### JACQUELINE NOLAN-HALEY, *INFORMED CONSENT IN MEDIATION: A GUIDING PRINCIPLE FOR TRULY EDUCATED DECISIONMAKING*

74 Notre Dame L. Rev. 775, 781, 787–792 (1999).

Informed consent is an ethical, moral, and legal concept that is deeply ingrained in American culture. In those transactions where informed consent is required, the legal doctrine requires that individuals who give consent be competent, informed about the particular intervention, and consent voluntarily. Informed consent is the foundational moral and ethical principle that promotes respect for individual self-determination and honors human dignity.

* * *

*Values Informed Consent Serves in Mediation*

In mediation practice, the principle of informed consent is not an end in itself but is a means of achieving the fundamental goal of fairness. Fairness requires that parties know what they are doing when they decide to participate in mediation, that they understand all aspects of the decisionmaking process, including their right to withdraw consent and discontinue negotiations, and that they understand the outcome reached in mediation. Toward this end, the principle of informed consent in mediation protects the psychological and legal interests associated with the values of autonomy, human dignity, and efficiency.

*Autonomy in Mediation Enhanced Through Informed Consent*

* * *

Respect for autonomy and its legal equivalent, the right of self-determination, is widely accepted as the intrinsic value of mediation, and the principle of informed consent provides the structural framework through which this value is measured in mediation. The value of autonomy in mediation lies in what Gerald Dworkin has described as its "intrinsic desirability of exercising the capacity for self-determination." This capacity for self-determination is described in the Code of Professional Conduct for Mediators as the "fundamental principle" of mediation. Mediation theorists and practitioners repeat the theme, emphasizing the self-governance and empowerment aspects of mediation.

The idealized vision of autonomy in mediation, "mediation autonomy," is grounded in relational and communal values. As a governing principle, it is concerned not just with one's self but with the other party to the dispute. Mediation autonomy is exercised in cooperation with the other party. In this regard, Lon Fuller's classic definition characterizes mediation's "capacity to re-orient the parties toward one another, not by imposing rules on them, but by helping them to achieve a new and shared perception of their relationship, a perception that will redirect their attitudes and dispositions toward each other." Central to his definition is an understanding of "mediation autonomy" as a relational concept. Thus, unlike the way that autonomy is expressed and understood in traditional liberal theory with its emphasis on privacy and self, mediation autonomy is connected to other human beings; it requires cooperation and collaboration with other persons whose values may differ.

Mediation autonomy has two components which are linked to the principle of informed consent. First, conceptually, the principle of autonomy distinguishes mediation from the adjudicatory dispute resolution processes. Instead of allocating decisionmaking power to a third party, the parties who are affected by a dispute retain such power. Second, mediation autonomy operates as a corrective to paternalism. As a limiting principle, it gives the mediator power to control only the process in which parties' decisionmaking occurs, while the parties retain the power to decide and control the outcome.

*Human Dignity Protected Through Informed Consent*

The principle of informed consent promotes respect for the fundamental value of human dignity in several aspects of mediation decisionmaking. First, the value of dignity is most frequently associated with the right to participate in decisionmaking. When disputing parties can participate directly in the bargaining process, their perceptions of procedural fairness are enhanced. Second, the principle of informed consent guards against unwanted intrusions into highly personal aspects of parties' lives. There is the potential for a high degree of personal exposure in mediation that makes parties' privacy interests vulnerable. As described in one informed consent form: "Mediation may involve the risk of remembering and disclosing unpleasant events. Your disclosures may lead you to feel vulnerable, and the negotiations you enter into can arouse emotions, such as fear and anger, or feelings of anxiety, uncertainty, or frustration." When parties can decide for themselves whether they can tolerate this kind of exposure or personal invasion, the value of human dignity is enhanced.

Third, the principle of informed consent promotes understanding and alleviates the fears associated with lack of information. When parties come to mediation without sufficient knowledge of what is occurring, there is a greater likelihood that they will consciously or unconsciously resist mediation and thus never fully give consent to participate.

Finally, recognition of individual human dignity contributes to a mediation process that is free of fraudulent and coercive influences. The principle of informed consent requires that mediators be honest with both parties and disclose whatever information is necessary to prevent deliberate fraud, manipulation, and trickery. This aspect of the human dignity value of informed consent operates throughout the mediation process.

*Efficiency Promoted by Informed Consent*

The principle of informed consent promotes educated decisionmaking and thus contributes to efficient dispute resolution.

It makes agreements more stable and durable. The idea of consent promotes satisfaction with the mediation process, results in greater compliance with mediated settlement agreements, and realizes greater overall efficiency. The factual disclosures encouraged by the practice of informed consent enhance the settlement process. This allows for decisionmaking that is the product of reasoned judgment based on a sound factual foundation. Informed consent leaves parties with the feeling that the outcome was fair, and thus, there is less likelihood that parties will attempt to rescind or repudiate their agreements.

---

## U.N. SECRETARY-GENERAL, *STRENGTHENING THE ROLE OF MEDIATION IN THE PEACEFUL SETTLEMENT OF DISPUTES, CONFLICT PREVENTION AND RESOLUTION: REPORT OF THE SECRETARY-GENERAL*

U.N. Doc. A/66/811 (June 25, 2012) Annex I: United Nations Guidance for Effective Mediation pp. 23, 24 (2012). Reprinted with the permission of the United Nations (data downloaded 2/1/19).

*Consent*

21. Mediation is a voluntary process that requires the consent of the conflict parties to be effective. Without consent it is unlikely that parties will negotiate in good faith or be committed to the mediation process.

22. A range of issues can affect whether conflict parties consent to mediation. The integrity of the mediation process, security and confidentiality are important elements in cultivating the consent of the parties, along with the acceptability of the mediator and the mediating entity. However, the dynamics of the conflict are a determining factor, and whether parties consent to mediation may be shaped by an interest to achieve political goals through military means, by political, ideological or psychological considerations, or by the actions of external players. In some instances, parties may also reject mediation initiatives because they do not understand mediation and perceive it as a threat to sovereignty or outside interference. In a multi-actor conflict, some, but not all, conflict parties may agree to the mediation, leaving a mediator with the difficult situation of partial consent to commence a mediation process. Moreover, even where consent is given, it may not always translate into full commitment to the mediation process.

23. Consent may sometimes be given incrementally, limited at first to the discussion of specific issues before accepting a more comprehensive mediation process. Consent may be conveyed explicitly or more informally (through back channels). Tentative expressions of consent may become more explicit as confidence in the process increases.

24. Once given, consent may later be withdrawn, especially when there are differences within a party. Armed or political groups may splinter, creating new pressures on the negotiations process. Some splinter groups may pull out of the mediation all together and seek to derail the process.

*Guidance*

25. Mediators need to create a common understanding with the conflict parties on the mediator's role and the ground rules of the mediation. This understanding may be affected by formal mandates for the potential mediation effort or by informal arrangements with the parties. Based on this, mediators need to:

> Understand whose consent is necessary for a viable mediation process to start. If only some of the conflict parties have agreed to the mediation, the mediator may need to engage with the consenting parties and gradually expand the consent base. Such a judgement of "sufficient consent" should be based on an analysis of the different constituencies and an assessment of the possible impact of an initially limited mediation process, as well as the potential for excluded parties to derail the process.
>
> Cultivate consent, in order to create the space for, and a good understanding of, mediation. Informal contacts allow parties to test the waters without committing to a fully-fledged mediation process; this can help address possible fears or insecurities.
>
> Engage with local and community-based actors or organizations, including women's groups, as well as external actors with access to and relationships with conflict parties to encourage the use of mediation.
>
> Use confidence-building measures at different stages to build trust between the conflict parties and between the mediator and the parties, as well as confidence in the mediation process.

Be consistent, transparent and even-handed in managing the mediation process, and respect confidentiality.

Periodically assess whether the process has sufficient consent and be prepared for fluxes in consent throughout the mediation, working to bring the conflict parties back into the process and drawing on the influence of their backers or other third parties as appropriate.

---

## C. Impartiality and Neutrality

There is a wide variance in the mediation literature regarding the definitions of impartiality and neutrality. In some cases, they are used interchangeably as demonstrated in the statement—"the mediator is an impartial or neutral third party who assists disputing parties in managing their dispute." But, as discussed earlier in Chapter 1, the two terms can be distinguished. Impartiality is considered a fundamental mediation norm whereas neutrality is a contestable one. A common understanding of these terms and that adopted in this book is that impartiality refers to the mediator's relationship to the parties while neutrality refers to the mediator's view of the outcome.[2]

An impartial mediator does not favor one party in a mediation over the other. Standard definitions of mediator impartiality hold that the mediator is free from favoritism and bias. For example, the Model Standards of Conduct for Mediators require that mediators conduct the process in an impartial manner and avoid conduct that gives the appearance of partiality. Some standards such as the Swiss Chamber of Commerce Mediation rules link impartiality with the notion of independence, "The mediator is impartial and independent." (Rule 4)

A neutral mediator is essentially indifferent towards the outcome. Her role is to assist the parties in coming to an agreement that they favor, not necessarily one favored by the mediator. In the political context of mediation, the United Nations has made it clear that neutrality is not synonymous with impartiality.

In the following excerpt, the U.N. Secretary-General's report discusses impartiality as a fundamental norm in mediation, but it

---

[2] Douglas N. Frenkel & James H. Stark, The Practice of Mediation 88 (3rd ed. 2018).

distinguishes and limits the role of neutrality where universal values and principles are at stake.

## U.N. SECRETARY-GENERAL, *STRENGTHENING THE ROLE OF MEDIATION IN THE PEACEFUL SETTLEMENT OF DISPUTES, CONFLICT PREVENTION AND RESOLUTION: REPORT OF THE SECRETARY-GENERAL*

U.N. Doc. A/66/811 (June 25, 2012) Annex I: United Nations Guidance for Effective Mediation pp. 24, 25 (2012).
Reprinted with the permission of the United Nations (data downloaded 2/1/19).

26. Impartiality is a cornerstone of mediation—if a mediation process is perceived to be biased, this can undermine meaningful progress to resolve the conflict. A mediator should be able to run a balanced process that treats all actors fairly and should not have a material interest in the outcome. This also requires that the mediator is able to talk with all actors relevant to resolving the conflict.

27. Impartiality is not synonymous with neutrality, as a mediator, especially a United Nations mediator, is typically mandated to uphold certain universal principles and values and may need to make them explicitly known to the parties.

*Guidance*

28. To address the issue of impartiality, mediators should:

Ensure and seek to demonstrate that the process and the treatment of the parties is fair and balanced, including through an effective communications strategy.

Be transparent with the conflict parties regarding the laws and norms that guide their involvement.

Not accept conditions for support from external actors that would affect the impartiality of the process.

Avoid association with punitive measures against conflict parties by other actors and minimize public criticism of the parties as much as possible, while maintaining frank exchanges in private.

Handover to another mediator, or mediating entity, if they feel unable to maintain a balanced and impartial approach.

## IV. LAWYER'S DUTY TO INFORM CLIENTS ABOUT MEDIATION

Given the importance of fairness and justice in mediation and the critical role of self-determination, does this raise questions about informing clients about mediation? Whose responsibility should it be to inform clients? What role should lawyers play in this regard?

Enthusiasm for ADR processes, in particular the mediation process, has motivated several countries to implement policies that would require lawyers to inform their clients about the option of mediation when attempting to manage or resolve legal issues. Italy, for example, has imposed a strict requirement as a way to promote mediation awareness. Lawyers have a duty to inform clients about the option of mediation and to try to resolve disputes using mediation. A litigant can even void the attorney-client contract if counsel fails to provide detailed information about mediation. Likewise, in Ireland lawyers have a statutory obligation to inform their clients about the advisability of using the mediation process to resolve their disputes.

On the other hand, in the United States there is a debate about the extent to which rules should require attorneys to discuss ADR with their clients and whether this should be an ethical obligation. The ABA Model Rules of Professional Responsibility are not specific on this topic: Model Rule 1.2(a) requires lawyers to "abide by a client's decisions concerning the objectives of representation" and obligates lawyers to "consult with the client as to the means by which they are to be pursued." Numerous commentators argue lawyers should instead have an explicit obligation to advise clients on the advantages and disadvantages of appropriate dispute resolution processes. Others oppose this on the ground that it would add inflexibility, increase representation costs, and become a source of malpractice claims.

State mediation legislation typically does not cover this topic, but court rules are used in some states to promote discussion of alternatives to litigation. In Minnesota, a rule that requires parties to consider using ADR in every case is coupled with authority for judges to order mediation. There is evidence that use of mediation increased after this rule was adopted.

## V. ETHICAL ISSUES IN ONLINE MEDIATION

Virtual mediation has assumed a strong presence in the field of ODR. Given the steady growth of on-line mediation activity, questions regarding regulation and accountability arise. Do the Model Standards of Conduct for Mediators apply to virtual mediators? If not, what ethical standards govern or should govern this practice? The important role of technology has spawned the idea that there are "fourth" and "fifth" parties in virtual mediation. Who are these "fourth" and "fifth" parties and what ethical standards apply to them? Thus far, limited guidance has been available.

In the following excerpts, Susan Nauss Exon describes the "fourth" and "fifth" parties in virtual mediation and Leah Wing, co-director of that National Center for Technology and Dispute Resolution, outlines ethical principles for online dispute resolution.

## SUSAN NAUSS EXON, *ETHICS AND ONLINE DISPUTE RESOLUTION: FROM EVOLUTION TO REVOLUTION*

32 Ohio St. J. on Disp. Resol. 609, 664 (2017).

### *The Fourth Party*

The most notable distinction of ODR is the recognition that additional parties play a vital role in virtual mediation. In 2001, Ethan Katsh and Janet Rifkin coined the "fourth party," referring to the technology that provides communication channels for online participants. The fourth party is more than the technology itself; it "is a shared perception, a product of individual and collective consciousness empowered by a multitude of social, cultural, and technical tools." It also changes the dynamics of virtual mediation.

For example, automated procedures provide "assisted decision-making and negotiation support and threaded discussion technology," which helps make decisions in situations that used to require human interpretation of factual information. Elaborate decision trees are created using sophisticated "branching technology." The system asks the user a series of questions to create an accurate description of the dispute. By applying law or other standards to the factual description, the system provides a conclusion in the form of a likely outcome. This conclusion provides greater access to justice because it allows lawyers to offer better advice to clients and facilitates more informed decisions. Additionally, the software creates a record so that participants may review statements and offers made by various parties, and the sequence in which those statements and offers were made. A virtual mediator may capitalize on the recorded language by reintroducing it to illustrate the extent to which parties' interests are aligned.

The fourth party also enables mediators to modify their behavior. Mediators may conduct concurrent caucuses simultaneously with a joint session, avoiding parties' frustrations with the amount of time a mediator may spend with others or interruptions in the flow of negotiations.

Mediators may engage in "pre-communication reframing." This technique allows mediators to capitalize on the asynchronous text-based nature of virtual mediation by directing reframed communication back to the sending party before being communicated to the other party, providing a means to coach good communication skills. Pre-communication reframing differs from similar face-to-face communication in which a party communicates to the other party directly and then the mediator reframes in front of everyone. One easily can see how ODR, including virtual mediation, is changing. No longer does virtual mediation simply imitate face-to-face mediation. The fourth party is creating its own dispute resolution process.

### *The Fifth Party*

Whereas the fourth party is technology, the fifth party is the provider of the technology. For instance, the mediator may own third party tools. The fifth party normally provides a website to enable email, chat, and/or other communication capabilities. Visualize the fifth party as the supplier of a technique since the fifth party does not use the e-mail or chat facilities.

## LEAH WING, *ETHICAL PRINCIPLES FOR ONLINE DISPUTE RESOLUTION: A GPS DEVICE FOR THE FIELD*

3 Int'l J. Online Disp. Resol. 12, 24–27 (2016).

### *Preamble*

The Ethical Principles for Online Dispute Resolution (ODR) are designed to enhance the quality, effectiveness and scope of dispute resolution processes with technological components. Taken together, they can provide a touchstone for best practices, standards, rules, qualifications and certification efforts in dispute resolution and related fields that address dispute resolution processes and practices.

* * *

With the knowledge that there is a diversity of perspectives and practices, and that there will be a constant innovation of new technologies impacting the ways we use, foster and transform conflict, it is worthwhile to formulate and continue to revisit ethical principles to inform, guide and inspire best practices.

* * *

It is likely that more specific or additional principles may be articulated in the future from within particular sectors and jurisdictions. These, instead, are offered as core, shared values and as a living document that can respond to new conditions, technologies, stakeholders and knowledge—to prove sustainable to those relying on it.

*Accessibility.* The design and implementation of efficient and effective processes provide for their usage, not only to the broadest range and number of people, but also by accounting for the reality of cultural differences within and between jurisdictions, as well as differential access to resources and experiences of marginalization that can hinder access to dispute resolution and justice processes, whether formal or informal. ODR systems and processes effectively facilitate and do not limit the right to representation for parties in processes of dispute resolution.

*Accountability.* The development and implementation of ODR systems, processes and practices are accountable to the institutions, legal frameworks and communities that they serve.

*Competence.* ODR systems, processes and practitioners will be competent in or provide access to relevant technological or human competency required for the effective implementation of the dispute resolution process that they undertake to assist with. This includes but is not limited to relevant dispute resolution, legal, and technical knowledge; languages; and culture.

*Confidentiality.* The development and implementation of ODR systems, processes and practitioners maintain confidentiality in accordance with all legal obligations and in a manner that is consistent, in particular, with the principles of Legal Obligation, Informed Participation, Security and Transparency.

*Empowerment.* ODR systems and processes are designed and implemented in ways that seek to enable growth and positive change for individuals, relationships, systems and society, thereby increasing access to justice and enhancement of choices and effective decision making opportunities.

*Equality.* ODR processes are designed and implemented in ways that treat all participants with respect and human dignity; that system design and processes enable silenced or marginalized voices to be heard and actively seek to ensure that privileges and disadvantages are not replicated in the experience of participation; that no participant is placed at a higher risk than others; and, therefore, that ODR processes are designed to respond effectively to the reality that some contexts may put some at more risk than others.

*Fairness*. ODR processes are designed and implemented to facilitate and uphold due process, without bias or benefits for or against individuals or groups, including those based on algorithms. They are responsive to and reflective of the communities and stakeholders they serve.

*Honesty*. ODR processes are designed and implemented with the intention that data is gathered, managed and presented in ways to ensure it is not misrepresented or presented out of context.

*Impartiality*. ODR processes are designed and implemented, and practitioners function with commitment to reducing bias in the delivery of the process. This includes accounting for technological and other conditions that could structure patterns of privilege in process and outcome for repeat players with particular attention to the principles of Accessibility, Fairness and Transparency.

*Informed Participation*. In the development and implementation of ODR systems and processes active effort is made to ensure (1) explicit disclosure to participants of all information about risks and benefits of the process, (2) the competency of participants to evaluate the information about participation in the process, (3) understanding by participants of the information, (4) whenever possible, the voluntary acceptance by the participants of the risks of participating; and whenever voluntary consent is not possible due to the mandatory nature of participation than that is made transparent.

*Innovation*. Online dispute resolution continues to innovate to improve the delivery of dispute resolution services and benefits more fairly, effectively and efficiently in ways that increase peace, trust and access to justice.

*Integration*. ODR processes are effectively integrated both internally within a system and externally with other systems, networks and entities. Technology serves the dispute resolution process as seamlessly as possible. The application of technology and of dispute resolution is designed and implemented in the context of their linkages with other existing systems and networks and of knowledge that new ones will emerge. This is implemented with special attention to the integration with public entities to enhance inclusiveness and access to justice.

*Legal Obligation*. The design and implementation of ODR systems and processes uphold the laws of relevant jurisdictions and ensure that relevant laws are known and followed in the context of the principles of Accessibility, Informed Participation and Transparency.

*Neutrality*. ODR systems and practitioners function with independence from the disputing parties, and any conflicts of interest are made transparent.

*Protection from Harm*. ODR design and implementation seek to prevent and minimize harm and risk for those involved in dispute resolution processes, with particular attention to those most marginalized and with least access to justice.

*Security*. All reasonable efforts are made to ensure that the data and communication between the parties and other entities linked to ODR processes are secure to the fullest extent of the law, making transparent any known limitations.

*Transparency*. All reasonable efforts are taken to make transparent the true purposes, risks and legal obligations inclusive of but not limited to: the form and legal jurisdiction of dispute resolution processes; the identities, affiliations, obligations and conflicts of interest of the parties, entities and systems; and the data security, confidentiality and privacy policies and systems involved.

---

## VI. NOTES AND QUESTIONS

1. *Truthfulness in Mediation:* Empirical studies show that cultural differences result in different attitudes about ethical negotiating behavior. For example, research conducted by Rivers and Lyte discuss what they describe as "ethically ambiguous" negotiation tactics which they define as "maneuver[s] used in the course of a negotiation that may be regarded as wrong by at least some individuals who participate in or observe the negotiation." Two examples offered by the authors are falsely promising to reward the other party at a future time, and offering misleading information to support your case. Recalling the material in Chapter 3 on culture, and given the differences among cultures do you think it is possible or even advisable to have uniform ethical rules regarding truthfulness in international mediation? *See* Cheryl Rivers & Anne Lytle, *Lying Cheating Foreigners!! Negotiation Ethics across Cultures*, 12 Int'l Negot. 1 (2007).

2. This chapter discusses research conducted in Australia showing that mediators have different views on the meaning of justice in mediation. Consider the following findings. Mediators all agreed on the importance of impartiality and neutrality but some mediators

were more willing to intervene when they considered "unfairness" to be involved. Given such findings, do you think it is feasible or even desirable to draft guidelines on what constitutes ethical mediation practice? *See* Mary Anne Noone & Lola Akin Ojelabi, *Ethical Challenges for Mediators around the Globe: An Australian Perspective,* 45 Wash. U.J.L & Pol'y 145 (2014).

3. With respect to the value of neutrality in mediation, Carol Izumi has argued that "the veneer of neutrality is stripped away by research findings that show convincingly that mediators fall far short of the ethical duty to treat parties impartially and without bias." In your view, is it possible for mediators to eliminate or reduce bias in the mediation process? If so, how may this be achieved? *See* Carol Izumi, *Implicit Bias and the Illusion of Mediator Neutrality,* 34 Wash. U.J.L. & Pol'y 71, 155 (2010).

4. What are the differences, if any, in the Model Standards of Conduct for Mediators definition of impartiality and that of the United Nations in its document, United Nations *Guidance for Effective Mediation, Report of the Security General* (2012)?

5. Consider the following description of the mediator's responsibility in China—

> Mediators are governed under the Mediation Regulations of 1989. These rules are important because they are not necessarily Maoist in ideology, nor are they strictly Confucian based. Rather they combine elements of both ideologies, producing a list of wide ranging guidelines for mediators to follow. Under the rules, mediators should educate the public during mediation, but not necessarily about Maoist ideology. Mediators should apply the "laws, regulations, rules and policies" of the government, but where there are no clear laws, mediators should appeal to "social morality."

To what extent can it be said that mediators acting under this description are impartial or neutral? *See* Kevin C. Clark, *The Philosophical Underpinning and General Workings of Chinese Mediation Systems: What Lessons Can American Mediators Learn?* 2 Pepp. Disp. Resol. L.J. 117, 128 (2001).

6. Some scholars have suggested creating a separate set of standards for the "fourth" and "fifth" parties in online mediation and dispute resolution. Do you agree that there is need for separate standards or could the Model Standards of Practice for Mediators with its focus on third-party neutrals be adapted to meet the needs presented by the "fourth" and "fifth" parties? *See* Susan Nauss Exon, *Ethics and*

*Online Dispute Resolution: From Evolution to Revolution,* 32 Ohio St. J. on Disp. Resol. 609 (2017).

7. Do you agree with Waldman and Ojelabi that self-determination and autonomy should not be the single basis to guide mediators' conduct? If so, what principles should have priority in guiding mediators' behavior?

8. Should lawyers have a duty to inform clients about mediation? Would it make a difference if a lawyer believed that mediation was not an appropriate option in a particular case?

# Chapter 6

# COMBINING MEDIATION WITH OTHER ADR PROCESSES

## I. INTRODUCTION

While Chapter 2 examines mediation used by the courts to encourage settlement, this chapter focuses on the combination of mediation with other ADR processes. Parties can do this in multiple ways, and the flexibility of these combinations offers parties an opportunity to structure and control their own resolution method. One of the most common combinations is with arbitration. While many legal practitioners think of arbitration as the process of choice for transnational disputes, it is now criticized as too slow and expensive, having become too much like judicial proceedings. This has created a desire to integrate mediation with arbitration in order to increase efficiency through settlement. In addition, when parties choose to include an arbitration stage as part of a combination with mediation, it can solve one of the major drawbacks of relying solely on mediation—the uncertainty of reaching a resolution. An adjudication step provides assurance that if the parties do not agree to settle their dispute it will nonetheless be resolved in a final and binding way.

There are indications of strong interest globally in combining an adjudicatory process with mediation. At the Global Pound Conference in 2016–2017, stakeholders met at 28 events held in 24 locations around the world to discuss ways to improve commercial dispute resolution. The delegates, with additional participants on line, voted on answers to a series of core questions designed to assess the current dispute resolution landscape and evaluate paths for improvement. One of the key themes that emerged from the voting was a sense that effective dispute resolution currently involves "[c]ombining adjudicative and non-adjudicative processes (e.g. arbitration/litigation with mediation/conciliation)." This was also a very popular choice as a priority for improving the future of commercial dispute resolution.[1]

Mediation is combined with other dispute resolution processes in multiple ways. "Mixed modes" is a general term used to describe both actual combinations of processes and more informal ways that neutrals encourage settlement, including using techniques drawn from other processes.[2] This chapter will focus on functional combinations of processes. First, in Part II, it will discuss multi-tiered dispute resolution clauses, in which parties agree to use a series of separate processes, often including mediation, in a sequence. Then the rest of the chapter will examine multiple ways that parties use mediation in tandem with arbitration.

Under the status quo, mediation and arbitration are the most usually combined processes. The blend can become a hybrid process with its own characteristics that functions differently from either of the component stages. Part III introduces the structures that are most commonly used to combine mediation with arbitration. Part IV then looks at the combination through the eyes of arbitrators, where mediation serves as a settlement process prior to, or during, an ongoing arbitral proceeding. Part V presents a view from the perspective of parties who desire mediation, but who want to add arbitration to aid with the enforceability of their resolution.

Part VI examines one of the major issues with combining processes: the identity of the neutral(s). The processes can be conducted by the different neutrals, but using the same neutral is an attractive way for parties to reduce costs. This practice, however, raises concerns that it will diminish the likelihood of reaching an agreement in mediation, undermine mediation confidentiality protections, and damage the integrity of the subsequent adjudicative process if there is no settlement. Practitioners in different legal systems differ regarding the extent to which having the same neutral is a concern. Part VII explores how different legal and social cultures affect views regarding combining neutral roles along with combining processes.

---

[1] Global Pound Conference Series: Global Trends and Regional Differences, https://www.globalpound.org/.

[2] *See generally* Thomas J. Stipanowich & Veronique Fraser, *The International Task Force on Mixed Mode Dispute Resolution: Exploring the Interplay between Mediation, Evaluation and Arbitration in Commercial Cases,* 40 Fordham Int'l L.J. 839 (2017).

The last two sections explore legal frameworks for combining mediation and arbitration and possibilities for safeguarding important values such as confidentiality and the integrity of adjudication. Part VIII discusses some of the approaches that countries have taken through legislation, and how arbitration and mediation institutions handle these issues. Part IX looks at ways dispute process design can be used to reduce the tensions inherent in combining mediation and arbitration and then considers conditions under which parties can exert self-determination through consent to waive due process rights for pragmatic reasons.

## II. SEQUENCES OF SEPARATE PROCESSES: MULTI-TIERED DISPUTE RESOLUTION CLAUSES

One way that mediation is combined with other processes is with a design that takes the parties through a sequence of distinct stages, which are typically laid out in advance in a dispute resolution agreement. These multi-tiered agreements are also called escalation clauses or step clauses. The steps are treated as separate processes and, if they involve neutrals, the neutral is different for each step. The sequence typically starts with a relatively inexpensive consensual process such as negotiation or mediation. The final step is adjudication (arbitration or, more rarely, litigation), which is used only if the earlier steps in the sequence are exhausted without a settlement. When the parties are able to settle their dispute at an early stage in the sequence, they gain the benefits of using a consensual mechanism. But if they are unable to reach a resolution, they have a plan—and an agreement to use that plan—in place. Ultimately resorting to an adjudicatory process is often disruptive, expensive, and time-consuming—features the parties hoped to avoid by using a multi-tiered procedure—but it provides an assured final resolution to a dispute that cannot be settled by other means.

Arbitration has not always lived up to the hope that it would provide a time- and cost-effective alternative to court processes, and the addition of earlier steps is an effort to resolve disputes with lower costs, less confrontation, and reduced disruption to business relationships. If these earlier steps do not lead to settlement, they add cost to the overall process. But they can also narrow and more clearly define the issues, making eventual adjudication more efficient. The motivation for using tiered clauses has been described as follows:

> [The clause] specifically addresses the concerns for relationship preservation and the need for process economy by maximizing collaborative efforts as the primary tool. The Clause has the added benefit of providing a schematic for well-defined ADR process features. . . . Certainly, settlement achieved by party-principle negotiations lessens relationship risks and dispute expense, particularly when compared with the contentious, expensive, and laborious court system. [This] approach at least provides the opportunity to maintain if not enhance customer, supplier, and employee relationships, which can be costly to establish, difficult to keep, and deadly to lose.[3]

A common, off-the-shelf, structure used in step clauses is to engage first in negotiation, followed (if necessary) by mediation, followed (if necessary) by arbitration. The parties can, however, design a sequence to fit their circumstances and goals. For example, they may choose to start with mediation. Or, to enhance the likelihood of settlement, parties may find it useful to include an additional intermediate stage. One goal for such a step is to provide the parties with additional information in a context that promotes settlement. It can be followed by a "loop-back," which is a return to a consensual process for another attempt at an agreement. By avoiding adjudication unless absolutely necessary, this design can help preserve relationships and keep the decisionmaking power with the parties. Early neutral evaluation is one useful format for an intermediate step designed to provide information that can stimulate settlement. In this process, an expert provides a non-binding assessment of the issues in the case. Another process with a similar goal is the mini-trial, in which party representatives present their cases in an abbreviated hearing to senior management personnel, who then negotiate or mediate.

Another alternative is to include a quasi-adjudicative step involving a decision. Expert determination is one quasi-adjudicative procedure that is especially suited for multi-tiered contracts when the parties anticipate that a dispute will involve complex legal or factual issues, or a valuation. The decision by the expert binds the parties unless it is challenged in a subsequent phase of the proceedings. Dispute boards are a special form of expert determination, most commonly used in construction contracts. An

---

[3] Robert N. Dobbins, *The Layered Dispute Resolution Clause: From Boilerplate to Business Opportunity*, 1 Hastings Bus. L.J. 161, 163–64 (2005).

appointed panel of experts monitors performance and decides disputes between the parties as soon as they arise during the course of the construction project. This helps keep disputes from escalating and prevents them from interfering with ongoing work under the contract.

The goals of having a multi-tiered dispute resolution plan can be achieved only if the parties actually participate in the early stages of the sequence of processes. Thus enforceability of the clause is an important consideration.[4] Legal systems vary in how they regard multi-tiered dispute resolution clauses, with some countries treating them under substantive contract law rules and others, especially in continental Europe, regarding the breach of an obligation to engage in a dispute resolution process as a procedural violation. Enforcement issues arise if one of the parties files a litigation or arbitration claim without first fulfilling its obligations under the agreement to use a preliminary process. In general, when the parties have drafted an enforceable multi-tiered dispute resolution agreement, the court or arbitral panel may dismiss the claim or stay the proceedings while the parties engage in the agreed dispute resolution process(es). To be enforceable, a multi-tiered agreement should, at a minimum, commit the parties to mandatory use of the dispute resolution steps, specify the order of the steps, indicate a time limit for each step in order to trigger the following step, and provide procedures for conducting each of the processes.

The following excerpt acknowledges the advantages of using a sequence of processes, but also notes one of the major limitations of multi-tiered clauses: the practical aspects of developing a resolution may not fit well with a series of separate distinct processes. Thus the parties may benefit from more flexible or more integrated combinations with mediation. These combinations are discussed in the remainder of the chapter.

## THOMAS J. STIPANOWICH & ZACHARY P. ULRICH, *COMMERCIAL ARBITRATION AND SETTLEMENT: EMPIRICAL INSIGHTS INTO THE ROLES ARBITRATORS PLAY*

6 Y.B. on Arb. & Med. 1, 8–9 (2014).

Stepped dispute resolution provisions in commercial contracts are a straightforward response to the reality that most business

---

4 *See generally* Ewelina Kajkowska, Enforceability of Multi-Tiered Dispute Resolution Clauses (2017).

disputes are amenable to a negotiated resolution, and that there are multiple benefits associated with early, informal resolution of disputes. Stepped approaches are intended to function as a series of sieves or filters to cull out all of the issues and controversies that may be resolved short of binding adjudication. Where direct negotiation between representatives of the parties is unavailing, the intervention of a mediator may help break the logjam and craft a workable resolution.

But the linear arrangement of elements in multi-stage dispute resolution templates does not take account of the reality that dispute resolution is very often "non-linear." It is frequently not viewed as possible or practicable to settle a case before the filing of an arbitration demand. This may be because of differing (and often, unrealistic) expectations on the part of counsel or parties regarding the likely disposition of issues should the case go to trial or arbitration or the settlement value of a case, the perceived need for more information, or other factors. . . . When settlement does not occur during the preliminary stages of dispute resolution, the arbitration proceeding becomes the backdrop against which negotiated settlement discussions will occur. In many such cases, mediation is postponed until a relatively late stage in the pre-hearing process when discovery is completed or well-advanced.

---

## III. STRUCTURES USED FOR BLENDING MEDIATION AND ARBITRATION

In addition to forming a key step in multi-tiered dispute resolution clauses, mediation can be combined with arbitration in ways that create new processes with their own advantages, and drawbacks. The following excerpt describes the three most important combinations: med-arb, arb-med, and arb-med-arb (also called mediation windows). In considering their characteristics, it is important to distinguish between two alternative formats: they can be used either with different neutrals for mediation and arbitration or with the same neutral. Using the same neutral can save time and money because there is no need to find a second neutral, and that neutral does not need to be educated about the case. But having a neutral "change hats" also introduces ethical challenges regarding impartiality. Moreover, when a neutral switches from facilitating participation as a mediator to deciding as an arbitrator, the blended hybrid may not function well, and having the same neutral may pose a threat to due process or natural justice values.

## ELLEN E. DEASON, *COMBINATIONS OF MEDIATION AND ARBITRATION WITH THE SAME NEUTRAL: A FRAMEWORK FOR JUDICIAL REVIEW*

5 Y.B. on Arb. & Med. 219, 221–22 (2013).

*Structures for the Combination of Mediation and Arbitration*

The most common combination of mediation and arbitration is med-arb, in which the parties attempt to resolve their dispute using mediation and proceed to arbitration only if they are not successful in reaching a settlement. Commentators praise this combination as offering the parties flexibility and efficiency. . . . . The particular advantage of the med-arb format is that if mediation is successful as the first phase of the process, this means the parties can dispense with adversarial proceedings and entirely avoid the expense of arbitration.

In arb-med, the order of the processes is reversed. After a hearing, the arbitrator formulates an award, but does not share it with the parties. A common procedure is to place it in a sealed envelope. The parties then proceed to mediate their dispute. If they are successful, their agreement is the outcome of the process. If they are unable to agree, the envelope is opened and the award becomes binding. With this sequence, the parties can draw on the development of the case in adjudication to assess its strengths and weaknesses and thus inform their settlement process. Notably, this process can avoid many of the concerns associated with med-arb (discussed below) in that the neutral can conduct the mediation without fear that information he learns will contaminate the arbitration process. But it is not a cost-saving device; the parties must bear the expense of both an arbitral hearing and mediation even if they are able to settle the dispute. As a result, while some neutrals favor arb-med, the process is less popular than med-arb due to the practical cost barriers.

Mediation may also be conducted in the midst of an ongoing arbitration. Termed "mediation windows" or "arb-med-arb", this procedure (using separate neutrals) is authorized by the American Arbitration Association (AAA) Commercial Arbitration Rules, and is a feature of some international commercial arbitrations. In a multi-hearing arbitration, mediation can take place during a period when no hearings are scheduled, so it need not disrupt the arbitration process. It offers both flexibility to schedule the mediation at the time most conducive to settlement and the prospect of substantial savings in arbitration fees.

---

There are other design variations as well. For example, mediation can be combined with last-offer arbitration in a process dubbed MEDLOA. A mediator and arbitrator can work together in what is termed co-med-arb. There is also shadow mediation, in which a mediator observes the arbitration process and steps in when appropriate to facilitate settlement. Unfortunately, even the basic combinations (med-arb, arb-med, and arb-med-arb) lack standard definitions. As Dilyara Nigmatullina notes, to some the term med-arb means that the same neutral will preside over both stages. To others, that is not implied. For some, the parties must agree on the combination prior to engaging in dispute resolution. For others, a second stage can arise organically during a settlement process. Thus it is particularly important for parties to be specific, not just about which process will come first, but also about the details of how the combination will operate.[5]

The extent to which various forms of combinations are used is uncertain. A 2013 survey of arbitrators reported by Stipanowich and Ulrich asked about experience in combined processes using the same neutral. Only about one-quarter indicated this experience. However, in a related survey of mediators, more than half indicated some experience acting as the same neutral in both processes.[6] In contrast, a 2014 study by Dilyara Nigmatullina examined experience with combined processes more generally, with or without the same neutral. She found that 35% of the respondents (whose regional representation was concentrated in continental Europe and common-law countries in Asia) reported experience with a combined process during the prior five years. The most common experience was not with the same neutral in a combined process but with sequential use of processes using a different neutral at each stage.[7] She also found that almost all the respondents recognized benefits from combinations and supported their wider use in some configuration.[8]

---

5 Dilyara Nigmatullina, Combining Mediation and Arbitration in International Dispute Resolution 21–22 (2019).

6 Thomas J. Stipanowich & Zachary P. Ulrich, *Commercial Arbitration and Settlement: Empirical Insights into the Roles Arbitrators Play,* 6 Y.B. on Arb. & Med. 1, 26–28 (2014).

7 Nigmatullina, *supra* note 5, at 89.

8 *Id.* at 113, 115.

## IV. ARBITRATORS' ATTITUDES ABOUT THEIR ROLE IN SETTLEMENT

Because the dominant international dispute resolution process is arbitration, many view blended processes through that lens—as a means to terminate an adjudicatory process. Just as in litigation, parties in arbitration often seek a more cost-effective resolution by attempting to settle their dispute. This raises important questions about what role arbitrators should play in settlement processes. Depending on an arbitrator's philosophy, she may engage in a range of settlement initiatives:

- suggesting that parties try to negotiate a settlement of the case or use a separate neutral as a mediator
- actively participating in settlement negotiations with the parties
- proposing a settlement formula
- meeting with parties separately to discuss settlement options
- hinting at the possible outcome of the arbitration
- rendering a "case evaluation"

The more extensive and intensive an arbitrator's intervention, the more controversial it becomes.

The following two excerpts concern arbitrators' views of their appropriate role in promoting settlement during the arbitration process, typically in what is called arb-med-arb, with the arbitrator serving as a mediator. The first selection discusses findings from a survey of experienced arbitrators. While the researchers found that rates of settlement during arbitration are increasing, they also found that arbitrators hold very different views about their appropriate level of involvement in settlement. The second excerpt examines the question as part of a larger debate about the role of tribunals in international arbitration. The authors argue that facilitating settlement should not be seen as incompatible with the role of an arbitrator as a decisionmaker, and urge arbitrators to promote settlement in response to parties' needs.

## THOMAS J. STIPANOWICH & ZACHARY P. ULRICH, *COMMERCIAL ARBITRATION AND SETTLEMENT: EMPIRICAL INSIGHTS INTO THE ROLES ARBITRATORS PLAY*

6 Y.B. on Arb. & Med. 1, 5–7 (2014).

The role of arbitrators in promoting the informal settlement of disputes before them is a subject that is ripe for deliberation and debate. The topic is intertwined with concerns regarding efficiency and economy in arbitration, which in recent years has been the subject of continuing attention and discussion. . . .

Responses to the CCA [College of Commercial Arbitrators]-Straus Institute Survey indicate that, as was the experience in recent decades with litigated cases, settlement during the course of arbitration procedures, and prior to award, is becoming increasingly prevalent. Curiously, however, many experienced arbitrators apparently do not perceive their arbitral role as extending to the promotion of settlement. The roots of such perceptions are unclear, but may in some cases reflect an all-consuming focus on the arbitrator's adjudicative function. This focus may be reinforced by the sense of discomfort some may feel about shifting to a facilitative role, either because it requires different skills and a different mindset, or because it is viewed as incompatible or even detrimental to the arbitral role. (As we will see, however, it is possible for arbitrators to play a role in settlement without actively facilitating or mediating.) For some, a perhaps-unconscious motivation to ignore opportunities to promote settlement may lie in the desire to maintain sufficient hours of commercial arbitration work in an increasingly competitive environment.

On the other hand, many experienced arbitrators are conducting themselves as proactive managers of the case before them, and many perceive a connection between their activities and settlement. One of the most effective means by which arbitrators "set the stage" for settlement is by ruling upon dispositive motions . . . . A sizable minority of Survey respondents have gone so far as to take more direct action in facilitating settlement, sometimes by embracing dual roles in resolving a dispute (that is, by serving as both a mediator and an arbitrator).

## KLAUS PETER BERGER & J. OLE JENSEN, *THE ARBITRATOR'S MANDATE TO FACILITATE SETTLEMENT*

40 Fordham Int'l L.J. 887, 888–90 (2017).

"Procedural efficiency," "case management," and "proactivity"—these buzz words currently dominate the realm of international arbitration. Most stakeholders have realized that a considerable decrease of the time and costs an international arbitration requires is vital to its future success. There is widespread agreement that crucial to ensuring procedural efficiency is a decisive and proactive arbitral tribunal. There is less agreement regarding another important means of increasing efficiency: settlement facilitation by the arbitrator.

Whether an arbitrator can and should take a proactive approach and get involved in the parties' settlement efforts has been the subject of a controversial debate throughout the past decades. To a large extent, this debate has not yielded definitive answers. At its core lie differing perceptions of the arbitrator's mandate. Is his or her role limited to *deciding* the parties' dispute by rendering an award or should he or she endeavor to *resolve* it, which may include getting involved in settlement discussions between the parties? The answer to that question still markedly depends on the legal backgrounds of those who participate in the debate. While common law arbitrators are more inclined to view their role solely as decision-makers, lawyers with a civil law background follow a more liberal approach and advocate a proactive arbitral role in the parties' settlement attempts.

Historically, such clashes of the civil law and common law traditions have existed in many areas of international arbitration. Today, in a world in which all stakeholders have realized and accepted the need for efficiency and predictability, most of these clashes have been resolved in a more or less pragmatic fashion. Instead of the legal background influencing an arbitrator's procedural conduct, there is an "increasing convergence of approaches used by chairpersons in international arbitration [which] increases the predictability of the international arbitral process." Indeed, it can be considered a hallmark of the modern international arbitrator that he or she is able to adopt different styles of procedural conduct, depending on the specificities and intricacies of the case: "By drawing on a variety of legal traditions but wedding themselves to none, truly transnational arbitrators can promote the effective resolution of disputes by offering unique procedural solutions tailored to the parties' needs."

There is no reason why settlement facilitation by international arbitrators should be an exception. This Article argues that what should guide the arbitrator who is faced with the question whether to facilitate settlement between the parties are not his or her legal upbringing and cultural convictions. Neither should misconceptions about what settlement facilitation actually is deter arbitrators from exploring that option. Rather, the arbitrator should solely be guided by what the parties and the intricacies of the case require. Recent surveys and developments indicate that parties in many cases require their arbitrators to facilitate settlement between them. This Article advocates that this need should not be discarded as incompatible with the arbitrator's mandate. Rather, it is compatible with the arbitrator's judicial role as a decision-maker that he can get involved in settlement discussions with the parties.

---

## V. MED-ARB AS A SOLUTION TO ENFORCEMENT ISSUES

While the previous section looked at combining mediation and arbitration from an arbitration perspective that values the benefits of settlement, there are also reasons to combine the processes from the point of view of parties who wish to engage in mediation. Mediation offers no guarantee of a final resolution, but that can be provided by adding an adjudication step in the event that the parties do not reach an agreement. Moreover, even when the parties do agree to settle their dispute in mediation, they can face enforcement difficulties. The legal landscape for settlement is changing with a new international convention on enforcing mediated settlement agreements. (See Chapter 4 for more details.) Currently, however, one of the motivations for combining arbitration with mediation is to turn a settlement agreement into an arbitral award, which can then benefit from the well-established legal framework for awards' enforcement. This framework is provided by the United Nations Convention on the Recognition and Enforcement of Foreign Arbitral Awards (the New York Convention). As Bobette Wolski discusses in the next excerpt, however, there are important considerations in structuring the combination of mediation with arbitration in order to ensure that the New York Convention will apply.

### BOBETTE WOLSKI, *ARB-MED-ARB (AND MSAS): A WHOLE WHICH IS LESS THAN, NOT GREATER THAN, THE SUM OF ITS PARTS?*

6 Contemp. Asia Arb. J. 250, 261–62 (2013).

In many jurisdictions there is provision for a settlement reached in the course of arbitral proceedings to be recorded as a consent award or "an arbitral award on agreed terms". Such an award may be made "if requested by both parties and accepted by the tribunal". Although the New York Convention is silent on this point, there is wide consensus that these consent awards can be recorded and enforced as arbitral awards under the Convention.

These provisions were designed to encourage parties to an arbitration to settle. Today, they are also used strategically to increase the prospects of enforcing an MSA [mediated settlement agreement]. The timing of mediation in relation to the arbitration is all-important. In order to come within the terms of the New York Convention and similar arbitral systems, the parties must first enter into an agreement to arbitrate a present or future dispute. If the parties commence mediation first and settle their dispute, arguably, there is no dispute on which to base an arbitration agreement. Put another way, to take advantage of arbitration laws in most jurisdictions, the agreement must be reached as a result of a process which began as arbitration, not as a result of one which began as mediation. Some commentators caution that parties who seek a binding MSA and who wish to ensure the applicability of the New York Convention are best advised to agree to submit the dispute to arbitration and at a minimum, to convene the arbitral tribunal before commencing mediation.

---

## VI. BENEFITS AND PROBLEMS WITH USING THE SAME NEUTRAL IN A COMBINED PROCESS

There are many benefits to combining mediation and arbitration. When the parties are able to settle the dispute, they benefit from all the advantages of mediation:

- reduced time and cost of the process
- tailored outcomes that might not be possible through adjudication
- opportunities for the parties to continue a business relationship

Settlements that the parties achieve in mediation during an arbitral proceeding may be issued by the arbitral tribunal in the form of consent awards, which gives them the benefit of the strong international regime for enforcing arbitral awards. And if mediation does not lead to settlement, the arbitral process will result in a final outcome in the form of an arbitral award.

The assessment of advantages and disadvantages becomes more complex when the same neutral presides over both the mediation and arbitration phases of a combined process and this hybrid process is controversial. It is seen by some as "the best of both worlds," with the combination able to offer advantages that neither mediation nor arbitration alone can offer. Others view it as an "ethical disaster."[9] This section examines the issues from multiple perspectives.

In the first excerpt, Fan Kun discusses the perspectives of both supporters and opponents of combining arbitration with mediation using the same neutral, focusing on their views of the goals of the process and its advantages and drawbacks. The second excerpt asks if one neutral can serve in two processes. Harold Abramson contrasts the benefits of using the same neutral in med-arb or arb-med-arb with the risks this can create. These include legal challenges and difficulties in preserving the integrity and functioning of both the mediation and arbitration stages of the process. The third excerpt, by Ellen Deason, concentrates on drawbacks that stem from using the same neutral in med-arb. There are practical and functional limitations on settlement. And, even more importantly, using the same neutral creates concerns for due process and threats to important values in both the mediation and the arbitration phases of the combined process. In the final excerpt, Bobette Wolski summarizes and compares the disadvantages of the med-arb process when used with different neutrals (which she calls "med-arb (diff)") and with the same neutral ("med-arb (same)").

## FAN KUN, *AN EMPIRICAL STUDY OF ARBITRATORS ACTING AS MEDIATORS IN CHINA*

15 Cardozo J. Conflict Resol. 777, 777–78 (2014).

Whether an arbitrator can and should act as a mediator in a pending arbitration is one of the most controversial issues in international arbitration. While mediation is not a new concept for the West, the practice of having the same person acts as both an arbitrator and a mediator in one proceeding has aroused great debate

---

9 Nigmatullina, *supra* note 5, at 29.

in theory and practice. The debate gives rise to delicate ethical issues, and touches the very core of arbitration, i.e., the mission of arbitrators.

The supporters consider that the arbitrators' mission is to ensure that arbitration in general provides the parties with a menu of processes that may assist them in resolving their disputes in the most effective way, which includes assistance in reaching a fair resolution of their differences at the earliest practical time. Thus, the arbitrators' role will include the facilitation of settlement. Another justification for the arbitrators' facilitation of settlement is based on the parties' freedom of choice. If the parties want the arbitrators to carry out a conciliatory role, to use caucus in mediation, and to shift their hat back as arbitrators if the mediation fails, such agreement should be respected. Furthermore, settlement facilitation by arbitrators can be a useful tool to enhance the efficiency of arbitration and to improve the administration of justice.

The opponents of the combination of arbitrator and mediator consider the goal of arbitrators to be solely ensuring that the arbitral process was conducted fairly and resulted in an enforceable award. Thus, promoting settlement should fall beyond the mission of the arbitrators. The main argument against the arbitrators' facilitation of settlement is the risk of a breach of due process and natural justice. Fundamental to the notion of natural justice is the right to know and be able to answer an opponent's case. The rule of due process' governing of disputes' fair hearing on the merits forbids ex parte communications with the decisionmaker. However, the process of mediation often presupposes that there is a separate meeting with the parties (caucusing). During these caucuses, information communicated confidentially to the mediator is not known to the opposing party, and it is not subject to response or clarification by the opposing party. In consequence, the other party may be deprived of its due process right to rebut those facts. Another drawback to the combined approach is the fear that, in the event that the settlement fails and the arbitration continues, the impartiality of the mediator-turned-arbitrator may be affected, mainly because of the confidential information he or she obtained during the mediation phase, which is not part of the record. On the other side of the debate, there is the concern that if the parties anticipate the mediator's potential reversion to arbitrator, in which role she might decide the case if the mediation fails, they might be less candid than they would be with a "pure" mediator. This concern may weaken the effectiveness of the mediation process.

# HAROLD I. ABRAMSON, *PROTOCOLS FOR INTERNATIONAL ARBITRATORS WHO DARE TO SETTLE CASES*

10 Am. Rev. Int'l Arb. 1, 3–4 (1999).

*Can One Neutral Serve Two Processes?*

Practitioners and scholars have debated extensively whether one neutral can serve as both arbitrator and settler in the same case. The benefits are self-evident. Arbitrators who settle cases can save parties time and money. Savings accrue because the case settles rather than continue in the arbitration proceeding. Furthermore, the case settles without adjourning the arbitration to select a mediator who must then be educated about the dispute at a rescheduled session. These savings are magnified in international arbitrations where communications and scheduling of sessions are more difficult among neutrals, parties and attorneys who are from different countries. It is for these reasons that when everybody is already convened in one location for the arbitration proceeding, parties can find the option of the arbitrator settling a case to be extremely attractive.

The primary risk is that one neutral may not be able to perform effectively the two distinctively different roles of arbitrator and settler in the same case. In order to preserve the integrity of each process, the neutral must simultaneously maintain her impartiality as arbitrator and her flexibility as settler.

The neutral must figure out how to preserve her impartiality when trying to settle a case. Settlers, for instance, may solicit confidential information for purposes of settlement, hold ex parte meetings (caucuses), engage in "reality testing," and even assess merits of claims (evaluations). These initiatives may benefit the settlement process but may expose the arbitration process to legal attack. A party may challenge the arbitrator or the award on the grounds that the arbitrator was influenced by information learned during settlement efforts. A party also may claim that the arbitrator prejudged the case during settlement efforts when she offered an evaluation of the merits of the case. A party might even complain that the arbitrator retaliated against the party in the arbitration proceeding for not heeding her advice during settlement discussions. Therefore, arbitrators face the daunting risk of engaging in settlement initiatives that may disqualify them as arbitrators. In trying to reduce this risk, arbitrators may feel compelled to limit their use of some basic techniques that might otherwise make settlement efforts effective.

Other problems arise when the same neutral serves two processes. For settlement efforts to be successful, parties must talk candidly with the neutral. Parties may be reluctant to talk candidly for strategic reasons when they realize that the neutral may later serve as the arbitrator. . . .

## ELLEN E. DEASON, *COMBINATIONS OF MEDIATION AND ARBITRATION WITH THE SAME NEUTRAL: A FRAMEWORK FOR JUDICIAL REVIEW*

5 Y.B. on Arb. & Med. 219, 224–27 (2013).

### *Concerns for the Functionality of Combinations of Mediation and Arbitration*

All of the combinations of mediation and arbitration offer an advantage over either process alone in that they allow the parties to find their own solution (in mediation), while ensuring that the dispute will be resolved even if the parties fail to reach an agreement (through arbitration). While this is advantageous, there are practical difficulties that parties should be aware of when they select a combined process. One is that not all neutrals are qualified for both roles. The appropriate skills are very different; a judicious decision-maker who runs an efficient adversary evidentiary hearing may not be effective in working directly and more informally with the parties to facilitate their own agreement, and vice versa. Some even regard these roles as "fundamentally incompatible" because they are so diametrically opposed.

Moreover, whenever arbitration follows mediation, there is an inherent functional limitation on the potential effectiveness of the mediation step. In med-arb or arbitration windows, the knowledge that the mediator may become a decision-maker may make parties less willing to share information with the neutral during the mediation. Because revealing interests or a bottom-line might influence the neutral's decision, parties may strategically hesitate to provide any information they think could hurt their position in arbitration. For some parties, there may also be a tendency to use mediation to lay the groundwork for arbitration by trying to shape the views of the person who will become the ultimate fact finder. Both of these approaches to mediation will limit the effectiveness of the neutral and of the parties' ability to interact productively during the process to the detriment of prospects for reaching an agreement.

Given the consensual nature of mediation and agreements to engage in arbitration, and the flexibility afforded parties to design their own settlement processes, parties are free to elect a combined process despite these practical and functional limitations. Parties may be willing to accept these shortcomings as a trade-off for the efficiency, the opportunity to structure their own outcome, and the assured finality offered by combining mediation with arbitration. Other aspects of the combination, however, create process concerns . . . . .

*Process Concerns for a Mediated Agreement from a Combined Process*

[T]he combination of mediation with arbitration creates [a] potential source of pressure on mediation norms. Because the parties are aware that the neutral will render an award if they cannot resolve the dispute themselves, it is thought that they have an additional impetus to settle in mediation. While this can be considered a strength of the combined process, if mishandled, the impetus may become coercion. There is a fear that if a neutral wields his decision-making authority as a "big stick," it can undermine party self-determination. Particularly if the neutral has signaled his perspective on the issues, the neutral's ultimate power can lead to an agreement that does not truly represent the will of the parties.

*Process Concerns for an Arbitral Decision from a Combined Process*

When a combined process moves from mediation to an arbitral decision with the same neutral, the potential for information flows within the structure poses additional risks to process norms. The concerns fall into two categories: mediation process norms reflected in confidentiality principles and adjudicative process norms for arbitral decision-making. These process protections promote important goals: to help the parties trust the mediation process (and thus make it more effective) and to protect the integrity of the adjudicatory process.

Mediation confidentiality principles are at stake with combined processes because in an effective mediation phase the neutral will learn information that would not ordinarily be introduced in the arbitration phase. The discussions may include bottom lines, the degree of flexibility in demands or offers, or self-evaluations of weaknesses in the merits of the case. This information may be irrelevant or, more seriously, prejudicial to a decision about the dispute.

Mediation confidentiality serves to insulate participants from disclosures that could affect them in later proceedings and is thus an important principle embodied in procedural rules, statutes, and ethical guidelines for mediators. . . . . The theory (and experience) is that settlement will be more effective if the parties feel free to explore "trial balloons" and express their interests, needs, and priorities. In a process involving one's adversary, confidentiality protections are necessary if parties are to express themselves freely without fear that information they share will be used against them if the dispute is not resolved in mediation.

Arbitral adjudicative principles are also at stake. Our conception of arbitration as an adjudicative process includes at its core an opportunity for parties to be heard and the right to be treated equally. This principle of equality is ensconced in the UNCITRAL Model Law on International Commercial Arbitration and many national laws. It makes combinations of mediation and arbitration problematic in that a party who is not privy to communications between the neutral and the adversary in a mediation may have no knowledge of those communications and thus no opportunity to be heard on issues they raise. Moreover, the knowledge the neutral gains in mediation may lead a party to doubt that neutral's ability to maintain impartiality as a decision-maker. These doubts can be especially strong when the parties have met separately with the neutral in caucuses during the mediation phase. Because of the confidentiality of caucuses, neither party knows what the other side conveyed and thus does not have an effective opportunity to counter that information or cross-examine its source.

## BOBETTE WOLSKI, *ARB-MED-ARB (AND MSAS): A WHOLE WHICH IS LESS THAN, NOT GREATER THAN, THE SUM OF ITS PARTS?*

6 Contemp. Asia Arb. J. 250, 258–60 (2013).

Different models of med-arb have emerged over time. The most well-known models are med-arb (diff) and med-arb (same). In med-arb (diff), the mediation and arbitration phases are undertaken by different third party interveners. The obvious disadvantage of this process is that two third parties have to be educated about the dispute and on two separate occasions if settlement is not reached in mediation. This involves additional time and resources. The additional cost may be offset somewhat by authorizing the mediator to provide the arbitrator with an agreed list of issues in dispute as well as an agreed list of issues not in dispute. The list may be entered into evidence in the arbitration with the agreement of the parties. The advantage of med-arb (diff) is that it avoids potential problems which arise whenever the same third party undertakes the roles of mediator and arbitrator.

In med-arb (same), the same third party first acts as a mediator and then, if necessary, makes a decision on any unresolved issues. There are a number of potential problems with this process. In fact, these problems arise whenever arbitration follows mediation and the same third party conducts both processes. The following behavioral problems may be encountered:

1. The parties might be reluctant to disclose information in a separate session with the mediator for fear that the information will harm them in a subsequent arbitration.

2. Rather than using a separate session to discuss previously undisclosed interests and exploring options for settlement, the parties might treat a separate session as an early trial run of the arbitral hearing, putting their 'best case' to the would-be-arbitrator.

3. If the mediator suggests terms of settlement, the parties might feel unduly pressured to settle on those terms. Suggestions by the mediator might be perceived to foreshadow the outcome of a later arbitration. If the parties settle on these terms, they might feel that they were compelled to do so. The consensual nature of mediation may be undermined.

In some countries, med-arb (same) also raises concerns about procedural fairness (or due process) in that:

1. In a separate session, one party might disclose information which has some bearing on the arbitration. Since the other party may not know that the information was revealed, he or she will not respond to it in a later arbitration.

2. The parties might disclose information in separate sessions which should have no bearing on the arbitrator's decision but which nonetheless causes the mediator/ arbitrator to become biased or at least, to be perceived as biased.

---

## VII. VARIATIONS IN LEGAL CULTURE

Many of the concerns expressed in the previous section about the disadvantages and risks of combining mediation and arbitration with the same neutral come from a common-law perspective. These views are not universally held. In several continental European countries and in many Asian countries, neutrals and parties are more receptive to blended roles than are participants in the United States. Views tend to vary with the cultural background of neutrals and parties, especially the legal culture of settlement in the judicial system and society's attitudes toward conflict and harmony.

One way to look at cultural differences is through the lens of common- and civil-law traditions. Commentators have noted that judges in civil-law systems are more likely to encourage settlement, but attitudes about blending processes do not split cleanly along this line; they appear to be influenced by the example of judicial behavior in specific countries. For example, in Europe, arbitrators in Germany, Switzerland, and Austria have historically integrated encouraging settlement into adjudicatory proceedings more than in some of the other civil-law countries such as France. This stems from the role of the judiciary in those countries, as explained by Klaus Peter Berger:

> [The] proactive role of the arbitrator as "dispute-resolver", rather than a mere "dispute-decider", is deeply rooted in the traditional role of domestic judges in those jurisdictions. The statutory mandate of those judges is not limited to that of a decision-maker. It always includes the active promotion of an amicable settlement of the parties' dispute . . . .[10]

It is possible, however to draw general contrasts between legal systems, and a survey of arbitration practitioners completed in 2004 indicates how much attitudes have traditionally differed. It inquired about arbitrators getting directly involved in a settlement process, in effect acting as mediators. Respondents from civil law countries were familiar with this practice (especially those from Germany), and few had objections to it. In contrast, those from common-law countries (especially the United States) typically responded that they had "practically never" seen arbitrators get involved as mediators, and two-thirds of them regarded it as inappropriate.[11] The settlement

---

[10] Klaus Peter Berger, *The Direct Involvement of the Arbitrator in the Amicable Settlement of the Dispute: Offering Preliminary Views, Discussing Settlement Options, Suggesting Solutions, Caucusing*, 35 J. Int'l Arb. 501, 504 (2018).

[11] Christian Buhring-Uhle, Lars Kirchhoff, & Gabriele Scherer, Arbitration and Mediation in International Business 122 & Figs.11–12 (2006). This is consistent with an earlier 1994 survey in which German respondents reported that they "often" encountered arbitrators participating in settlement negotiations while U.S. participants reported that they "very rarely" saw arbitrators do this. When asked about the propriety of arbitrators participating in negotiations, 92% of German respondents thought it was appropriate, while 71% of U.S. respondents rejected this

rate in arbitration cases also differed; it was higher in civil law jurisdictions. For example, German respondents reported a settlement rate (69%), twice that of American respondents (33%). Hybrid processes are also used in several Latin American countries. In some, legislation sets the legal culture regarding combining processes. For example, in Brazil, arbitrators have a duty to conciliate at the beginning of arbitration under the Brazilian Arbitration Act.[12]

There is also significant regional variation between practices in East Asia and the West. East Asian arbitrators tend to play a significantly more active role in settlement. In a 2006–2007 survey, practitioners from East Asia were much more likely to report that arbitrators engage in settlement activities than were Western respondents:[13]

- suggesting settlement negotiations to the parties (40% East Asia; 16% West)
- regularly participating in settlement negotiations (30% East Asia; 16% West)
- meeting separately with the parties (26% East Asia; 8% West)
- suggesting a settlement formula (17% East Asia; 4% West)

The most complete combination of the role of mediator and arbitrator is found in China. In some other Asian countries the practice is to suspend arbitration hearings during mediated settlement attempts. But in China, the process is thoroughly integrated—mediation may occur during an ongoing arbitration with no clear distinction between the arbitration and mediation phases of the process. A survey in 2011–2012 of active Chinese arbitrators found that they consider it appropriate to suggest mediation to the parties at the arbitrator's own initiative (91.7% of respondents); meet with the parties separately during mediation (80.6%); and make a

---

role for arbitrators. Christian Buhring-Uhle, Arbitration and Mediation in International Business 189–96 (1996).

[12] *See* Pedro Alberto Costa Braga de Oliveira, *Designing Effective Med-Arb and Arb-Med Processes in Brazil,* 2 NYSBA New York Dispute Resol. Law., Spring 2009, at 89.

[13] Shahla F. Ali, Resolving Disputes in the Asia-Pacific Region: International Arbitration and Mediation in East Asia and the West (2011).

settlement proposal (27.8% at arbitrator's initiative and 63.9% with a joint request from the parities).[14]

The extent to which arbitrators act as mediators in China is influenced by multiple cultural factors—both social and legal. In the first excerpt below, Fan Kun relates the use of mediation during arbitration to several of the cultural dimensions introduced by Geert Hofstede (which are discussed in Chapter 3). Second, Christine Kang describes how Chinese settlement practices during arbitration have been influenced by the tradition of Confucianism, the extensive use of mediation by the judiciary, and the influence of the China International Economic and Trade Arbitration Commission (CIETAC), which was the first institution for international arbitration in China. In sum, social attitudes and legal practices may shape participants' attitudes toward having one neutral serve two different roles.

## FAN KUN, *AN EMPIRICAL STUDY OF ARBITRATORS ACTING AS MEDIATORS IN CHINA*

15 Cardozo J. Conflict Resol. 777, 786 (2014).

Psychologists have increasingly recognized the important role that culture and cultural values have in shaping conflict and conflict resolution. It has been argued that in societies where interpersonal relationships are more stable and long-lasting, procedures that allow for compromises are preferred. China is a very long-term-oriented society, according to Professor Geert Hofstede's definition of cultural dimensions. In a society where relationships play an essential role not only for social, but economic reasons[, p]arties tend to seek an arbitrator who is often viewed as someone who is familiar with the parties and their dispute. Moreover, parties seek an arbitrator who will not only end their dispute, but will also assist them in reaching a mutually agreeable solution with as little loss of face as possible. Power distance may be another cultural dimension relevant to dispute resolution. Research shows that people with a high level of power distance place less weight on procedural justice than on distributive justice concerns. In other words, procedural fairness was considered to be less important by those who accept the legitimacy of the authority (high on power distance). Chinese culture places a high level on power distance, i.e., China is a society which believes that inequalities between people are acceptable. The Chinese parties may care less about the due process and natural justice concerns raised

[14] Fan Kun, *An Empirical Study of Arbitrators Acting as Mediators in China*, 15 Cardozo J. Conflict Resol. 777, 790–91 (2014).

by the opponents of arb-med, and they may focus more on having the disputes resolved in the most efficient manner. As a result, arbitrators acting as mediators may be easily acceptable in China.

## CHRISTINE KANG, *ORIENTAL EXPERIENCE OF COMBINING ARBITRATION WITH CONCILIATION: NEW DEVELOPMENT OF CIETAC AND CHINESE JUDICIAL PRACTICE*

40 Fordham Int'l L. J. 919, 921–24 (2017).

The "combination of arbitration with conciliation" is a hybrid dispute settlement mechanism that permits the parties to make use of conciliation in the process of arbitration, which is well known as the "oriental experience" or "Chinese experience." It is widely used in arbitration proceedings by almost all of the 235 Chinese arbitral institutions . . . . . It is also explicitly supported by the Arbitration Law of the People's Republic of China ("PRC Arbitration Law"), which allows the arbitral tribunal to proactively conciliate the dispute during arbitration proceedings and even requires the arbitral tribunal to do so if the parties voluntarily apply for conciliation. If the parties reach settlement during conciliation in the arbitration proceedings, the arbitral tribunal shall issue a conciliation statement recording the claims and the terms of the settlement between the parties, which will be signed by the arbitrators, sealed by the arbitration institution, and served on the parties. Specifically, the PRC Arbitration Law vests in the conciliation statement with the "same legal force as that of an arbitral award" rendered based on the merits of case.

Indeed, the combination of arbitration with conciliation is vibrant and widely applied in most arbitral proceedings in China. . . . . [I]t is typical in practice for the arbitral tribunal, when having a clearer picture about what has taken place between parties at the end of the oral hearing, to invite the parties to consider whether they would like the arbitral tribunal to conciliate their disputes. . . .

Rome was not built in a day. To figure out the reasons why the combination of arbitration with conciliation is so popular in China, one should look at the historical background of the Chinese arbitration practice. The combination of arbitration with conciliation has been deeply rooted in the Chinese arbitration practice for over half a century. . . . . CIETAC conducted arbitration in the mediation-arbitration ("med-arb") model at the very beginning, as it tried every effort to conciliate the dispute before rendering an award. The first CIETAC Arbitration Rules, promulgated in 1988, set up a rule explicitly vesting in the arbitral tribunal with the authority to conciliate disputes. In 1994, the PRC Arbitration Law accepted this mechanism in its text honoring the successful CIETAC experience of combining arbitration with conciliation. Subsequently, many newly established Chinese arbitral institutions also adopted a similar mechanism in their arbitration rules. Therefore, the combination of arbitration with conciliation has developed for more than half a century in China and has been strongly promoted by both Chinese law and the leading Chinese arbitration institutions. Given the leading role of CIETAC in creating and promoting the combination of arbitration with conciliation, the oriental experience is considered the main characteristic of the CIETAC arbitration practice. . . .

Among all kinds of factors contributing to the success and popularity of conciliation in Chinese dispute resolution practice both in litigation and in arbitration, the Confucianism that advocates harmony and opposes litigation is widely regarded as the philosophical basis of conciliation in China. The prominent character of Chinese society given that the basic unit of traditional Chinese society was not based on individuals but rather every small community causes people to gravitate towards conciliation rather than adversarial proceedings. Besides the long-standing and deep-rooted culture and social factors, China's government intensively promotes conciliation and other alternative dispute resolution mechanisms. The conciliation is regarded as an important part of harmonious society, a political goal of the Chinese Central Government of the day, and has been strongly promoted for decades. Following this guideline, the Chinese Supreme People's Court and the Ministry of Justice officially required the Chinese courts to promote and enhance conciliation in judiciary practice. Since recently, the conciliation was further elevated to an unprecedented priority in the Chinese judiciary practice as one of the alternative dispute resolution methods for the purpose of achieving the rule of law in China.

---

## VIII. LEGISLATION AND INSTITUTIONAL RULES

### A. Legislation

Most arbitration and mediation legislation is silent on combining these processes. The UNCITRAL Model Law on International Commercial Mediation and International Settlement

Agreements Resulting from Mediation (described in more detail in Chapter 4) establishes a default rule that prohibits a mediator from serving as an arbitrator for the same or related dispute. However parties can elect to use the same neutral by mutual agreement. (See Box 1.) This Model Law has been adopted by 33 nations.

**1. Example of a Default Prohibition on Using the Same Neutral**

**UNCITRAL Model Law on International Commercial Mediation and International Settlement Agreements Resulting from Mediation** (2018).

Art. 13. Unless otherwise agreed by the parties, the mediator shall not act as an arbitrator in respect of a dispute that was or is the subject of the mediation proceedings or in respect of another dispute that has arisen from the same contract or legal relationship or any related contract or legal relationship.

Several nations, however, have enacted arbitration legislation that explicitly allows combinations with mediation using the same neutral. The supportive approach of China's arbitration legislation, which permits arbitrators to mediate with the acceptance of the parties, is described in the excerpt above. Singapore has a provision that permits combinations using the same neutral with written consent of the parties. It addresses concerns about the enforceability of arbitral awards that result from a combined process by prohibiting challenges to the result of an arbitration on the ground that the arbitrator served as a mediator. (See Box 2.) Hong Kong has an almost identical provision in its Arbitration Ordinance.[15]

Some of the national laws that authorize combinations using the same neutral attempt to address the problems associated with this practice. Singapore uses a disclosure approach to try to minimize due process problems in subsequent arbitration while also preserving flexibility to use caucuses during the mediation phase. If the neutral obtains any confidential information during mediation and the case does not settle, before resuming arbitration the neutral must disclose to all the parties "as much of that information as [the arbitrator] considers material to the arbitral proceedings." This provides a safeguard against the danger that an arbitrator will decide a case based on confidential information received during the mediation.

15 Cap. 609 Hong Kong Arbitration Ordinance § 33.

Again, Hong Kong follows the same pattern. But it is reportedly not popular with Hong Kong mediators, who see it as undermining the assurances of confidentiality that are essential for process. (See Chapter 4 for more on confidentiality protections.) They predict that with disclosure looming, parties will not engage in the candid and open communication that is crucial for a successful mediation. They also argue that arbitrators have not been trained with mediation skills. For both these reasons, they believe that the parties are less likely to obtain the benefits of a mediated settlement with a combined process under these rules.[16]

**2. Example of Legislation Permitting the Same Neutral**

**Singapore International Arbitration Act** § 17 (2012).

17. Power of arbitrator to act as conciliator.

(1) If all parties to any arbitral proceedings consent in writing and for so long as no party has withdrawn his consent in writing, an arbitrator or umpire may act as a conciliator.

(2) An arbitrator or umpire acting as conciliator—

(a) may communicate with the parties to the arbitral proceedings collectively or separately; and

(b) shall treat information obtained by him from a party to the arbitral proceedings as confidential, unless that party otherwise agrees or unless subsection (3) applies.

(3) Where confidential information is obtained by an arbitrator or umpire from a party to the arbitral proceedings and those proceedings terminate without the parties reaching agreement in settlement of their dispute, the arbitrator or umpire shall before resuming the arbitral proceedings disclose to all other parties to the arbitral proceedings as much of that information as he considers material to the arbitral proceedings.

(4) No objection shall be taken to the conduct of arbitral proceedings by a person solely on the ground that that person had acted previously as a conciliator in accordance with this section.

Australia has taken a somewhat different approach that relies on renewed party consent along with disclosure before arbitration

16 Nadja Alexander, *Opening the Mediation Window in the Arbitration House*, 20 Canadian Arb. & Med. J. 37, 38 (2011).

with the same neutral can follow mediation. This approach, and criticisms of the way it operates in practice, is described in the following excerpt.

## BOBETTE WOLSKI, *ARB-MED-ARB (AND MSAS): A WHOLE WHICH IS LESS THAN, NOT GREATER THAN, THE SUM OF ITS PARTS?*

6 Contemp. Asia Arb. J. 250, 263 (2013).

The "solution" adopted in . . . . Australia's new commercial arbitration legislation is based on the consent of the parties. The parties must be given several opportunities to opt out of the arrangement if they have concerns about the same person serving as arbitrator after a failed mediation. The parties must give explicit consent: at the outset, to the same person acting as both arbitrator and mediator; to that third party holding separate sessions in mediation; and after a failed mediation has been terminated, to the same third party proceeding to arbitrate. In order for consent to proceed to arbitration to be meaningful, the drafters of the legislation reasoned that the parties must know what was said in separate sessions in mediation. . . . [T]he mediator-arbitrator is required to disclose to the parties any confidential information learned during separate sessions which the arbitrator considers material to the arbitration. These provisions have been criticised on two grounds. First, the third party is placed in the difficult position of having to determine whether or not something said in a separate session is "material" to the arbitration. Second, if information from a separate session is disclosed, inroads are made into the confidentiality of separate sessions. The parties are unlikely to be candid and forthcoming in separate sessions if they know that information might be passed onto the other party. In the view of one author, "these apparent attempts to encourage the practice of arb-med . . . . is, in reality, more likely to discourage the practice."

---

## B. Institutional Rules and Guidelines

Arbitral institutions' rules increasingly have provisions on using mediation and there are many variations in their approaches. They all typically provide that a settlement will be entered as a consent award based on the agreed terms. As shown by the examples below, however, the rules differ on how they coordinate the two stages of the process and how they treat the question of using the same neutral.

As mentioned in the excerpt by Christine Kang, CIETAC, the first institution for international arbitration in China, has supported combined processes from its founding. Currently the rules provide for parties to use conciliation by the arbitral tribunal during the arbitration, or use a settlement process conducted outside the tribunal. The tribunal may conciliate the dispute only if both parties wish to conciliate, or if one party wishes to conciliate and the other consents. The tribunal must terminate the conciliation at the request of either party. If that happens, or if the parties fail to reach a settlement agreement, arbitration proceeds.[17]

In contrast, under the International Centre of Dispute Resolution of the American Arbitration Association (ICDR) rules, mediation is generally an independent process. Mediation may proceed concurrently with arbitration under the ICDR Mediation Rules. The mediator shall not be appointed as the arbitrator for the arbitration proceedings unless the parties agree to use the same neutral.[18] The International Chamber of Commerce (ICC) approach is similar, with an independent proceeding under the ICC Mediation Rules that can proceed in parallel with adjudication. Again, there is a default rule that the mediator shall not act in any judicial or arbitral proceeding related to the dispute unless the parties agree otherwise. [19] The International Centre for the Settlement of Investment Disputes (ICSID) has a new set of Mediation Rules, which prohibit a mediator from acting as an arbitrator, counsel, expert, witness, judge, or in any other capacity in any proceeding relating to the dispute that is the subject of the mediation, unless the parties agree otherwise.[20]

In Singapore, there are not only separate mediation rules, but the case is sent to a different institution for mediation with a different neutral. The Singapore International Arbitration Centre (SIAC) allows disputes to be mediated at the Singapore International Mediation Centre (SIMC) during the arbitration proceeding, provided there is an arb-med-arb agreement between the parties and provided the arbitral tribunal has stayed the case. If no settlement is reached in mediation, the case returns to arbitration at SIAC[21]

---

17 CIETAC Arbitration Rules Art. 47 (2014).

18 ICDR International Dispute Resolution Procedures Art. 32 (2014).

19 ICC Mediation Rules Art. 10(3) (2014).

20 ICSID Mediation Rules Art. 8(7).

21 Arb-Med-Arb Protocol, SIMC.

CEDR, the Centre for Effective Dispute Resolution, a dispute resolution organization based in the United Kingdom, convened a commission to review settlement practices in arbitration and make recommendations to improve this aspect of international arbitration. The Commission concluded that, unless the parties agree otherwise, an arbitral tribunal should take steps to assist the parties in reaching a negotiated settlement of their dispute. But it asserted that the primary responsibility of an arbitral tribunal is to produce an award that is binding and enforceable. In order to protect that function, the Commission decided that a tribunal should not act in any way to make an arbitral award susceptible to challenge when helping the parties with settlement. Specifically, an arbitrator or tribunal should not meet separately (caucus) with a party or obtain information that is not shared with the other parties. That is because this aspect of med-arb or arb-med-arb poses a threat to the integrity of the arbitration process. An exception can be made if meeting separately is acceptable in all the court systems that might consider the validity of the award, or if the parties consent. [22] Coupled with their recommendations to discourage arbitrators from obtaining confidential information during a mediation phase, however, the Commission adopted provisions allowing arbitrators to engage in activities that many regard as controversial.[23] The following excerpt describes the measures arbitrators may use to facilitate settlement under the CEDR rules and voices criticisms of these methods.

## THOMAS J. STIPANOWICH & ZACHARY P. ULRICH, *COMMERCIAL ARBITRATION AND SETTLEMENT: EMPIRICAL INSIGHTS INTO THE ROLES ARBITRATORS PLAY*

6 Y.B. on Arb. & Med. 1, 14–15 (2014).

*Arbitrators Directly Facilitating Settlement: The CEDR Commission*

The work of the CEDR Commission on Settlement in International Arbitration represents the first major international effort to focus specifically on settlement during arbitration. Its stated intent is establish a broad-based international consensus on the role of international arbitrators in facilitating settlement, but although the effort is in many respects commendable it envisions roles for

---

[22] CEDR Commission on Settlement in International Arbitration: Final Report 2–3 (2009). https://www.cedr.com/about_us/arbitration_commission/Arbitration_Commission_Doc_Final.pdf.

[23] *See* CEDR Rules for Facilitation of Settlement in International Arbitration, Art. 5. https://www.cedr.com/about_us/arbitration_commission/Rules.pdf.

arbitrators in the active facilitation of settlement that fall well short of a consensus model and are in some respects controversial.

To some extent, the *CEDR Recommendations* and *CEDR Rules for Facilitation of Settlement in International Arbitration* cover ground also touched upon by other recent guidelines, including the notion of conducting arbitration proceedings "in conjunction with other processes to achieve efficient and cost-effective outcomes," the value of multi-tier dispute resolution clauses and the use of a "mediation window" during arbitration.

Central elements of the Rules, however, are drawn from German, Swiss and Chinese practices that are not universally embraced. The Rules state that in the absence of a contrary written agreement arbitrators may take any of the following measures for the purpose of facilitating settlement:

> 1.1. provide all Parties with the Arbitral Tribunal's preliminary views on the issues in dispute in the arbitration and what the Arbitral Tribunal considers will be necessary in terms of evidence from each Party in order to prevail on those issues;
>
> 1.2. provide all Parties with preliminary non-binding findings on law or fact on key issues in the arbitration;
>
> 1.3. where requested by the Parties in writing, offer suggested terms of settlement as a basis for further negotiation;
>
> 1.4. where requested by the Parties in writing, chair one or more settlement meetings attended by representatives of the Parties at which possible terms of settlement may be negotiated.

These provisions go well [beyond] the scope of other initiatives . . . . by projecting arbitration tribunals into a much more forthright role as settlement masters. Many arbitrators are likely to be uncomfortable with presenting preliminary views or findings, offering suggested settlement terms, or facilitating settlement discussions. Any or all of these approaches may be seen by some as undermining perceptions of arbitral impartiality, or taking arbitrators well beyond their adjudicative comfort zone into a realm that may require different skills and a different mindset. Others may be reasonably concerned about the ability of arbitrators to filter out communications made during settlement discussions in arriving at an award; or how and when an arbitration tribunal decides settlement facilitation should occur; how tribunals are to reach a consensus on preliminary views or findings; and how they are collectively to facilitate settlement between the parties.

Despite these concerns, the *CEDR Rules* offer a platform for beta-testing of procedures that thrust arbitrators into the heart of the settlement dialogue, and a tangible alternative for those parties and arbitrators who are comfortable with the CEDR format. For the time being, however, many parties and arbitrators may be reluctant to make the leap afforded by the *CEDR Rules*.

## IX. SAFEGUARDS THROUGH PROCESS DESIGN AND PARTY CONTROL THROUGH CONSENT AND WAIVER

This final section introduces some steps that arbitral institutions, arbitrators, and parties can take to avoid or minimize the dangers med-arb can pose to effective mediation, confidentiality, and adjudicatory due process principles. Under principles of self-determination, parties should be free to decide that they want to use of a combination of mediation and arbitration in some form. In that case, the first excerpt proposes some protective design configurations. Note that many of these designs involve some form of compromise as they attempt to offer ways to obtain many of the benefits of a combined process while also preserving parties' rights to due process in adjudication and to confidentiality in mediation.[24]

Under the same principles of self-determination, however, parties can waive those rights. This raises important questions about appropriate conditions for consent. For example, while the CEDR Commission determined that arbitrators should not meet separately with parties during mediation, it recognized that some parties will nonetheless want to use caucuses. It therefore recommended safeguards for arbitrators who use separate meetings in facilitating settlement. These safeguards concern the conditions for party consent.[25] In the following selection, Ellen Deason draws on the CEDR safeguards and on U.S. court decisions on waiver in the context of med-arb to propose standards for informed consent by

[24] For a thorough examination of potential design options for combinations of mediation and arbitration, see generally Nigmatullina, *supra* note 5.

[25] CEDR Commission on Settlement in International Arbitration: Final Report, App.2 (2009).

parties who desire to use a process that contemplates arbitration following mediation.

## ELLEN E. DEASON, *COMBINATIONS OF MEDIATION AND ARBITRATION WITH THE SAME NEUTRAL: A FRAMEWORK FOR JUDICIAL REVIEW*

5 Y.B. on Arb. & Med. 219, 245–48 (2013).

*Protecting Process Rights through Design and Consent*

When a party agrees to arbitration, [according to *Mitsubishi Motors Corp. v. Soler Chrysler-Plymouth, Inc.,* 473 U.S. 614, 628 (1985)] it "trades the procedures and opportunity for review of the courtroom for the simplicity, informality, and expedition of arbitration." This does not mean, however, that when a party agrees to a combined process it necessarily gives up the fundamental process rights of equal treatment and an opportunity to be heard that are associated with arbitration as well as litigation. Nor does an agreement to use a combined process necessarily surrender the confidentiality rights associated with mediation. The combined process can be designed to minimize, and to some extent avoid, these problems, although these solutions often come with the price of decreased efficiency. Alternatively, parties can waive their rights, but in this situation courts should ensure that this waiver was both knowing and voluntary.

The most straightforward way to design a combined process that avoids the problems is to employ separate neutrals. There are ways to do this that retain at least some of the practical advantages of a same-neutral design. For a mediation windows process that can take place in the midst of arbitration, a separate neutral can serve as a "stand-by mediator" who observes the arbitration and reads the briefs. This neutral is then already educated about the dispute in case the parties want to attempt mediation. By integrating the two processes to this degree, the design improves efficiency over two separate processes involving different neutrals. With a panel of three arbitrators, some separation between neutral functions can be achieved if the two party-appointed arbitrators take on the role of co-mediators, excluding the presiding arbitrator from the mediation process. Then if there is no settlement the arbitral decision is left to the presiding arbitrator who has not heard any confidential communications during mediation.

Another way to retain an opportunity for the parties to settle the case in mediation without information flowing into arbitration is to use the arb-med process. Although, as noted, this design eliminates the cost savings associated with a med-arb settlement because the parties must incur the expense of the arbitration in any event, it does offer the advantage of finality if mediation fails, with the lesser expense of only one neutral.

It is also possible to conduct the mediation without using caucuses. While the mediator may still learn things that are irrelevant or prejudicial to the arbitration, at least all the parties would be aware of these communications, and would have an opportunity to respond. This no-caucus approach is consistent with the recommendations of the CEDR Commission on Settlement in International Arbitration, which reviewed settlement practices and drafted rules and guidelines designed to promote improvements. The rules developed by the Commission provide that an arbitral tribunal shall not "meet with any Party without all other Parties being present; or obtain information from any Party which is not shared with other Parties."

If the parties want separate meetings, however, their effect on adjudicatory norms can be minimized using the approach of the Hong Kong Arbitration Ordinance, which permits an arbitrator to serve as a mediator with the parties' written authorization. If the neutral obtains any confidential information during mediation and the case does not settle, before resuming arbitration he must disclose to all the parties "as much of that information as the arbitrator considers is material to the arbitral proceedings."

Absent a protective design for a combined process, the parties may alternatively waive their rights. But the nature of the combined process they have agreed to use, and the extent of their waiver, must be clear. This is important not only to protect the rights of the parties, but to ensure enforcement of a resulting award. Courts undertaking review of such waivers should not be bound by the deferential standards of the FAA [U.S. Federal Arbitration Act] because, . . . . if valid, the waiver of a fundamental aspect of arbitration should remove it from the scope of the FAA's coverage of "arbitration."

The following proposal for standards for consent is drawn from the court decisions that have carefully considered the appropriate conditions for waiver and from the recommendations of the CEDR Commission on Settlement in International Arbitration. First, consent should be contained in a written agreement signed by the parties. This is consistent with the FAA's writing requirement for an enforceable arbitration agreement and with the Uniform Mediation Act's writing requirement for waivers of the mediation privilege.

Second, the consent should include a clear definition of the processes that the parties will use in mediation and in presenting their cases to the decision-maker. In order to dispense with a hearing or other submission of evidence in the arbitration phase, the agreement needs to specifically authorize the arbitrator to rely on information presented during the mediation. [When] a confidentiality statute provides a mediation privilege or prohibits a decision-maker from relying on communications made in mediation, the parties need to satisfy the statutory standards for waiving the confidentiality requirements. With regard to the mediation process, the agreement should specify whether ex parte contacts are permitted and, if they are, how the neutral is to handle information gathered during caucuses. This may include a requirement that the neutral disclose information learned in confidence in the mediation.

Third, if the agreement was made before the dispute arose or before the mediation phase of the combined process, it should be affirmed by the parties before proceeding (or returning) to arbitration. [As described by CEDR, consent] given after the mediation phase is "particularly important because it is given in the knowledge of developments during the mediation." Without an option to select a new neutral at this stage, a party may argue that its consent was not given on a fully informed basis in that it was not aware the neutral would learn of matters that were discussed in the mediation.

It is important that the parties understand the full implications of their consent to use the same neutral and to the procedures they have selected. They need to appreciate that the neutral's functions during the mediation phase are inconsistent with expectations for an arbitrator's behavior and that the mediator is likely to learn information that would otherwise be confidential and that might influence her later judgment as an arbitrator.

---

In the final excerpt, Harold Abramson proposes twelve protocols that arbitrators should embrace if they decide to settle a case. Many of them consist of practices followed in stand-alone mediation. The rest relate to issues that arise from combining the two processes with one neutral. While these are written as recommendations for arbitrators, they are also design options that parties could impose on arbitrators in a dispute resolution agreement. Some of protocols modify the mediation process in ways that turn it into what Abramson calls "quasi-mediation." This is because they restrict the activities of an arbitrator who is mediating in order to protect the parties' due process rights in a resumed arbitration.

## HAROLD I. ABRAMSON, *PROTOCOLS FOR INTERNATIONAL ARBITRATORS WHO DARE TO SETTLE CASES*

10 Am. Rev. Int'l Arb. 1, 2, 7–15 (1999).

International arbitrators can safely encourage parties to settle. They can suggest that parties consider settling or trying mediation with another neutral of their choice. When taking these initiatives, arbitrators stay out of direct participation in settlement negotiations.

Arbitrators also might dare to participate directly in settlement efforts. This initiative is controversial and fraught with risks. . . . . Ideally, I think international arbitrators should stay out of the direct settlement business. I favor the optimal arrangement in which the neutral who tries settling a case is different from the neutral who decides the case. This arrangement preserves the impartiality of the neutral as decisionmaker while giving the neutral as settler the maximum flexibility to do her job well.

But as a pragmatist, I worry about lost opportunities for settlement in international arbitrations. In many international disputes, it can be extremely cumbersome to convene all the parties and attorneys. The first opportunity for the participants to meet face-to-face may not arrive until the first day of the arbitration hearings (or the night before in a foreign city while recovering from jet-lag.) This first opportunity to meet may be the first real opportunity for participants to discuss settling the case. In this paper, I consider whether these settlement discussions can be facilitated by the arbitrators. This may be feasible when done under strict safeguards. When participants agree to follow carefully crafted protocols, this suboptimal arrangement may be capable of preserving the impartiality of arbitrators while offering limited opportunities for efficient, cost-effective, and fair settlement of disputes.

* * *

*Protocols for Arbitrators Settling Cases*

Parties and neutral(s) should adopt protocols that will reduce the inherent risks that arise when one neutral serves two processes. Any protocols must manage the tension between the need to preserve the impartiality of the arbitrator and the need to give the neutral sufficient flexibility to conduct effective mediations or quasi-mediations. This tension erupts when the neutral as mediator contemplates caucusing with one party or providing an evaluation of the case. Does the use of these two settlement techniques by a neutral inherently compromise the appearance of impartiality of the neutral when she resumes arbitrating? The tension also surfaces when the neutral as mediator learns information during settlement efforts that should be disregarded by the neutral in the arbitration proceeding. Is it possible for the neutral to erect a mental wall that strictly separates information, insights, and views developed during settlement efforts from the record of evidence developed in the arbitration proceeding?

The antagonism against the same neutral serving as both mediator and arbitrator in the same case is reflected in the clear prohibition found in most arbitration and mediation rules. But most rules authorize an exception: they permit parties to waive this prohibition. For this waiver to be meaningful, the consent must be informed and uncoerced. Informed consent can be achieved through a discussion of the protocols described below. The protocols elaborate on a number of issues that participants should consider before giving consent. Uncoerced consent is more likely when a party first suggests that the participants try settling than when an arbitrator makes the suggestion. An arbitrator's suggestion may be interpreted as an order that if not followed will alienate the arbitrator. Nevertheless, arbitrators can try to broach the topic tactfully and creatively. For example, they might sincerely advise the parties that they routinely and non-judgmentally ask whether any parties are interested in trying to settle the case. . . . .

(1) *Neutral is Trained in Both Processes.* The neutral who serves as both settler and arbitrator should be trained in the ethics, norms, and techniques of each process. The neutral must strive to maintain the integrity of each separate process, and this is no easy task. Only an exceptionally qualified neutral is likely to succeed.

(2) *Neutral Consents to Serve Both Roles.* The neutral should carefully consider whether to assume both process roles. The neutral should first assess whether she has the expertise to perform both roles (Protocol 1). The neutral also should ascertain whether the mandate to preserve her impartiality as an arbitrator prevents her from serving effectively as a settler. Finally, the neutral should make an independent assessment as to whether the particular case is ripe for settlement.

(3) *Neutral as Settler Will Respect Principle of Party Self-Determination.* When trying to settle a case, the neutral should respect the right of each party to enter into a voluntary, uncoerced

agreement. Each party should be free to determine whether or not to settle. This principle of party self-determination is adopted in the mediator's code of conduct. This principle can be easily violated in an arrangement in which the settler also has the power to decide the case. This arrangement may create a coercive atmosphere for settlement. As a result, the neutral as settler must be especially careful to avoid any initiatives that may be viewed as coercive in order to preserve the principle of party self-determination.

(4) *Clients with Settlement Authority Will Be Present.* Settlement efforts are usually more successful when the settlement process includes active participation by not only attorneys but also their clients—the people with the personal knowledge of the dispute, personal interest in the outcome, and settlement authority. Real mediations in the United States succeed in part because of the unique opportunity for attorneys and clients to meet with their counterparts in a non-adversarial and confidential setting. However, the familiar division of roles between attorneys and clients in the U.S. is not necessarily followed in civil-law jurisdictions. In other countries, clients may perform less active roles and their attorneys may possess greater settlement authority and personal knowledge of the clients' situation, especially in business matters. Therefore, this protocol may need to be modified to accommodate different cultural practices while ensuring that the people with broad settlement authority and personal knowledge participate in settlement efforts.

(5) *Documents and Statements in Settlement Process are Confidential.* Parties and neutral(s) should execute a confidentiality agreement that prohibits introducing in the arbitration proceeding any information disclosed or developed in the settlement process and that is otherwise not independently discoverable. . . .

(6) *Neutral as Settler Will Not Evaluate Merits, Evidence or Reasonableness of Positions.* Any evaluation by the neutral as settler poses a significant risk of compromising the neutral's impartiality if she resumes the role of arbitrator. The arbitrator who offers an evaluation during the settlement process may appear to have prejudged the case when the arbitration proceeding resumes. When the neutral returns to arbitrating, the neutral also may discover that her evaluation may have contaminated her view of the record in the arbitration proceeding. This protocol barring evaluations directs the neutral as settler to resist slipping prematurely into an adjudicatory mindset. This prohibition should reinforce the wall that separates the settlement process from the arbitration process.

This restriction should not be interpreted to bar a mediator or quasi-mediator from helping the parties evaluate their case. The settler can still ask even-handed questions about the quality of evidence, credibility of witnesses, clarity of law, and likelihood of success in the arbitration proceeding. The settler can introduce the use of decision tree analysis to help the parties assess alternatives to settlement. The settler can even encourage the parties to bring in a jointly-selected expert to evaluate decisive aspects of the case, such as conflicting evidence or conflicting interpretations of law.

This protocol, followed by mediators who subscribe to a facilitative style of mediation, eliminates a tool for settlers who use their personal evaluations as a technique to break impasses and prod settlements. Even though I strongly recommend against the use of evaluations, I realize that some participants may still want to take the risk and seek evaluations from arbitrators-turned-settlers. In these circumstances, participants should limit evaluations to matters not likely to be adjudicated in the arbitration, such as future-oriented issues or compromised-based solutions that do not clearly reflect who has the stronger case.

(7) *Neutral Will Not Caucus, Unless Parties Agree to Exception.* When to use caucuses and how best to use them are debated among mediators. Some mediators even advocate avoiding caucuses altogether because the private meetings between the neutral and one side may interfere with the opportunity for parties to work with each other to resolve their own problems.

Arbitrators turned settlers increase the risk of compromising their appearance of impartiality when they hold private meetings. The excluded party may become concerned that the neutral played one party against the other during settlement efforts. The excluded party also may become suspicious that the other party corrupted the neutral's view of the case under circumstances where the excluded party could not challenge the information. Presumably for these reasons, international practitioners have judged caucuses as the least appropriate technique for the arbitrator-turned-mediator.

Barring caucuses means eliminating a tool that many quasi-mediators and mediators consider vital for settlement efforts to be successful. Many settlers believe that private meetings create a unique and safe opportunity for neutrals to help parties vent and release anger, clarify positions and interests, and assess the acceptability of alternative settlement options. In private confidential sessions, parties may be more inclined to engage in reality testing with the settler and openly recognize weaknesses of their own case as well as strengths of the other side. The private meetings also can create an environment in which parties may feel secure to reveal their real interests to the neutral, who can then use this information to help parties explore mutually acceptable solutions.

After weighing the risks and benefits of using caucuses, parties might still want the settler to use caucuses. Parties may decide to permit the use of caucuses generally or restrict their use to less risky settings. Caucuses are less risky when the settlement effort is focused on forward-looking solutions such as a continuing business relationship instead of backward-looking issues of the type that typically arise in the arbitration. . . . .

(8) *Parties Agree to Reconfigure Arbitration Panel to Suit Settlement Process.* Arbitrators can take many different pathways toward helping parties settle a case. Each pathway offers different ways for preserving the impartiality of the neutral as arbitrator while opening opportunities for settlement. Many of these pathways are built around the flexibility offered by the usual international tribunal of three arbitrators. Five configurations are considered here, although other permutations can be imagined.

First, when a typical panel of a neutral chair with two party-appointed arbitrators is constituted, the two party-appointed arbitrators could work together as a settlement team without the participation of the chair. This arrangement would preserve the neutrality of the chair who would not be tarnished by settlement efforts. . . . .

Second, the typical panel of a neutral chair with two party-appointed arbitrators could be reconfigured so that the chair serves as the settler, preserving the relative impartiality of the party-appointed arbitrators. . . .

Third, when three neutral arbitrators are selected, one could serve as a settler while the other two function only as arbitrators. This arrangement would preserve the impartiality of two arbitrators. . . . .

Fourth, three arbitrators, whether all neutral or with two party-appointed ones, could serve as a settlement team. This arrangement poses a significant risk of the impartiality of the arbitrators being compromised as settlement efforts are tried. Under these circumstances, the arbitrators should limit themselves to serving as quasi-mediators who employ relatively safe initiatives such as encouraging the participants to try settling the case on their own, requesting parties with settlement authority to be present, helping participants define legal and factual issues in dispute, or suggesting at a propitious moment that the parties "split the difference." If the issues in the settlement process are limited to forward-looking ones, the settlement team might try a broader range of settlement initiatives.

A fifth pathway may be possible in the rare case when a single international arbitrator is selected. This pathway should be a narrow one. A sole arbitrator should be limited to the roles of a quasi-mediator who employs only a few selected and safe initiatives. This restriction is necessary because of the inherent difficulty in preserving the appearance of impartiality of a single arbitrator who tries to settle a case.

(9) *Arbitrator Will Not Be Influenced by Information Revealed in Settlement Process.* The neutral must erect a mental wall to guard against information learned in the settlement process from contaminating her understanding of the record in the arbitration proceeding. The neutral as arbitrator should not be influenced by off-the-record information and insights gleaned from settlement efforts. This fundamental tenet can be too easily violated when a neutral is in the throes of an actual case. The neutral as arbitrator must tenaciously strive to make any decisions based on the arbitration record in order to preserve the integrity of the arbitration process.

(10) *Parties Agree Not to Challenge Arbitrator or Award Based on Combined Roles.* When an arbitrator has tried to settle a case, his impartiality as an arbitrator and the fairness of the arbitration process can be easily challenged by a dissatisfied party. A party who is willing to consent to the combined roles should waive any later objections related solely to the arbitrator trying to settle the case. Any challenges should be restricted to cases in which a party can make a clear showing that the arbitrator prejudged the case or improperly considered information learned in the settlement process.

(11) *Settlement Initiatives Will Not Unduly Delay the Arbitration Proceeding.* Parties who are anxious to conclude a dispute frequently resist settlement efforts out of concern that the efforts might delay the arbitration proceeding. They are concerned that settlement efforts might extend the arbitration proceeding due to time lost trying to settle or worse yet time lost due to repeating the arbitration selection process because disqualified arbitrators must be replaced. To guard against unduly prolonging the arbitration proceeding, parties could agree to continue the arbitration proceeding in parallel with settlement efforts, or parties could

negotiate a short timetable for suspending the arbitration proceeding. To guard against disqualification of the settling arbitrators, parties and neutrals should strictly follow the other protocols.

(12) *Parties Consent to Combined Processes.* The parties serve as the ultimate safeguard of the arbitration process. No settlement initiatives by arbitrators should be tried unless the parties consent. This is a vital and indispensable requirement. In order to increase the likelihood of parties making an informed decision, parties should be given a copy of these protocols and a disclosure statement on the advantages and risks of the neutral serving two processes. Parties and neutral(s) may even develop their own set of protocols and then sign an agreement to abide by them.

---

# X. NOTES AND QUESTIONS

1. What is the difference between a process design that incorporates mediation into a multi-stage dispute resolution clause and one that uses it in a combined process? If the difference is that the processes are separated more with a multi-stage agreement, isn't there also a continuum of "blending" even in combined processes?

2. Lawyers tend to recycle boilerplate dispute resolution clauses without considering tailoring them to the circumstances of the parties. What might explain this? Can you think of ways to encourage more sophisticated approaches to dispute system design?

3. Does combining processes (with or without the same neutral) offer more benefits in some industries than in others? Is it more useful in a commercial dispute, rather than in an investment dispute where one party is a national government? Does the nature of the relationship between the parties matter?

4. How are the operation and values of mediation and arbitration changed when they are combined? Does it matter if the result is considered to be merely a combination of these well-known processes or is instead treated as a blended hybrid with characteristics and issues of its own? What are the consequences of this choice for the regulation of the hybrid process?

5. What do you see as the most significant issues regarding the combination of mediation with arbitration using the same neutral? Are you more concerned with the integrity of mediation, of adjudication, or of both?

6. What do you think of the assertion that a neutral who transitions from mediator to arbitrator can build a mental wall to ignore information that the neutral learned during the mediation stage? Can this assertion stand in light of developments in cognitive science suggesting that human brains have difficulty disregarding information, even when they know it is irrelevant?

7. What do you make of the varied attitudes in different legal cultures toward combining processes and using the same neutral for all the stages? Some commentators have observed that while procedures for arbitration generally are becoming more harmonized globally, combinations of mediation and arbitration are not following that trend. Do you think it is important to have a uniform world-wide approach to combining mediation with other processes in light of the growth of transboundary disputes? If so, what would you do about differences in the level of comfort with various procedures that characterize different legal cultures?

8. Are you personally comfortable with combining mediation and arbitration with the same neutral? How do you think your attitude might be influenced by your own legal culture?

9. Which design options or legislative/institutional approaches do you most favor as a way to safeguard confidentiality and due process? Is there any way to fully protect both mediation confidentiality and due process values in arbitration when using the same neutral? What good is a so-called quasi-mediator who doesn't caucus and limits her involvement in the mediation stage? How would you make the trade-off in values that are implicated when using the same neutral?

10. Do you agree with Ellen Deason's emphasis on the conditions for party consent and the suggestion to use an opt-out procedure with combinations of mediation and arbitration with the same neutral? Would there be unintended consequences? For example, would giving parties an opportunity to obtain a new arbitral tribunal following an unsuccessful mediation encourage them to manipulate the process to obtain a more favorable neutral?

11. Is having a set of protocols such as those proposed by Harold Abramson (or safeguards like them) necessary? Abramson describes a colleague who reported that he had served on an international arbitration panel that violated almost every one of the protocols Abramson proposes, but still was able to settle the case successfully. What might have happened, however, if the case had not settled? Would the parties have been comfortable proceeding to an arbitral decision?

12. How might the protocols proposed by Abramson be viewed by arbitrators and parties in China? In Germany? Are there costs (monetary or otherwise) to observing them?

# Chapter 7

# INTERNATIONAL MEDIATION IN THE CONTEXT OF INVESTOR-STATE DISPUTES

## I. INTRODUCTION

This chapter explores the increasing importance of the mediation process in the context of domestic and international disputes regarding foreign direct investment (FDI).[1] FDI refers to the processes by which companies establish operations and acquire strategic assets in a country other than their own. The country where the investment occurs is commonly referred to as the host State, and the entity or individual establishing the business is the foreign direct investor.

Our global economy, with its increased interconnectivity, has expanded the landscape in which not only businesses, but all of us, operate. This high level of interdependence between world markets has had a profound impact on our domestic economies. In order to remain competitive, companies in many industries, both old and new, have been propelled to cross national borders and engage in FDI looking for affordable resources, efficient operations, and market expansion. Globalization has increased customers' and companies' access to information, services, products, and markets. Yet it has also

1 *E.g.*, United Nations Conference on Trade and Dev., *Investor-State Disputes: Prevention and Alternatives to Arbitration, in* UNCTAD Series on International Investment Policies for Development (2010), https://unctad.org/en/docs/diaeia200911_en.pdf; United Nations Conference on Trade and Dev., Investor-State Disputes: Prevention and Alternatives to Arbitration II (Susan D. Franck & Anna Joubin-Bret eds., 2011) [hereinafter *Prevention and Alternatives*], https://unctad.org/en/Docs/webdiaeia20108_en.pdf; United Nations Conference of Trade and Dev., *Investor-State Dispute Settlement: A Sequel, in* UNCTAD Series on Issues in International Investment Agreements II (2014), https://unctad.org/en/PublicationsLibrary/diaeia2013d2_en.pdf; Transnational Dispute Mgmt, Reform of Investor-State Dispute Settlement: In search of a roadmap (Jean E. Kalicki & Anna Joubin Bret eds., 2014), https://www.transnational-dispute-management.com/journal-browse-issues-toc.asp?key=52.

posed new political and economic challenges and disparities, and produced significant disruption.

Unlike international trade, which is based on transactional exchanges of goods and services between the domestic sectors of two countries, FDI requires the establishment of operations in a foreign jurisdiction. This endeavor often entails a long-term commitment and the development of a more significant business relationship between the foreign investor and host State. Foreign investors need to have powerful incentives to expand operations outside their own jurisdictions, where they enjoy the competitive advantage of interacting within their own language, culture, and legal system. Yet by going outside their national borders, companies can gain access to more natural resources, strategic assets, new markets, and higher efficiency. Similarly, there are also important incentives for host States to attract and retain foreign investors, as they often provide increased access to new capital, knowledge, and jobs.

Nonetheless, the business relationship between foreign investors and host States can give rise to complex conflicts that may escalate into significant and intense disputes. Historically, the focus of investor-State dispute resolution has been on investor-State arbitration at the international level. Even though conciliation, and more recently, mediation, have been available as alternatives, they have not been as widely used to date.

However, due to the relational nature of FDI, facilitative processes, such as mediation, constitute an important addition to the roster of dispute resolution processes at the international level because they promote mutually satisfying resolutions by increasing the parties' level of self-determination. In this regard, business relationships can be strengthened by developing options that go beyond the baseline of legal remedies, which often end up damaging the business relationship.

Furthermore, mediation has recently been considered as a part of Conflict Management Mechanisms (CMMs)[2] at the domestic level,[3] where host States are developing their internal problem-solving

---

[2] Roberto Echandi, *Complementing Investor-State Dispute Resolution: A Conceptual Framework for Investor-State Conflict Management*, *in* Prospects in International Investment Law and Policy 270, 270–305 (Roberto Echandi & Pierre Sauvé eds., 2013) (pioneering a framework for CMMs).

[3] *See* Lisa Blomgren Bingham, *Opportunities for Dispute Systems Design in Investment Treaty Disputes: Consensual Dispute Resolution at Varying Levels*, *in Prevention and Alternatives*, *supra* note 1, at 33–37 (arguing that dispute systems design can be used at different levels that range from global to community).

techniques to promote investment retention and expansion within their jurisdictions. This emerging emphasis on early interventions aims to prevent a conflict from escalating into a full blown legal dispute at the international level.[4] This new focus, with an emphasis on investment retention or divestment prevention, can be a significant factor in creating the incentive to use mediation both domestically and internationally.

First, Part II of this chapter provides a short overview of the historical evolution of dispute resolution methods used to address investor-State disputes, as these disputes have a unique nature, given the intersection of the private and public spheres in a cross-cultural setting. Next, Part III looks at the relational aspect of FDI and suggests that the mediation process can play an essential role in managing conflict and addressing disputes, given its ability to address issues that require options beyond the legal realm, which often include business and political matters. Then, Part IV discusses the development of the IBA Investor-State Mediation Rules as a necessary regulatory framework for investor-State mediation at the international level. It explores the new opportunities for tailoring the mediation process and the role of experts to the parties' preferences. Finally, Part V addresses the recent developments of investor-State mediation and system design at the domestic level. It examines the potential of mediation to function as part of Systemic Investor Response Mechanisms (SIRMs) and Shared Decisions System Design (SDSD) in order to retain and expand foreign investment.[5]

## II. THE EVOLUTION OF DISPUTE RESOLUTION PROCESSES: ADDRESSING THE UNIQUE NATURE OF INVESTOR-STATE DISPUTES

Mediation can provide unique opportunities to strengthen the business relationship between the host State and foreign investor. As a dispute resolution process that can also focus on interests instead of merely rights, it expands the decision-making power of the parties to resolve their own disputes with the guidance of a mediator. In

---

[4] Roberto Echandi, *Investor-State Conflict Management: A Preliminary Sketch,* 1 TDM (2014), https://www.transnational-dispute-management.com/article.asp?key=2083.

[5] Roberto Echandi & Mariana Hernandez Crespo Gonstead, *Investor-State Conflict Management, in* Elgar Encyclopedia of International Economic Law 335–38 (Thomas Cottier & Krista Nadakavukaren Schefer eds., 2017).

order to fully grasp the benefits of mediation in the FDI field,[6] it is critical to gain a historical perspective of some of the challenges faced by both foreign investors and host States, the complexity of their interactions, and an overview of the development of dispute resolution processes.

Historically, foreign investors have been primarily concerned with the risk of investing in the unstable environment found in developing countries. In order to secure their investments, the foreign investors initially utilized methods such as gunboat diplomacy. Yet this power-based system relied on coercive resolution processes or political pressure. In the 1960s, bilateral investment treaties (BITs) were introduced to provide greater investment security through a rule-based system that provided opportunities to resolve disputes using arbitration. Arbitration provided investors with a way to directly recover in the case of a violation by the host State.

Yet given the relational nature of FDI, an adjudicative process where there is a clear winner and loser can leave the business relationship strained or dissolved.[7] For example, one of the most prominent recurring challenges for host States is attracting and retaining foreign investors, as there are numerous political, legal, economical, and cultural factors affecting the decision to enter into and continue business relationship. In order to address this, interest-based processes such as negotiation, conciliation, and, most recently, mediation have been increasingly considered[8] to resolve investor-State disputes at the international level, and in some cases even included in treaties. Additionally, at the domestic level, CMMs have emerged, as systems created to implement problem-solving

---

6 Int'l Mediation Inst. Inv'r-State Mediation Task Force, Response to ICSID on its Invitation to File Suggestions for Rule Amendments (2017), https://icsid.worldbank.org/en/amendments/Documents/20.%20IMI.pdf

7 Mariana Hernandez Crespo, *From Paper to People: Building Conflict Resolution Capacity and Frameworks for Sustainable Implementation of IIAs to Increase Investor-State Satisfaction, in Prevention and Alternatives, supra* note 1, at 55.

8 *See generally* S.I. Strong, *Beyond International Commercial Arbitration? The Promise of International Commercial Mediation*, 45 Wash. U.J.L. & Pol'y 11 (2014) (analyzing why arbitration is still the preferred method for resolution of international commercial disputes, and suggesting reforms to facilitate the use of international commercial mediation).

techniques to manage investor-State conflict before it escalates into a legal dispute.[9]

## A. Overview of Investment Treaty Arbitration (ITA)

With the introduction of investment treaties, arbitration gained primacy in the international realm. Arbitration has played an essential role in moving the resolution of investor-State disputes from a primarily power-based system to a rule-based dispute resolution system. However, given the unique nature of the investor-State relationship, in some instances other methods may be better suited to address the particular type of dispute and the goals of the parties.

When a foreign company brings a claim against a sovereign state, the stakes are high and the implications are systemic. Therefore, in some cases, an adjudicative process may be insufficient to fully address the interests of all stakeholders affected by the dispute. This is partly due to the fact that adjudicative processes can only provide for damages and injunctions, unlike facilitative processes which can provide a broader range of mutually satisfying options memorialized in the agreement. This is particularly relevant given that the investor-State dispute arises in the context of a long-term business relationship rather than a series of transactions.

Susan D. Franck has been one of the primary experts leading the charge in forging the relationships between the international investment law and dispute resolution communities to pave the way forward for a dialogue. In the following excerpt from the first chapter of her book, she discusses the role of Investment Treaty Arbitration (ITA) for disputes arising under international investment treaties in the context of the historical development of international investment conflict resolution. She explores a matrix of dispute resolution options which consists of two dimensions: (1) informal versus formal and, (2) adjudicative versus non-adjudicative mechanisms.

## SUSAN D. FRANCK, ARBITRATION COSTS: MYTHS AND REALITIES IN INVESTMENT TREATY ARBITRATION

(10–11, Oxford University Press, 2019).

ITA is a hybrid *sui generis* creature that owes its doctrinal and policy basis to both public and private international law. For private

[9] For the definition of CMMs, see Echandi & Hernandez Crespo Gonstead, *supra* note 5.

law, it involves the rights of private individuals, their commercial activities, and vindicating rights using adjudicative forums and fiscal awards of damages. From a public law perspective, ITA involves the law of state responsibility, state regulatory conduct, and states' capacity to craft international law instruments that voluntarily set boundaries on their own regulatory capacity in a bid to incentivize private commercial activity.

ITA is a relatively new international law phenomenon but fits within a larger historical framework. For centuries, people made their way to other countries searching for economic opportunities. Sometimes this involved trade in goods or services; other times, there were more developed commercial enterprises with deeper commitments. Whenever people are involved in commercial activity, there is inevitably friction that can transform into investment-related conflict and escalate to crystalized disputes. Historical options for addressing conflict included: ignoring investment conflict and accepting it as a cost of doing business (and pricing commercial risks accordingly), obtaining political risk insurance coverage and passing the cost of conflict onto a secondary market, soliciting the investor's home state to privately engage in diplomacy on investors' behalves, engaging in "gunboat diplomacy," or making formal declarations of war to protect the underlying economic interests. Over time, formal adjudicative rule-of-law options developed, including espousal of investors' disputes in a public international venue or state-to-state adjudication.

One might conceptualize these conflict management options as quadrants with two dimensions. The first dimension involves informal versus formal options; and the second dimension involves adjudicative or non-adjudicative mechanisms. As dispute resolution options are not a pure binary continuum, managing conflict requires broader options including: (1) informal non-adjudicative options, such as those related to private negotiation and mediation, (2) informal adjudicative options, such as expert determination or assessments by ombuds, (3) formal non-adjudicative options, including diplomacy, gunboat diplomacy and declarations of war; and (4) formal adjudicative options, including national courts or other international courts and tribunals. *See* Figure 2. Methods are not per se "right" or "wrong"; rather optimal choices require contextual evaluation of how well processes meet stakeholder needs.

| | Rulemaking or Non-Adjudicative | Adjudicative |
|---|---|---|
| **Formal** | **Formal Rulemaking:** Diplomacy, Declarations of War, Treaty Drafting, Free Trade Commission Statements, Negotiated Rulemaking | **Formal Adjudication:** International Courts and Tribunals, International Arbitration, National Courts |
| **Informal** | **Informal Rulemaking:** Negotiation, Mediation, Dispute Prevention Policies, etc. | **Informal Adjudication:** Early Neutral Evaluation, Expert Determination, Ombuds |

Figure 1.2: Matrix of Dispute Resolution Options in International Investment Law

Within that framework, other areas of international law—particularly international economic law in areas like international trade—have become more judicialized. Following a strong current in a related discipline, international investment law developed in a similar direction of valuing formalized adjudication.

History also explains this evolution. In the past, foreign investors were caught between a rock and a hard place when trying to obtain redress for state activity arguably harming their investment. Investors had a limited range of non-adjudicative, direct options. Investors were dependent upon: internal capacity to absorb losses, ability to negotiate directly with host States, or political capital and willingness of their home state to use diplomacy to secure favorable outcomes. Without a clear, independent, reliable and predictable adjudicative baseline, the non-adjudicative options meant commercial risk and uncertainty. While investors could manage risks with their local counterparties, they had limited capacity to manage risks involving host State regulation, particularly when local expertise is limited or sovereign immunity prevented redress. This could make investment either untenable or lead investors to pass the cost of uncertainty onto the market through increased costs.

---

In the following excerpt, Jeswald Salacuse discusses the increased use of arbitration in investor-State disputes and the costs associated with this mechanism. In addition, he explores the unique nature of investor-State disputes and the potential that other dispute resolution mechanisms may have to resolve these disputes.

## JESWALD W. SALACUSE, *IS THERE A BETTER WAY? ALTERNATIVE METHODS OF TREATY-BASED, INVESTOR-STATE DISPUTE RESOLUTION*

31 Fordham Int'l L.J. 138, 138–43, 146–47, 154–56 (2007).

The rapid growth over the last two decades in the total stock of international investment . . . . ha[s] quite naturally led to an increase in potential and actual conflicts between investors and host countries. Parallel to the growth in international investment has been the rapid increase in international investment treaties among states, which now number nearly 2500 and involve some 180 different countries. These agreements, which include bilateral investment treaties ("BITs"), regional agreements such as NAFTA, free trade agreements ("FTAs"), and special purpose accords such as the Energy Charter Treaty, are often concluded between industrialized countries and developing nations in order to protect and promote investment among the countries concerned. In general, these agreements do two things: (1) they subject host countries to a set of international legal rules that they must respect in dealing with foreign investors and their investments and (2) they grant investors the right to bring a claim in international arbitration autonomously and without regard to the wishes of their home country against host country governments that allegedly violate those rules. Such treaties enable investors to convert a "conflict" (i.e., a perceived difference of interests) with host governments, which might otherwise be settled through informal means or domestic courts, into a public international law "dispute" (i.e., a conflict that is activated by the parties) to be settled by an international arbitration tribunal outside the jurisdiction of the host country.

These two factors—the increase in international investment and the increase in international investment agreements—have together led to a growth in the number and severity of treaty-based disputes between host states and individual investors. An increasing number of such disputes are being settled through international arbitration.

* * *

Investor-State disputes arising under international investment treaties are not ordinary commercial disputes. Treaty-based investor-State disputes are special, and their special nature must be understood because it affects the ways in which the disputants approach their conflict and the utility and effectiveness of dispute resolution techniques employed to resolve that conflict.

First, such disputes are not a matter of simple contract claims governed by contract law. They are disputes governed by public international law in the form of treaties—instruments of international law—solemnly entered into by two or more states. . . . .

Second, at the heart of many investor-State conflicts is a public policy question. . . . . The resulting arbitration decision or other form of settlement has significant implications for the ability of sovereign governments to regulate enterprises within their territories. . . . .

Third, because they involve public policy issues, investor-State disputes are political in nature and often become highly politicized, as political groups, non-governmental organizations, the media, and ultimately the general public come to have definite views on the dispute and how it should be settled. . . . .

Fourth, underlying the dispute is an intended long-term investment relationship: A complex connection, often amounting to a state of interdependence, between the investor and the host country. In cases of privatization of public services, such as water, gas, or telecommunications, the investor and the host country are linked in a more or less permanent relationship that is very difficult to unravel, far more difficult than that arising out of a simple contract of sale of a commodity in international commerce. . . . .

Fifth, the amounts of money at stake in the dispute are large, sometimes staggeringly so, reaching in some cases to hundreds of millions, even billions of dollars. . . . .

Moreover, the costs of an investor-State arbitration are usually substantially greater than those in an ordinary commercial dispute and may prove to be a significant burden for developing countries. In addition to indirect costs such as the time of government officials and corporate executives devoted to preparing and participating in the case, the direct costs usually consist of two elements: (1) the expenses of party's legal representation and (2) each party's share of the costs of administering the arbitration. . . . A more typical investor-State case is perhaps *Int'l Thunderbird Gaming Corp. v. United Mexican States*, a NAFTA case under United Nations Commission on International Trade Law ("UNCITRAL") rules. There, the total cost of the proceeding was US$3,170,692, including US$405,620 in arbitrators' fees and approximately US$99,632 in various administrative expenses, US$1,502,065 in Mexico's legal representation costs, and US$1,163,375 in Thunderbird's costs of representation.

* * *

The growing number of investor-State disputes may impose indirect burdens on governments as well. Investment policy, like any other government policy, needs to be sustained by a degree of popular support. The public's realization of the costs incurred by host countries as a result of investor-State, treaty-based disputes, which are often accompanied by significant publicity and media comment, may lead to declining support for foreign investment and for the policies of economic liberalization that many countries have adopted over the last two decades. . . .

In addition to the cost incurred by host countries and the investors, investor-State arbitrations may also have negative consequences for international relationships between host countries and investor home countries. A high-profile, hotly litigated arbitration between a foreign investor and a host country can negatively affect governmental and public opinion in the investor's home country toward the host country.

Despite the examples of investors who have won large awards as a result of a treaty-based, investor-State arbitration, the idea that investor-State arbitration is a road to vast riches for investors is a gross exaggeration. . . . The costs to the investor have several dimensions. First are the financial costs incurred by the investor in hiring legal representation and paying its share of the arbitration's administrative costs. Second are costs incurred by having to devote significant executive time, effort, and concentration to the arbitration rather than to the investor's core business. Third are the relationship costs. A transnational corporation requires productive relationships with the host governments, business communities, and publics of the countries in which it operates. . . .

* * *

To resolve a dispute, disputants can theoretically resort to one of four basic dispute settlement processes. These four basic processes, with numerous variations, include: (1) negotiation, whereby the parties themselves through direct discussion of their conflict agree to settle their dispute, a process that sometimes results in a renegotiation of their underlying transaction or relationship; (2) mediation (often referred to as "conciliation" in international business and investment disputes) or other forms of voluntary third-party intervention, by which a non-disputant third person assists the disputants to resolve their conflict; (3) arbitration, by which the parties to the dispute agree to submit their dispute to a third person for a decision and to abide by that decision; and (4) adjudication by a court of law or some other governmental authority. . . . . [T]hese four dispute resolution processes form a continuum from negotiation on the one hand to adjudication on the other.

As the parties in conflict move along the continuum, they increasingly lose control of their dispute and are increasingly subject to the actions of a third party. . . . .

* * *

Lawyers and many executives tend to view arbitration and adjudication as the principal ways of resolving international investment disputes. These two dispute settlement processes, however, suffer from several disadvantages. They are costly, time-consuming, unpredictable, lack finality in some cases, and destroy the business relationship between the disputants in nearly all cases. . . . . Accordingly, given the ever-present potential for conflict in international investments, the parties to international transactions, particularly in long-term arrangements, should consider the role of negotiation and mediation in resolving eventual disputes. Moreover, they might even build these dispute settlement processes into their transaction from the very beginning of their dealings together, before any conflict has arisen.

---

## B. The Role of Conciliation

Even though investor-State arbitration has been the most commonly used dispute resolution mechanism for foreign investors and host States, in the past several decades other methods such as conciliation have provided the parties with higher levels of party self-determination. In the conciliation process (discussed briefly in Chapter 1), the parties, rather than the conciliator, make the final decision. The conciliator, as a third-party neutral, guides the process and sponsors the terms of the settlement, thereby assisting the parties in their efforts to reach an agreement. While conciliation may be highly beneficial, there is potential for misuse in some cases. In the following excerpt, Jack Coe highlights some key features of conciliation, as well as the potential strengths and weaknesses of the process.

## JACK J. COE JR., *TOWARD A COMPLEMENTARY USE OF CONCILIATION IN INVESTOR-STATE DISPUTES—A PRELIMINARY SKETCH*

12 U.C. Davis J. Int'l L. & Pol'y 7, 15–18 (2005).

[D]isputants engage in conciliation voluntarily in the sense that unlike arbitration, the process cannot put an end to the dispute without both disputants agreeing to terms of settlement, and those terms of settlement will ordinarily have been generated by their active participation in the collaborative process. Consequently, disputants retain control of the outcome, and to a large degree, of the process as well; as a by-product they may avoid disputed law and facts to craft durable solutions not dependent on assigning rights and duties. The shift from adjudicating legal issues to identifying shared interests and acceptable accommodations allows the parties to not only avoid the risk of zero-sum outcomes but to possibly transform a legal dispute into a restructured relationship, enlarging the value of the relationship to each.

In conciliation, the neutral plays an essential role; it is typically the conciliator who successfully sponsors terms of settlement, terms that might be rejected if they emanated directly from a disputant. . . . .

Because conciliation need not be pleadings-intensive or dependent on adducing full proofs, it can produce results with greater speed and less expense than arbitration. . . . .

Among the weaknesses typically associated with conciliation are: that it relies on voluntary, good faith participation (and, as a corollary, that it can be exploited for delay by an insincere but cunning disputant); that it is not certain to yield an outcome and thus may prove to be a waste of resources; that its effectiveness depends to an extent on the timing of the intervention; and that convening and reconvening the disputants can be difficult. Additionally, where no mechanism exists to transform the mediated agreement into an award, enforcement of the result (effectively a contract) may be more arduous than with an award or court judgment. These are traits that any system of mixed conciliation would do well to confront, as more fully addressed below. Nevertheless, these perceived liabilities have not prevented relative success in the private commercial setting, where conciliation is credited with impressive rates of settlement.

# III. THE ESSENTIAL ROLE OF MEDIATION: EXPANDING THE FOCUS TO ACKNOWLEDGE THE RELATIONAL ASPECT OF FOREIGN DIRECT INVESTMENT (FDI)

Besides addressing the unique nature of investor-State disputes, it is important to expand the focus from merely resolving a dispute, to deepening the understanding of the investor-State business relationship. To this end, processes such as mediation can contribute the necessary paradigm shift from mainly securing investments through rights, to strengthening investor-State cooperation through the mutual satisfaction of stakeholder interests. Furthermore, the mediation process can allow for a more systemic approach which integrates the differences of the stakeholders into the process in an effort to produce more effective interactions. In the following excerpt, Mariana Hernandez Crespo Gonstead discusses some of the benefits that may come from shifting the focus from merely resolving a specific dispute, to also including options to strengthen the business relationship through the maximization of joint gains.

## MARIANA HERNANDEZ CRESPO, *FROM PAPER TO PEOPLE: BUILDING CONFLICT RESOLUTION CAPACITY AND FRAMEWORKS FOR SUSTAINABLE IMPLEMENTATION OF IIAS TO INCREASE INVESTOR-STATE SATISFACTION*, *IN* UNITED NATIONS CONFERENCE ON TRADE AND DEVELOPMENT, INVESTOR-STATE DISPUTES: PREVENTION AND ALTERNATIVES TO ARBITRATION II

55–58 (Susan D. Franck & Anna Joubin-Bret eds., 2011).

Building conflict resolution capacity consists of enabling stakeholders with the necessary skills to assess, to manage and to resolve conflict, while knowing when to employ a wide range of facilitative and adjudicative processes. Since the 1970s in the United States, lawyers have been developing conflict resolution capacity. This trend has been of special importance to the business sector, whose need for a cost-effective and relationship-driven method for dispute resolution has led it to turn to processes besides traditional adjudication. . . .

A framework for the satisfaction of investor-State interests expands beyond merely an adversarial model of zero-sum adjudication of rights (such as arbitration) to a broader spectrum of options that also includes interests-based methods (such as mediation, among others). If the investor-State business relationship is to be strengthened, stakeholders could emphasize an overarching principle of knowledge building and concrete areas of strategic development.

* * *

*A paradigm shift: From strictly protecting investor's positions to satisfying investor-State interests through the maximization of joint gains*

IIAs [international investment agreements] are designed around the need for foreign investors to protect their capital from the adverse consequences of social, economic, or political instability in the host country. This approach focuses on protecting investor's positions through a so-called "Bill of Economic Rights." Investment security is achieved by guaranteeing these rights through the use of arbitration. As with any adjudicative process, arbitration operates under a rights-based, zero-sum assumption in which one party necessarily wins while the other party loses. In such a paradigm, the losing party is nearly always unsatisfied. The absence of the satisfaction of both parties is not optimal and can weaken the ongoing investor-State relationship.

Rather than focusing strictly on protecting investors through a positions-based paradigm, a shift needs to be made to an interest-based paradigm. Broadening the focus could allow the parties to cooperate when addressing investor-State interests, leaving the protection of the investor's rights as the last and final resort. If the maximization of joint gains becomes the main focus, three areas of strategic development (implementation committees, dispute and conflict management systems design) could help to provide the necessary framework for sustainable implementation.

* * *

Maximizing joint gains begins by discovering the underlying interests and values of each party. It is critical not just to know the parties' positions (what they want) but their interests (why they want it) and their values (why it is important to them). Moreover, when parties express their interests and values to one another, it can create a bond of solidarity between them. This bond can be a catalyst in the creative process, encouraging them to consider the satisfaction of all the parties' interests when creating options.

**Table B.5.2. A paradigm shift: From protection to the maximization of joint gain**

| *From* | *To* |
|---|---|
| Protection | Cooperation |
| Investor's positions | Investor-State interests |
| "Bill of Economic Rights" | "Joint Gains Maximization" |
| Arbitration awards | Implementation Committees, DSD and CMSD |
| Investment security | Investor-State sustainable business relationship through maximization of joint gains |

*The Overarching Goal: Sustainable Investor-State relationship*

In order to maximize joint gains, besides a paradigm shift from rights to interests, the relationship between the foreign investor and the host country needs to be placed at the centre of a sustainable framework.

An analogy that could illustrate the dynamic of the relationship between a foreign investor and a host country is that of a renter of a room in a landlord's home. Just as a renter is subject to the rules of the house and vulnerable to the decisions of the landlord, so too the foreign investor has to operate within the framework of the host country's political, social, and economic landscape. Under the current structure of IIAs, if the renter (foreign investor) was not satisfied with the landlord's (host country's) implementation of some aspects of the agreement, no matter what kind of dispute, the main recourse available is to sue the landlord (arbitration), likely resulting in the severance of the relationship. Rather than resolving tensions with extreme options, IIA disputes might consider other options. Foreign investors have a significant relationship with the host country, made up of joint human resources, environmental concerns, and an interlocking of the foreign entity into the larger economic network of the country. That relationship is generally worth preserving. By the time conflict arises there is a substantial interconnection between the two entities, even if through a myriad of representatives. The central issue in developing a sustainable relationship between investors and host States is the marked gap between the IIA rights and offered IIA remedies—namely the arbitration process. Focusing on after-the-fact monetary solutions as a catch-all, without considering more constructive processes, inhibits the growth of the relationship.

*Ongoing knowledge building: A key to developing conflict resolution capacity*

Ongoing knowledge building is critical for sustainable implementation of IIAs, given the intricacies of the investor-State relationship. The longer an association endures the more intertwined become its nexuses. Ongoing knowledge building is vital and should be an overarching principle for designing a sustainable framework of implementation.

To strengthen investor-State relationships, some principal areas should be considered, including: (1) moving from the particular to the systemic by identifying patterns of behaviour, incentive, resistance and culture, (2) learning from failure through systemic introspection using reflective practices, and (3) applying the knowledge built toward a future strategy. Reflecting on assumptions and testing hypotheses are a central component of developing stakeholder's conflict resolution capacity.

* * *

[M]ediation can be highly effective, but may not be most appropriate in every case. Susan Franck contends that it is important to explore all dispute resolution options across the continuum, determining how to best facilitate "an effective, efficient, and fair and legitimate process for resolving investment treaty conflict." Others have suggested that relevant factors should be taken into account when determining whether mediation is an appropriate forum, despite all the benefits that mediation offers, including speed, cost, innovative solutions, and preserving the relationship between the parties. Laurence Boulle pointed out that a diagnosis of the appropriateness of mediation is necessary, noting specific cases when complex factors affected the determination. Andrea Schneider stressed that these options would operate under the shadow of investment arbitration.

---

# IV. INTERNATIONAL ADVANCEMENTS: TRENDS IN INVESTOR-STATE MEDIATION AND NEW OPPORTUNITIES FOR TAILORING PROCESSES AND THE ROLE OF EXPERTS TO THE PARTIES PREFERENCES

In recent years, significant developments have taken place in investment treaty conflict resolution. There is evidence that parties have been opting for processes beyond arbitration, sometimes settling on their own after the process has commenced.[10] The inclusion of mediation as an explicit dispute resolution process in the next generation of treaties,[11] has elevated it to equal standing with arbitration. Yet for mediation to be a viable alternative[12] in the context of FDI, the development and implementation of a regulatory framework has been essential. Without it, sovereign governments and foreign investors may not consider mediation as a possible option, given the lack of clear guidelines and familiarity with the process. In this regard, the IBA Rules for Investor-State Mediation have significantly contributed to both the legitimacy and structure needed to encourage the use of mediation in investor-State disputes.

Moreover, these rules have also played a critical role in addressing some of the unique challenges of investor-State disputes, while still maintaining the necessary flexibility to accommodate the broad range of investors and host States. These rules highlight the opportunity for process choice and design through the use of a mediation management conference and the introduction of the option for co-mediators. These features can be of critical importance for foreign investors and host States attempting to solve disputes, given the complexity of a private-public dispute, which is sometimes intensified due to cultural differences. Providing the parties with an opportunity to tailor the process with assistance from a team of mediators that share their cultural ties, might significantly contribute to enhancing the quality of process and the sustainability of the agreement.

---

[10] Roberto Echandi & Priyanka Kher, *Can International Investor-State Disputes be Prevented? Empirical Evidence from Settlements in ICSID Arbitration*, 29(1) ICSID Rev. 41, 63–65 (2014).

[11] *See* European Comm'n, EU-Vietnam Trade and Investment Agreements (Authentic Text as of August 2018), Annex 15-C: Mediation Mechanism, http://trade.ec.europa.eu/doclib/press/index.cfm?id=1437.

[12] *See generally* Anna Spain Bradley, *Integration Matters: Rethinking the Architecture of International Dispute Resolution*, 32 U. Penn. J. Int'l L. 1 (2010).

## A. Trends in Investor-State Dispute Resolution

In the following excerpt from the final chapter of her book, Susan D. Franck discusses the untapped potential of non-adjudicative methods in resolving conflicts between foreign investors and host States. She brings awareness to the current cost of arbitration and suggests that if both investors and states adopt a broader perspective on conflict management, they might be able to determine the appropriate process for resolution. She also notes how UNCITRAL's Convention on the Enforcement of Mediation Settlements, ICSID's proposed Mediation Rules, and the mediation references in the EU-Canada Comprehensive Economic and Trade Agreement (CETA), provide the "legal infrastructure to support non-adjudicative methods."

## SUSAN D. FRANCK, ARBITRATION COSTS: MYTHS AND REALITIES IN INVESTMENT TREATY ARBITRATION

(309–14, Oxford University Press 2019).

As the only realistic adjudicative and viable dispute resolution method in treaties, it is unsurprising that investors and counsel focus on arbitration as the primary conflict management method. There are, however, a suite of options, including ombuds, negotiation, early neutral evaluation, fact-finding, mediation, or the small claims facility discussed earlier.

Costs data suggests that alternatives to arbitration are warranted to provide more flexibility and expanded options. To the extent that investors, states, and counsel are economically rational actors (while recognizing people are predictably irrational but domestic politics impacts states' rational decision-making), stakeholders require data to aid appraisals of ITA's [Investment Treaty Arbitration's] net value. Net value permits stakeholders to assess adjudicative options, like arbitration, explore viability of alternative processes for managing conflict to identify *appropriate* dispute resolution (ADR) strategies. The objective should be to avoid disputes where possible, manage conflict when it arises, and engage in systematic consideration of dispute resolution options to "fit the forum to fuss." Part of making strategic choices involves understanding outcome probabilities given the variables involved and likely costs of pursuing different methodologies. . . .

* * *

For all final cases (including cases where investors lost), the average award was around US$16.6 million, meaning average total PLC [party legal costs] and TCE costs [tribunal costs and expenses] were roughly 60% of average awards. Reframed to focus on the subset of claims where investors obtained a damage award, the average amount awarded of US$45.6 million, meaning average total PLC and TCE was around 22% of average awards. Meanwhile, Chapters 6–7 demonstrated that the baseline for when and how tribunals shifted costs remained relatively uncertain, with a reliable (but not guaranteed) pattern that winning investors reliably obtained more beneficial cost shifts than winning states. The only certain fiscal risk was: parties paid up-front costs of their lawyers and advances to arbitrators and institutions. Chapter 6 estimated, for every year of ITA, each party spent roughly US$1.5 million (using aggregated averages), and one might legitimately question whether those fees could be put to a better use and whether negotiated settlements could facilitate more cost-efficient results while placing control of outcomes squarely in parties' hands.

Where ultimate substantive outcomes and cost-shifting assessments are generally uncertain *ex ante*, costs data and possibility of a win (or risk of loss) offer baselines for decision-making. Investors may find it useful to incorporate the data, use it to judge risk, and have those assessments inform dispute resolution choices, including the most likely alternatives to negotiated settlements. Cognitive illusions could facilitate investors' incentives to settle. As Chapter 2 explains, when claimants are faced with the low probability of a gain, cognitive illusions of positive framing and loss aversion facilitate investors being inclined to actively pursue adjudication; whereas, if there is a medium-to-high probability risk—which Chapter 5 suggests is likely given large claims—investors' predictable incentive should be to settle and take a lower, but certain, outcome.

The ultimate focus should be on crafting appropriate dispute resolution. Mediation, negotiation, or working with an ombuds office (or lead government agency), particularly when combined with Dispute Systems Design to identify methodologies for channeling conflict, provide core infrastructure supporting alternatives for extracting value from dispute resolution, decreasing direct costs, avoiding indirect costs (like diverting key personnel from productive activities), and maintaining relationships, particularly when investors continue to do business within the state or region. Approaching conflict management with a broad perspective and eye towards effective use of adjudication alternatives has resolved disputes about government conduct, regulatory conflicts, and public policy issues, including environmental disputes. A broader perspective on conflict management, searching for appropriate tools, opens doors to dispute prevention and fostering relationships that constructively promote investment retention and expansion in collaboration with local communities. [. . . .]

* * *

The functional value of non-adjudicative alternatives is increasing, as innovations create legal infrastructure to support non-adjudicative methods by decreasing transaction costs and facilitating easier adoption. In 2018, there were major innovations regarding the use of alternative methods, like mediation. The draft UNCITRAL Convention on the Enforcement of Mediation Settlements (the Singapore Convention) was finalized; and once open for signature in August 2019, it will likely serve as the "New York Convention" for mediated settlements with streamlined enforcement. UNCITRAL relatedly promulgated a Model Law on international mediation and settlements.

While exceedingly formal, ICSID's proposed Mediation Rules and CETA's mediation references are a light nudge in the right direction. The EU's draft negotiating text with Chile is even more direct about mediation procedures and ethical standards for mediators. The IBA has guidelines that offer a preliminary framework for investment treaty-related mediation, and the Energy Charter Conference adopted a Guide on Investment Mediation. Meanwhile, the International Mediation Institute promulgated mediator competency standards for investment treaty disputes; and ICSID encourages dispute prevention and conflict management as part of best practices, even offering mediator training.

Scholars also focus on non-adjudicative methodologies for investment treaty disputes. Perhaps it is little wonder, if mediated settlements mean disputes can be resolved within weeks (or months) rather than years and on creative terms acceptable to both parties. One wonders, as Everett Rogers suggested new innovations begin when older innovations saturate a market, whether mediation will become the new wave and, over time, commonplace.

Even though arbitration has been the most widely used method for dispute resolution in investor-State disputes, mediation has been gaining traction recently. For example, Frauke Nitschke, notes that "[a] new generation of treaties refer specifically to mediation as an alternative or additional means of solving investment disputes."[13] She provides a number of examples of treaties that reference or include mediation, such as: EU-Canada Comprehensive Economic and Trade Agreement (CETA), Central American Free Trade Agreement (CAFTA), and Investment Agreement for the Common Investment Area of the Common Market for Eastern and Southern Africa (COMESA).

Additionally, studies, such as the one discussed below, have shown that in investor-State disputes, parties tended to negotiate amicable settlements soon after commencing the arbitration claim. This prompt reaction demonstrates the willingness of parties to look for options beyond compulsory arbitration. In these cases, it seems that adjudication does not fully meet their needs and interests or provide the desired outcomes. Therefore, both investors and host States are opting for the available alternative processes to resolve their disputes. This trend can be explained by a variety of reasons, but it will certainly lead to new developments regarding the processes and timing of both conflict management mechanisms and investor-State dispute resolution. In the following excerpt, Roberto Echandi and Priyanka Kher provide empirical evidence for this trend.

## ROBERTO ECHANDI & PRIYANKA KHER, *CAN INTERNATIONAL INVESTOR-STATE DISPUTES BE PREVENTED? EMPIRICAL EVIDENCE FROM SETTLEMENTS IN ICSID ARBITRATION*

29 ICSID Rev. 41, 63–65 (2014).

Our hypothesis was that if settlements are taking place so early in the arbitration process that the parties have not used the process to assess the strength of their respective claims and arguments, then the real need for a tribunal elucidating a disagreement of law or fact would be questionable. It would then follow that in such situations, ICSID arbitration would be dealing with disputes that, had there been a proper outlet for the parties to resolve them at the domestic level, may have been prevented from escalating to international adjudication.

This study revealed that 92 cases, representing 22 percent of the total arbitration proceedings registered in ICSID between 1970 and

---

[13] Frauke Nitschke, *The ICSID Conciliation Rules in Practice*, *in* Mediation in International Commercial and Investment Disputes (Catharine Titi & Katia Fach Gómez eds.) (forthcoming).

2012, were settled before an award on the merits was rendered, as a result of an agreement between the parties. Out of those 92 cases, 36 of them—representing 39 percent of the total—took place during what we denominated as 'Phase 1' of the arbitration proceedings—that is, between the time the arbitration was registered and the constitution of the tribunal.

* * *

In sum, the findings of our research tend to support three key ideas. First, the fact that substantial negotiation activity is already occurring in investor-State arbitration supports the notion that the very availability of compulsory arbitration, and in particular the prospect of facing an adverse award, increases the possibility that respondent State governments will seriously consider amicable settlement, as an option to resolve a dispute with affected investors. Second, the gradual development of a body of jurisprudence interpreting international investment law over the past two decades seems to have contributed to assisting the parties in better assessing the probability of getting a favourable award, and pursuing more informed settlement negotiations.

Third, the significant—and growing—number of arbitration disputes settled at early stages of the proceedings reveals the potential for establishing mechanisms to enable States and investors to effectively manage their conflicts and find mutually agreed solutions before such grievances escalate into international arbitration. Such mechanisms could not only reduce the growing caseload, but more importantly, could strengthen the relationships between investors and host States by promoting problem solving without incurring the economic and political costs of international arbitration.

---

## B. IBA Rules for Investor-State Mediation

The IBA Rules for Investor-State Mediation created a regulatory framework that helped fill a void in the current system, which was primarily focused on arbitration. These rules have provided necessary guidelines for the mediation process, ensuring that the parties consider the significant procedural options available and make informed decisions. This framework allows both governments and foreign investors to align their choices with their needs and interests, and thereby potentially enhancing the level of satisfaction with the mediation process.[14]

While the rules suggest specific procedures, there is also room for flexibility. As noted in Article 1, the parties can "exclude or vary any of these rules at any time." In this way, the rules offer the maximum level of party self-determination, while still providing a set of default options. In the following excerpt, Anna Joubin-Bret, a co-chair for the IBA Rules Committee, highlights some of the key features of this regulatory framework. The IBA Rules are available on the ICSID website.[15]

## ANNA JOUBIN-BRET, *INTERNATIONAL DISPATCH: INVESTOR-STATE DISPUTES*

20 Disp. Resol. Mag. 37, 39–40 (Fall 2013).

*IBA Rules for Investor-State Mediation*

The IBA's rules have a broad scope that applies to the mediation of investment disputes or conflicts involving a state or a state entity and an investor. Parties may consent to mediate in advance under an investment law, treaty, or specific contract with a mediation provision. Mediation can also be an option at any point by mutual agreement of the parties. These are default rules that parties can modify or amend by agreement, which gives everyone flexibility, the chance to tailor the mediation process to their own needs, along with the comfort that comes from knowing that if they can't agree on the changes, they can always fall back on the IBA's guidelines. Since the IBA rules on ISM [Investor State Mediation] have been adopted they have been used in an ICSID conciliation case at the request of the parties.

---

14 Barton Legum, Ana Joubin-Bret & Inna Manassyan, *Rules for Investor-State Mediation: Draft Prepared by the International Bar Association State Mediation Subcommittee, in* Prospects in International Investment Law and Policy 265 (Roberto Echandi & Pierre Sauvé eds., 2013); *see also* Susan D. Franck, *Using Investor-State Mediation Rules to Promote Conflict Management: An Introductory Guide*, 29 ICSID Rev. 1, 66–89 (2014); Anna Joubin-Bret & Barton Legum, A Set of Rules Dedicated to Investor-State Mediation: The IBA Investor-State Mediation Rules, 29 ICSID Rev. 1, 17–24 (2014).

15 Int'l Bar Ass'n Mediation Committee, State Mediation Subcommittee, IBA Rules for Investor-State Mediation 2–9 (2012), https://icsid.worldbank.org/en/Documents/process/IBA%20Rules%20for%20Investor-State%20Mediation%20(Approved%20by%20IBA%20Council%204%20Oct%202012).pdf.

*Minimal Formalities*

Article 2 of the rules provides for the commencement of the mediation process with a minimal requirement of formalism and timing constraints. Mediation may take place before arbitration or litigation, after arbitration has begun, or while a case is pending case before the domestic courts of the state party.

*Pre-Mediation Conference*

To allow for process organization and an early assessment of the dispute and the interests of the parties, the rules provide for a mediation management conference, which is an opportunity for the parties to clarify important issues such as the authority or mandate for both parties to negotiate, the language, timetable, and format of the proceedings and communication between the parties and the mediator. Through this management conference, the parties and the mediator can adapt the process to their own needs.

*Co-Mediation*

These disputes often involve parties who do not speak a common language, do not come from the same legal tradition, have cultural and background differences, and most important, are politicians or civil servants who represent the sovereign state. Being able to use co-mediators, which is permitted under the rules, can help bridge cultural and language gaps. The drafters felt that this feature could make it easier for state representatives to "buy into" the mediation process.

*Party Control*

The rules also make clear the role and involvement of the parties in the conduct of the mediation process and the decision. The parties control the process at all times. The mediator may make procedural decisions after consultation with the parties, but the parties retain control over the process at all times.

*Institutional Support*

The rules allow recourse to an arbitration and mediation institution to support and facilitate the meetings, logistics, and venue for the mediation. The drafters felt that the informal and ad-hoc character of a mediation could be an obstacle for state parties and that the availability of services by an institution could generate additional confidence in the process. Under the IBA rules, ISM can be administered by any arbitration institution.

*Confidentiality and Transparency*

The rules provide for privacy of the process and the communication of information to the mediator and set a default rule of confidentiality for all information prepared or exchanged during the mediation. This confidentiality and transparency is important, given the participation of a sovereign state and implications on public funds and governance. In the last decade, various stakeholders have criticized arbitration for its confidential character, and arbitration rules have been amended to accommodate requirements of transparency. Drafters of the IBA Mediation Rules addressed both issues specifically and opted not to leave them to the parties. Confidentiality, however, does not extend to the fact that a mediation is taking place or to the outcome of the mediation, unless the parties specifically agree to keep this information confidential.

---

## C. Opportunities for Investor-State Mediation and Process Design in the Context of the IBA Rules

The variety of mediation models discussed in Chapter 1 bring new possibilities to the realm of investor-State disputes. These models allow the parties to achieve outcomes that are unattainable through arbitration. For example, facilitative mediation allows the parties to explore their interests, evaluative mediation provides parties with the opportunity to explore the strengths of their legal claims, and transformative mediation can assist the parties in altering their interactions through empowerment and recognition. Yet in order to maximize the benefits of the different models of mediation, it is necessary to tailor the process to the needs and preferences of the parties.

The pre-mediation conference, established in the IBA Investor State-Mediation Rules, presents an opportunity for the assessment of the parties' process preferences, goals, interests, and values, in order to select or design the appropriate mediation process for their dispute. Furthermore, the parties may decide to consider or design processes other than mediation. In the following excerpt, Nancy Welsh and Andrea Schneider emphasize the need to identify the goals of the parties in order to align them with the selected investor-State mediation process.

## NANCY A. WELSH & ANDREA K. SCHNEIDER, *BECOMING "INVESTOR-STATE MEDIATION"*

1 Penn. St. J.L. & Int'l Aff. 86, 95–96 (2012).

It is essential, though, to consider mediation in context, and this requires a brief discussion of the other procedures available to investors and states. Generally, three such procedures come to mind—negotiation, conciliation, and arbitration. The mediation model. . . . offers something new in comparison to these procedures—a third party's assistance in facilitating the parties' communication, information-sharing and negotiation and an explicit opportunity to identify and focus on the discussion of interests. . . .

A procedure called "mediation" is likely to be useful in the investor-state context, but mediation's value will depend upon the particular model that is integrated, and whether it responds to the parties' needs and complements the other available processes in this dispute resolution system. Thus, key actors must devote some time and attention to identifying the key goals and essential practices that should characterize the process that "becomes investor-state mediation."

---

In order to align the goals of the parties with the mediation process, especially given the systemic nature of investor-State disputes, Dispute Systems Design (DSD) can provide the framework for an effective methodology. DSD has been defined as "the applied art and science of designing the means to prevent, manage, learn from, and resolve streams of dispute or conflict."[16] In the following excerpt, Susan D. Franck explores the potential of DSD as a tool to solve and prevent investor-State disputes.

---

16 Lisa Blomgren Amsler, Alexander B. Avtgis, & Michael Scott Jackman, *Dispute System Design and Bias in Dispute Resolution,* 70 SMU L. Rev. 913, 915, 916 (2017); *see also* Cathy A. Costantino & Christina Sickles Merchant, Designing Conflict Management Systems (1996); William L. Ury, Jeanne M. Brett & Stephen B. Goldberg, Getting Disputes Resolved: Designing Systems to Cut the Costs of Conflict (1988); Stephanie Smith & Janet Martinez, *An Analytic Framework for Dispute Systems Design,* 14 Harv. Negot. L. Rev. 123, 126 (2009).

## SUSAN D. FRANCK, *INTEGRATING INVESTMENT TREATY CONFLICT AND DISPUTE SYSTEMS DESIGN*

92 Minn. L. Rev. 161, 177–78, 181–84 (2007).

A properly designed dispute resolution system can draw conflict to the surface and channel its productive forces. Dispute Systems Design (DSD) is the systematic process of creating a dispute resolution system that harnesses the positive aspects of conflict or at least minimizes the negative aspects.

DSD is not a dispute resolution methodology itself. Rather it is the intentional and systematic creation of an effective, efficient, and fair dispute resolution process based upon the unique needs of a particular system.

The objective of DSD is to design better dispute resolution systems. It does so by (1) analyzing parties' patterns of disputing to diagnose the current system, (2) designing methods to manage conflict more effectively with practical principles, (3) approving and implementing the design architecture, and (4) testing and evaluating the new design to make appropriate revisions prior to disseminating the process to the rest of the system. . . . .

* * *

Systematic consideration is critical. Various commentators suggest the dispute resolution system is in crisis and its utility is subject to debate. Meanwhile, the United Nations Commission on Trade and Development (UNCTAD) suggests these challenges "could be addressed by improving the dispute settlement procedures" and the International Centre for the Settlement of Investment Disputes (ICSID) has made certain procedural changes with the intent of improving the process of resolving disputes by arbitration. This puts the evolution of investment treaty disputes at a unique historical junction: we are simultaneously presented with concerns about the system's efficacy and the opportunity to improve its future development.

* * *

Investment treaties and DSD share at least one core concern: both are interested in the effective management of conflict. . . . . DSD offers an approach to conflict management focused on effectively and fairly managing individual cases on a systematic basis. . . . .

Effective use of DSD to manage investment treaty conflict is likely to reduce the transaction costs of dispute resolution. This could decrease investment risks, lower the cost of investing, and produce economic incentives that make host governments more attractive investment opportunities. . . .

Without effective dispute resolution, the goal of using investment treaties to promote investment is undermined. Investors need security, transparency, predictability, reliability, and certainty in the planning of their investments and the resolution of related disputes. Poorly planned and poorly managed dispute resolution increases the cost of resolving disputes, amplifies investment risk, and generates investment disincentives. On a larger scale, the poor management of investment treaty conflict could undermine the success of the investment treaty regime. If DSD can improve the dispute resolution system and promote efficient conflict management, it is worthy of consideration.

---

When using DSD to tailor the mediation process to the parties' preferences, the cultural aspects described in Chapter 3 need to be taken in to account, as they can play a critical role in both external matters, such as communication preferences, and internal cognitive processes such as interpretation. This is especially relevant in the context of investor-State disputes, given the inherent nature of the cross-cultural business relationship. In the following excerpt, Rebecca Golbert reminds us of the need to recognize the impact of culture on our own approach to conflict, the role of the third-party in mediation, and the broad spectrum of expectations with regard to neutrality.

## REBECCA GOLBERT, *AN ANTHROPOLOGIST'S APPROACH TO MEDIATION*

11 Cardozo J. Conflict Resol. 81, 86–88 (2009).

Augsburger draws our attention to the cultural diversity of conflict and conflict resolution practices. He writes, perhaps somewhat idealistically:

> From culture to culture, each has developed its unique patterns of managing differences and resolving disputes. Each constructs its repertoire of conflict behaviors, its hierarchy of values, [and] its code of laws. The study of conflict patterns is the study of contrasts. Out of the same basic needs, fears, and hopes, humans have created ways of dealing with competition, frustration, and aggression that reverse and reflect each other and that would, if brought together, complete each other.

* * *

While a range of social and legal mechanisms for resolving conflict exists across cultures, Augsburger emphasizes mediation as the most frequently used process of dispute settlement in traditional societies. . . .

It is worth examining in greater detail what is meant here by mediation and third party roles and processes. Avruch refers to a diversity of possible third party roles and points to the complexity of the term "mediator." Augsburger offers a continuum of mediator roles—including observer, chairperson, enunciator, prompter, leader, and arbiter. He suggests that the strategy of the mediator frequently changes along with the stages of the mediation, shifting from a more facilitative role as observer, chairperson, or enunciator to a more evaluative or directive role as prompter, leader, or arbiter.

Based on the ethnographic record, both scholars question the presupposition within the North American model of mediation that the ideal mediator should be completely impartial and unbiased and unconnected to the parties or the dispute. Avruch writes, "[t]he ethnographic record in general does not support the existence of the uninvolved third party as either the norm or the ideal (and how could it be in small-scale, multistranded societies?)." Augsburger describes mediators in a traditional model of mediation as "recognized communal leaders or trusted go-betweens from the social context. They are personally embedded in the social networks and remain in relationship with parties in the dispute both during and after the resolution."

---

As values are at the core of culture, and usually investor-State disputes involve parties who may not share a similar culture, the assessment of values becomes of particular relevance in the selection and design of dispute resolution processes. To address these cultural differences in the design of the mediation process, in the following excerpt, Mariana Hernandez Crespo Gonstead explores the use of the Cultural Value Discernment (CVD), previously discussed in Chapter 3, as a relevant tool in the context of investor-State disputes.

## MARIANA HERNANDEZ CRESPO GONSTEAD, *A NEW DANCE ON THE GLOBAL STAGE: INTRODUCING A CULTURAL VALUE-BASED TOOLBOX TO OPTIMIZE PROBLEM-SOLVING, INNOVATION, AND GROWTH*

34 Ohio St. J. on Disp. Resol. (forthcoming 2019).

[The use of a tool known as] [t]he Cultural Value Discernment (CVD), can play a critical role in process design, especially when it is necessary to enhance understanding between the parties in an effort to strengthen their business relationships. This is particularly significant in the context of investor-State disputes, given the complexity of the cultural dynamics that can be present. The Cultural Value Discernment (CVD) could help identify the different cultural values of host countries, foreign investors, and communities in order to adapt the processes and roles accordingly.

Because foreign investors might not share the culture of the host state or the communities in which they operate, gaining understanding of the parties' most significant values embedded in their cultures constitutes a critical initial phase. Deepening the knowledge of what is important to the parties can contribute significantly to the design of the process and the determination of parties', attorneys', and mediators' roles, making them consistent with their values.

A process design that is consistent with the values of the parties can not only be more effective, but it can also enhance understanding between foreign investors and host States. This deepening of understanding between the two is essential to promote investment retention and enhance the host state's investment climate.

---

### D. The Possibility of Co-Mediation in the IBA Rules

Another significant feature of the IBA Investor-State Mediation Rules is the possibility of co-mediation. Given the different cultural differences often found in the investor-State relationship, it is particularly important to provide both parties with an option to select a mediator who shares similar cultural ties in order to help interpret the parties' frame of reference. This could be essential for enhancing understanding and reaching a mutually satisfying agreement. While using one mediator may work for some parties and disputes, in other cases the parties may be better served by the use of co-mediators. In the following excerpt, Mariana Hernandez Crespo Gonstead expands upon this idea, and describes how co-mediation, previously discussed in Chapter 3, can be used to aid culturally diverse parties in resolving investor-State disputes.

## MARIANA HERNANDEZ CRESPO GONSTEAD, *A NEW DANCE ON THE GLOBAL STAGE: INTRODUCING A CULTURAL VALUE-BASED TOOLBOX TO OPTIMIZE PROBLEM-SOLVING, INNOVATION, AND GROWTH*

34 Ohio St. J. on Disp. Resol. (forthcoming 2019).

Specifically, co-mediation in investor-State disputes offers untapped opportunities to enhance understanding between culturally diverse parties. In investor-State mediation there may be cultural tensions between the parties regarding the expectations of the process and/or the role of the mediator. One of these critical tensions could be related to the neutrality of the mediator. Some parties may prefer a neutral mediator, while others may prefer a mediator with shared cultural ties. To address this tension, co-mediation provides an opportunity for each party to select the mediator of their choice, which may enhance their level of satisfaction with the process, and potentially lead to a more sustainable agreement. Although co-mediating across cultures might pose its own challenges given the potential stark cultural differences between the mediators themselves, in this multi-cultural world, co-mediation cannot be overlooked as an option to address the needs of culturally diverse parties.

---

# V. DOMESTIC DEVELOPMENTS: USING INVESTOR-STATE MEDIATION AND SYSTEM DESIGN FOR EFFECTIVE CONFLICT MANAGEMENT TO PREVENT DISPUTES, AND PROMOTE INVESTMENT RETENTION AND EXPANSION

The use of investor-State mediation also has the potential to strengthen the investor-State relationship at the domestic level, as it can contribute to managing conflict before it escalates into an international legal dispute. In particular, domestic conflict management efforts have become more relevant, given the current focus on investment retention and expansion. To this end, investor-

State dispute settlement[17] at the international level, although necessary, is not sufficient to improve the investment climate in a given country. While investor-State dispute settlement allows for the resolution of the issue at hand, conflict management mechanisms are necessary to enhance the on-going relationship between foreign investors, host States, and local communities.

### A. Systemic Investor Response Mechanisms (SIRMs) and Shared Decisions System Design (SDSD)

Governments have a greater capacity to manage conflicts at the local, state, or national levels through CMMs than when legal disputes have escalated into an international arbitration process. Some investor-State conflicts occur because governments are not monolithic, but rather are an amalgamation of agencies and federal, state, and local authorities. Given this structural complexity, it is a challenge to coordinate governmental actions with foreign investors. To this end, host States can greatly benefit from developing their own processes, such as a SIRMs. Originally developed by Roberto Echandi and implemented by the World Bank Group, SIRMs can act as an essential framework to ensure fluid and coherent government interactions with foreign investors.[18]

In the G-20 Compact with Africa, SIRMs are defined as "[a]n early warning and tracking mechanism to identify and resolve complaints . . . . that arise from government conduct . . . . ultimately preventing legal disputes and facilitating harmonious relations between investors and governments. [It] . . . . enables countries to collect data and helps identify patterns in government-generated grievances affecting investments. [It] . . . . quantifies investment retained or expanded as a consequence of addressing grievances, [and] . . . . investment lost as a consequence of not addressing them."[19]

Collaborative design systems such as SDSD can operate within SIRMs in cases where there are multiple stakeholders involved and the issues are systemic. SDSD provides a framework to integrate the investor, the community, and the host State's government in the

---

[17] European Comm'n, Investor-to-State Dispute Settlement (ISDS): Some Facts and Figures (2015), http://trade.ec.europa.eu/doclib/docs/2015/january/tradoc_153046.pdf.

[18] Echandi, *supra* note 2.

[19] World Bank Grp., The G-20 Compact with Africa 23 (2017), https://www.compactwithafrica.org/content/dam/Compact%20with%20Africa/2017-03-30-g20-compact-with-africa-report.pdf.

decision-making process on issues directly affecting their daily lives. Mediation is considered an integral part of SDSD and can be used to manage differences before conflict arises, during the rule making process, implementation, and conflict management. It can also be used to manage the investor-State relationship at different stages: rule-making, implementation, and conflict management. In the following excerpt, Mariana (Hernandez Crespo) Gonstead defines SIRMs and SDSD and explores how they could be used in the context of natural resource seeking investment to manage conflict efficiently and effectively at the domestic level. She argues that mediation can be an essential process in enhancing the investor-State and community relationship.

## MARIANA HERNANDEZ CRESPO G., *A NEW CHAPTER IN NATURAL RESOURCE-SEEKING INVESTMENT: USING SHARED DECISIONS SYSTEM DESIGN ("SDSD") TO STRENGTHEN INVESTOR-STATE AND COMMUNITY RELATIONSHIPS*

18 Cardozo J. Conflict Resol. 551, 556, 574–75, 580–81, 584, 618–19 (2017).

Through the use of what I have called Shared Decisions System Design ("SDSD")—participatory processes put in place to promote public decision-making of systemic impact—civic society can be engaged, together with the foreign investor and host State, as active participants along the policy continuum: upstream (decision-making), midstream (implementation), and downstream (resolution/ enforcement).

* * *

The final guiding principle to the preservation of investor-State satisfaction and, ultimately, the recipe for investment retention, involves the principles of SIRMs and SDSD. The protocols designed by SIRMs have been part of pilot projects developed and implemented by the Investment Policy and Promotion Team of the World Bank Group. On top of the seven components of the previously known CMMs, SIRMs now track the investment retention and expansion that occurs, due to the capacity developed to address issues in a timely manner. This information is obtained through an information technology tool. Besides problem-solving techniques, Echandi's SIRMs also include what I have conceptualized as Shared Decisions System Design, in order to craft decision-making processes to address matters of systemic impact.

The protocols for the design and carrying out of SIRMs are not a one-size-fits-all program, but serve as a guide to help stakeholders adopt a program that meets their specific needs. These protocols detail the following seven elements, geared toward generating further research that can be utilized in constructing a specific program: (1) stocktaking, or diagnosing the types of disputes experienced in a given State based on where they occur, when they occur, and how often they occur; (2) establishing a national Lead Agency with the necessary capacity to administer conflict management policies and negotiate investment treaties; (3) information sharing and open channels of communication need to be developed between the Lead Agency and other agencies that deal regularly with the foreign investors. They need to be knowledgeable about the contractual obligations of the host State, so everyone is aware of what has taken place at the national level. Similarly, they need to be able to provide clarification or point the investors to CMMs in case of a potential conflict; (4) Early Alert Mechanisms that warn the government of potential conflicts before they escalate into a dispute through a notice of intent and a value claim; (5) problem solving methods that determine whether a conflict can be managed by means of administrative review, which is preferable, or whether further recourse to preventative ADR mechanisms would be necessary. Shared Decisions System Design (SDSD) come into play when participatory processes need to be put in place to make decisions that will have systemic impact; and (6) Political Decision-Making and Enforcement stresses the need for the agreed solution to be approved by the highest decision-making authority in the host State to ensure implementation.

* * *

SDSD originates from the notion of collaborative governance, which Lisa Blomgren Amsler has defined as "the integration of reasoned discussions by the citizens and other residents into the decision-making of public representatives, especially when these approaches are embedded in the workings of local governance over time." This concept could play a critical role in settling the upheaval and stabilizing the sociopolitical environment, creating necessary conditions to accommodate long-term investments.

In the FDI arena, policy makers face the challenge of developing channels for participation at the local level that are able to not only prevent and manage conflict, but also encourage collaborative work among foreign investors, local government, and the community. In helping face this challenge, the field of DSD can assist in crafting interactions along the policy continuum of collaborative governance—where citizens participate together with the government in the decision-making process in areas such as deliberative democracy, collaborative public management, and alternative dispute resolution.

* * *

[Multi-party mediation as an integral element of SDSD, can contribute to the enhancement of the investor-State and Community relationship and play a critical role in public dispute resolution.] For example, if one of the goals of the parties was to preserve the relationship, perhaps mediation, in which parties could potentially reach a mutually beneficial agreement, would be more appropriate than an adjudicative process, where one party would win and the other would lose, possibly eroding the relationship.

* * *

The new chapter [For investor-State. . . .] places a new emphasis not only on remedies for specific disputes, but also on strengthening the investor-State relationship. Such a shift of emphasis could also help the international investment regime gain the stability associated with developing countries that fulfill their obligations under these treaties.

Investor and State interests can best be fulfilled through the development of decision-making processes that involve civic participation and engaging stakeholders early on and then throughout the entire relationship (i.e., along the policy continuum). Protecting investors' rights is not enough; fulfilling investor-State interests is also critical. Sustainable and fruitful investor-State relations require a system of joint gains involving the satisfaction of all the parties' interests. Attempting to secure investment without citizen participation could limit the radius of BITs' success. Long-term sustainability could be realistically hoped for only when the interests of both investors and the citizens that comprise the State are met, thus enabling relationships to be built upon maximization of joint gains.

These interests can be fulfilled if conflict management takes place during a preventative stage, before conflict escalates to the level of dispute through the use of Conflict Management Mechanisms. Furthermore, it would be vital to implement the Systemic Investment Response Mechanisms developed by Echandi, along with Shared Decisions System Design I have proposed in this Article, in order to implement participatory decision-making processes to address matters of systemic impact. By promoting participation of stakeholders—representatives of the community, the State, and the foreign investor—SDSD could serve as an important tool to advance inclusion and contribute to the legitimacy of the system. In this way, these new measures can contribute to promoting investment retention and expansion.

---

The following excerpt presents specific examples of countries who have designed their own domestic systems in an effort to identify conflict before it escalates into a dispute. Nancy Welsh and Andrea Schneider highlight some of the potential risks of designing domestic conflict management mechanisms without input from the foreign investor.

## NANCY A. WELSH & ANDREA K. SCHNEIDER, *BECOMING "INVESTOR-STATE MEDIATION"*

1 Penn. St. J.L. & Int'l Aff. 86, 95 (2012).

A few states, however, have expanded the usual list of options available in the investor-state context by establishing new structures and procedures designed to encourage early communication and information-sharing between states and investors, thus identifying difficulties before they escalate into disputes or resolving such disputes very early on. Examples include Peru's coordination and response system, including its Special Commission; China's domestic administrative review process; and Colombia's establishment of a lead agency model. Interestingly, the state officials leading these efforts have the *potential* to serve a "quasi-mediator" function, meeting many of the needs that would otherwise fall to third party mediators using the [facilitative/evaluative] model of mediation . . . . Trust, however, is the key. If investors perceive these quasi-mediators as biased against them—as insufficiently benevolent, insufficiently even-handed, or insufficiently open-minded—then investors are unlikely to perceive their procedures as fair. Mediation involving an outside mediator is likely to be perceived as more procedurally just—or fairer—and thus preferable. At the very least, then, the easy availability of a corps of outside, independent and trusted mediators, as an alternative to the state's judicial or administrative officials, has the potential to incentivize the state to make its own processes equally even-handed, in order to attract foreign investors.

---

### B. Introduction of the Cultural Value Integration Spectrum (CVIS) in System Design

Another aspect to consider when designing the mediation process, SIRMs, or SDSD is the cultural compatibility of the parties and the possible level of discerned integration of their cultures. In the investor-State context, parties often come from different backgrounds, and therefore the foreign investor and host State might not have a shared culture. While culture informs personal values, at the same time values are at the core of culture, and it is important to take into account the differing value systems of the parties at the mediation table. The Cultural Value Discernment (CVD), previously discussed in Section IV of this chapter, is a critical tool that allows for tailoring the process and when necessary the overall system design, so that the process or system is aligned with the values of the parties.

Once the values have been identified, the Cultural Value Integration Spectrum (CVIS), can be an effective tool to help determine the level of integration of the cultural values, spanning from co-existence, to collaboration, to complementarity. In the following excerpt, Mariana (Hernandez Crespo) Gonstead revisits the CVIS, previously discussed in Chapter 3, in the context of investor-State disputes, as an essential tool to assist the process of assessing and understanding the value compatibility of stakeholders.

### MARIANA HERNANDEZ CRESPO GONSTEAD, *A NEW DANCE ON THE GLOBAL STAGE: INTRODUCING A CULTURAL VALUE-BASED TOOLBOX TO OPTIMIZE PROBLEM-SOLVING, INNOVATION, AND GROWTH*

34 Ohio St. J. on Disp. Resol. (forthcoming 2019).

The Cultural Value Integration Spectrum (CVIS) can be used as a tool to provide the information needed to assist the stakeholders' mutual discernment of the appropriate level of assimilation or integration between the host State, foreign investor, and local community. In the context of Foreign Direct Investment (FDI), the Cultural Value Integration Spectrum (CVIS) is especially critical given the private-public nature of the relationship and the multiplicity of cultures. At a minimum, the foreign investor brings a corporate culture, the host State brings a government culture, and the community where the investment takes place adds a local culture.

In order to facilitate this discernment, the Cultural Value Integration Spectrum (CVIS) is conducted through three steps: first, the identification of stakeholders' values through the Cultural Value Discernment (CVD); second, an assessment of the stakeholders' value compatibility and the level of integration of their cultural values on a spectrum that goes from co-existence, to collaboration, to complementarity; third, based on the information gained in the first two steps, appropriate processes and systems can be designed for dispute resolution.

The Cultural Value Integration Spectrum (CVIS) can promote participatory based dispute resolution methods (i.e. facilitative processes), leading to integration, promote persuasion based methods (i.e. adjudicative processes) leading to assimilation, or combine elements of both in a hybrid process. For example, the different approaches of mediation, such as facilitative, evaluative, transformative, and narrative, can be utilized to assist foreign investors, host States, and communities in the designing of processes for decisionmaking and dispute resolution that take into account the appropriate level of cultural integration determined by the Cultural Value Integration Spectrum (CVIS). Reflecting stakeholders' values in the processes can make interactions between foreign investors and host States more efficient and effective. Also, this tailoring of the process has the potential to make the host State more attractive to the foreign investor and can serve as a strategy to promote investment retention and expansion.

---

## VI. NOTES AND QUESTIONS

1. The move to a primarily rule-based system that sets rules for host States, grants rights to foreign investors, and enables them to bring claims through arbitration has not been without controversy. Yet it allowed the move from the mainly power-based system and also allowed an interest-based system to emerge, which now includes processes such as investor-State mediation. Now that there are three systems in place to address conflicts and resolve disputes, can you think of situations where it would be best to use a power-based strategy (i.e. pressure), a rules-based strategy (i.e. arbitration), an interest-based strategy (i.e. mediation), or a combination of any of the strategies?

2. Taking into account the unique nature of investor-State disputes, how would processes such as negotiation, conciliation, and mediation address the five essential considerations identified by Jeswald Salacuse, listed in Part II?

3. As a foreign investor think of a possible conflict that could arise with the host State. To resolve this conflict, you need to select an appropriate process for resolution. Would mediation be the preferred option? What criteria would you use to make your decision? Would the criteria be the same if you take the systems approach that encompasses all the stakeholders affected by your decision? Who would you identify as stakeholders? If you are the host State, would any of your answers change? Could you design a process or system that satisfies the interests of both the foreign investor and the host State?

4. Some have argued that the flexibility provided by the IBA rules is one important feature, given the diverse preferences in the world for both interactions and conflict resolution. *See* Susan D. Franck, *Using Investor-State Mediation Rules to Promote Conflict Management: An Introductory Guide*, 29 ICSID Rev. 66 (2014). For example, differences in communication styles, ways of building trust, and desired levels of disclosure can affect the satisfaction of the parties and impact the outcome. What are some of the advantages of having a flexible set of rules to accommodate diverse cultural preferences? What are some of the issues that are presented by this flexibility? Would a more rigid set of rules that mandate specific options be preferable? What are some of the advantages of having a defined procedure? Who should make the decision? Whose preferences should be adopted for all to follow? What values would those preferences advance?

5. Article 9 in the IBA rules introduces the "mediation management conference." What could the parties do to maximize this opportunity to discuss and design the process? How could this mediation management conference be used to tailor the mediation process to the parties' preferences when there are cultural differences?

6. Articles 4 and 6 in the IBA rules regulate the designation of co-mediators. In what context would one mediator, rather than two, be preferable? When would two mediators be more desirable? What factors would you take into account when choosing the co-mediators? What are some of the challenges that having co-mediators can pose? How can they be overcome?

7. Part V examined some of the current efforts to address conflict at the domestic level before it escalates to a legal dispute at the international level. To this end, conflict management mechanisms were discussed. If the goal is to move from investor-State dispute prevention to investment retention or divestment prevention, how can mediation at the domestic level be used to strengthen the business relationship? What are some of the benefits and challenges of addressing conflict before it escalates into a legal claim? How can

some of the features of the different mediation models discussed earlier in this book, be used at the domestic level to manage conflict?

8. The Cultural Value Integration Spectrum (CVIS) was presented as a tool to "provide the information needed to assist the stakeholders' mutual discernment of the appropriate level of assimilation or integration between the host State, foreign investor, and local community." Given that the cultures of the foreign investor, host State, and local communities may be significantly different, especially in the context of natural resource seeking investments (mining, oil, and other natural resources), the CVIS might be especially relevant in order to understand what is important to each of them, and allow them to make informed decisions when selecting the appropriate process. Can you think of the factors that you would take into account in order to decide the desired level of integration (co-existence, collaboration, or complementarity)? If mediation is determined to be the appropriate process, how would the level of integration affect the mediation model selected?

# Chapter 8

# PEACEMAKING MEDIATION

## I. INTRODUCTION: MEDIATION AND DIPLOMACY

Mediation is part of a wide spectrum of processes for peacemaking and diplomacy. Negotiation between diplomats is the classic example of preventative diplomacy. There is also the practice of Track II negotiations between non-official but influential members of a community who are able to facilitate dialogue among parties in conflict. Arbitration has been used successfully in resolving international boundary disputes. Transitional justice approaches have elements of mediation, working with victims, offenders, and the community. Finally, consensus building processes in the public sphere rely in part on mediation approaches to identify positions, interests, and values of different stakeholders.

In this chapter we focus on the increasingly important role of mediation in international conflict resolution. Article 33 of the United Nations Charter lists mediation as one of several processes for States to manage their disputes. Ethnic groups within states also employ mediation to resolve seemingly intractable conflicts. Finally, there is a growing interest by the World Bank and other international institutions in promoting mediation practices to resolve conflict.

This Chapter discusses some of the major decisions that must be made in planning for mediation in conflict cases. It explores concepts of fairness and success in mediation, and considers various models of mediation practice. The following excerpts discuss the historical foundations of peacemaking mediation, and the role of self-determination in the political context.

## A. Historical Role of Mediation in Peacemaking

### JOHN D. FEERICK, *THE PEACE-MAKING ROLE OF A MEDIATOR*

19 Ohio St. J. Disp. Resol. 229, 230 (2003).

Mediation, or the intervention of third parties, has been a tested and tried means of dispute resolution since the earliest history of the world. It was widely used in both Rome and Egypt and by the Greek city-states in connection with their wars. Indeed, emperors and rulers at different points in history were called on to assist in the resolution of disputes involving other states and nations. Louis IX became world renowned in that role, sought both from inside and outside his country to arbitrate and mediate disputes. More recently, we have witnessed a former President of the United States, Jimmy Carter, playing such a role on the world stage, and his former Secretary of State, Cyrus Vance . . . . . played such a role as well. The citation accompanying the Nobel Peace Prize given to President Carter spoke admiringly and deservedly of his role in mediating disputes.

Hugo Grotius, the father of international law, spoke often of the importance of mediation and other forms of dispute resolution as a way to avoid or end hostilities. Given the consequences of war, Grotius emphasized the importance of using such approaches, pointing to historical and successful examples of third party intervention. Not surprisingly, the United Nations Charter singles out mediation as a major tool of dispute resolution.

---

## B. The Role of Self-Determination in the Political Context

The principle of self-determination is considered a foundational value of mediation. However, in the context of international mediation, self-determination is linked to sovereignty and takes on broader meaning. The following excerpt discusses the concept of self-determination in relation to both international law and dispute resolution.

## JACQUELINE NOLAN-HALEY, *SELF-DETERMINATION IN INTERNATIONAL MEDIATION: SOME PRELIMINARY REFLECTIONS*

7 Cardozo J. Conflict Resol. 277, 280–82 (2006).

### *Self-Determination in Public Mediation*

The concept of self-determination in public international mediation must be understood in relationship to both international law and dispute resolution principles. As a substantive principle of international law, the historical roots of self-determination in the West have been traced to the exodus of the Hebrews from Egypt, while its modern engagement began at the Versailles Peace Conference. President Woodrow Wilson championed the ideal of self-determination and introduced it to the League of Nations in 1919 as "the right of every people to choose the sovereign under which they live, to be free of alien masters, and not be handed about from sovereign to sovereign as if they were property." Article I of the United Nations Charter continued the self-determination theme by describing the development of ". . . . friendly relations among nations based on respect for the principle of equal rights and self-determination of peoples. . . . ." as one of the purposes of the United Nations. Over the twenty years following adoption of the Charter, understandings of the substantive legal principle of self-determination evolved into recognition of it as a fundamental right. In 1966, two United Nations Covenants on Human Rights included acknowledgment of the right of self-determination for the contracting parties by connecting it to political, civil, economic, social and cultural rights. Article I of both Covenants on Human Rights states:

"All peoples have the right of self-determination. By virtue of that right they freely determine their political status and freely pursue their economic, social and cultural development."

The legal right to self-determination that allows people or groups to choose their own forms of political government is a well-established part of international law in the anti-colonialist context. It also prohibits foreign military occupation and requires access to government for all racial groups. Beyond these three areas, the boundaries of the right of self-determination as a substantive international legal principle are unclear. Should it be limited to situations of colonial rule? To the claims of indigenous peoples? Who are the "people" for whom the right attaches? Who belongs to the group and who decides?

## II. MEDIATION IN OPERATION: CHALLENGES

There are a number of practical challenges that must be considered in connection with the practice of mediation. What is the appropriate time for a third party to enter into a conflict? Who are the stakeholders and how should they be included in the mediation process? How should we define a quality agreement in mediation that has long-term durability? Finally, how do we determine whether mediation has been successful in the long run? The following sections discuss these concerns.

### A. Timing the Entry into a Conflict Situation

When is a conflict ripe for intervention by a third party? When are parties ready to mediate? It is generally understood that the best time to attempt to resolve a dispute is at the early stages, before it becomes transformed into violent conflict. Waiting to intervene has costs which are described in The Manual for UN Mediators—"The longer a conflict persists, the more intractable it becomes, making its resolution ever more difficult; its impact on people, communities, institutions of state and the sub-region ever more devastating; and the cost of rebuilding ever more expensive."[1]

In the following excerpt, William Zartman discusses the concept of ripeness and explores the idea of opportunities as entryways into a conflict. He focuses on cases of missed opportunities in collapsed states when ripe moments for conflict resolution were not seized effectively.

### WILLIAM ZARTMAN, *COWARDLY LIONS: MISSED OPPORTUNITIES FOR DISPUTE SETTLEMENT*

18 Ohio St. J. on Disp. Resol. 1, 2–6, 12–15 (2002).

*Opportunities*

Opportunities are favorable moments for achieving a purpose—a suitable combination of conditions for accomplishing a goal. The opportune moment to do something is not just "whenever," but is contextually determined in relation to the conflict. Interventions require an "entry point" or occasion that invites foreign action. Need alone does not justify action; there must be some definable opening for external parties to enter, and if there is not, it must be created. Opportunities or entry points can be defined by event or by context.

---

1 Connie Peck, A Manual for UN Mediators: Advice from UN Representatives and Envoys 5 (2010).

Events that require or justify a mediatory reaction can be either scheduled or unscheduled. In a few instances, a scheduled event such as an election requires a response that could make a major difference in the subsequent course of actions. Examples include the fraudulent count announced after the 1985 elections in Liberia, where American rejection would have triggered both internal and external reactions; or the cancellation of the November 1987 elections in Haiti, which occasioned a cut in aid but little more; or the restoration of Aristide in 1994, which was not followed by measures to restore the state as well; or the 1996 elections in Yugoslavia, where the opposition received polite notice from Washington but no help.

More frequently, unscheduled events or crises invite an external response. The 1995 shelling of Sarajevo galvanized the NATO allies into intervention in Bosnia, and the 1991 advances of the Eritrean and Tigrean rebels on Addis Ababa brought in United States mediation. But neither the 1988 massacre of dispossessed Somali tribesmen in Hargeisa, the 1991 and 1993 military and civilian riots in Kinshasa and other Zairean cities, the 1995 and 1996 pogroms of targeted ethnic groups in the Kivus of eastern Zaire, the 1991 military coup against the elected Haitian government in Port au Prince, nor the 1994 unconstitutional installation of a new president in Haiti brought any effective response. In an event-defined opportunity, scheduled or unscheduled, the response must be immediate; otherwise, the opening closes and the justification appears lame.

When there is no event, scheduled or unexpected, to require a response, the opportunity is to be found more broadly in the context of the conflict. Significantly, this is the more frequent case. The established model indicates that a ripe moment for initiating mediation is composed of a mutually hurting stalemate, out of which parties seek or are responsive to help in extricating themselves.

* * *

Parties to conflicts have repeatedly allowed ripe moments to slip away as evidenced by the following: in Lebanon in March 1978, July 1982 and March 1984, factions engaged in a civil war were deadlocked and hurting but not helped out of their impasse; in Liberia in June 1990, in April 1992 or July 1993, parties were brought to a ceasefire but no effective measures for ending the conflict. Other instances when ripe moments for conflict resolution were missed existed in June 1990 when the Yugoslav republics were deadlocked over the future of the federation, in October 1998 when the Serbian government and the Kosovars were at an impasse over the Kosovo issue, and in Somalia in March-June 1991 just after Siad Barre's fall. A mutually hurting stalemate may motivate conflicting parties themselves to negotiation but it is often the vehicle for third party intervention if the parties are not motivated to seize the moment on their own.

But in some instances, there was only a soft stalemate with a painful but bearable effect, and the interveners were required to create an event or an opportunity to justify their action. Intervention therefore had to be sold to the conflicting parties themselves (as well as to the interveners' public); it was a lifebuoy thrown to a swimmer rather enjoying the excitement of the surf and oblivious to the approaching tidal wave that was visible to the thrower. The image shows that a soft stalemate requires third party intervention, even more than does a hard or hurting stalemate. In these instances, the opportunity is artificial, to be constructed out of the unstable conflict or impending collapse before it really blows up at a less convenient time for both conflicting parties and vulnerable bystanders.

* * *

Finally, there are moments of opportunity when the conflict undergoes a momentary calm, opening the possibility of creating a longer lasting, more stable outcome. It is generally evident that measures are needed to make the pause in the conflict permanent by addressing the causes of the conflict and establishing mechanisms to prevent its reoccurrence. The opportunity may come from an informal lull in the conflict, from a more explicit ceasefire, or even from a meeting of the parties. The point is that it offers an opening for specific measures for it is not self-perpetuating and will fall apart at the next incident if not seized and solidified. In half the instances, third parties took advantage of a momentary lull to summon the conflicting parties to a conference to fill the political vacuum and reinstitute the state, but then failed in reality because they did not invest commensurate energy in follow-through.

In sum, the opportunity is defined as a moment in the conflict or collapse when the external party can direct the conflicting parties' attention to constructive measures. While there is a specific element in the identification of opportunities—an event requiring a response, a stalemate impelling an exit—there is also a huge window for creativity. Opportunities can be inherently precise times or they can be broader time periods within which the particular moment is a matter of perception and creation.

* * *

Missed opportunities are not merely missed moments; they tend to be failures to gain entry into a whole phase of a conflict, after which entry is no longer or much more rarely possible, and the phase changes into something less penetrable. Opportunities are not revolving doors, where entry appears at regular intervals. They constitute a period of time in the life of the conflict when preventive diplomacy is possible and after which entry becomes much more difficult. Not only opportunities, but whole periods of opportunity were missed in Yugoslavia, Liberia, Haiti, Somalia, and Zaire-Congo. Consequently, these countries and their citizens, the regions, and the external powers have had to live with the consequences.

* * *

*Early Awareness and Early Action*

The strongest reason for early action, when options are still available, is that later action is more expensive, forced and constrained; inaction is costly in its consequences. In all of the cases, the US—to focus on the leading country—was obliged to enter the conflict late, after having avoided chances to take lesser action earlier. When it finally adopted a policy, substantial damage had already been done. Many of the deaths and displacements were accompanied by frightful human abuses—rapes, massacres, destruction of homes and places of worship, and other brutalities. These are some of the costs that need to be calculated in making the decision not to act.

In all of these cases, not only was it expensive to delay effective action in the conflict, it became impossible later to avoid involvement, with further expensive consequences. After the U.S. had dithered through the evolving Yugoslav disintegration in the early 1990s, it was unavoidably drawn in to handle the consequences in Bosnia, Kosovo, and Macedonia in the second half of the decade. After the U.S. pursued its contradictory appreciations of the Haitian crisis in the early 1990s, it was finally obliged to use full force in the middle of the decade; the U.S. declared victory and went back home. The U.S. and its Troika partners found themselves obliged to reckon with an intransigent, paranoid successor in dealing with Kabila's Congo after they avoided decisive measures at the beginning and into the middle of the 1990s in dealing with Mobutu's Zaire. The international community felt compelled to engage in truly shocking events in the successor situation after it had only looked on with shock at the final paroxysms of Siad Barre's regime—as the anguished discussions at the end of the Bush and the beginning of the Clinton administrations demonstrate. If external actors had continued to ignore these conflicts and collapses indefinitely, then the missed opportunities would only be humanitarian losses. But because the United States and other outside players eventually feel obliged to get involved when the situation is worse, early engagement becomes a matter of interest.

*Excuses*

In all thirty instances of missed opportunities in the six collapsing states, early warnings were more than adequate, proposed measures would likely have been successful, and the cost of collapse in terms of lives and money may have been much less than the final actual costs. In half the instances, the policy proposals involve merely strengthening initiatives that have already been taken. So why were the opportunities missed?

The most specific reason is that the measures were contrary to the policy supporting the status quo, even as the status quo was falling apart. . . .

Another reason opportunities were missed was a fear of casualties. The official fear of military deaths was encouraged by the Bush administration as early as 1991 by the manner the Gulf War was touted; the fear was then played to the hilt by the Clinton administration. Instead of developing such themes as leadership, post-Cold War order, U.N. usefulness to American objectives, regional security regimes, protection of human rights, and values as interest, the United States, joined by other Western countries, hid behind its own rhetoric about casualties even when the danger of deaths was minimal. As a result, it allowed forces of disorder and spirals of violence to prove its point. A little exemplary firmness in Liberia, Somalia, and Yugoslavia in 1990 or in Liberia, Somalia, Zaire, Yugoslavia, and Haiti in 1991 would have involved few or no troops and would have forestalled much larger troop use and danger later. The absence of such a response showed the forces of disorder in these countries that their actions were unchecked. Thus, a firm response not only inhibits specific disorder in the short run, but it also inhibits its escalation in the long run.

A third reason for the missed opportunities was a lack of mediation skills. Frequently, as in Lebanon, Liberia, and Somalia, mediation was attempted but failed because it was not well conducted. There were no skilled authoritative mediators, often because of a shortage of experience and training in the tough business of preventive diplomacy (especially in West Africa and the Middle East). Keeping the parties engaged, devising trade-offs, thinking through consequences and follow-through, working out details, installing dispute-resolution mechanisms, developing ties and relationships, were skills, which were absent in crucial conferences of the parties. Provision of a skilled mediator was required to complement the demarche.

---

## B. Identifying and Including All Stakeholders

Mediators should make every effort to insure that all stakeholders are represented at the table, whether or not all stakeholders recognize the existence of the other. Comprehensive inclusion helps to achieve a durable agreement. A good example of an inclusive model of negotiation is the approach of the Women's Coalition Party in the mediated negotiations leading up to the Good Friday/Belfast Agreement in 1998. The Women's Coalition Party insisted that all stakeholders be included at the table, including paramilitary parties. This approach differed from that of many other political parties who argued for the exclusion of certain groups from the peace talks, and then refused to speak with them when they were present.[2]

The following excerpt describes the views of the United Nations regarding the importance of providing for inclusion in mediated negotiations.

### U.N. SECRETARY-GENERAL, *STRENGTHENING THE ROLE OF MEDIATION IN THE PEACEFUL SETTLEMENT OF DISPUTES, CONFLICT PREVENTION AND RESOLUTION: REPORT OF THE SECRETARY-GENERAL*

U.N. Doc. A/66/811 (June 25, 2012), Annex I: United Nations Guidance for Effective Mediation, pp. 25, 26 (2012), reprinted with the permission of the United Nations (data downloaded on 2/1/19).

*Inclusivity*

29. Inclusivity refers to the extent and manner in which the views and needs of conflict parties and other stakeholders are represented and integrated into the process and outcome of a mediation effort. An inclusive process is more likely to identify and address the root causes of conflict and ensure that the needs of the affected sectors of

---

[2] Jacqueline Nolan-Haley & Bronagh Hinds, *Problem-Solving Negotiation: Northern Ireland's Experience with the Women's Coalition Symposium*, J. Disp. Resol. 387 (2003).

the population are addressed. Inclusivity also increases the legitimacy and national ownership of the peace agreement and its implementation. In addition, it reduces the likelihood of excluded actors undermining the process. An inclusive process does not imply that all stakeholders participate directly in the formal negotiations, but facilitates interaction between the conflict parties and other stakeholders and creates mechanisms to include all perspectives in the process.

30. It cannot be assumed that conflict parties have legitimacy with, or represent, the wider public. Mediation efforts that involve only armed groups may send the signal that violence is rewarded. In addition to generating resentment within other sectors of society, this could encourage others to take up arms in order to get a place at the negotiating table. Civil society actors can play a critical role in increasing the legitimacy of a peace process and are potentially important allies. Women leaders and women's groups are often effective in peacemaking at community levels and should therefore be more strongly linked to the high-level mediation process. However, support from civil society and other stakeholders cannot be taken for granted, as some of these actors may have hard-line positions and oppose the mediation.

31. In designing an inclusive process, mediators face a number of challenges. There may be instances in which not all conflict parties want to engage in mediation or have sufficient levels of coherence to negotiate, making only a partial process possible. Arrest warrants issued by the International Criminal Court, sanctions regimes, and national and international counter-terrorism policies also affect the manner in which some conflict parties may be engaged in a mediation process. Mediators need to protect the space for mediation and their ability to engage with all actors while making sure that the process respects the relevant legal limitations.

32. In seeking to broaden the process to other stakeholders, mediators may also face constraints from conflict parties who generally seek to determine who, how and when different actors are brought into the process. In some instances, more exclusive dialogue with conflict parties may be required to move the process forward expeditiously, for example in negotiating ceasefires, especially where parties feel too exposed politically or if their security may be compromised. Mediators need to gauge the comfort levels of conflict parties and convince them of the value of broadening participation. They also have to balance having a transparent process with protecting the confidentiality of the talks.

33. Mediators have to grapple with the potential tension between inclusivity and efficiency. Mediation processes become more complex (and may be overloaded) when the consultation base expands and/or multiple forums are used to engage actors at different levels. In addition, it may be difficult to engage interest groups that are not easily defined or lack clear leadership, for example social movements and youth groups. These kinds of issues put a premium on stakeholder mapping, planning and management of the process.

34. Building on a comprehensive mapping of all conflict parties and stakeholders, mediators should:

- Identify the level of inclusivity needed for the mediation to start and required for a durable peace that addresses the needs of all affected by the conflict.
- Communicate with any party or actor necessary to address the conflict, with the knowledge of the other negotiating parties.
- Limit contacts with actors that have been indicted by the International Criminal Court to what is necessary for the mediation process.
- Promote understanding among conflict parties of the value of broader participation and minimize preconditions for participation in the process.
- Ensure systematic and structured consultation with women's groups early in the process to allow for meaningful participation, with specific efforts to include them in the mediation process.
- Encourage conflict parties to include women in their delegations.
- Identify partners to help build the capacity of civil society and other relevant stakeholders to engage effectively.
- Develop mechanisms to broaden participation in the process, and to engage and include the different perspectives within civil society and other stakeholders, throughout the various phases of the peace process.
- Use different forms of media, including social media and opinion polls, to expand participation, inform and

engage the public and identify potential points of contention.

---

## C. Achieving Quality Agreements in Mediation

An important aspect of the mediation process is achieving agreements that are durable and of high quality. In the words of Lawrence Susskind and Jeffrey Cruikshank, a quality agreement should be "nearly self-enforcing," so that all the relevant parties realize that they are better off with an agreement than without one.[3]

In the following excerpt, the UN Secretary-General offers guidance on the importance of drafting peace agreements that are precise and aim to resolve the major issues that led to the conflict.

### U.N. SECRETARY-GENERAL, *STRENGTHENING THE ROLE OF MEDIATION IN THE PEACEFUL SETTLEMENT OF DISPUTES, CONFLICT PREVENTION AND RESOLUTION: REPORT OF THE SECRETARY-GENERAL*

U.N. Doc. A/66/811 (June 25, 2012), Annex I: United Nations Guidance for Effective Mediation pp. 30, 31, reprinted with the permission of the United Nations (data downloaded on 2/1/19).

*Quality peace agreements*

48. Different kinds of agreements are reached over the course of a mediation process, ranging from those more limited in scope, such as ceasefires or procedural agreements on the nature of talks, to more comprehensive peace agreements. Furthermore, mediation may be required in the implementation stage, although usually by another set of actors so as to avoid reopening the agreement to negotiations.

49. Peace agreements should end violence and provide a platform to achieve sustainable peace, justice, security and reconciliation. To the extent possible in each situation, they should both address past wrongs and create a common vision for the future of the country, taking into account the differing implications for all segments of society. They should also respect international humanitarian, human rights and refugee laws.

---

[3] Lawrence E. Susskind & Jeffrey L. Cruikshank, Breaking Robert's Rules: The New Way to Run Your Meeting, Build Consensus, and Get Results 133, 134 (2006).

50. Both the characteristics of the process and the contents of the accord determine the viability of a peace agreement. Its durability is generally based on the degree of political commitment of the conflict parties, buy-in from the population, the extent to which it addresses the root causes of the conflict, and whether it can withstand the stresses of implementation—in particular whether there are adequate processes to deal with possible disagreements that arise during implementation.

51. The implementation of peace agreements is often highly dependent on external support. The early involvement in the process of implementation support actors as well as donors can help encourage compliance with sometimes difficult concessions made during the negotiations. Although external support is critical to ensure that conflict parties have the capacity to implement the agreement, too much dependency on external assistance can undermine national ownership.

*Guidance*

52. To achieve a quality peace agreement, attention must be paid during negotiations and implementation to the process, substance and institutionalization of mechanisms that provide for the non-violent resolution of the conflict and prevent re-emergence of violent conflict. Mediators, conflict parties, other stakeholders and support actors should consider the following criteria:

- The agreement should aim to resolve the major issues and grievances that led to the conflict, either by addressing the root causes directly in the agreement or by establishing new mechanisms and/or institutions to address them over time through democratic processes.
- Where a comprehensive settlement appears unattainable, the mediator should establish with the conflict parties, and through broader consultations, what is the minimum that needs to be achieved in order to commence a peaceful approach to dealing with the remaining aspects of the conflict.
- When agreement cannot be reached on other sensitive issues, the mediator should also help the conflict parties and other stakeholders build into the agreement options or mechanisms for these issues to be addressed at a later time.

- Agreements should be as precise as possible in order to limit the points of contention that would have to be negotiated during the implementation stage.
- The gender dimension of all issues should be clearly articulated, as agreements that are gender neutral have often proven detrimental to the well-being, security and needs of women.
- Agreements should incorporate clear modalities for implementation, monitoring and dispute resolution to address disagreements that may arise during implementation. They should also include guidelines on priorities, the obligations of the respective parties and realistic timetables.
- Local capacity and existing national infrastructures to undertake conflict resolution should be evaluated and strengthened. Agreements should provide for strong dispute resolution mechanisms at different levels, including local and international actors as appropriate, so that problems can be addressed as they arise and not escalate.

---

## D. Defining Success in Mediation

How should we define success in mediation? Is it equivalent to notions of fairness? If so, whose perspective should control in this determination? Are we simply concerned with a fair process (procedural justice) or does a fair result (substantive justice) matter as well? The late Jacob Bercovitch reflects on these questions in the following excerpt.

### JACOB BERCOVITCH, *MEDIATION SUCCESS OR FAILURE: A SEARCH FOR THE ELUSIVE CRITERIA*

7 Cardozo J. Conflict Resol. 289, 291–94 (2006).

One of the central issues in the field of conflict resolution concerns the degree to which we can define a mediated or negotiated outcome as successful. How do we know that an outcome meets the criteria of success? How can we evaluate it? For example, how would we define the conclusion of the Camp David talks, where President Carter so ably mediated between the parties, and which produced a historic agreement between Israel and Egypt in 1978? Was that ground-breaking agreement successful? There will be as many opinions on that as there are commentators, but few will stop and think carefully about what it means to be successful at mediation or negotiation or how to recognize that success. Or to take another example, the Oslo talks which culminated in the signing of another historic agreement, this time between Israel and the PLO. Were the talks successful? Here, again, we may have as many different opinions as there are commentators. Clearly, we need to think more carefully about what constitutes a successful outcome, how to recognize it, and which factors may affect it.

* * *

*Categories and Criteria of Success?*

Broadly speaking, a given conflict management or a mediatory episode can be referred to as successful if it achieves 'fairness,' or 'effectiveness,' or any one or a combination of a plethora of applicable concepts. One of the things we note about success is that it is usually defined by reference to other abstract concepts (e.g. justice, fairness, satisfaction, etc.). This creates many problems for anyone wishing to evaluate the effects of mediation. How do we know justice has been achieved? Who defines it? An observer, a scholar or the parties themselves? And what if they disagree about what constitutes justice or fairness?

* * *

*Criteria for Success: From Abstract to Concrete*

The first criteria we need to evaluate is fairness. Fairness is an intangible abstraction. One cannot define fairness so stringently that it will not still be interpreted differently by different people, much like the term success itself. However, we do recognize that whatever it may be, fairness suggests to most people an even-handed procedure and equitable outcome that is indicative of some conception of 'success'. Sheppard presents a number of concrete indicators of fairness that serve to assuage concerns regarding the threat of abstraction including: levels of process neutrality, disputant control, equitability, consistency of results and consistency with accepted norms, all of which are relatively easily observed. Both Jameson, Susskind and Cruikshank present similar indicators of fairness (e.g. improvement of procedure and institution of precedent, access to information and opportunity for expression) that provide reasonably concrete concepts of fairness. However, while there are certain observable indices of fairness, both Sheppard, Susskind and Cruikshank talk about the importance of "perceived fairness" in proceedings. Indicators of fairness mean little to parties in conflict if they themselves do not think the proceedings are fair. This "perception of unfairness," justified or not, is often more crucial than any discussion of concrete measures of success. After all, the parties have to be convinced that what they experience is fair, and this conviction cannot be assessed a priori. Hence, while such indicators may emphasize balanced procedures, or even equitable solutions, if parties to it do not perceive that fairness, it is unlikely to have a direct link to success. As discussed in the previous section, this is typical of the assessment concerns that one faces when dealing with issues of perception and interpretation.

Thinking about fairness as one of the dimensions to evaluate mediation success is not without merit. It implies a number of qualities (even-handedness of process, equity of outcome) that may serve as indicators of a successful mediation. However, the perceptual nature of any interpretation of such an abstract concept as "fairness," incorporated with the very fluid nature of what fairness may entail in a given situation, means that interpretation begs as many questions as it provides answers.

In some respects, participant satisfaction seems like a better indicator of success. If parties in mediation are satisfied with the process or outcome, they are more likely to perceive it as a success and, as Sheppard indicates, are more likely to be committed to it. This in turn makes success more likely by producing other relevant dimensions of a successful outcome, such as stability. Sheppard identifies a number of measurable indicators, both with regard to process (privacy, level of involvement) and outcome (benefit, commitment).

However, as with fairness, party satisfaction is largely perceptual and has a very personal quality. Satisfaction is often deemed an almost emotional response to the achievement of a goal or attainment of some requirement. The sorts of goals taken into an event by those involved in conflict are personal in nature and formed by the specific configuration of their personality, environment, values, expectations, etc. This is neither unexpected nor unusual. While satisfaction is a personal quality, it does not mean we should abandon our quest to achieve outcomes that "satisfy" the parties. Categorically, we can say that an outcome that satisfies both parties (even if we don't quite know how to assess that) is more likely to be stable, longer-lasting, and, thus, more successful.

Perhaps the clearest concrete indication of a mediation success is the quality of effectiveness. Effectiveness is a measure of results achieved, change brought about, or behavioral transformation. Conflict management and mediation are processes of change.

Above all, they are designed to change the behavior and attitudes of the parties, even in a violent interaction. Hence, for mediation to be deemed successful, it must have some (positive) impact, or effect, on the conflict. Here, we are talking about such changes as moving from violent to non-violent behavior, signing an agreement, accepting a ceasefire or settlement, or agreeing to a U.N. peacekeeping force, among others. If any of these has occurred as a result of mediation, we can safely say that the mediation was effective, and thus successful. Effectiveness allows us to observe what has changed after a mediator has entered a conflict. It is to a large extent much less subject to perceptual disagreements and more easily observable and measurable.

Efficiency is the fourth criterion of successes and is primarily focused on the procedural and temporal dimension of conflict management. Efficiency addresses such issues as the cost of conflict management, resources devoted to it, timeliness and disruptiveness of the undertaking. In some respects, this may seem extraneous. If a mediation episode is effective in other ways, does efficiency matter? Once again, it must be stressed that conflict and its management does not tend to occur in a vacuum. Costs racked up to accrue benefits may be such that those benefits lose their sheen. Susskind and Cruikshank give efficiency the most weight. They suggest that "[f]airness is not enough. A fair agreement is not acceptable if it takes an inordinately long time to achieve or if it costs several times what it should have." An agreement may not be all that elegant, but if it is achieved within a reasonably short time without entangling too many people, there is much to be said for it.

None of these criteria can be used by itself as a total indication of success. A truly successful outcome is one that meets more than one or two criteria. Efficiency and effectiveness mean little if parties are not satisfied. Likewise, satisfaction and fairness mean little if mediation has proven to be ineffective in a practical sense. Stability can only be achieved when the parties are satisfied and the agreement is fair. These criteria can be analyzed independently, but in reality, they are all interdependent.

---

## III. MODELS OF MEDIATION

The fluidity of mediation practice in the context of international conflict gives mediators broad latitude in constructing a framework for the process. There are a number of different models of mediation practice. This section focuses on four different models: interest-based peacemaking, consensus building which is useful to reach agreement in the public square, what Melanie Greenberg refers to as "neutral, low-power models" which are common in American mediation practice, and finally, the good offices model which refers to the use of States and international organizations in mediating conflict between countries.

### A. Peacemaking Mediation

In the following reading, John D. Feerick discusses Senator George Mitchell's role in mediating the peace talks that led to the 1998 Good Friday/Belfast Agreement in Northern Ireland and his adaptation of American labor relations practices to that conflict situation.

### JOHN D. FEERICK, *THE PEACE-MAKING ROLE OF A MEDIATOR*

19 Ohio St. J. Disp. Resol. 229, 234–38 (2003).

Beginning in the 1980s and continuing through the mid-1990s, a number of important milestones occurred as a result of negotiations that took place between the British and Irish governments. These British-Irish agreements included: an Anglo-Irish Agreement in 1985, expressing a commitment that only the people of Northern Ireland could change its constitutional status; a Downing Street Declaration in 1993, setting out a general formula for participation in the peace talks by political parties associated with paramilitary organizations; and a Frameworks Document of 1995, creating the International Body on Decommissioning and setting a course for all-party negotiations. Also during this period the Irish and British governments had separate discussions with the political parties that had allegiances to them. Among these were discussions between the Irish government and the major Nationalist parties in the North, namely, the Social Democratic Labor Party and Sinn Fein (the political wing of the Irish Republican Army (IRA)). All of these discussions led to cease-fires in 1994 by the IRA and the Combined Loyalist Military Council. The British and Irish governments served a critical mediation function in laying the groundwork for the peace negotiations that began in June 1996.

*Senator George Mitchell and the Peace Process*

Senator Mitchell's appointment in 1996 to chair the all-party talks was foreshadowed by his assignments in Northern Ireland in 1995, after leaving the United States Senate. First he was appointed by President Clinton to organize a trade and investment conference. Then he was chosen as one of three members of the International Body on Decommissioning established by the Frameworks Document of 1995. In the process he became familiar with Northern Ireland, its people, leaders, and history. Many in Northern Ireland also came to know him. Looking more closely at the peace talks as a possible case study of mediation at its best, one finds the most careful of attention given by Senator Mitchell to every aspect of the process.

In a word, Senator Mitchell's style was one of extreme sensitivity to the process, the rules adopted, the views and positions of the parties, and to the independence of his office. Although his selection by the British and Irish governments to chair the talks was objected to by some of the political parties, he was given many opportunities to demonstrate his independence and he did so. At the very outset, he agreed, in the face of strong Unionist objections, to change the rules that had been agreed to by the British and Irish governments for the talks. The Senator said, "I felt throughout the discussions that ultimately my ability to be effective would depend more upon my gaining the participants' trust and confidence than on the formal description of my authority."

The multi-party talks began with the development of a set of rules of procedure, which took almost two months to put in place. By July 1996 there was agreement on the rules of procedure, which included provisions dealing with non-compliance by a party with respect to the conditions for entering into the talks, the formula for voting on proposals, and the confidentiality of the talks. A period of several months then followed to develop a very brief and general agenda for the opening plenary session, and on October 15, agreement was reached. Once a general agenda had been established, substantive negotiations could begin, taking place along three tracks or strands. However the issue of decommissioning—Unionists wanted paramilitary arms to be given up before negotiations could begin—arose postponing substantive negotiations for some months.

During discussions on decommissioning and subsequent negotiations, Senator Mitchell and his colleagues conducted many meetings with the parties through the use of strands to deal with global kinds of issues, subcommittees, smaller group meetings, and informal and individual meetings. They constantly put questions to the parties, asking for their responses and positions, both orally and in writing. They sought to understand each party's needs and fears and then to communicate them to the other parties as well as allowing the parties to directly communicate with each other through various formats. They created options for the parties to consider, drew them into every aspect of the process, and used caucuses, shuttle diplomacy, and smaller group discussions to find areas of agreement. Plenary sessions were convened judiciously to receive reports, to have exchanges at times, and to deal with important issues affecting the talks that had arisen. By November 10, 1997, opening discussions were complete and the parties were ready to get into active negotiations. To jump-start the negotiations, Senator Mitchell created a document identifying the key issues for resolution to generate some give and take. As he noted, "[o]nly when all of the issues were seen together could all the parties get a sense of where the necessary trade-offs and compromises might be made."

Throughout the negotiations, Senator Mitchell and his colleagues paid a great deal of attention to the importance of symbols, appearances, and ways to facilitate communications. For example, while most of the negotiations took place at Stormont, a suburb of Belfast, they were commenced in an undistinguished government office building rather than the building from which a Protestant-dominated Parliament once governed the North. Similarly, when some of the negotiations left Belfast, they were held in both London and Dublin so that both communities would not see a tilt in favor of the other. Care was also given to limiting the number of people who would be present at key meetings in order to encourage dialogue, and also to whether the presence of a stenographer or note taker might chill discussion. As the negotiations entered 1998, the agenda became more specific and the meetings more frequent with a deadline imposed to build a momentum toward an agreement. Senator Mitchell expressed the importance of a steadfast deadline in reaching an agreement:

> I began to think about a deadline, earlier than the one at the end of May that Blair had already set . . . . without a hard deadline these people just would not decide anything: the decisions are so fraught with danger for them that they would just keep talking and talking and talking. Eventually, this process would just peter out or, more likely, some dramatic outside event—some new atrocity—would just blow it up. Either way, it would fail. It had to be brought to an end; that was the only possible way to get an agreement. A deadline would

not guarantee success, but the absence of a deadline would guarantee failure.

Eventually Easter weekend of 1998 was set as the deadline and the parties unanimously agreed. On April 10, 1998, after nearly two years of talks and negotiations, an agreement was reached.

The process reflected a number of approaches and mechanisms used in the field of American labor relations, such as committees and subcommittees, smaller group discussions, and the creation of committees in the final agreement for issues that were not capable of resolution at the point of the final agreement. Far more than format, location, and the like was the constant sensitivity of the Senator to each of the parties engaged in the process. He met with them frequently and separately over every aspect of the talks, made sure their views were understood and advanced, sought their suggestions for solutions, and circulated to them for comment drafts of documents containing questions, issues, and options. The respect he gave to each made it their process and inspired confidence in him and his colleagues.

The manner in which Senator Mitchell conducted himself throughout the talks made its success possible. For example, despite the confidentiality of the talks, leaks were commonplace, and yet, the parties came to understand that the Senator (and his colleagues) would make no exception for themselves regarding the confidential nature of the talks. This proved providential because when the first draft of the final agreement was circulated in April 1998, confidentiality was of critical importance and when Senator Mitchell demanded it at that point, the parties complied. Also interesting to note, in terms of the personal role of a mediator, is the tone struck by Senator Mitchell in his public statements. When he spoke to the press at different junctures, his accounts of the negotiations were terse, but he always expressed hope that an agreement could be found. Nothing was conveyed that could be misinterpreted or that exalted the role or importance of the mediator. Throughout, Senator Mitchell helped build toward an agreement by reminding the parties that the people wanted peace and that the alternative to an agreement was not acceptable.

Senator Mitchell's service as chair of the peace talks was, I believe, a testament to the viability of American mediation in international dispute resolution. He brought to his assignment extraordinary personal qualities (most importantly listening, patience, and perseverance) and superlative experience at the center of American politics. The discipline that he brought to his office and the respect he gave to each party engaged in the process are a model for anyone asked to mediate a dispute, whether or not in a context of armed conflict.

---

Another example of peacemaking mediation is the use of consensus-building to reach agreement in the public square. The following excerpt describes a consensus building project, "Investing Social Capital: Exploring the Multi-Door Courthouse as a Catalyst to Maximize Latin American Dispute Resolution System," wherein, on three occasions, parties reached agreements in a participatory manner.

## MARIANA HERNANDEZ CRESPO, *BUILDING THE LATIN AMERICA WE WANT: SUPPLEMENTING REPRESENTATIVE DEMOCRACIES WITH CONSENSUS-BUILDING*

10 Cardozo J. Conflict Resol. 425, 432–33, 437–38 (2009).

### *Project Design: Creating the Foundation for Public Participation*

*A. Project Overview*

I wanted to examine whether tools such as the MDC [Multi-Door Courthouse] and consensus-building could be used to build the capacity of citizens meaningfully to participate in private and public dispute resolution processes, and whether the skills, knowledge and experiences learned in an inclusive deliberative process could be transferred to the civic arena. The goal of the Project was to engage various stakeholders in the issue of optimizing dispute resolution systems. By using consensus-building, I aimed to create a forum that allowed for inclusive, participatory deliberation. At a basic level, the Project was about bringing Brazilian citizens together to assess the state of dispute resolution in Brazil, and whether the Multi-door courthouse could help to optimize it. More broadly, however, the Project attempted to create a culture of inclusion in which citizens from a wide range of backgrounds and sectors were invited to participate in deliberations on an issue of public importance.

The Brazil Project sought to provide an innovative, participatory experience for citizen stakeholders in judicial reform. The Project aimed for collaborative, bottom-up participation in which participants were engaged at every stage of the deliberation process. The group of participants was comprised of representatives of seven sectors of society (lawyers, judges, law professors, law students, business leaders, low-income community leaders and representatives of non-governmental organizations). In this project, participants collectively identified problems, gathered relevant information, analyzed and interpreted that information, and developed action plans. They examined options for improving dispute resolution, specifically the Multi-Door Courthouse, a forum that directs incoming court cases to the most appropriate avenues for dispute resolution, as well as alternative methods (e.g., mediation or arbitration) and the traditional court. Through a specialized, virtual, on-line forum, volunteer participants first evaluated the current state of dispute resolution in Brazil. Second, they explored the use of judicial resources and the Multi-Door Courthouse as options to enhance dispute resolution opportunities. Finally, they proposed a systemic approach required for the implementation of their agreement.

### *B. Structure: Minipublics*

Currently, deliberative processes in Latin America are not fully participatory in two respects. First, the playing field is not level and is pitched in heavy favor of wealth and influence. Second, Latin Americans usually are asked to participate only at the information-gathering and implementation stages, but not in the idea-generation and decision-making stages.

In order to counteract the exclusionary forces that are so dominant in Latin American culture, the Project used the concept of the "minipublic" as its basic structure, following the work of Professor Archon Fung at Harvard's John F. Kennedy School of Government. A "minipublic" is an organization in which the diverse interests of society's sectors (in our case, the courts, NGOs, community leaders, lawyers, business groups, professors, and students) are self-consciously represented for the purpose of public deliberation. These types of groups aim to "improve[e] the quality of participation and deliberation" by offering a forum in which various sectors of society can be heard on issues of public importance. Fung notes that these types of participatory groups "rely upon the commitment and capacities of ordinary people to make sensible decisions through reasoned deliberation and empowered because they attempt to tie action to discussion."

I chose to create a hybrid minipublic, combining aspects of the educative forum and the advisory panel minipublic. The advisory panel minipublic emphasizes affecting the political process by creating linkages with policy makers. The educative minipublic's emphasis on inclusion and on creating an open forum for articulating and refining opinions in order to make informed decisions was appropriate to the Latin American context. By providing an environment where each participant's contributions are considered, the weaker voices that are more easily drowned out in public debate can be heard. In addition, the educative forum focuses on the provision of free access to information. Full participation by all sectors in the deliberative process, Fung acknowledges, is not automatic. He argues that public deliberation groups such as minipublics should be designed in a way that allows those unaccustomed to articulating and defending their interests in public to have the opportunity to develop that civic skill. Good facilitation, together with a carefully constructed minipublic, will ensure that "the weak, and not necessarily those with the best ideas or arguments, have ample time to speak and express themselves."

In the case of the Brazil Project, the structural design of a hybrid advisory-educative minipublic, as well as the emphasis on diversity and inclusion in the training, allowed the groups to counter socioeconomic and political inequalities, which are normally encountered in the public sphere in Latin America, and which pose a significant hindrance to free and open discourse. Moreover, all participants had access to the same bank of knowledge and skills, thus privileging no single group over another. Participants heard directly from experts and received information from all over the world during their information-gathering and deliberations, enabling stakeholders to make informed decisions for themselves.

### C. *Methodology: Consensus-Building Within and Across Sectors*

In order to create a deliberative experience that was as inclusive as possible, the Project adapted the consensus-building process created by Professor Lawrence Susskind of M.I.T. and the Harvard Program on Negotiation. Susskind has established a five-step process for building consensus aimed at creating more stable agreements than otherwise attained through traditional methods.

Consensus-building is distinguished from normal modes of decision-making because the process is based on several key premises. First, consensus-building is an ongoing process in which participation and dialogue are critical. Second, consensus-building does not mean that everyone must agree on one position. Third, each agreement created must be the best alternative to the status quo for all involved. Finally, because disagreement is at the core of the need for the consensus-building process, all minority opinions will be heard and will not be erased; hence, the final outcome will include all voices.

The above qualities made consensus-building the preferable methodology for the Brazil Project, since our primary goals were to involve all the sectors of society in addressing the problem of judicial reform and to create a space where all sectors could be heard. This approach also helped to involve participants at each stage of the decision-making process.

The Brazil Project used some of the latest technologies to link participants across a wide geographical area. Consensus-building was carried out through virtual dialogues, utilizing a creative combination of software, online discussion forums, conference calls, videos, and videoconferencing. Facilitators worked online with participants, both synchronously (using text, audio, and video chats) and asynchronously (using e-mail and threaded discussions) to ensure progress in the consensus-building conversation.

---

## B. Low Power Models of Mediation

What happens when the facilitative form of mediation, so prevalent in U.S. practice, is used to mediate violent conflicts? Melanie Greenberg describes the traditional facilitative model as a "neutral, low power model of mediation" and in the following excerpt she critiques its use in the case of violent conflicts.

### MELANIE GREENBERG, *MEDIATING MASSACRES: WHEN "NEUTRAL, LOW-POWER" MODELS OF MEDIATION CANNOT AND SHOULD NOT WORK*

19 Ohio St. J. Disp. Resol. 185, 186–89, 193–94 (2003).

Mediation is such a universal dispute resolution process, used in so many formal and informal settings around the world, that it is impossible to make a claim for American dominance of the field or American hegemony over any particular type of mediation. American diplomats use such a wide range of mediation styles in their mediation of international armed conflict (from Richard Holbrooke at one extreme, using NATO force as a backdrop to his muscular persuasion of the parties at Dayton, to George Mitchell in Northern Ireland, using only the force of his will and perseverance to influence the parties to reach the Good Friday Agreement), that there is no way to single out a typically American style.

However, there is one form of mediation that dominates the domestic landscape of American mediation, which mediators have used with wildly mixed results to resolve international armed conflict. This form of mediation, which I call "Neutral-Low Power Mediation" [hereinafter NLP mediation], would be instantly recognizable to anyone involved in a law school mediation seminar, a victim-offender mediation program, a community mediation program, a divorce mediation, a labor mediation, or a peer mediation program in an elementary school. While NLP mediation is neither a strictly American invention, nor exclusive to American conflicts, its pre-eminent role in the landscape of mediation in this country is extraordinary. . . .

*Characteristics of NLP Mediation*

The hallmark of NLP mediation is a mediator whose primary role is to help the parties in their own communication and negotiation. This form of mediation is typically an extension of the parties' own bilateral or multilateral negotiations, rather than a forum in which the mediator tries to browbeat the parties into agreement, or to push through solomonic judgments.

Within an NLP mediation, the roles of the mediator and parties are fairly circumscribed. The mediator can show a strong hand in shaping the process of the mediation, but not in influencing a particular outcome. Specifically:

- The mediator is expected to be neutral, with no bias toward any of the parties.
- The mediator typically brings no resources of his or her own and does not have power beyond moral persuasion to coerce a party into action.
- The mediator has full control of the mediation process, though parties usually have the power to accept or reject ground rules at the start of the mediation.
- The mediator keeps confidences and does not have the discretion to impart confidential information, even when it might benefit the parties.
- The mediator can ensure fair process but is not expected to impose a solution on the parties (though the mediator might suggest potential solutions, based on the parties' description of their own interests and potential areas of agreement).
- The mediator can help balance power dynamics within the mediation (for example, ensuring that each party gets equal time to talk, making sure each party has the resources to attend particular meetings, etc.) but

cannot unilaterally take measures to render a party more or less powerful in an absolute sense.

The parties, too, have obligations and powers within the NLP mediation:

- Parties are expected not to "forum shop" during the course of the mediation (though they may have recourse to the courts if mediation breaks down).
- Parties either help set the ground rules or agree to the mediator's ground rules.
- Parties are expected to participate in good faith, not using the mediation as a delaying tactic, venue for stonewalling, or means solely for extracting confidential information from another party.
- Parties agree to keep information revealed in the mediation confidential (unless there are agreements otherwise).
- Mediation may or may not be binding, depending on the context, the rules governing the mediation, and the desires of the parties.
- The solution "belongs" to the parties, and not to the mediator.

There are great advantages to NLP mediation. The process is transparent, nimble, and procedurally fair. It allows for creativity and catharsis. The outlook of NLP mediation is egalitarian and optimistic, with an emphasis on developing a roadmap for future action. These characteristics, especially when combined with the ability of participants to pursue more binding, judicial processes if the mediation breaks down, make NLP mediation a powerful and attractive tool for resolving a wide range of disputes.

However, there are disadvantages to NLP mediation, as well. NLP mediation is difficult to enforce, and does not work well to rein in spoilers. Procedural justice does not always lead to normative justice, and the lack of procedural safeguards can leave less powerful parties with no recourse. NLP mediation is not geared toward deep-seated societal conflict, which tends to require iterative, multi-level intervention, combining elements of muscular diplomacy, mediation, and grass roots initiatives.

The weaknesses of NLP mediation are amplified in contexts of violence, power asymmetry, and military crisis. In these situations,

NLP mediation has the potential to be not only ineffective, but also morally suspect and dangerous. In the United States, NLP mediation is not used in cases of violent crime (victim-offender mediation does not encompass crimes such as assault, rape or murder), and tends not to be used in contexts where the power imbalances between parties are so blatant and inexorable that any mediated resolution would be tainted (for example, sexual harassment suits). Beyond the boundaries of the United States, the use of NLP mediation in situations of armed conflict has led, in at least two very high profile cases, to great human suffering on the ground and shame for the international community.

While NLP mediation is usually taught as a neutral, transparent process, it is actually quite value-laden. Mediation often has a strong forward-looking component, rather than exclusive focus on adjudicating past wrongs. The mediator presumes good faith on the part of the parties. Issues of culture and power tend to be subjugated to a more neutral definition of interests and joint goals, even in more transformative settings.

These values and presumptions, which make the mediation process nimble and forward-looking in many contexts, can be disastrous in situations of deep-rooted, intractable conflict, in which leaders manipulate international intervention to suit their own strategic aims. Parties, even when they profess to be in good faith, often continue to shift the balance of the power on the ground, through violence, as the mediation is taking place. With the lack of an international police force, no entity can prosecute this extra-mediation violence, and the mediator must come to terms with the new power realities as the mediation unfolds. Power differentials between (and even among) the parties can hinder negotiation and can lead to coerced, ineffectual, or unjust agreements. The implementation of mediated peace agreements can be derailed by resentful, less powerful parties, or "spoilers" who never took part in the negotiations.

* * *

*Bosnia and Rwanda: Mediating Massacres*

In Bosnia and Rwanda, NLP mediation was an insufficient tool to stop the bloodshed or prevent genocide. In both cases, all the danger signs pointed to failure: the mediated agreements failed to satisfy powerful spoilers; the mediations took place on a highly visible stage, with top government leaders, during a time of crisis and tension; problem-solving trumped relationship building; and numerous red flags pointed to a lack of commitment by important parties.

The use of NLP mediation in Bosnia and Rwanda, rather than alleviating the conflict in those desperate countries, allowed intransigent and irredentist leaders breathing room to organize and conduct ethnic cleansing, and to pursue their military aims under cover of mediation. In Bosnia, the mediation was little more than a fig leaf for the assertive military intervention that the United States and the European Union were unwilling to employ in the conflict. In Rwanda, the mediation effort was sincere and well executed, but the lack of cohesion between the Hutu representatives, and the exclusion of powerful spoilers from the talks, led to a failure of implementation, and to the ensuing genocide. . . . . These cases illustrate the danger of trying to use mediation to create a safe space, while ignoring practical realities on the ground, power dynamics between the parties, and structural difficulties in the societies that make reconciliation extremely difficult.

---

## C. Good Offices Mediation

The traditional understanding of "good offices" refers to the use of third parties such as States or international organizations to assist conflicting countries in negotiating a resolution of their dispute. The United Nations, as the predominant international organization engaged in conflict resolution, frequently engages in good offices missions. However, without true consent of the parties involved in the conflict, "good offices" efforts may prove futile. The following excerpt discusses the United Nations "good offices" mission to Macedonia and describes some of the practical difficulties of mediating intrastate conflict when the host country has a reluctant attitude toward diplomatic efforts.

### DAVID J. LUDLOW, *PREVENTIVE PEACEMAKING IN MACEDONIA: AN ASSESSMENT OF U.N. GOOD OFFICES DIPLOMACY*

2003 BYU L. Rev. 761, 762, 789–91 (2003).

In March of 2001, ethnic Albanian rebels launched Macedonia into a violent civil conflict that made the international community hold its breath at the prospect of a new Balkan war. Until the hostilities of 2001, Macedonia had managed to remain virtually unsullied by the violent ethnic conflicts of its Balkan sister states. In part, Macedonia's success was due to recognition by the United

Nations ("UN"), the Organization for Security and Cooperation in Europe ("OSCE"), and other international actors of the fragile ethnic situation in Macedonia after the dissolution of the Communist bloc. As early as 1992, the international community had established preventive peacemaking and peace-building operations in Macedonia to monitor the situation and support the new democracy. The UN's deployment of troops to Macedonia from 1992 to 1999 played a key role in preventing a spillover of violence from Macedonia's Balkan sisters, but the Macedonian government consistently resisted "interference by the UN in sensitive internal matters, especially interethnic relations." The UN struggled to stabilize internal ethnic tensions through a "good offices" mandate due to the Macedonian government's unwillingness to address the roots of the conflict.

* * *

*Analysis: Preventive Peacemaking in Macedonia*

In Macedonia's case, as with a large number of post-Cold War conflicts, the inability of the international community to effectively "look in" hampered preventive peacemaking efforts. Former Secretary-General Boutros-Ghali described the paradox thus: "The United Nations . . . . now operates in a world where the major forces are global and internal. . . . . [T]he institutions created for peaceful and cooperative relations among States are now needed to sustain the States themselves from new global and internal pressures." No conflict is attributable to a single cause. In Macedonia, several factors led to the ignition of violence. Among those factors was the international community's difficulty in "sustaining" the state against "internal pressures" out of respect for the "political independence and sovereignty" of the new Macedonian nation.

After almost a decade's presence in Macedonia, the UN and other international actors were less successful in securing Macedonian peace than previously believed. Early peacemaking measures fell short of bringing about strong social institutions that could deal with and resolve internal ethnic difficulties. The question then arises: How can the international community effectively respect a state's sovereignty and influence democratic institution building in order to solve ethnic and internal tension before violence breaks out? In solving contemporary conflicts, William Zartman suggests that there may be a greater need not to respect sovereignty in the interest of peace:

> Since contemporary conflicts tend to be internal, the legitimacy of intervention is questionable. In a democratic age, people are sovereign and they get the government they

> deserve. . . . . The weak international law that does exist protects the sovereignty of states and their internal affairs from foreign interference, and for good reason: Relaxing the inhibitions on internal interference leaves power unrestrained and invites the strong to overrule the weak. The prohibition also protects would-be intervenors from involvement in cultures and arenas that are not their own. Ultimately, all these arguments are half-sound, reasoned justifications for inaction that are trumped by the need for action and responsibility.

Zartman's approach to conflict management—that responsibly dealing with conflict may mean trampling on sovereignty to some degree—has strong theoretical foundations in cases where violent conflict has already erupted, such as the ethnic cleansing in Bosnia or Rwanda. Harder questions arise when deciding if "the need for action and responsibility" may also trump sovereignty considerations if violence has not broken out, as was the case in Macedonia. Heeding the warning signs of "protracted social conflict" facilitates early action and international responsibility in preventing identity-based violence; however, such action must be tempered by respect for the political independence and sovereignty of the state. In theory, this respect for political independence was the foundation for the good offices mandate, but in practice an overly paternalistic UN signaled, at least in the mind of "adolescent" Macedonia, a degree of "disrespect" for the nation's sovereignty and its ability to solve its own problems. . . . . In this case, the UN's first mistake was authorizing a good offices mandate before consulting with Macedonia. The government viewed this ostensibly harmless act as meddlesome paternalism. The UN never overcame Macedonia's impressions of the good offices mandate. In fact, many of the UN's subsequent actions may actually have fortified the government's initial unwillingness to let the international community help with internal affairs.

---

# IV. NOTES AND QUESTIONS

1. In *International Peace Mediators and Codes of Conduct: An Analysis*, by Brenda Daly, Noelle Higgins and Sarah Bolger, The Journal of Humanitarian Assistance. August 4, 2010, available at https://sites.tufts.edu/jha/archives/756, the authors state that "As the field of international peace mediation has developed, there has been an increased focus on the need for some sort of guidelines and standards for practitioners. . . . . However, there is no universally

accepted code of conduct or set of guidelines and existing codes and guidelines vary greatly. This could lead to the practice of international peace mediation being 'more political than professional: such as in the case of EU Special Representatives who are generally chosen for political reasons rather than on the basis of "merit or professional standards." What danger do you seen in choosing mediators for political reasons? Are there any benefits to this method of mediator selection?

2. When is mediation not appropriate? Can you imagine situation where mediation would not be the appropriate response to conflict? For example, there might be some circumstances which might raise questions about the appropriateness of mediation, factors such as high levels of distrust, violence. Can you think of other factors?

3. In the case of violent conflicts, what alternative approaches to Neutral Low Power (NLP) Models of mediation (discussed in the excerpt by Melanie Greenberg) would you suggest?

4. In situations of intense violence with high levels of distrust, should international mediators take on the task of managing the risks of a negotiated settlement after it is signed? *See* Fen Osler Hampson, *The Risks of Peace: Implications for International Mediation,* 22 Negot. J. 13 (2006).

5. Is there an ideal time for third parties to enter into a conflict situation? William Zartman argues that conflicts are ripe for resolution when the parties reach a "mutually-hurting stalemate." However, the views expressed in *A Manual for UN Mediators: Advice from Representatives and Envoys* (2010) go beyond this framework and provide:

   > While a hurting stalemate may be one factor that leads to peace talks, other factors, such as a change in leadership or a change in the regional or geopolitical environment, can also do so. . . . As one UN mediator argues: "From a moral point of view, there's a lot to be said for UN involvement at an early stage. When the Organization becomes involved, it brings hope."

6. What is your view on the issue of ripeness? Is a "mutually hurting stalemate" likely to occur at the early stage of a conflict?

# Chapter 9

# CASE STUDIES

## I. INTRODUCTION

The topics discussed throughout this book have explored some common themes in the practice of mediation whether mediation arises out of contract, in community centers, or in court-connected programs. Despite how mediation occurs, it poses similar challenges in practice, with issues related to confidentiality, impartiality and fairness. But there are a rich variety of applications where mediation practice differs. In this chapter we highlight some specific applications of these differences that raise a number of significant questions. What are some of the ways that culture impacts the mediation model that is employed? How it is that parties from different countries both resist and embrace mediation? What indigenous forms of dispute resolution are related to mediation and to what extent do they have influence today? What are some of the lessons that can be learned from various countries' experience with mediation whether it is used in ending violent conflict or adapting ancient mediation practices to modern times? By exploring some of these questions this chapter can help us understand the difficulties of transplanting mediation from one culture to another. These questions can also help us gain awareness of our own values.

We have much to learn from the wisdom of other cultures and models when designing mediation programs. Case studies can inform design efforts by exposing policymakers to a range of possibilities and questions. For example, in designing mediation models what can we learn from a country such as China that has used mediation as a conflict resolution process for thousands of years? In developing peacemaking mediation models, what can we learn from the Navajo peacemaking courts? In attempting to introduce the concept of mediation to a country, how do we avoid the resistance problem that has occurred in Russia?

# II. SELECTED PERSPECTIVES ON MEDIATION PRACTICE

It is not possible to catalogue all the differences throughout the world regarding mediation practice. Instead, we have selected a wide variety of cultural and geographic points to offer a general description of what one scholar has referred to as the "variegated landscape of mediation."[1] These case studies should be read in contrast to the western models described in earlier chapters. All of them offer lessons. Some offer explicit lessons; others demonstrate by example. Some are informed by insider perspectives; others are seen through the lens of outsiders to the culture and this raises a number of questions. What is the role of culture in shaping dispute resolution mechanisms? What are the lessons to be learned from specific dispute resolution events that are contained in the tapestry of various approaches? How are these lessons tied to the customs and structure of a country's legal system and society?

This chapter begins with two case studies from Africa, discussing an example of customary dispute resolution in Ghana conducted by a traditional Queen Mother, and a forty-one day mediation process in Kenya led by the late UN Secretary-General Kofi Annan. Two different Asian perspectives are presented with excerpts on the general workings of Chinese mediation systems and the cultural underpinnings of mediation in Singapore. This is followed by a discussion of Russian resistance to mediation and then a shift to Native American peacemaking mediation. Finally, we offer a discussion of mediation in the contemporary Latin American context.

## A. Ghana

In some countries, the adjudication process blends with mediation/settlement processes. This is certainly true in the western African country of Ghana. Consider the following example of customary arbitration/adjudication from Ghana, conducted by a Queen Mother, the traditional dispute resolver of family and commercial disputes. Note the role that apology plays as this narrative evolves from an adjudication to a mediated settlement process.

---

[1] Manon Schonewille & Fred Schonewille, The Variegated Landscape of Mediation: A Comparative Study of Mediation Regulation and Practices in Europe and the World (Eleven International Publishing 2014).

## PAUL F. KIRGIS, *STATUS AND CONTRACT IN AN EMERGING DEMOCRACY: THE EVOLUTION OF DISPUTE RESOLUTION IN GHANA*

16 Cardozo J. Conflict Resol. 101, 104–07 (2014).

### *A Routine African Trial*

Nana Yaa Nyamaa II, the Paramount Queen Mother of Sunyani, holds court on Tuesday evenings. She is heir to a tradition of tribal chieftaincy that goes back centuries in Ghana. Enstooled in 1972 at age seventeen, she is part of the extensive hierarchy of Ashanti traditional authorities. Members of the Akan people, the largest ethnic group in Ghana, the Ashanti are the traditional tribal power in Ghana. The Ashanti had unified most of the modern territory of Ghana in the nineteenth century under their king, the Asantehene, who ruled his dominions from the Golden Stool in the Ashanti capital of Kumasi. They remain the most influential cultural force in Ghana today.

The Queen Mother's court is held in a large, open-air gazebo at her "palace," a small compound centered around her ranch-style home. Chiefs and queen mothers sit atop the social structure in Ghana and are often well off in relative terms. Most real property in Ghana is held in a system of allodial and usufructory rights, with the land ultimately vested in the "stool" on behalf of the entire community, living and dead. Male chiefs hold legal title in a capacity similar to a trusteeship. They are entitled to rents from the land, now collected in the form of taxes. Although they have lost much of their governing power, they remain essential adjudicators, hearing disputes involving Ghana's still vibrant customary law.

Queen mothers function like male chiefs, with certain differences. Queen mothers customarily have not been able to hold property, so they depend on the chief in their locale . . . . In addition, queen mothers were not included in the regional councils created by the English colonial administration, so they are not part of the governing structure in the same way as the men. Despite these limitations on their power, queen mothers are widely respected decision-makers. Lacking customary jurisdiction to hear land disputes, they hear mostly disputes involving family and commerce—traditionally the bailiwicks of women in Ghana. Men tend to take their disputes to chiefs; women tend to take theirs to queen mothers.

On this particular Tuesday, Nana Yaa is hearing a case involving two women, a wholesaler of dried fish and a retailer who had been unable to pay for a quantity of fish bought on credit. The wholesaler has brought her suit to the Queen Mother and paid the customary "token," a combination filing fee and consent to the Queen Mother's jurisdiction. The retailer has similarly accepted the Queen Mother's jurisdiction by paying her own token.

The Queen Mother sits on a slightly elevated chair with symbols representing her stool and a Catholic cross behind her, signifying her sources of authority. Six elders—five women and one man—surround her. Like all Akan chiefs and queen mothers, she has a linguist who serves as intermediary between her and the parties, required because in all formal settings chiefs and queen mothers do not communicate directly with an audience. The proceedings, conducted in the local language of Twi, open with the two parties taking an oath similar to the traditional Anglo-American courtroom oath.

The complainant speaks first. She explains that she sold about $1000 worth of dried fish to the retailer on credit. The retailer repaid half the amount on schedule but then stopped making payments. Eventually, the retailer repaid an additional $200, leaving a debt of about $300. The wholesaler went with her son to the retailer's home to demand payment of the remaining debt. When they got to the home, they found the retailer making a large pot of soup. This infuriated the wholesaler, who was being pursued by her own creditor (a fact the retailer did not know), and who did not have enough money to feed her own family. She picked up the pot of soup, took it off the stove, and threatened to take it with her. At her son's urging, however, she relented and put the soup bowl down the floor. The retailer responded by calling the wholesaler a witch, a serious charge. At least as much as the unpaid debt, it is this insult that has provoked the wholesaler to bring her case to the Queen Mother.

As the complaining wholesaler states her case, the Queen Mother occasionally interjects, through her linguist, to ask questions. At one point, the Queen Mother disallows a part of the wholesaler's testimony as hearsay. The retailer is then given a chance to cross-examine her before stating her own case. She explains that she was unable to make sales for a time because her father had died, a fact the wholesaler did not know. She expresses her outrage at the wholesaler's conduct in threatening to remove the soup. Taking the food from another person's house is a gross breach of local custom and tradition—a breach that, in the retailer's telling, justified her charge that the wholesaler was a witch. After she finishes her statement, the wholesaler is given a chance to cross-examine.

The case turns, dramatically, on the testimony of the only non-party witness called to testify, the wholesaler's son. His testimony is devastating to the wholesaler. He says that he had advised her not to take the soup and that he was ashamed when she did. The two women stand stiffly while he delivers this indictment. When he finishes, he asks for permission to speak with the two women privately. The proceedings are temporarily adjourned while he and the two parties leave the court to converse. They return with a proposed settlement. The son has agreed to take out a loan to give to his mother so that she can afford to supply new fish to the retailer, which will allow the retailer to resume sales and repay the wholesaler from the future profits. The retailer promises to pay in installments.

But the parties' agreement does not end the matter. The Queen Mother retains jurisdiction, and must accept any settlement. She indicates that she would have found for the respondent because taking another person's food from her house is so contrary to customary law that the retailer was justified in calling the wholesaler a witch. The Queen Mother forces the wholesaler to kneel before her and apologize to the Queen Mother, as representative of the community, for that breach of customary law before accepting the proposed settlement.

---

### B. Kenya

In the following excerpt, the authors offer a case study of a forty-one day mediation process that occurred in Kenya in 2008. Led by the late UN Secretary-General Kofi Annan, a team of mediators successfully ended a deeply rooted conflict in Kenya. In this detailed description, the authors describe the mediation strategies used and suggest key lessons to be learned from the mediation process.

## ELISABETH LINDENMAYER & JOSIE LIANNA KAYE, A CHOICE FOR PEACE? THE STORY OF FORTY-ONE DAYS OF MEDIATION IN KENYA

1–2, 22–25, International Peace Institute (2009).

At the heart of the successful forty-one-day mediation process in Kenya was the realization that this was a crisis that the world could not afford to ignore. For chief mediator Kofi Annan, however—making reference to the Chinese characters which make up the word—a crisis presents us with both danger and opportunity. On the one hand, the danger was that this East African nation, previously perceived as an island of political and economic stability and an essential hub for international activity, would allow the election crisis of 2007 to deteriorate into a catastrophic civil war along ethnic lines; as messages of hate penetrated the radio waves and a church full of fleeing women and children went up in flames, the echoes of Rwanda and Côte d'Ivoire made this danger a very real one. The opportunity, on the other hand, was that the crisis could be used to actually address deeply rooted problems: the simmering grievances, repeated ethnic migrations, and the cycles of dispossession which have characterized Kenya's colonial and postcolonial years. This was indeed an opportunity to create a political system which could attempt to address the vast disparities in wealth and the endemic sense of marginalization.

The mediation process, which began on January 22, 2008, three weeks after the postelection violence erupted across Kenya, was led by the Panel of Eminent African Personalities, 2 consisting of former President Benjamin Mkapa of Tanzania, former South African First Lady Graça Machel, and former UN Secretary-General Kofi Annan as Chairperson. The Panel was charged with helping the parties to the conflict ensure that an escalation of the crisis was avoided and that the opportunity to bring about a sustainable peace was seized as soon as possible. The unique team was mandated by the African Union (AU), relied on worldwide diplomatic support, and had the technical support of the United Nations, including the Department of Political Affairs (DPA), the United Nations Development Programme (UNDP), and United Nations Office in Nairobi (UNON), as well as the Geneva-based Centre for Humanitarian Dialogue (HD Centre).

On February 28, 2008, after six weeks of intense negotiations between the opposition Orange Democratic Movement (ODM) and the Government of Kenya's Party of National Unity (GoK/PNU) and a five-hour "end-game" with the principals, President Mwai Kibaki and the Honorable Raila Odinga, an Agreement on the Principles of Partnership of the Coalition Government was signed. For many, this was a triumph of African diplomacy, for some, it was the first realization of the international community's "responsibility to protect" (RtoP), enshrined in the 2005 World Summit Outcome Document, while for others, it was the avoidance of another genocide on African soil. It is impossible to know in exact terms what was prevented or what might have been, but all the warning signals indicate that a failure to solve this crisis may have resulted in significantly more violence, bloodshed, and loss of life, with huge implications for the entire region.

* * *

[The parties decided on the following four point agenda, referred to as the "Road Map:" (1) to undertake immediate action to stop violence and restore fundamental human rights and liberties; (2) to take immediate measures to address the humanitarian crisis, promote reconciliation, healing, and restoration; (3) to overcome the political crisis; and (4) to work on long-term issues and solutions]

When the Chairman of the Panel, Kofi Annan, said farewell to Kenya on March 3rd, six long and difficult weeks had passed. But this was only the beginning of an even longer and more difficult road ahead toward sustainable peace in Kenya. The technical elements of agenda item three were left in the hands of Attorney-General Amos Wako and a team of lawyers whose job it was to draft the necessary bills for the implementation of the power-sharing agreement into law, and 2 billion Kenyan shillings were pledged by the US in support of the speedy implementation of the agreement, in addition to the Sh1.75 billion already pledged by the US toward reconstruction. The negotiations over the root causes of the crisis, however, were left in the hands of Nigerian Foreign Minister Oluyemi Adeniji, who was tasked with addressing the last item on the agenda: the land issue, historical injustices, the cycles of dispossession, and the steps needed to move toward reconciliation.

There are key lessons to be learned from the crisis in Kenya. The February 28th Agreement was not a sufficient step, but it certainly was an important one toward peace in Kenya. With memories of Rwanda still in the minds of many, and the specter of Somalia not so far away, one shudders to think what might have been had the African Union not stepped in. Their swift action was a key element of the success in Kenya. This AU engagement highlights the importance of the partnership and the comparative advantages of regional organizations: speed was of the essence. The lives already lost and the families torn apart are irreversible tragedies; but the extent of the violence could have spread so much further, the number of deaths could have spiraled out of control and the crisis might have escalated from Kenya to the rest of the region, with devastating consequences for the entire African continent. All of this could have been had the African Union not acted on the basis of its Principle of Non-Indifference and Article 4(h) of its Constitutive Act. Few of us can feel indifferent in the face of mass killings and large-scale violence; but acting on that nonindifference, and doing so successfully, takes a great deal of resolve, commitment, and political will.

While the mediation was initiated by the African Union, the Panel realized that to be successful it would need the broader support of the international community, including African nations, the US, the EU, and the United Nations. It became clear that everyone was walking in the same direction and speaking with one voice. The mediation efforts in Kenya prove that when the international community has unity of purpose and stays the course, peace stands the very best chance of success; complex cases such as Darfur and the Democratic Republic of the Congo have proved that unity is not always a sufficient condition, but it certainly is a necessary one.

In addition to these broader lessons, there are also lessons to be learned regarding the specific conflict-resolution tools used in the course of the mediation. First, fostering the conditions for a single mediation process—with international support where possible—is an essential step to begin pursuing solutions meaningfully. In Kenya, Annan assured that, first and foremost, he had the African leaders behind him and that he also had the support of the international community and in particular the United States—which stepped in at pivotal moments to put pressure on the parties. While the process began with multiple mediator options, the Panel managed to assert authority over the process, and to generate enough worldwide support in order to ask the parties to accept its mediation as the only one they would engage in.

Second, civil-society actors have a vital role to play in the dialogue; even if involving them intimately in the negotiations around the table is not always practical, their consultative involvement early on helps shape the process in a way that ensures that the people have a voice and that the necessary pressure is put on the government during the implementation phase. In Kenya, the active involvement of the media, religious groups, business communities, and peace activists was crucial for creating an atmosphere that was conducive to fruitful negotiations and for generating that vital link between an elite-level process and the grass-roots realities, to avoid disenchantment or dangerous disconnect. Civil society engagement can be fostered and encouraged actively by mediators willing to take the time to listen to their views and engage them in the process where possible and appropriate.

Third, separating the short-term from the long term issues when drawing up a Road Map can prove essential in creating the much-needed nonviolent space for dialogue to proceed, as well as getting the parties used to agreement at a time when agreement with "the enemy" can be seen as a weakness. Putting the emphasis on ending the violence, over and above seeking "truth" about the elections, meant that Kenyan lives rather than political power were put at the heart of the peace process. Given that ending the violence and addressing the humanitarian situation also involved apolitical, or at least nonpartisan, discussions, it was easier to encourage the parties to agree, and to generate a sense of teamwork and compromise. Rapid agreement on the shorter-term agenda items, one and two, of the road map, was without doubt an important building block for the more difficult, long-term agenda items to follow.

Fourth, a carefully thought-out media strategy is essential both to ensure that the process within the room is not derailed by political-point scoring outside the room and to keep the people fully on board and correctly informed; it can also prove to be a useful tool in moving the process in the right direction. In Kenya, the Panel asked the parties early on to avoid making inflammatory statements to the press about the details of what was going on behind closed doors; when it seemed that they were not keeping their promises and that press statements risked sowing the seeds of failure, the decision to take the parties to an undisclosed location, where the media could no longer play a role, may have actually prevented the talks from deteriorating into exchanges of accusations and finger-pointing. It certainly helped get things back on track, and created a temporary space where the media was no longer a political tool. On the other hand, the Panel made it their priority to keep dialogue with the people of Kenya as frequent and open as possible, while shielding them when necessary from destructive events behind closed doors which may have made them lose hope; the translation of almost all press conferences into Swahili by a prominent figure, such as President Mkapa, formed a vital part of the media strategy. The media was also a very useful tool to put pressure on the parties when necessary, to add momentum or to plant the seeds of desirable outcomes in the minds of the government, the people of Kenya, and the international community. For the Panel, the media provided a perfect means by which to test terms such as "grand coalition" and "new government," helping to make compromise seem inevitable.

Fifth, an emphasis on pragmatism can help overcome political differences. Turning political questions into technical ones, postponing divisive debates over appellations, and focusing on practicalities rather than the "big picture" can all be useful strategies in helping negotiators to work as a team and to put peace before political aspirations or concerns. In Kenya, the use of technical experts—be they humanitarian, electoral, legal, or political—was an essential part of helping the parties to understand which solutions were feasible given the explosive environment in which they were operating; they also helped orient the parties to a problem-solving framework and away from adversarial negotiation strategies.

Sixth, understanding that negotiations are a process, rather than an event—and that the process is owned by the parties themselves—is integral to a holistic approach to peacemaking. Expectations can be managed more fruitfully if dialogue is engaged in as part of a process, rather than simply a political exercise or event; the process has its own inherent worth, and trusting that the process will be constructive also means being patient. The Panel reminded the parties to have patience when they appeared frustrated, and reminded them of progress already made when they were despondent; similarly, the Panel was flexible and open enough to see the talks as a process, one which needed their full engagement if they were going to succeed. Annan's decision to stay was part of this realization and certainly helped the parties to realize he was certainly not in transit, but as much a part of the process as the parties. That said, while the mediator is a part of the process, the process always belongs to the parties. This was essential in the final stages of the peace process in Kenya: suspending the talks was the mediators' decision, but it was based on actions by the parties; and the ability to save the talks from collapsing lay with the parties, not the mediator.

Lastly, creativity, flexibility, and awareness of timing are crucial. A mediation process is inherently unpredictable, and the mediator must try to constantly reassess, remain open to ambiguity, and to offer new options when necessary. In Kenya, for example, one of the major obstacles was finding a solution which would create a prime-ministerial position which was nonexecutive but still meaningful; Annan's proposition to make this a nonexecutive position with substantial powers and special responsibility delegated from the powers of the president was a midway, creative solution that satisfied both parties.

Political will and mediation skills, however, would have been useless without the desire for peace on the part of Kenyans themselves. The spirit of compromise can only come from the parties. Whether peace will be sustained in Kenya will depend first and foremost on the people of Kenya and on their willingness to implement and keep the agreement they have reached. They must tackle the root causes of the conflict—the issues of land, dispossession, poverty, and injustice—which were the underlying and deep-seated reasons for the explosion of violence during the 2007 elections. They must also continue to enjoy the sustained and undivided support of the international community, when needed, in consolidating the peace achieved. Kenya may have made some impressive strides toward peace but it has a long way to go before it can affirm that it fully avoided the dangers of civil conflict and entirely embraced the opportunity to address underlying factors which could lead to a more just, equitable, and prosperous society. Above all, peace in Kenya would not have been possible if the people of Kenya had not wanted it; peace cannot be imposed.

### C. China

It is generally understood that the Chinese approach to mediation is more directive than that employed in many western countries including the United States. Are there any lessons that Americans, in particular, can learn from a culture that has employed mediation for thousands of years? In the following excerpt, an American author discusses numerous lessons that Americans can learn by studying Chinese mediation systems.

## KEVIN C. CLARK, *THE PHILOSOPHICAL UNDERPINNING AND GENERAL WORKINGS OF CHINESE MEDIATION SYSTEMS: WHAT LESSONS CAN AMERICAN MEDIATORS LEARN?*

2 Pepp. Disp. Resol. L. J. 117, 134–38 (2001).

### 1. *Morality in Mediation*

The biggest lesson that can be learned from the Chinese model is that there is a place for morality in mediation. Confucian mediations were based upon morality and offered mediators an opportunity to reinstall moral values in disputants. By appealing to morality, Confucian mediators were able to get the disputants to agree to an end to a dispute.

In America, "morality" often has a pejorative meaning with a large segment of the population. Perhaps readers of this article are exclaiming that they have no interest in forcing their values upon another individual, particularly one involved in a dispute. The author would agree with this assertion, and add that mediators should not force moral values on to disputes, but rather should appeal to disputants to recognize moral values. Much like the method of asking party A to understand party B's arguments and grievances, an appeal to morality causes each side to see the right and the wrong in their actions. Questions presented in caucuses such as "Can you see what's wrong with X position?" or "do you think that's right?", where the question is honestly presented and the outcome honestly sought, may yield an epiphany for some disputants. This moral lesson is important not only for settling current disputes, but could have an effect on future behavior.

A possible example of where the exploration of morality would be pertinent and helpful is during a divorce mediation. For example, if both the husband and wife were unfaithful to each other, an appeal to explore one's morality would help the couple go "below the line," and possibly explore the issues that led to their predicament. Furthermore, an exploration of their immoral behavior may lead to an understanding, which in turn may prevent future immoral behavior.

Mediators should not make moral judgments about their disputants, and invariably if they do, they should not vocalize these judgments nor allow these moral judgments to affect their ability to mediate the dispute. Moral counseling in the mediation context is a thought provoking exercise, and the Chinese have proven that its use facilitates agreement.

2. *The Power of a Mediator*

The second lesson presented is a caveat to the first. The mediator has a tremendous amount of power, and that power should not be used lightly. In China, mediation was historically used as an element of social control. In Maoist China, mediation was used to suppress the masses and instill communist ideology in disputants.

American mediators should realize, and never forget, the inherent power that they possess in mediation. The commonly defined role of mediator, the facilitative negotiator, describes the mediator's importance and power in the dispute resolution process. Parties seeking an end to often bitter disputes are looking towards their mediator for guidance, support, and recognition. This is not a job for the half-hearted, and should not be undertaken lightly. Those who are in it purely for selfish reasons have no place at the mediation table. Being a mediator is not merely a job, but is also a belief in the power of reconciliation.

3. *Materialism, Personal Advancement, and Lack of Community are Counterproductive to a Successful Mediation*

Just as the mediator must remember their place in a mediation, a disputant must also be aware of counter-productive attitudes. Traditionally, one of the positive forces promoting settlement in mediation in China was the sense of community one felt, a value that governed over all other values. Where the sense of community decreases, so too will the desire to go to mediation. Currently in China's major cities, mediation is becoming less and less prevalent. There is a direct correlation between this and the economic growth and personal advancement being experienced by the citizenry. Thus, as Chinese disputants become more interested and focused on their self-interests, they are more likely to avoid mediation.

American mediators should be cognizant of these self-interest centered values, and when they appear in a mediation, the mediator should not be afraid to call a caucus and point out counterproductive attitudes. While Americans are generally more individualistic then their Chinese counterparts, this does not mean that all Americans lack a sense of community. There is a direct link between a lack of community and a lack of settlement, for if there is no appeal to save the relationship, both to the person and to the community, the desire to do save the relationship and end the dispute is lessened, and the potential for settlement ultimately decreases. American mediators should appeal to disputants' sense of community as a means of encouraging dispute resolution.

*4. The Mediators Qualifications*

Anyone can be a mediator, and anyone can set a charge for their services, but a truly successful mediator is one educated in the field. Chinese mediators are not required to have any legal background, nor are they required to have any formal training. Consequently, they are not paid very well. Though this situation is changing, and the Chinese government is increasingly offering more training to their mediators, there are a significant number of mediators in China who are uneducated.

American mediators can take an important lesson away from the Chinese situation: the power of knowledge. There is no substitute for becoming educated in the mediation process, for just being a past participant is not enough to qualify one later as a mediator. To know how the process works is only half the battle. American mediators should seek to educate themselves on why the process works. Only a combination of the two can adequately prepare one for the duties associated with mediating a dispute.

*5. The Inherent Limitations of Mediation*

Mediation is neither applicable nor practicable for all types of disputes. In China, mediation has traditionally been used to resolve family disputes and neighbor disputes. In the cities, where different types of disputes have arisen, mediation has proven ill-suited to deal with economic disputes. In 1995, the Chinese government created an arbitration program to deal with economic and contractual disputes.

In America, mediation is used to solve all types of disputes. From divorces to contractual violations, there are few civil disputes that cannot go to mediation. This general willingness to mediate, if the parties so desire, misses the lesson being taught by the Chinese—some disputes need to go to arbitration or litigation. In order to be more effective as mediators, parties and their advocates need to be aware of all of their dispute resolution alternatives. Some disputes require a finding of fact, not a finding of common ground. Unfortunately, the recognition of what dispute resolution procedure to undertake is not the choice of the mediator, but rather the choice of the parties. However, mediators can play a role in this selection process by informing potential parties of the mediation process, its goals and outcomes, and its limitations. In order to utilize the mediation process properly, mediators must inform some potential clients that mediation is inappropriate to settle their dispute.

### 6. *The Importance of Conciliation*

There is a turning point in every settled dispute when the parties realize that their actions have contributed to the dispute. This does not mean that there was a right and a wrong; rather this means that both sides realize that they were right and they were wrong. In Chinese mediation, an important element of mediation is self-criticism. During this stage, each disputant asks himself or herself "What did I do to cause this?" Here, one is reminded of the old adage: It takes two to tango.

America mediators can take a valuable lesson away from the importance of conciliation. It is critical for the mediator to make disputants aware of their contribution to the dispute. Often times, a disputant's awareness of her own contribution to the dispute leads to a solution for the dispute. Further, an important step in repairing the damage done to the disputants' relationship is a gesture of conciliation. Far from mandating a conciliatory gesture, encouraging such a gesture, either jointly or singularly, can vastly improve the chances of mediating a settlement. Often times, such gestures tell the other party that their message or quarrel is being heard and understood. One of the main reasons parties are in mediation in the first place is that they are unable to "hear" what the other party is saying. Acts of conciliation open these channels.

---

## D. Singapore

The following excerpt explores the intersection between culture and mediation. Writing from a Singaporean perspective, the author discusses differences between Asian and Western models of conflict resolution and the cultural assumptions inherent in each model. He also formulates a framework to understand concepts such as belonging, status, communication, and face.

## JOEL LEE, *CULTURE AND ITS IMPORTANCE IN MEDIATION*

16 Pepp. Disp. Resol. L. J. 317, 319–20, 322–30, 332–36 (2016).

In the past, one could delineate a cultural community or group along national or ethnic lines. These would be the days when cultural anthropologists like Margaret Mead could observe a group or community like the Samoans, and identify their cultural traits. Of course there would be exceptions, but in those days, one could be fairly sure it was an exception and not the norm. This was possible because there was very little cross-grouping "contamination" or influence: the Samoans had very little exposure to other cultural influences, whether through travel or other means. There was, therefore, the illusion of sameness, which in that time was relatively reliable.

With the advent and development of modern travel, communication, and of course, the Internet, this is no longer true. The lines between cultural communities and groupings are blurring. It is now increasingly possible for a Chinese person to be born in Singapore, grow up in New York, be educated in the United Kingdom, and end up living and working in Hong Kong. It would be a mistake then, to assume that one was dealing with a Singaporean Chinese person. This individual may not manifest any characteristics of what it might mean to be Singaporean Chinese. Further, exposure to movies, music, and other forms of media could also mean that any individual that we look at may manifest different sub-cultures depending on the context he or she is put in. In the context of business, the person may manifest characteristics of typical "western" business values. However, in a martial-arts context, we may see the manifestation of a sub-culture that is very different from the behaviors and values that are typical of that individual. Put simply, the illusion of sameness is gone.

* * *

It would be very odd and politically incorrect for one to suggest that, in relation to mediation, culture was unimportant or insignificant. However, looking at this question in the cold light of day, it is a fair question. Does culture really have such a significant impact on human interactions, specifically mediation?

There has always been a tension between two schools of thought: the "Universalists" and the "Culturalists." The "Universalists" believe that all conflicts are fundamentally universal in nature. Humans manifest universal patterns of behavior, and a general and universal model of conflict resolution applies by recognizing universal human needs and addressing them. Culture plays a minimal, if not non-existent, role in the resolution of disputes.

The "Culturalists," on the other hand, believe that we are more different than we are similar. While group characteristics and traits do exist, culture is complex, dynamic, and multi-dimensional. It is personal to the individual and any model of conflict resolution can only be a generalization, which is at best, a guide.

Of course, it is important to note that the "Universalists" and the "Culturalists" form two extreme ends of a continuum and where one stands within that continuum determines how one approaches conflict resolution theory and practice.

This was precisely where Singapore found itself in 2003. The commonly used model of conflict resolution in Singapore (and many other jurisdictions) at the time was the facilitative interests-based model. The question posed was whether this model of conflict resolution was appropriate in the Asian context. If it was, what modifications, if any, needed to be made to take into account relevant cultural differences? If it was not appropriate, then what model should replace it?

* * *

Before looking at how Singapore dealt with this question, it is useful to make a contextual segue. Singapore is a small island state, with an area of approximately seven hundred square kilometers and a population of five million people. Its population is made up of many ethnicities, including: Malays, Chinese, and Indians among others. Modern-day Singapore was founded by Sir Stamford Raffles in 1819, colonized by the British in 1824, and subsequently occupied by Japan during the Second World War. After the Japanese surrender, Singapore reverted to British rule and remained a British colony until its independence in 1965.

Singapore has since become a developed country with all the trimmings of modernity and a robust economy. The country is governed by a democratically elected unicameral parliament and the legal system is based on the English common law system.

Historically, there are indications that disputes were resolved through indigenous forms of mediation practiced among the ethnic groups. The mediators were often religious and community leaders who had standing and credibility in their respective circles. Under

British influence, these traditional methods of dispute resolution eventually gave way to litigation in the courts as a primary way to resolve disputes, which brought with it the attendant tangible and intangible costs.

The modern history and development of mediation in Singapore has been explored elsewhere, both inside and outside this volume. The writer will not seek to repeat any of that here; save to say that since 1994, mediation has taken root in the form of the Primary Dispute Resolution Centre in the Subordinate Courts, Community Mediation Centres, and the Singapore Mediation Centre. In each of these contexts, disputes between parties of different races, ethnicities, and, increasingly, nationalities are mediated regularly.

* * *

This segue was important for two purposes. First, it provided those unfamiliar to Singapore with some contextual background. Second, it illustrated that, in the melting pot of races that is Singapore, it would be absurd to say that culture was not important. If it is sometimes perceived that culture is not often discussed in Singapore, this is due to the fact that it is so much a part of Singapore life that talking about it would be odd; as if it was something unusual.

* * *

From 1994 to 2003, mediation training and practice overseas, in particular "Western sources" such as those in the United States, Australia, and the United Kingdom, had a heavy influence on modern mediation practice (including training and accreditation). As mentioned, this is the facilitative interests-based model and, while it worked well enough most of the time, there was no denying that it was not always a comfortable fit.

Considering that one view asserts that mediation has its roots in the Asian culture, this irony was not lost on the former Chief Justice Dr. Yong Pung How, who remarked that Singapore had to relearn mediation from the West. It is therefore not surprising that the Singapore Mediation Centre was tasked with looking at whether the facilitative interests-based model was appropriate for the Asian context.

A working group was convened to study this question and was faced with the dichotomous choice of "West versus East." The working group rejected this distinction and proceeded from the assumption that the interests-based model of conflict resolution provided a functional paradigm that was universal to the human condition. What sometimes caused an uncomfortable fit with cultures outside the West were the cultural assumptions inherent within the model that had their origin in the West. These assumptions were: (1) the primacy of the individual and the individual's expectation of autonomy; (2) the priority of the interests of the individual; (3) the premium placed on direct and open communication for constructive conflict management; and (4) the importance of maintaining a good working relationship for constructive conflict resolution. The operational behaviors that flowed naturally and unconsciously from these assumptions are illustrated in Figure 1 below:

**Figure 1.**

| WESTERN-ORIENTED CULTURAL ASSUMPTIONS OF THE INTERESTS-BASED MODEL | RESULTING FEATURES/ STRATEGIES OF THE INTERESTS-BASED MODEL |
|---|---|
| Primacy of the individual and the individual's expectations of autonomy | Western-oriented assumption puts disputing parties first and in the center. |
| | Mediator is an external neutral party who facilitates the process and has low substantive authority. Parties know best and are therefore most well placed to decide on the form of mediation process and shape of mediated outcome. |
| | Interactions are kept informal to encourage parties to negotiate and take decisions. |
| Priority of interests of the individual | Western-oriented assumption gears the mediation process towards helping parties maximize and satisfy individual interests. |
| | Interests include those of self and immediate family members. |

| | |
|---|---|
| Direct and open communication is constructive for conflict management | Open debate and confrontation is acceptable. |
| | Explicit expression of feelings, views, and concerns is encouraged to "air" grievances. |
| | Joint sessions perceived to be beneficial as flow of information may create new levels of understanding and create options for settlement. |
| | Mediator facilitates process by asking questions to surface underlying interests and hidden emotions and turn them into issues for joint discussion. |
| Unconditionally constructive approach to maintaining good relationship for optimal outcome | Cultivation and maintenance of good relations to facilitate securing a good outcome. |
| | In view of objectives, the same approach to relationship building is generally taken for one and all. |

* * *

By identifying these "Western" cultural assumptions and replacing them with cultural assumptions appropriate to the context of Singapore—and other cultures that share its heritage—it was possible to preserve the usefulness of the interests-based model of conflict resolution—its functional paradigm—and harmonize it with the culture of Singapore in application—its operational paradigm. These "Asian" assumptions (in juxtaposition to the ones earlier identified) were: (1) the primacy of social hierarchy and the individual's expectations to fulfill roles in any hierarchical relationship; (2) priority is given in observing proper conduct; (3) communication and conduct is geared towards preserving harmony, relationships, and face; and (4) one approaches context-dependent relationship maintenance as a way of life.

Before looking at the impact these assumptions have on the operational aspects of implementing the interest-based model, it is important at this point to highlight two observations. First, there is no suggestion that these assumptions represent the values system of all Asians, and no attempt to prescribe any "Asian Model" of mediation. That would be an absurd proposition. It simply offers *one* Asian perspective—that of Singapore—and provides a methodology by which academics and practitioners of mediation in other contexts may choose to contextualize the interests-based model for their own cultures.

Secondly, it is important to highlight here that by inserting these "Asian" assumptions into the conflict resolution model, the functional paradigm of using "interests" to resolve the dispute remains untouched. What changes are the operational aspects of implementing the interests-based model. The operational behaviors that flow naturally and unconsciously from these assumptions are illustrated in Figure 2 below:

**Figure 2.**

| SUGGESTED ASIAN-ORIENTED CULTURAL ASSUMPTIONS | RESULTING FEATURES/ STRATEGIES OF THE INTERESTS-BASED MODEL |
|---|---|
| Primacy of social hierarchy and the individual's expectations to fulfill roles in hierarchical relationships. | Asian-oriented assumption requires the mediator to be at the heart of the mediation. |
| | Mediator has high social status and is expected to lead and guide. |
| | Parties expect guidance from the mediator, and are expected to value and respect his opinions. |
| | Interactions with an authority figure in the form of a mediator may be expected to be formal. |
| Priority in observing proper conduct. | Interests include those of self, immediate family members, and wider groups, and group interests may have priority, |

| | |
|---|---|
| | especially in a dispute with another in-group member. |
| Communication and conduct gearing towards preserving harmony, relationships and face. | Disputants may be more reserved and reticent, and prefer to communicate through non-verbal cues or in more subtle ways. |
| | Unearthing issues that should be left unspoken may lead to embarrassment and disengagement from the process. |
| Context-dependent relationship maintenance a way of life. | Cultivation and maintenance of good relations with in-group members is a matter of priority and an end unto itself. |
| | Any interest in cultivating or maintaining relationships with out-group members is similar to the original Western interests-based model. |
| | Nature of relationship (in-group/ out-group) dictates appropriate approach to issues of relationship. |

By juxtaposing the operational behaviors from both values system, it is clear that certain tensions can arise. It can be illustrated as Figure 3 below:

**Figure 3.**

| RESULTING FEATURES/ STRATEGIES OF THE INTERESTS-BASED MODEL—WESTERN ASSUMPTIONS | RESULTING FEATURES/ STRATEGIES OF THE INTERESTS-BASED MODEL—ASIAN ASSUMPTIONS | TENSIONS CREATED IN THE ASIAN CONTEXT DUE TO INCOMPATIBLE CULTURAL CHARACTERISTICS |
|---|---|---|
| Western-oriented assumption puts disputing parties first and in the center. | Asian-oriented assumption requires mediator to be at the heart of the mediation. | A party-centric process may leave mediator and parties feeling out of place. |
| Mediator is an external neutral party who facilitates the process and has low substantive authority. | Mediator has high social status and is expected to lead and guide. | A mediator who does not assume position of authority may be deemed ineffective. |
| Parties know best and therefore most well placed to decide on form of mediation process and shape of mediated outcome. | Parties expect guidance from mediator, and are expected to value and respect his opinions. | A mediator who holds back on giving guidance may be viewed to have abdicated his responsibilities. |
| Interactions are kept informal to encourage parties to negotiate and take decisions. | Interactions with an authority figure in the form of mediator may be expected to be formal. | Individuals not accustomed to being the sole locus of decision-making. They may be frustrated if prompted to take decisions without any assistance in the form of inputs from an authoritative source. |
| | | Interactions with the mediator on egalitarian terms may be a breach of social etiquette and cause discomfort. |
| Western-oriented assumption gears | Interests include those of self, immediate | Satisfying and maximizing individual |

| | | |
|---|---|---|
| mediation processes towards helping parties maximize and satisfy individual interests. | family members, and wider groups and group interests may have priority, especially in a dispute with another in-group member. | interests may not be considered "proper conduct." |
| Interests include those of self and immediate family members and these take priority above all else. | | |
| Open debate and confrontation acceptable. | Disputants may be more reserved and reticent, and prefer to communicate through non-verbal cues or in more subtle ways. | Pursuit of individual rights and search for collaborative solution to problems do not justify open confrontation. Open confrontation disrupts harmony. |
| Explicit expression of feelings, views and concerns encouraged to "air" grievances. | Unearthing issues that should be left unspoken may lead to embarrassment and disengagement from the process. | Joint sessions for open discussion may be perceived as face threatening. There may be a preference for private sessions. |
| Joint sessions perceived to be beneficial as flow of information may create new levels of understanding and create options for settlement. | | |
| Mediator facilitates process by asking questions to surface underlying interests and hidden emotions and turn them into issues for joint discussion. | | |

| | | |
|---|---|---|
| Cultivation and maintenance of good relations to secure a good outcome or facilitate future dealings. | Cultivation and maintenance of good relations with in-group members a matter of priority and an end unto itself. | Requiring a one-size fits all approach to relationships is a blunt instrument with no nuance. |
| In view of objective, same approach to relationship building generally taken for one and all. | Any interest in cultivating or maintaining relationships with out-group members is similar to the original Western interests based model. | Requiring parties to build a relationship where none is valued can cause discomfort |
| | Nature of relationship (ingroup/out-group) dictates appropriate approach to issues of relationship. | Not recognizing that the relationship is the substance can give rise to a conflict of expectations between the mediator and the parties. |

* * *

[The following section discusses the notions of status, belonging, communication and face.]

As mentioned earlier, it would be inaccurate to make a general assertion that, in an "Asian" context, one must use indirect language and that face concerns are prevalent. There are many instances in Asia where parties communicate directly and do not seem concerned about helping the other party preserve "face." While one could dismiss these instances as anomalies, the writer submits that there is coherence and consistency in these behaviours, and a framework underlies and guides them. This section seeks to formulate this framework so as to assist readers in traversing this challenging area.

As a preliminary point, it is useful to define some of the terms that the framework will revolve around. The first is the notion of *status*. This is expressed by Hofstede as Power Distance and is measured by the Power Distance Index (PDI). This is a measurement of how society handles inherent inequalities, which may result from prestige, wealth, and power. Put simply, some cultures are more hierarchical than others. Hierarchical societies (i.e. societies with a high PDI) have a more defined sense of roles and obligations and there are clear decision makers (usually at the top of the hierarchy). Status, seniority, age, and even gender, therefore, matter. Societies that are more "flat" (i.e. societies with a low PDI) tend to be comfortable with shared authority, more diffused roles, and have a preference for consensus.

It is important to note that the PDI is, as with many other things, contextual. Within a society that that has a low PDI (e.g. the USA), there are certain contexts within that society that may exhibit a higher PDI. The military and the legal profession are two examples of groups that generally exhibit a higher PDI. Conversely, within a society that has a high PDI, some contexts within that society may manifest a lower PDI.

The second is the notion of *belonging*. This is expressed by Hofstede as Collectivism/Individualism and is measured by the Individualism Index (IDV). This is a measurement of the relationship and extent of integration between the individual and the group that prevails in a given society. Put simply, cultures that have a high IDV tend to play down relationships and focus more on the individual and individual rights. Conversely, cultures with a low IDV tend to be collectivist and focus more on close ties between individuals. As with the PDI, there may be contexts within a high IDV culture where they may manifest a lower IDV and vice versa. Individuals within the same collective or grouping can be referred to as being "ingroup." Those not within the same collective or grouping can be referred to as being "out-group." Of course, these are static snapshots of the relational belonging between two individuals. It can be that the relational belonging is in transition (i.e. two individuals are moving from an out-group relationship to an in-group relationship or vice versa) either by design or circumstances.

The next notion to consider is *communication*. For the purposes of this paper, this amorphous concept can be split into direct and indirect communication. Direct and indirect communications are often associated with low-context and high-context communication respectively. Put simply, a direct or low-context communicator derives meaning primarily from the words that the speaker uses. Similarly, they will seek to transmit meaning primarily with words. Very little meaning, if any, is derived or transmitted via the context, hence the reference to low-context communication. A direct communicator who does not feel able to commit to the deal that is on the table may simply say, "This is not a good deal for me. I cannot agree."

On the other hand, an indirect or high-context communicator derives and transmits meaning not just from words but also through contextual cues and clues. Taking the same message from the previous paragraph, an indirect communicator may say, "Let me take this proposal back to consider it," but give off non-verbal cues indicating that he is just being polite.

At this point, it is useful to make three points about the nature of direct and indirect communication. First, it is important to be clear that both forms of communication seek to convey the same message. Those that engage in direct communication will simply say what they mean. Those who engage in indirect communication will find some other way to convey this message that requires the listener to read between the lines. This could even be expressed as a metaphor.

Secondly, because we have a preference for our own style of communication, this often leads to each type of communicator attributing negative intentions to the other type of communicator. Direct communicators may perceive indirect communicators to be "shifty," "evasive," and "unwilling to communicate." On the other hand, direct communicators are perceived as "insensitive," "abrasive," and "brash."

Thirdly, direct and indirect communication is not a digital either-or distinction. Instead, it is an analogue distinction that traverses a continuum. Put another way, it is not useful or easy to say whether any piece of communication is "direct," or "indirect." One can more usefully say that one piece of communication is more direct or indirect than another piece of communication.

Fourthly, accepting the preceding point will affect how we think about our communication styles. While there are "tests" or survey instruments that one can take to determine whether one is a direct or indirect communicator, it is probably more useful to think of these as indicators of one's communication style preferences. Instead of being a single point on the direct-indirect communication continuum, our communication style preference is more of a range within this continuum. Put another way, our communication style preference is a continuum within a continuum; for some, their range could be greater or narrower than someone else's.

Fifthly, different people will perceive the same phrase differently depending on their communication style preferences. A person who is closer to the indirect end of the direct-indirect continuum would likely consider phrases that are considered indirect by those on the other end of the continuum to be direct. Therefore, even when a person who was closer to the direct end of the continuum restated a phrase more indirectly, it may not be heard by one on the indirect end of the continuum as being indirect.

Finally, since we are able to operate inside a range within the direct-indirect continuum, most people exercise some discretion and choice about where within their range they will communicate. What guides this choice can be the values they have about communication (it is important to be open and direct) or the model of mediation being used (in the interests-model of mediation, as practiced in many western jurisdictions, direct communication is prescribed) or the context and conditions that the mediation is being conducted in (where there is a concern about preserving the harmony of the collective and saving face of individuals, indirect communication may be prescribed).

The final notion to look at is the concept of *face*. This is a difficult concept to define. It is sometimes expressed in some western contexts as ego or pride and can include the concern for dignity, honor, and status. Some provide a four quadrant framework encompassing face saving, asserting, restoration, and giving. For our purposes, it is not necessary to delve into the intricate complexities of face. It is sufficient to make two observations.

First, a person can either save one's own face or give the other person face. While it is possible to say that one "saves the other person's face," for the purpose of this piece, we will take this to mean the same thing as giving the other person face. Further, while it is possible to say, although admittedly an uncommon formulation, that one "asserts one's own face," for the purposes of this piece, we will take this to mean the same thing as saving one's own face.

Secondly, what does it mean exactly, in behavioral terms, to save or give face? The starting point is the assumption that where there are no face considerations, two parties will communicate with each other in a direct manner and can reasonably expect and assert for what they are entitled to in terms of, *inter alia*, respect, behavior, or rights. We will take this to be the norm.

When face considerations come into play based on the first observation above, two scenarios arise. In the first scenario, Party A may feel a need to give Party B face. Behaviorally, this means that Party A may communicate indirectly, manifest patterns of deference, and assert for less than what she or he is entitled to. In the extreme, Party A may even completely refrain from asserting for his or her entitlement. In the other scenario, Party A may feel the need to save face. Behaviorally, this means that Party A may communicate directly, manifesting patterns of dominance and authority and asserting exactly what she or he is entitled to. In the extreme, Party A may even assert for more than his or her entitlement, perhaps to the point of seeming unreasonable. Essentially, in this context, deviating from the norm can be seen as a manifestation of giving or saving face. In the context of mediation, the need to give or save face may also manifest as a reluctance to talk about certain things in joint session. Put another way, a private session can be a very useful tool to manage face considerations.

---

## D. Russia

Not every country and culture has embraced the mediation process. In the following excerpt the author discusses the resistance of Russian citizens to the introduction of mediation into the legal system and attempts to explain this phenomena. This case study illustrates some of the challenges involved in transplanting mediation from one culture to another.

### KATHRYN HENDLEY, *RESISTANCE, INDIFFERENCE OR IGNORANCE? EXPLAINING RUSSIANS' NONUSE OF MEDIATION*

32 Ohio St. J. on Disp. Resol. 469, 470–81, 484–89, 491–92 (2017).

Russia is a late developer as to mediation. In contrast to the United States, Western Europe, and the Far East, where mediation has been available for decades, legislation authorizing mediation in Russia went into effect only at the beginning of 2011. Although Russian law scholars greeted this institutional innovation with enthusiasm, ordinary Russians paid little attention. Few have taken advantage of it. The leaders of the Moscow-based Center for Mediation and Law argue that "[a]bsolutely all experts agree that the development of mediation in Russia has been very weak." The Russian scholarly literature is replete with explanations for the nonuse of mediation. Most focus on the shortcomings of the legislation, with an occasional nod to the potential role of legal culture. Given the historical preference for doctrinally-driven research, the failure to ground theory in empirical data is not surprising. This article, which analyzes Russians' views of mediation gleaned through a series of 2014 focus groups, begins to fill that gap.

* * *

*The introduction of mediation in Russia*

Russia would seem to be an ideal candidate for mediation. Russians' preference for working out problems on their own ought to have created a welcoming environment. Moreover, its courts are straining under an ever-increasing caseload. Between 1995 and 2015, the number of cases resolved by Russian trial courts more than quadrupled. Alla K. Bol'shova, the former chairman of the Moscow city *arbitrazh* court, [This is a state court that deals with most cases related to busineses. ed.] fears that the current burden on the courts is not sustainable. The VII All-Russian Congress of Judges in December 2012 agreed that the introduction of mediation "will permit the improvement of the quality of justice and provide a reliable guarantee to citizens of access to justice within a reasonable time." Thus, much as in Western countries, mediation was adopted in Russia with the dual goals of ameliorating judges' workload and improving the quality of litigants' experiences.

* * *

The law opens the door to mediation in most civil cases, regardless of whether they are brought in the courts of general jurisdiction or the *arbitrazh* courts. Its use is forbidden in cases involving third parties or in collective labor disputes. It also prohibits its use in criminal or other cases of public concern. This has been interpreted to preclude mediation in disputes with the state.

In Russia, as elsewhere, settlement is distinguished from mediation. This makes sense. Settlement generally involves the parties finding a compromise on their own, whereas mediation assumes this has proven impossible and contemplates bringing in a mediator to help the parties. Disputants are permitted and encouraged to settle at every stage, including before coming to court. Along similar lines, the language of the law would seem to open the door to trying mediation both in the lead up to the lawsuit and after it has been filed. But pretrial mediation is allowed only if it is contemplated in the agreement that establishes the parties' relationship. This is rarely found. As a practical matter, therefore, mediation is possible only after a lawsuit has been initiated. When judges accept a case for trial, they send an order (*opredelenie*) to the litigants detailing the time and place for the hearing and laying out their rights and duties. Among those is the right to bypass the court for mediation. When the parties appear before the judge, the procedural codes obligate her to remind them of this option. If they are amenable, then the case is stayed for up to sixty days while the parties work with a mediator. If the parties are able to resolve their dispute, they emerge with a "mediation agreement" (*mediativnoe soglashenie*) that is reviewed by the court. Judges do not pry into the merits of the resolution; so long as it is within the bounds of the law, they approve it, thereby terminating the lawsuit. If a resolution proves elusive, even with the help of a mediator, then the parties return to court and resume their adversarial stances. Much like mediation the world over, the proceedings are deemed confidential. The parties cannot rely on what they learned to bolster their cases, nor can they call mediators as witnesses.

*The Use (or Nonuse) of the Law*

Iaroslav B. Zhelobov, the chairman of the Pushkin district court in St. Petersburg, speaks for the judicial corps generally when he argues that "from the point of view of the judicial community, mediation is needed." Iakovlev buttresses these sentiments. Not only does he see value in the potential to divert cases away from the courts, but he also believes that helping parties to find a way through their problems creates more stable solutions.

* * *

Litigants, on the other hand, have mostly given the cold shoulder to mediation. Beginning in 2014, national-level data on the use of mediation has been included in the annual statistical report on the activities of the courts of general jurisdiction. . . . . [L]ess than one tenth of a percent of all civil cases were resolved via mediation. Mirroring Western experience, litigants tend to be more open to trying this alternative approach when tussling with those closest to them. Almost a quarter of all cases mediated involve inter-familial disputes. When we look at the number of cases mediated as a percentage of all similar cases, inheritance disputes, which also typically pit family members against one another, emerge as being friendly to mediation. In both categories of cases, just over 0.02 percent of disputes were resolved through mediation. A similar level of usage is visible for consumer disputes. Unlike family and inheritance squabbles, consumer claims involve parties operating at arms' length. Some Russian retail establishments have begun including mandatory mediation clauses in their form documents, which helps explain the higher than average propensity to resort to mediation.

* * *

These data do not break down mediation use by region or by courts within regions. Russian scholarship occasionally provides a glimpse of this reality. The limited data does suggest that the use of mediation is concentrated in a few regions where local administrators have embraced it wholeheartedly. Training judges helps. Judges who have received formal training on mediation are more likely to encourage parties to try it. In several regions, such as St. Petersburg, Voronezh, Ekaterinburg, and Pskov, mediation centers have been created and have secured funding to pay the costs of mediation for interested litigants as part of limited-time pilot projects. In these regions (as well as several others), mediators are available in the courthouse, thereby eliminating the need for litigants to seek them out independently. All of these incentives have boosted the use of mediation, but even with them, very few parties have been willing to try it. For example, in the Pushkin district court of St. Petersburg, where the chairman is an unabashed cheerleader for mediation, only 52 cases were mediated from October 2011 to October 2012. This accounted for less than 2 percent of its 2012 civil caseload. Mediation was successful in 40 of these cases (77 percent). The bulk of these cases were family disputes (68 percent). The remainder were fairly evenly divided between labor disputes and consumer claims. Judges reported that even when mediation failed to produce concrete results, they nonetheless observed behavioral changes. Parties who had tried mediation were more willing to listen to each other and to restrain their emotions in court. More importantly, they were better able to clearly formulate their arguments which allowed their cases to proceed more quickly. Such comments echo the observations of Western judges.

Vasilii Nechaev, Deputy Chairman of the Russian Supreme Court, argues in favor of parties, themselves, resolving disputes. He bemoans the "adversarial nature of trials. There is always a dissatisfied party. Practice shows that if a decision is reached through mediation, then, as a rule, the parties will respect it." Along similar lines, Zhelobov told of a family transformed through their participation in mediation. He strong-armed former spouses into trying mediation in a contentious child custody case in which the husband had been stalking his ex-wife. With the help of the mediator, they came to better understand each other's positions and found a mutually acceptable resolution. The judge said that, even though they remained divorced, he sometimes sees them walking together with their children near his courthouse in St. Petersburg. According to those who have tracked mediated cases, no one has yet recanted an agreement made through mediation or tried to reopen the dispute.

* * *

*Russian Scholars' Explanation for the Nonuse of Mediation*

The failure of Russian litigants to use mediation has not gone unnoticed by the Russian scholarly community. Much ink has been spilt in an effort to explain the failure of mediation to take hold.

* * *

Given its civil law legal heritage, Russian legal scholars tend to focus on the letter of the law. As one analyst cogently argued: "The essential shortcomings of the legal regime constitute the basic explanation for the unpopularity of mediation today." Others agree. Of course, no law is ever perfect. Russia's mediation law is no exception.

A critique that has consistently dogged the law is its terminology. There are several words that can be used for mediation. [The term used by Russian law *posrednik*, is a word that has several meanings.]

* * *

Scholars also fault the law for a lack of clarity on who can serve as a mediator. The requirements under the law are threefold: (1) at least 25 years of age; (2) university degree; and (3) training as a mediator. The scholarly literature focuses largely on the third prong. There seems to be a yearning for more specificity as to the approach and content of the training. At present, a number of mediation centers have established training programs and each pursues its own path. At a public round-table, several judges expressed concern over the lack of regulation, suggesting that some sort of accreditation process for mediators would be welcome.

Another sticky issue is whether public officials—especially judges—should serve as mediators. The law establishes a default rule prohibiting state officials from serving as mediators, though it opens the door to exceptions. A draft law that would create such an exception for retired judges and other courthouse personnel was floated in 2012, but came to naught. Russian judges are keen to carve out this exception, pointing to the success in Belarus and Japan of judicial mediators. In support, they point to the Russian past. Nineteenth-century Russian justices of the peace were encouraged to conciliate among litigants. My own observational research in Russian courts documents that judges frequently intercede with parties to help them find mutually acceptable compromises. In doing so, they skirt the line between judge and mediator, though both allow them to maintain their neutrality.

* * *

An insufficient supply of qualified mediators has also been cited by several scholars as a deterrent to the use of mediation. Though training centers have sprung up, there is little doubt that the system could not cope if litigants began to opt for mediation routinely. But to claim that a shortfall in mediators lies at the root of the nonuse of mediation would seem to put the cart before the horse. After all, as one group of Moscow scholars acknowledged, "most [Russian] citizens know nothing about mediation."

* * *

### *Ordinary Russians' Attitudes Towards Mediation: Insights from the Focus Groups*

* * *

The most striking finding that emerges from the focus groups is the profound lack of popular knowledge of mediation. Even though over 60 percent of the participants had court experience, not a single person was aware that they could have opted for mediation. This reality upends my initial hypothesis that having court experience would matter because it would bring a familiarity with mediation. Both neophytes and court veterans were equally ignorant. It also confirms Russian scholars' intuition that the unfamiliarity with mediation constitutes a significant constraint on popular use.

Court veterans' obliviousness reveals that judges are either failing to inform them about their right to mediate or are doing so ineffectively. As I noted earlier, the procedural codes require judges to educate litigants on this score, both orally and in writing. But the written notification is far from conspicuous. It is buried in a sea of legalese in a small font on the back side of the document that notifies parties of the time and place of their hearing. My observational research in Russian courts reveals that judges' recitations of parties' rights and duties are often rendered in a rapid monotone that leaves litigants more confused than educated. Few ask clarifying questions, preferring to let the unfamiliar language wash over them.

The focus group participants were not surprised or angered by this gap in their knowledge of the Russian legal environment. Much like the participants in my earlier Russian focus groups, they cheerfully described themselves as "legally illiterate." Their reactions to learning of mediation were varied. Non-Moscow participants assumed that it was available only in the capital. Voronezh residents were uniformly surprised to find out that they had a well-respected and centrally located mediation center. Several assumed that the failure of news to spread meant that it was not helpful. As Nadia, a 33-year-old Voronezh doctor put it: "It seems to me that there must be few positive results [from mediation] because if the pluses outweighed the minuses, then I think information about it would have been shared more widely." All participants agreed that "word of mouth" (*serefannoe radio*) would be the most effective way to stimulate knowledge and use.

Much as the legal experts predicted, the focus group members were flummoxed by the terminology of the law. No one had positive associations with the word *posrednik.* Vladimir, a 45-year-old Muscovite, spoke plainly on this score: "Who are these *posredniki*? We all know who they are. These are the bandits from the 1990s who would arrive and announce: 'You are going to pay and we will provide a roof (*krysha*).' They then went to others and said: 'You can't do business here because this is our territory.' " This understanding of a *posrednik* as a goon or enforcer was consistent across the focus groups, raising doubts as to whether the word can be rehabilitated and repurposed. *Mediator*, by contrast, had no negative connotations, but was simply unknown to the participants. Many of them correctly surmised that it was a foreign word, which was a mark against it. In time, it may come to be part of the popular vernacular. No one brought up *primiritel'*, Iakovlev's suggestion as a substitute for these contested terms, suggesting that it was also a non-starter.

* * *

Needless to say, none of the participants had read the law. The moderator explained its terms in broad strokes. Their biggest criticism was one that was absent from the scholarly literature. To a person, they could not understand why the law authorized mediation only after a lawsuit had been filed. Iulia, a 34-year-old Voronezh accountant, succinctly expressed the views of her colleagues when she commented: "Well, then, what's the point?" They argued that mediation would make more sense before disputes were brought to the courts. In their view, filing a lawsuit tended to harden the parties' positions, complicating compromise. As Aleksei, a 28-year-old Moscow bank manager commented: "the mentality of those who litigate—on principle, they don't want to talk . . . .; they're not interested."

Unlike the scholars, who are aware of the battles and compromises that lay behind the law, the focus group participants came to mediation with fresh eyes. They questioned its institutional structure, which scholars accepted as a given. The participants' first reaction was that the moment for mediation has passed once the lawsuit has been filed. Their logic is compelling, but falls victim to political realities. Had legislators opted for this more informal structure, it would have opened a Pandora's Box of problems of enforcement. In its current form, judges act as the guarantors of the process; they will not endorse a mediation agreement that violates the law. Moreover, a court-endorsed mediation agreement has the same legal force as a judicial opinion, allowing parties to seek a court order (*ispolnitel'nyi list*) without having to return to the merits of the case.

* * *

But the participants' critiques go deeper. They are generally satisfied with the court as the default venue to resolve vexing problems and are dubious as to the need for mediation. Some—mostly court veterans—saw the potential for mediation to ease the burden on courts. They recognized that mundane cases could be diverted to mediation. But the majority of participants were more resistant to the charms of mediation. Maksim, a 36-year-old Voronezh taxi driver, described it as "completely superfluous." David, a 32-year-old dispatcher at a Moscow transportation company, expressed a commonly felt frustration: "This is simply puzzling. So, this mediator gets involved at the court. But the trial is already underway and I retained a lawyer (*advokat*) from the outset, to whom I already paid money and signed a contract so that I can win the case. So why is [mediation] needed? If I already have an *advokat*?" David's comment reveals two sources for this skepticism, namely the cost and the function of mediators.

* * *

Cost was the most common objection to mediation raised by the focus group participants. As a rule, they recoiled at the prospect of having to pay for mediators' services. The response of Klavdia, a 41-year-old Moscow insurance agent, was telling. She said: "We already paid for the complaint, we already showed up in court and paid for the case. Is this free?" There was a consensus that the filing fees (*gosposhlina*) ought to cover any and all expenses related to the dispute. When the moderator explained that the services of mediators was not included, the displeasure was palpable. The participants saw this as paying twice for the same service. Even more troubling to them was the uncertainty as to the cost (which stands in contrast to *gosposhlina*, which is calculated as a percentage of the amount sought).

Once reconciled to paying mediators, participants argued in favor of a results-based payment scheme. Put more bluntly, they believe that mediators should only be paid if they are successful in bringing the parties together, thereby averting lawsuits. As Mikhail, a 51-year-old Voronezh engineer, put it: "It's ok if it's expensive, but there should be a small advance payment. The remainder should come from the person at fault."

* * *

Mikhail's comment illustrates his lack of understanding of the mediation process. He sees it as being a battle where someone emerges as victorious. But the beauty of mediation is that it allows parties to abandon this construct and work through their problem collaboratively. Egor, a 65-year-old Muscovite who, as the chairman of a housing committee, was an experienced litigator, resisted the idea that a mutually acceptable solution could emerge through mediation. He remarked: "This simply couldn't happen—that both sides are content." Although a few participants recognized that the non-adversarial nature of mediation potentially allowed disputants to maintain a cordial relationship, most shared the confusion of Mikhail and Egor. Many saw the mediator as replicating the function of their lawyer, as David's earlier remark reflects. For example, when the idea of asking a third party to intercede in a dispute was first raised by the moderator in the Moscow group with court experience, Nadezhda, a 48-year-old housewife responded with several questions: "When you say intermediary (*posrednik*), do you have in mind an *advokat*? . . . An *advokat* is, in principle, a *posrednik*."

She and her fellow participants had trouble trusting in the neutrality of any third party. They were suspicious that he would inevitably favor one of the parties. Indeed, Evgeniia, a 42-year-old Novosibirsk municipal official, dismissed the very idea as a "fairy tale." To some extent, their misgivings tap into their view of human nature, which has been colored by Russia's long struggle with corruption. Many saw judges as inherently venal and assumed that the same would be true of mediators. Nadezhda summed up this position: "Someone is paid off and then you are left with nothing." The participants struggled to wrap their minds around the role of mediators; their instinct was to put them into the familiar boxes of decision-makers or lawyers. They could not see that the very fact that a mediator lacks a dog in the fight ought to ensure his neutrality and ought to eliminate any incentive for under-the-table payoffs.

The focus group participants' bewilderment over the role of mediators led them to wonder who could and should serve as a mediator. No consensus emerged. Some thought legal training was critical, while others felt that training as a psychologist would be useful. Several advocated for psychologists with legal education, though presumably these are few and far between. In most groups, the discussion quickly moved away from formal educational prerequisites to the personal qualities that a mediator ought to have. Harkening back to the concerns over corruption, all agreed on the need to be able to stand up to intimidation. Putting it more colorfully, Fedor, a 25-year-old Novosibirsk worker, cautioned against having a "meek dandelion" serve as a mediator. Just as important was an ability to work with people of all stripes and to convince them to shift their positions. Many were skeptical that a mediator could effect a settlement. They pointed out that people who end up in court tend to be intransigent. Iulia summarized this position regarding the second scenario dealing with a home repair: "If I don't agree to an amount, then no one can force me. If I decide on 5,000 rubles and they propose 7,000, I will tell them to get lost. . . . . They'll tell me to take it to court. The situation will remain conflictual." Others questioned whether a mediator would be able to win the confidence of the parties. Anna said that many of her neighbors would simply "shut the door in your face and refuse to talk." Not everyone was so dismissive. Some saw the potential value to having a neutral third party who can break down the barriers between the parties. But everyone agreed that the impetus for mediation would have to come from the disputants. The consensus was that forcing it on the parties would be counterproductive.

Just as problematic was the question of mediator accountability. A lively debate arose in most groups over whether mediators ought to work under the auspices of the state or whether they ought to operate independent of the state. Fedor advocated state control. Like many others, he saw *advokaty*, who have to pass something akin to a bar exam, but then are independent to pick their clients, as a good model. An equal number expressed concern over contributing to the ever-increasing size of the state bureaucracy. A few veered into a conspiratorial view of mediation as a way of providing sinecures for the children of the political elite.

* * *

*What is to be done?*

* * *

Making mediation mandatory in some or all cases might help close this gap. Comparative experience indicates that mediation is slow to integrate itself into the legal culture when it is entirely voluntary. Yet voluntariness is a foundational principle of mediation, which Russia has endorsed. Other countries have mandated mediation in some or all cases as a prerequisite to bringing a dispute to court. Because parties are not required to persevere through a mediated settlement, but can walk away at any time, they reason that this requirement does not compromise the voluntariness of the process. Although making mediation mandatory has sometimes backfired, the evidence shows that many parties who are railroaded into mediation find it helpful, even when it fails, and that they opt for mediation on their own volition when other problems arise.

Russian scholars are aware of the positive effect elsewhere of mandatory mediation. Some wonder whether Russia ought to require mediation as a prerequisite to litigation in some or all cases. The law is silent on this question. At a 2012 round-table discussion, Bol'shova, a former *arbitrazh* judge, argued that Russia has a historical legacy to draw upon. She reminded her colleagues of the requirement for industrial enterprises to send a letter laying out their grievances, known as a *pretenziia*, before initiating a lawsuit during the Soviet era and the early post-Soviet years. She claimed that this *pretenzionnyi* system forestalled upwards of 90% of disputes from proceeding to court. While not advocating a return to the past, she favors making pre-trial mediation mandatory for economic disputes. Reshetnikova, a current *arbitrazh* judge, likewise supports mandatory mediation for such disputes. Others are less confident that the principle of voluntariness can be maintained if mediation becomes a requirement. Valerii S. Seleznev, the chairman of the Duma's property committee, spoke for many when he dismissed the idea of mandatory mediation as "something absolutely incomprehensible." The courts are only beginning to weigh in. When a retailer tried to have a case dismissed because the disgruntled consumer failed to live up to a mandatory mediation clause, the Irkutsk court invalidated the clause, arguing that mediation is inherently voluntary, so cannot be compelled. Of course, courts would quickly change their tune if the law itself was amended to require mediation.

---

## E. Latin America

# MARIANA HERNANDEZ-CRESPO, *30 YEARS OF DISPUTE RESOLUTION IN LATIN AMERICA*

ABA Dispute Resol. Mag. 48, 50–51, Spring 2015.

*Regional Debate*

*Second-Class Justice*

The emphasis on the use of dispute resolution mechanisms has been to provide access to justice for those who cannot afford the formal and traditional justice system; to date, the traditional formal justice system remains reserved for those who can afford the cost of litigation. For many, mediation, the most-used dispute resolution process, has become not one option but the only option.

The debate in this area has revolved around mediator quality and protection of parties' rights. Currently, with the exception of Colombia and Argentina, most countries in Latin America do not require mediators to have a law degree, and in most countries, a mediated agreement can be enforced as a judgment. Countries such as Chile, Costa Rica, Guatemala, Paraguay, and the Dominican Republic, however, do require that a judge homologate, or approve, the mediation agreement so that it can be enforced as a judgment. Legal representation in the mediation process is generally voluntary, although countries such as Argentina and Honduras (with exceptions) require the presence of lawyers in the mediation process.

*Mandatory Court-Connected Mediation*

The tendency to promote court-connected mediation has also been a topic of debate in Latin America. Colombia and Argentina have significant experience in this area. Most recently, Chile experimented with a voluntary mediation process in the context of family law but ended up making mediation mandatory.

Even though some data suggests that mandatory court-connected mediation reduces the number of cases that end up in court, there is not enough information to establish a causal effect between mediation and the number of cases in courts. The drop in trials could be due to the cost of the process, the cost of legal representation, or general distrust in the judicial system.

*Social Conflict*

So far, most efforts to promote ADR in the region have concentrated on private disputes: the casas de justicia, for example, were designed primarily to resolve private-sphere disagreements.

But these efforts could be used as building blocks for collaborative governance, including making policy through dialogue and deliberation, implementing policy through public policy ADR, and enforcing policy through public dispute resolution. Expanding the focus to include social conflict could contribute to the promotion of socio-political stability by addressing larger challenges, such as disputes between communities, between local governments, and even between foreign investors and local authorities or local businesses.

Throughout Latin America, wide gaps between the rich and poor persist. ADR reforms could be expanded to engage the large number of people who have historically been excluded from the decision-making processes that affect their lives. If designed and implemented carefully and creatively, ADR processes may be able to provide the structures for participation in the public sphere and potentially enhance individual conflict resolution capacities.

*Conclusion*

Remarkable progress has been made in the last 30 years with the development of dispute resolution legal frameworks and innovative initiatives aimed at promoting access to justice. Yet without efficient and reliable civil systems of justice, dispute resolution mechanisms cannot operate effectively. Therefore, a civil system reform is an indispensible next step.

New regional trends might benefit from a more systemic approach, one that integrates the civil procedure reforms with the dispute resolution initiatives that already exist and engages each country's citizens in the process of reform through dispute system design. Furthermore, one of the major lessons of the last 30 years has been the need for evaluation to build knowledge and strengthen future efforts.

Finally, if dispute resolution efforts were expanded to address social conflicts, these experiences could provide significant opportunities for civic engagement and promote socio-political stability. The world has yet to see what Latin Americans could achieve if reformers designed participatory systems through which citizens could enhance their capacities to collaborate in the public square.

---

Latin America has developed a specific model of dispute resolution, the *Casas de Justicia,* which is based on the framework of the multi-door courthouse. It generally works at redressing small grievances in low-income urban communities and rural areas. In the follow excerpt, the author discusses the use of mediation as an access to justice vehicle in Latin America and integration of mediation into Latin America through the *Casas*. The author also discusses the challenges mediators face in enabling citizens to develop problem-solving capacity.

## MARIANA HERNANDEZ-CRESPO, *FROM NOISE TO MUSIC: THE POTENTIAL OF THE MULTI-DOOR COURTHOUSE (CASAS DE JUSTICIA) MODEL TO ADVANCE SYSTEMIC INCLUSION AND PARTICIPATION AS A FOUNDATION FOR SUSTAINABLE RULE OF LAW IN LATIN AMERICA*

2012 J. Disp Resol 335, 366–67, 380 (2012).

The promotion of mediation in Latin America has been used, for the most part, as a way to provide access to justice for low-income communities and to reduce the cost of dispute resolution. Although mediation has been promoted through court-connected efforts in some countries, various mediation projects operate outside the judicial system. Yet, when parties from low-income communities are unsatisfied with the results of their mediation processes, financial and, in many cases, geographical limitations can make it difficult for them to seek justice through adjudication. Furthermore, as with arbitration awards, a congested judicial system can undermine the enforceability of the mediation agreement.

*Casas de Justicia* have also been promoted in several countries of the region as part of efforts to expand access to justice, with the aim of advancing pro se, legal education, human rights, and the de-judicialization of dispute resolution. The concept of the *Casas de Justicia* is a variation of the multi-door courthouse model, which has been developed to a lesser degree as oficinas multi-puertas (multi-door offices). The *Casas de Justicia* are generally located in marginalized areas, whereas the oficinas multi-puertas are located in urban areas as part of the court system.

* * *

ADR was also established as an essential component of the *Casas de Justicia* model. In this regard, mediation was promoted to advance access to justice by enabling citizens to reach "more equitable and accessible justice, while maintaining a sense of respect for local leadership and customary law." The Peace Accord on indigenous rights mandated that the Guatemalan government recognize Mayan or customary law practice within the legal system, as long as such actions are not in violation of human rights. As a result, ADR, and specifically the mediation process, emerged as a way to integrate elements of local practices into the justice system.

In addition, mediation was promoted as a means of increasing access to justice and reducing backlog in the courts. To this end, it "provides decentralized justice at the community level, providing more power to individuals and civic organizations in resolving their own disputes." Moreover, mediation, as a significant element of *Casas de Justicia,* was intended to be a mechanism through which citizens could not only save time and money, but also gain access to justice "in their own community and language."

---

### F. Native American Peacemaking Mediation

In the following excerpt, the author describes the problem-solving, consensus-based approach of Navajo justice and peacemaking. Notice the focus on interdependency and the importance of relationships.

## ROBERT YAZZIE, *LIFE COMES FROM IT: NAVAJO JUSTICE CONCEPTS*

24 New Mexico L. Rev. 175, 179–87, 189 (1994).

Vertical justice looks back in time, to find out what happened and assess punishment for it. We may never know what really happened. Vertical justice does not look to the future. It does not try to find out what went wrong in order to restore the mind, physical well-being, the spirit, and emotional stability. I insist that any definition of "law" must contain an emotional element: one of spirit and feelings. Where the feelings of parties are separated from the process and the decision does not address them, dissatisfaction follows. Where the legal system ignores the emotions of the parties, there can be no restoration of relationships.

Vertical adversarial adjudication relies upon power, force and coercion. Where powerful figures abuse their authority, there is authoritarianism and tyranny. Navajo thought recognizes the danger of hierarchical or vertical systems. There is a Navajo maxim that one must "beware of powerful beings." Likewise, coercion is so feared in Navajo ethics that the invocation of powerful beings (e.g. calling upon them to use their force against another)—a form of coercion—is considered to be witchcraft. The inappropriateness of the vertical system, as imposed upon Indian nations in modern systems of law and courts becomes more obvious when it is compared to the "horizontal" Navajo approach.

*[The Navajo System: "Horizontal" Justice]*

The "horizontal" model of justice is in clear contrast to the "vertical" system of justice. The horizontal justice model uses a horizontal line to portray equality: no person is above another. A better description of the horizontal model, and one often used by Indians to portray their thought, is a circle. In a circle, there is no right or left, nor is there a beginning or an end; every point (or person) on the line of a circle looks to the same center as the focus. The circle is the symbol of Navajo justice because it is perfect, unbroken, and a simile of unity and oneness. It conveys the image of people gathering together for discussion.

Imagine a system of law which permits anyone to say anything during the course of a dispute. A system in which no authority figure has to determine what is "true." Think of a system with an end goal of restorative justice which uses equality and the full participation of disputants in a final decision. If we say of law that "life comes from it," then where there is hurt, there must be healing.

Navajo concepts of justice are related to healing because many of the principles are the same. When a Navajo becomes ill, he or she will consult a medicine man. Patients consult Navajo healers to summon outside healing forces and to marshal what they have inside them for healing. A Navajo healer examines the patient to determine the illness, its cause and what ceremony matches the illness to cure it. The cure must be related to the exact cause of the illness because Navajo healing works through two processes: first, it drives away or removes the cause of illness; and second, it restores the person to good relations in solidarity with his or her surroundings and self.

The term "solidarity" is essential to an understanding of both Navajo healing and justice. Language is a key to law, and those who share common understandings of the values and emotions which are conveyed in words are bonded through them. Words are signs which also convey feelings. The Navajo understanding of "solidarity" is difficult to translate into English, but it carries connotations which help the individual to reconcile self with family, community, nature, and the cosmos-all reality. The sense of oneness with one's surroundings, and the reconciliation of the individual with everyone and everything, makes an alternative to vertical justice work. Navajo justice rejects simply convicting a person and putting them in prison; instead it favors methods which use solidarity to restore good relations among people. Most importantly, it restores good relations with self.

Navajo justice is a sophisticated system of egalitarian relationships where group solidarity takes the place of force and coercion. In it, humans are not in ranks or status classifications from top to bottom. Instead, all humans are equals and make decisions as a group. The process—which we call "peacemaking" in English—is a system of relationships where there is no need for force, coercion or control. There are no plaintiffs or defendants; no "good guy" or "bad guy." These labels are irrelevant. "Equal justice" and "equality before the law" mean precisely what they say. As Navajos, we do not think of equality as treating people equal *before* the law; they are equal *in* it. Again, our Navajo language points this out in practical terms.

* * *

Clanship-*dooneeike'* is a part of the Navajo legal system. There are approximately 210 Navajo clans. The clan institution establishes relationships among individual Navajos by tracing them to a common mother; some clans are related to each other the same way. The clan is a method of establishing relationships, expressed by the individual calling other clan members "my relative." Within a clan, every person is equal because rank, status, and power have no place among relatives.

The clan system fosters deep, learned emotional feelings which we call "*k'e.* ". The term means a wide range of deeply-felt emotions which create solidarity of the individual with his or her clan. When Navajos meet, they introduce themselves to each other by clan: "I am of the (name) clan, born for the (name) clan, and my grandparents' clans are (name)." The Navajo encounter ritual is in fact a legal ceremony, where those who meet can establish their relationships and obligations to each other. The Navajo language reinforces those bonds by maxims which require duties and mutual (or reciprocal) relationships. Obviously, one must treat his or her relatives well, and we say: "Always treat people as if they were your relative." That is also *k'e*.

Navajo justice uses *k'e* to achieve restorative justice. When there is a dispute the procedure, which we call "talking things out," works like this: Every person concerned with or affected by the dispute or problem receives notice of a gathering to talk things out. At the gathering everyone has the opportunity to be heard. In the vertical legal system the "zone of dispute" is defined as being only between the people who are directly involved in the problem. On the other hand, as a Navajo, if my relative is hurt, that concerns me; if my relative hurts another, I am responsible to the injured person. In addition, if something happens in my community, I am also affected. I am entitled to know what happened, and I have the right to participate in discussions of what to do about it. I am within the zone of a dispute involving a relative. In the horizontal system the zone is wider because problems between people also affect their relatives.

The parties and their relatives come together in a relaxed atmosphere to resolve the dispute. There are no fixed rules of procedure or evidence to limit or control the process. Formal rules are unnecessary. Free communication without rules encourages people to talk with each other to reach a consensus. Truth is largely irrelevant because the focus of the gathering is to discuss a problem. Anyone present at the gathering may speak freely about his or her feelings or offer solutions to the problem. Because of the relationship and obligation that clan members have with each other, relatives of the parties are involved in the process. They can speak for, or speak in support of, relatives who are more directly involved in the dispute.

* * *

Traditional Navajo civil procedure uses language and ceremony to promote the process of talking things out. Navajo values are expressed in prayers and teachings using the powerful connotative force of our language to bring people back to community in solidarity. Navajo values convey the positive forces of *hozhooji,* which aims toward a perfect state. The focus is on doing things in a "good way," and to avoid *hashkeeji naat'aah,* "the bad or evil way of speaking."

The process has been described as a ceremony. Outside the Navajo perspective, a "ceremony" is seen as a gathering of people to use ritual to promote human activity. To Navajos, a ceremony is a means of invoking supernatural assistance in the larger community of reality. People gather in a circle to resolve problems but include supernatural forces within the circle's membership. Ceremonies use knowledge which is fundamental and which none of us can deny. Traditional Navajo procedure invokes that which Navajos respect (i.e. the teachings of the Holy People or tradition) and touches their souls. Put in a more secular way, it reaches out to their basic feelings.

For example, traditional Navajo tort law is based on *nalyeeh,* which is a demand by a victim to be made whole for an injury. In the law of *nalyeeh,* one who is hurt is not concerned with intent, causation, fault, or negligence. If I am hurt, all I know is that I hurt; that makes me feel bad and makes those around me feel bad too. I want the hurt to stop, and I want others to acknowledge that I am in pain. The maxim for *nalyeeh* is that there must be compensation so there will be no hard feelings. This is restorative justice. Returning people to good relations with each other in a community is an important focus. Before good relations can be restored, the community must arrive at a consensus about the problem.

Consensus makes the process work. It helps people heal and abandon hurt in favor of plans of action to restore relationships. The dispute process brings people together to talk out a problem, then plan ways to deal with it. The nature of the dispute becomes secondary (as does "truth") when the process leads to a plan framed by consensus. Consensus requires participants to deal with feelings, and the ceremonial aspects of the justice gathering directly addresses those feelings. If, for any reason, consensus is not reached (due to the human weaknesses of trickery, withholding information or coercion), it will prevent a final decision from being reached or void one which stronger speakers may force on others.

There is another Navajo justice concept which we must understand for a better comprehension of Navajo justice, and that is distributive justice. Navajo case outcomes are often a kind of absolute liability where helping a victim is more important than determining fault. Distributive justice is concerned with the well-being of everyone in a community. For instance, if I see a hungry person, it does not matter whether I am responsible for the hunger. If someone is injured, it is irrelevant that I did not hurt that person. I have a responsibility, as a Navajo, to treat everyone as if he or she were my relative and therefore to help that hungry person. I am responsible for all my relatives. This value which translates itself into law under the Navajo system of justice is that everyone is part of a community, and the resources of the community must be shared with all. Distributive justice abandons fault and adequate compensation (a fetish of personal injury lawyers) in favor of assuring well-being for everyone. This affects the legal norms surrounding wrongdoing and elevates restoration over punishment.

Another aspect of distributive justice is that in determining compensation, the victim's feelings and the perpetrator's ability to pay are more important than damages determined using a precise measure of actual losses. In addition, relatives of the party causing the injury are responsible for compensating the injured party, and relatives of the injured party are entitled to the benefit of the compensation.

* * *

The Navajo Peacemaker Court makes it possible for judges to avoid adjudication and avoid the discontent adjudication causes by referring cases to local communities to be resolved by talking things out. Once a decision is reached, it may (if necessary) be capped with a formal court judgment for future use.

The Navajo Peacemaker Court takes advantage of the talents of a *naat'aanii* (or "peacemaker"). A *naat'aanii* is a traditional Navajo civil leader whose authority comes from his or her selection by the community. The *naat'aanii* is chosen due to his or her demonstrated abilities, wisdom, integrity, good character, and respect by the community. The civil authority of a *naat'aanii* is not coercive or commanding; he or she is a leader in the truest sense of the word. A peacemaker is a person who thinks well, who speaks well, who shows a strong reverence for the basic teachings of life and who has respect for himself or herself and others in personal conduct.

A *naat'aanii* acts as a guide, and in a peacemaker's eyes everyone—rich or poor, high or low, educated or not—is treated as an equal. The vertical system also attempts to treat everyone as an equal before the law, but judges in that system must single out someone for punishment. The act of judgment denies equality, and in that sense, "equality" means something different than the Navajo concept. The Navajo justice system does not impose a judgment, thereby allowing everyone the chance to participate in the final judgement, which everyone agrees to and which benefits all.

Finally, *naat'aanii* is chosen for knowledge, and knowledge is power which creates the ability to persuade others. There is a form of distributive justice in the sharing of knowledge by a *naat'aanii*. He or she offers it to the disputants so they can use it to achieve consensus.

Today's consumers of justice in the Navajo system have a choice of using the peacemaking process or the Navajo Nation version of the adversarial system. The Navajo justice system, similar to contemporary trends in American law, seeks alternatives to adjudication in adversarial litigation. The Navajo Nation alternative is to go "back to the future" by using traditional law.

* * *

Traditional peacemaking is being revived in the Navajo Nation with the goal of nourishing local justice in local communities. The reason is obvious: life comes from it. Communities can resolve their own legal problems using the resources they have. Local decisions are the traditional Navajo way, in place of central control. Everyone must have access to justice that is inexpensive, readily available and does not require expensive legal representation. Peacemaking does not need police, prosecutors, judges, defenders, social workers or the other agents of adversarial adjudication. Peacemaking is people making their own decisions, not others forcing decisions upon them. . . . .

. . . Navajo peacemaking is not a method of alternative dispute resolution; it is a traditional justice method Navajos have used from time immemorial.

---

## III. NOTES AND QUESTIONS

1. Do you see any similarities between the process conducted by the Queen Mother in Ghana and the med-arb and arb-med processes described in Chapter 6?

2. Some scholars have reported a lack of knowledge by parties about mediation programs in some U.S. courts. Does this compare to Russia's experience described earlier in this chapter? *See* Donna Shestowsky, *When Ignorance is Not Bliss: An Empirical Study of Litigants' Awareness of Court-Sponsored ADR Programs,* 22 Harv. Negot. L. Rev 189 (2017).

3. Are you persuaded by the arguments for making mediation mandatory in Russia?

4. To what extent are lessons from the United Nations-led mediation in Kenya transferable to other conflicts? For example, do you think that a United Nations team would have the same success in Afghanistan?

5. The excerpt from the article by Clark draws conclusions regarding the lessons that American mediators can learn from Chinese mediation systems. Do you think that a person from China would draw the same lessons?

6. The readings discuss how policymakers were able to identify western cultural assumptions and replace them with cultural assumptions appropriate to the context of Singapore in order to preserve the usefulness of the interest-based model of conflict resolution. Are you able to identify western cultural assumptions and replace them with the cultural assumptions appropriate to the context of your cultural heritage?

7. In Steven Weller, John Martin and John Paul Lederarch et al, *Fostering Culturally Responsive Courts: The Case of Family Dispute Resolution for Latinos,* 39 Family Court Rev. 185, 198 (2001), the authors report on a study of Latinos in court-connected mediation in the United States, and suggest how court mediation services can

be improved to better reflect the culture-based needs and expectations of this growing group in U.S. society. In contrast to the Anglo-American, mostly neutral model of mediation, they argue that for Latino families, "the mediator must take more of an assertive role, that of mediator, counselor, educator, translator, spokesperson, and guide." Do you see any similarities with this role and that of the Navajo peacemaker?

8. In the Middle Eastern context, Mohammed Abu-Nimer describes a community dispute resolution process in a Palestinian village in Northern Israel and identifies some basic assumptions of that conflict resolution process. These assumptions include the following:

    a. "[C]onflict resolution aims to restore social order and the disrupted balance of power, rather than to change power relationships or the status quo."

    b. "The group, not individuals, is a central locus of action."

    c. "[F]uture relationships are very crucial elements in settling a dispute . . . . ."

    d. "[C]onflict is negative, threatening, and disruptive to the normative order and needs to be settled quickly or avoided."

    Do these assumptions resonate with any of the other cultures described in the case studies in this chapter? *See* Mohammed Abu-Nimer, *Conflict Resolution Approaches, Western and Middle Eastern Lessons and Possibilities,* 55 Amer. J. of Economics and Sociology 35, 46 (1996).

9. What are the advantages and disadvantages of using mediation as an access to justice vehicle in Latin America?

# Index

**References are to Pages**